Davidson
2003

THE *PASSION PLAY*

136.

f.136   The opening of *Passion I* showing one of the large red numerals inserted by the scribe to divide the play into pageants. The capital N at the foot of the page is one of the seventeenth-century quire signatures, probably inserted when the manuscript was bound as part of Sir Robert Cotton's library. Photograph reproduced by permission of the British Library (BL MS Cotton Vespasian D VIII).

THE
PASSION PLAY

FROM THE
N. TOWN MANUSCRIPT

·

EDITED BY

PETER MEREDITH

LONGMAN
LONDON AND NEW YORK

Longman Group UK Limited,
Longman House, Burnt Mill, Harlow,
Essex CM20 2JE, England
and Associated Companies throughout the world

Published in the United States of America
by Longman Inc., New York

First published 1990

British Library Cataloguing in Publication Data
[British Library. Manuscript. Cotton Vespasian D viii]
The Passion play: from the N. town Manuscript.
I. Meredith, Peter, *1933–*
822'.2

ISBN 0-582-49079-0

Library of Congress Cataloging-in-Publication Data
Ludus Coventriae. Passion play.
The Passion play from the N. Town manuscript / edited by Peter
Meredith.
p.   cm.
Includes bibliographical references.
ISBN 0–582–49079–0
1. Jesus Christ – Drama.   2. Passion-plays.   3. Mysteries and
miracle-plays, English.   I. Meredith, Peter.   II. Title.
PR1261.P38L83   1990
822'.1 – dc20   89–13122 CIP

Set in Bembo (Linotron 202) 10/12

Produced by Longman Singapore Publishers (Pte) Ltd.
Printed in Singapore

CONTENTS

PREFACE

My basic aim in the editions of both the *Mary Play* and the *Passion* has been to present a text as uncluttered as possible by the later additions and alterations present in the manuscript. In the case of both plays this can only be done up to a point. With the *Mary Play*, however, there is at least relative certainty about the nature of the ending, and therefore the shape and direction of the play is known. With the *Passion* the ending is lost. It is still possible to disentangle the Play from other material in the second part (*Passion* II), but there is no way of knowing how or where in Christ's death and resurrection the story ended. In this edition, therefore, I have printed *Passion* II as it is in the manuscript but have tried by means of an extensive commentary (in introduction, notes and Appendix 4) to show as far as I can tell what was and what was not part of the play.

The first part of the play (*Passion* I), however, is a different matter altogether. Here the additions are obvious and the structure and meaning of the play can be clearly seen. In the text of *Passion* I which follows the additions have therefore been removed and are printed as Appendices 1 and 2.

It is a source of surprise to me that *Passion* I, a separate play by any criteria, is still so often treated as part of a cycle. There is of course no reason why it should not also be investigated as part of an early attempt to create a new cycle play, but this should be done with an awareness of just how incomplete that attempt was. It seems to me far more valuable to consider *Passion* I as a play in its own right than as part of an uncertain and incomplete enterprise.

The staging of the N. town plays has, like the dramatic form, too often been treated as a single homogeneous whole. That there are similarities of a general kind between the staging of the various parts seems to me to be likely, but there is no point in trying to think in terms of an integrated set for the pageants, the *Mary Play* and the

Passion. Even the two parts of the *Passion* (being one year apart) are quite different in their requirements.

Seeing the N. town manuscript as a collection of incomplete plays imperfectly blended together should not be a cause for gloom. To be certain about what is not, is a surer foundation for judgement than uncertainty about what is. Besides which, we are not unfamiliar with incomplete works in dealing with medieval English literature and drama. At least we can be sure that somewhere in East Anglia there was a person or place of sufficient dramatic vitality to be handling material as diverse as a devotional *Mary Play*, a series of pageants, some of great skill and theatrical effectiveness, a procession of apostles and others, and a two-part *Passion Play* – and, as well, to be thinking of combining them all into a cycle to end all cycles.

The modern stage history of the N. town *Passion* in some form stretches back to the early years of this century. The *Passion Play* (or Passion sections from the whole manuscript) formed the text of the 'blasphemous' production by Nugent Monck in 1909 (or 'non-production' since owing to the action of the Lord Chamberlain it never took place), later re-created for private performance at the Maddermarket Theatre in Norwich in 1938, and finally publicly performed there in 1952. Between then and now the whole manuscript has been used at various times to provide a 'cycle', as at Tewkesbury, Grantham, Coventry, Lincoln and Winchester – the last using a circular, open-air playing-space and large perimeter scaffolds. (For a guide to productions, see the list at the end of John Elliott's *Playing God: Medieval Mysteries on the Modern Stage* (Toronto 1989).) In Toronto in 1981 there was the first modern attempt to perform the *Passion Play* as a separate entity, in a modernised version by Stanley J. Kahrl, using the stage directions of the manuscript to create a place-and-scaffold set in the quadrangle of Victoria College (see reviews in *Research Opportunities in Renaissance Drama* and *Medieval English Theatre* listed in the Bibliography). Moreover, ever since the late fifteenth century, or early sixteenth, sections of the *Passion* have clearly been extracted for separate production, and with so good a text it is not surprising to find that this tradition is still being followed.

It is a very long time ago that I first started thinking about the manuscript of the N. town plays and in the course of the years that have intervened I have talked to many people about different aspects of it; my gratitude is no greater to those I can remember than to those I have forgotten – it is not they who are forgettable but I who am forgetful – and I offer my thanks and apologies to the forgotten ones. Of those I can remember I should like first to repeat my *Mary Play* list: Richard Beadle, Arthur Cawley, Stanley Kahrl, Stephen Spector, Meg Twycross, and to add Lesley Jeffries (who made me a computer user), Lynette Muir (my French connection), Richard Rastall, John E. Tailby (my German aide), Veronica O'Mara, JoAnna Dutka and Theodore de Welles. To them all I am most grateful, even if at times I appear to have ignored their advice, forgotten their warnings, and gone off on my own. Those blundering wanderings are mine and not theirs. My students at Leeds, both undergraduate and post-graduate, and for a while those in Toronto, have again been of invaluable assistance, for their interest and enthusiasm and for showing me what did not need explaining. I am extremely grateful to the University of Leeds for creating the machinery for arranging study leave, and to the School of English, and in particular my medievalist colleagues, for generously allowing me to benefit from the arrangement. I have also used up much in the way of typing time and goodwill and I should like to thank especially Mrs Pamela Armitage for all her skill and assistance. Finally (apart from thanking my family who have almost all left home in the course of this book) I should like to say what a pleasure it has been to work with such patient and good-humoured publishers as Longman.

Peter Meredith *Bramley, November 1988.*

To my wife, who will be glad to see
the back of it, and to those who stayed
and those who flew.

INTRODUCTION

THE MANUSCRIPT

Form and Purpose

The late fifteenth-century N. town manuscript (British Library Cotton Vespasian D VIII) which contains the *Passion Play* consists of a proclamation, or banns (Block, pp. 1–16), describing a series of forty pageants, and a text of what appear to be forty-one pageants (wrongly numbered forty-two), almost entirely written in the hand of a single scribe. The proclamation (ff. 1–9v) describes each pageant in turn, e.g. 'In þe ffyrst pagent we þenke to play . . .', 'In þe secunde pagent by godys myth . . .', normally devoting a stanza or two to each. The stanzas are thirteeners[1] except for those describing pageants 13 and 14 which are quatrains, and those describing pageants 23/24 and 37/38 where in each case a thirteener (divided into four lines and nine) is shared between two pageants. That the descriptions of 13 and 14 were intended to be in thirteeners is clear from the space which has been left in the manuscript for the completion of the stanzas, and which is still empty. This section of the manuscript has therefore an orderly, regular appearance with account being taken of material to be entered in the future. The only hint of disorder lies in the altered numbers of pageants 8–14 (renumbered 10–16).[2]

The pageant texts which follow the proclamation (ff. 10–225) are each numbered in the right margin with a large red arabic numeral from 1 to 42 (17 has been inexplicably omitted).[3] So far (almost) so good. Unfortunately this superficial regularity and numerical near-fit conceals complex varieties of re-organisation, half-attempted integration, botching and patching. Apparently a series of pageants matching the proclamation has been stretched and distorted to absorb a separate play on the early life of Mary (*The Mary Play*) and a separate two-part *Passion Play*. Two pageants unmentioned in the proclamation have been added, one written out again by the scribe (the *Purification*) and one inserted in its original form (the *Assumption of the Virgin*). At least one other pageant (*Noah*) has been substantially revised. The absorbing of the *Mary Play* is described elsewhere but the scribe's methods can be seen even more clearly in *Passion* I, the first part of the *Passion Play*, where material has been baldly inserted into the play from other, most probably pageant, sources (see below 'Passion I' and Appendices 1 and 2). Though the text is sometimes blended with some care there is no attempt at creating or presenting an integrated staging.

The result is a remarkably comprehensive coverage of the history of mankind from Creation to Doomsday, but one which theatrically veers uneasily between different styles of presentation. It is not unplayable as a whole, though unwieldy, but it looks not so much like the carefully thought-out text of a theatrically minded writer as the minute by minute adjustments and second thoughts of a scribe concerned primarily with following his own (or another's) desire for completeness.[4]

It should be clear from what has been said that the manuscript is not a straightforward cycle of pageants. It contains part of such a cycle and it contains the proclamation for such a cycle, but it also contains some quite different dramatic pieces. It is now impossible to be sure what the main scribe or those who were directing him were attempting to achieve. It does seem, however, as if the project was never completed, or else that it was never intended to achieve more than a rough 'workshop' form. There is conflicting evidence here. We have on the one hand a half-finished correction of the proclamation numbering and an attempt to integrate diverse dramatic texts. On the other hand if we turn to the added *Assumption* pageant we find something apparently rather different. This pageant is a separate booklet written by another scribe and simply bound into the manuscript. The main scribe has, however, numbered it and rubricated it to bring it visually into line with his own work.[5] If the whole manuscript was intended to be only a rough copy, why did he bother? The answer lies again, I think, in half measures. The main scribe could have written the pageant out again if he had wanted to produce a truly homogeneous manuscript. Instead he has done enough to give it the rough appearance of homogeneity.

The same patching is apparent elsewhere. The first part of the *Passion Play* was, like the *Assumption*, a separate booklet (though larger), which has been bound into the manuscript. In this case it was a manuscript that the main scribe had written himself at another time. Originally it was larger and included a description of a procession. Part of this has been removed, but one leaf still survives because the opening of the description of the procession has been written on the other half of one of the bifolia containing the text of the play (f. 163 contains the procession, f. 156, its counterpart, contains ll. 779–824 of *Passion* I). He could have removed the leaf with the procession on it and copied out again the text of the play which would have been lost, but he chose half measures once again.

The form of the manuscript is, then, clear. It is a collection of miscellaneous texts roughly integrated with some concern for appearance and some for comprehensibility. It is not a prestige manuscript in any way; is it then in some way a 'workshop' copy? And if so, what sort of workshop? It could be a theatrical one, representing the text of plays drawn together for the use of a particular place or a particular group. But why in that case not keep them separate? This would be of far more practical use than a manuscript hard to follow and a play of dauntingly unwieldy proportions. Would the 'workshop' of a theatrical entrepreneur make any more sense? If this were a manuscript for lending-out, it could serve a multitude of purposes: a two-part Passion Play, a St Anne's day celebration (or any feast of the Virgin Mary), a cycle of varying size, or any number of smaller plays, to be performed anywhere (the 'N' town of the proclamation). This is certainly how it has been used. Marginal annotations in *Passion* II indicate sections divided off for day's performances and marginal alterations and additions to the text suggest the use of the manuscript as a 'drawing-board' for the creation of new versions of these and other sections (see Appendix 5, below).

The lending-out of play manuscripts certainly occurred in France. Mons in 1501 hired the text from Amiens and adapted it for its own purposes. There is also evidence from France of poets being hired to write or adapt plays for particular occasions.[6] Perhaps the 'property players' at work in East Anglia in the sixteenth century dealt in texts as well as the more obvious stage properties. Would Richard Gibson, Henry VIII's resourceful Yeoman of the Revels, have had a use for such a manuscript, or Gover Martyn in his dealings with towns like New Romney?[7] Certainly the retention of what are almost multiple endings for the *Mary Play* would make sense in such a context, but again it has to be remembered that the semi-integrated form of the manuscript does not make multiple use easy.

If this was the purpose of the manuscript, a text to be lent or hired out, or one which could be used in a variety of situations, where might such a manuscript have been written? It does not look like the work of a professional scriptorium, unless it was intended to be copy for the production of a finished version,[8] but nevertheless the hand is a competent and usually neat one and the scribe obviously had the training to cope with the lay-out of a large and complex manuscript and the skill to deal with a number of changes of plan, even if he did not always carry through his intentions. The hand is similar in general appearance and skill to many of those working on vernacular manuscripts during the later fifteenth and early sixteenth centuries, e.g. the hands in the Paston letters (though more formally presented) or those of the Northampton *Abraham and Isaac* and the Reynes *Commonplace Book* (though less stylish), and it is far more controlled and skilful than that of the slightly later *Mary Magdalen*.[9] It is therefore not enough by itself to indicate where the manuscript came from or for whom it was written.

What of the content of the manuscript apart from the plays? It has sometimes been suggested that the marginalia imply an 'ecclesiastical' origin.[10] Apart from the fact that 'ecclesiastical' could mean anything from a church building fund to a monastic liturgy, there is some doubt about whether the marginalia that exist are properly so called. The most useful comparison here is with the Reynes *Commonplace Book*.[11] This consists of a miscellaneous collection of information, some of practical use in the handling of affairs – assize of bread and ale, weights and measures, arabic numerals, instructions about various legal matters, charms, recipes for ink; some of a more abstract interest – the number of the drops of Christ's blood shed in his Passion, the age of the Virgin Mary, a poem about Anne, lists of the Magi, the twenty-four elders, the twelve apostles, notes on Adam and on Septuagesima. These latter snippets of information reflect just the same kind of interest as the marginalia of the N. town manuscript: liturgical – the day of the translation of Mary Magdalene and of the birth of Adam (f. 74v); the holy family – the five Annes (f. 37v), the relatives of Mary (f. 37); biblical 'facts' – the dimensions of Noah's ark and the depth of the flood (f. 24). Reynes's book demonstrates how an interest in such 'ecclesiastical' material can very easily be of lay origin; besides which his book also reveals an interest in plays (see below 'Dramatic and social context').

Other play manuscripts, although many of them come from the same area of the country and some are of a similar date, do not help much to suggest the kind of people likely to be commissioning or compiling the N. town manuscript because in every case their origin is as uncertain. The Croxton *Play of the Sacrament*, with its list of twelve characters and the assurance that 'ix may play yt at ease', is not necessarily aimed at a group of professional touring players. Many different kinds of groups may have found it useful to know what kind of doubling could be used. Even the earlier *Castle of Perseverance* with its stage plan gives no firm evidence of the kind of performance groups for which it was written down. The commonest arrangement in East Anglia, outside Norwich and the other large towns, seems to have been for groups of towns or villages to join together, often only financially, to put on a play – perhaps in aid of church funds (see below 'Dramatic and social context'). Under such circumstances any religious play manuscript could have been of use and anyone who could have supplied such a manuscript of value to the community. We do not seem to be dealing here with regular performance and therefore there is a need for publicising date and place. Which is no doubt the reason for the inclusion of a substitutable 'N. town' or a blank in the surviving banns, and of dates and times of performance: 'A sunday next . . . at vj of þe belle' (*N. town*), 'on Monday' (*Croxton*), 'þis day seuenenyt . . . be vnderne of þe day' (*Castle of Perseverance*). If we cannot be sure of the purpose of the N. town compilation, at least it seems likely that this is the performance context of its various parts and of many of the other surviving East Anglian plays.

Play and pageants

It is sometimes implied or stated that the present *Passion Play* is a revision of earlier pageants (those described in the Proclamation) to make a continuous play. While it is impossible to disprove this it seems to me that in the case of *Passion* I and the first part of *Passion* II (up to l. 880) this is unlikely. The demonstrable overlaps between the episodes in the play and the Proclamation are not numerous. *Passion* I deals with the events from the beginning of the Conspiracy against Christ to his taking in the garden of Gethsemane. The scribe has numbered the play as a series of pageants, 25 to 27 (Proclamation 23 to 25). The descriptions in the Proclamation only very inadequately describe the play episodes. The first description (one of the 'half-stanza' ones) runs:

> In þe xxiij^ti pagent, Palme Sunday,
> In pley we purpose for to shewe,
> How chylderyn of Ebrew with flourys ful gay,
> Þe wey þat Cryst went þei gun to strewe.

The text to which this applies, numbered 26 in the manuscript, contains two prologues, of the Demon (I. 1–124), and of John the Baptist (I. 125–64); the beginning of the conspiracy (I. 165–342); the fetching of the ass (Appendix 1); the preaching of Peter and John (I. 343–98); and the entry into Jerusalem with the healing of the blind (I. 399–442). Moreover the incident to which the description refers is contained in a stage direction (or at most a stage direction and four lines of text).

The second description runs:

> In þe xxiiij^te pagent, as þat we may,
> Cryst and his apostelys alle on rewe,
> The mawndé of God þer xal they play;
> And sone declare it with wordys fewe.
>   And than
> Judas þat fals traytour,
> For xxx^ti platys of werdly tresour,
> Xal betray oure Savyour
>   To þe Jewys, certan.

Here, the text, numbered 27, has Christ's lament over Jerusalem and his preparation for the Last Supper (I. 343–518); a continuation of the conspiracy (I. 519–82); the anointing of Christ by Mary Magdalene, and the foretelling of the betrayal (Appendix 2); Judas's betrayal (I. 588–662); and an extended Last Supper – 'declare it with wordys fewe'? – (I. 663–884). Not only is the emphasis wrong but the order is reversed.

The final section, numbered 28, is the shortest (under 200 lines) and the least complicated. Its only unusual feature is the visit of Magdalene to the Virgin Mary at the very end, and this is not contained in the Proclamation.

The same is broadly true of the first part of *Passion* II. In the second part a simple mixing of pageant and play material largely takes over. (For a detailed description of the relation between play and Proclamation, see Appendix 4).

More important than the lack of overlap between play and Proclamation however, is the fact that so much of the play is devoted to the very episodes which are most unlikely to occur in separate pageants – e.g. the linking/walking speeches like Peter's sermon (I. 343–74) or Christ's words to his disciples as he walks towards Simon's house (I. 495–502) – and the considerable sections of the play which make sense only in continuity – e.g. the interrelatedness of first Annas's and then Caiaphas's doubts about Christ, the necessity of a meeting, the involvement of the Pharisees (I. 165–342); all of which seems far too long for a pageant but is appropriate to the opening of a play (nearly 200 lines simply to decide to conspire).

Furthermore, when what appears to be pageant material is introduced into *Passion* I, the stanza form used (wholly in one case and partly in the other) is one which is common in the pageant part of the manuscript but does not appear at all in the *Passion Play*, the thirteener. It might be expected that if the *Passion Play* were a revision of existing pageant material this would show more in the type of stanza used.

Passion I

It is important to take the two parts of the *Passion Play* separately because their manuscript origins and the treatment given them by the scribe are quite different. As has already been said, *Passion* I is a separate booklet bound into the present manuscript but written in the same hand throughout, that of the main scribe, before the compilation was made. It is therefore in every sense a separate play. There is no evidence, even, to suggest that it had a second half, except that if it did not it was a rather odd series of episodes to choose. The only interference with the original play by the scribe occurs on f. 143 and ff. 149–51.

The first is the interpolation of the incident of the fetching of the ass (Appendix 1), on a single leaf (f. 143), probably originating from old pageant material. The incident is not mentioned in the Proclamation description, but that description is a very short one (see above p. 6). This addition was clearly written out by the scribe specially to be incorporated here, making use of a piece of scrap paper (it had several large ink blots on it before he wrote his text). The purpose of the addition seems to have been simply to supply an incident that was not present – and is not necessary.

The second interference is a somewhat longer interpolation. This occurs between ff. 148 and 152 and consists of two sections continuous in the manuscript: the repentance of Magdalene (f. 149) and

the foretelling of the betrayal (ff. 150–1) (Appendix 2). These three
leaves, now called quire O, have been interpolated between two
original quires, now N and P. In both cases the additions have no
necessary narrative or dramatic purpose and seem to be merely the
result of the scribe's desire for all-inclusiveness.

In view of the distinct and separable nature of these interpolations,
it is fair to say that the form that *Passion* I took is clear. I would not go
so far as to say that we have the original or even the final form. The
prologues are not perhaps as well integrated with the play as one
might have expected, nor is their relationship to each other entirely
clear. There are elaborate stage directions for much of the play but
there are none for the prologues and some of those later in the play
tend to be more narrative than practical – but what medieval English
play does have consistently full stage directions? It looks like a play in
the course of development, and we are lucky that it reached the
relatively developed stage that it has and that it is so free from the
scribe's adaptation.

Passion II

The second part of the *Passion Play* shows at first every sign of being
a similar text to the first part. It looks like a separate play, with a
prologue that links it in some detail with the events already played
'þe last 3ere' (II. 6). The two quires on which much of it is written
show signs of having been a separate manuscript. Around f. 184,
however, there is clearly some kind of disruption. Two leaves, ff.
184–5, have been interpolated into the middle of the quire, but the
text that they contain is continuous with what precedes and follows
it and is not detachable in the way that the interpolations into *Passion*
I are. Moreover, at the place about a third of the way down f. 183v
where the writing becomes somewhat cramped, no doubt signalling
the introduction of ff. 184–5, a new stanza form appears, the romance stanza. It seems that this marks the end of *Passion* II as an
entity and the beginning of the scribe's somewhat undigested mixing of play and pageant material. After II. 880 there are far more
romance stanzas than any other, while before that line there are no
romance stanzas and the quatrain is far and away the commonest
form. It would be wrong to base conclusions simply on stanza
forms, but when the evidence they provide is taken with the manuscript evidence, it overwhelmingly suggests the introduction of new
material. The later material in the play is not in the same order as it is

in the Proclamation but it is often close to it in content, and the conclusion seems inescapable that the scribe is blending *Passion Play* and pageant text in a rather unsubtle way; see Appendix 4.

LANGUAGE AND PLACE

The evidence set out in the *Linguistic Atlas of Later Middle English* indicates that the main scribe of the N. town manuscript learned to write in south-west Norfolk.[12] There seems no good reason for doubting that the 'placing' of the scribe serves in a general sense to 'place' the plays. Though scribes could and did move considerable distances away from their places of origin, the authors of the *Atlas* suggest that the commonest pattern was for them to work within their local area (I, p. 23). The manuscript is not a prestige one. Its composition shows general competence rather than exceptional skill and there is nothing in it to suggest a home other than Norfolk or its immediate neighbours. That the scribe was trained in the general area of East Harling does not give the plays a definite home but it does make an East Anglian, and more specifically a Norfolk, provenance likely. The authors of the *Atlas* also draw attention to the variety of forms available to a Norfolk scribe (II, p. x) and both parts of the *Passion Play* reflect this variety.

In many respects the language of the *Passion Play* is similar to that of the *Mary Play*, but there are differences which no doubt reflect the different origins of the texts and the different periods at which the scribe was writing. It must be borne in mind that unlike the *Mary Play*, *Passion* I at least was once a separate manuscript and written at a separate time; though how much time elapsed between the writing of *Passion* I and that of the rest of the manuscript it is impossible to know. In discussing the language I shall follow the order of the discussion in the *Mary Play* Introduction.

Most consistent of the scribe's characteristic spellings is again *x-* for *xal*, *xulde*, etc. which is a common East Anglian feature. There are only five intrusions into this pattern from *sch-*, *sh-* spellings (*schal* I. 145, 899, II. 393; *schuld* I. 715; *shal* II. 1473). Even rarer are the extensions of *x-* outside the pattern: *xad* 'shed' (I. 798) and *xamefullest* 'most shameful' (II. 61). In the variations between *-ght* and *-th/-tht/-t* there is not only further evidence for East Anglian provenance but also evidence for the differing origins of the parts of the *Passion Play*. In the ratio of spellings the *Passion Play* partly differs from the *Mary Play*, but it also differs within itself. This is worth looking at in a little more detail. On a crude count, in the second part of *Passion* II (II. 800 onwards) *-ght* spellings outnumber the others by a little under 2:1 (79:47). This is similar to the *Mary Play* (89:48) and to the texts here printed as Appendices 1 and 2 where *-ght* is also the predominant form (17:4), though the sample is far smaller. In *Passion* I, however, the situation is reversed and the *-th/-tht/-t* spellings outnumber the *-ght* by 42:1 (84:2) and this pattern is similar in the first part of *Passion* II where *-ght* spellings are outnumbered by nearly 15:1 (74:5). This does not prove a close relationship between the composition or copying of *Passion* I and *Passion* II(a), but it does point to *Passion* II(b) as the odd man out and to a closer relationship, in one way at least, between this part and the rest of the manuscript. Examples of *-th/-tht/-t* spellings are: *bryth* 'bright', *nyth* 'night', *almythty* 'almighty', *lytys* 'lights', *knytys* 'knights'.

Numerically far less significant are two other East Anglian features: the use of *qw-/qwh-* for *wh-* and the use of *-t/-ht/-ght* for various verb inflections in *-th*. Examples of the former are: *qwan* 'when', *qwat*, *qwhat* 'what', *qwere*, *qwher* 'where', *qweche*, *qwych* 'which'; and of the latter: 3 sg. pr. *dystroyt*, *fortyfyet*, *prayt*, imp. pl. *goht*, *heryght*. Other East Anglian characteristics are the forms: *hefne* (15:13 *hevyn*), *kend(e)* (8:1 *kynde*), *mende* (7:0), *werd(e)* (11:6 *werld(e)/world(e)*), *erde/herd* (2:3 *erth(e)*), *erdon* (1:3 *erand/herand/errandys*). *Curyng* and *recure* are used with their East Anglian meanings of 'covering' and 'obtain', and the word *thyrknes* (cf. *therkeness*, *Mary Play* l. 1009) occurs in Appendix 3, l. 27.

Because of the variations between *-ght* and *-th/-tht/-t* on the one hand and the *-t/-ht/-ght* spellings for *-th* on the other (mentioned above), and because of the pronunciation /t/ for *-th*, there are many confusions in the spelling of final *-t*: *abowth* 'about', *eneryth* 'inherit', *perfyth* 'perfect', *mownth* 'mount', *Egythp* 'Egypt', *whath* 'what'. The variation *qw/qwh* and *wh/w* in words like 'where' and 'what' produces comparable variations in the spelling of other words with initial *w*: e.g. *whare* 'ware', *whysshe* 'wish', *whith* 'wight' (creature), *whe* 'we', *whylde* 'wild'. There are many other spelling variations current in East Anglia but elsewhere as well: e.g. *e* for *i* not only in *kende/mende* but also, for example, in *ceté* 'city', *jebet/gebettys* 'gibbet(s)', *hedyr* 'hither', *hese* 'his', *meracle* 'miracle', *pelere* 'pillar', *pety* 'pity', *tekyl* 'tickle', *velany* 'villainy'. Initial *h* is occasionally omitted in words of both French and English origin, but more often it is added before an initial vowel: e.g. *a*, *ast*, *an* (forms of 'have'); *habyl* 'able', *habundawns* 'abundance', *hasayd* 'assayed', *hendles* 'endless', *heuermore* 'evermore', *hylle* 'ill', *howth* 'aught'. Spellings *were/ware/wore* are the result of blending of dialect forms of English and Scandinavian origin. The scribe also sometimes joins unstressed *it* (represented by *d* or *t*) onto the associated verb, e.g. *tys* 'it is', *applyed* 'apply it', *levynt* 'leave it', *settynt* 'set it'.

The inflections used in the play are among those normal in the area. For verbs, *-th* is the commonest ending by far for the third person singular present indicative, but uninflected forms occur (e.g. *perverte* I. 218, *werke* I. 322, *drynke* I. 821), occasional syncopated forms (II. 361, 658sd), and once the Northern *-s* rhyming with a pair of *-s* present plural verbs (I. 39). The present plural is normally uninflected but there are a considerable number of examples with *-n* (the ratio is considerably more than 2:1 in favour of the uninflected), there are a few with *-th* (I. 195, II. 63, 68, 875), and three with Northern *-s* (I. 36, 37, II. 665) all in rhyme position. The imperative singular and plural is most commonly uninflected but the plural occasionally has *-th*. The infinitive is also normally uninflected but *-n* appears quite frequently (the ratio is about 4:1). The past tense seldom takes *-n* and the past participle varies between being uninflected and *-n*. The present participle is almost invariably *-yng(e)* though there are three examples of *-ande*, all rhymes (I. 134, 136, 139). For stylistic variation some use is made of auxiliary *do*, especially in the 3 sg. pr. *doth* and the preterite *dede*.

The first part of the *Passion Play* is the only place where there is some consistency of usage of *þu* and *ȝe*. *Ȝe/ȝow* is used by their servants to Annas and Caiaphas (except for one *ȝe* by Caiaphas to the messenger, I. 255) and by the Virgin Mary and Magdalene in the short scene at the end of the play. In the second part there is no overall consistency and no subtlety in the usage. The forms of third person plural pronouns are those to be expected in this area: *thei/þei*, *hem*, *here* with occasional variation (*them/þem* 13 examples, *þer(e)* 7 examples, against *hem* 72 and *here* 46).

METRE, LANGUAGE AND STYLE

In *Passion* I the commonest stanza forms are the quatrain (122 examples) and the octave, or double-quatrain, rhyming *ababbcbc* (71). There are a very small number of subsidiary forms: five couplets, a couple of single lines and a single octave rhyming *abababab* which opens the play. The scribe is normally reliable in indicating stanzas, though he occasionally omits his stanza marker (the *capitulum*) and occasionally misplaces it. In one case he imposes his own idiosyncratic pattern, when he divides Demon's prologue into quatrains on the recto of the leaf and octaves on the verso (I. 1–124). He does not indicate any twelve-line stanzas in this part of the *Passion* though there is a good deal of stanza-linking of octaves and quatrains.

In *Passion* I the couplet appears only during the Last Supper (if we discount the two single lines at I. 341–2 which are unlikely to be intended, and do not deserve to be considered, as a couplet). The first example (I. 763–4) contains the repeated words of Christ as he gives the sacramental wafer to each of the disciples:

> This is my body, flesch and blode,
> Þat for þe xal dey upon þe rode.   (I. 763–4)

The words echo those of gospel and mass 'Hoc est enim corpus meum' and the couplet form underlines their solemnity by isolating them, this isolation being emphasised by the repetition. The pattern of repetition is broken by Christ's question and Judas's reply in the form of another couplet. The next couplet again breaks a series of repetitions, this time of the single or half line 'Lord, it is not I', the denial by the disciples of Christ's betrayal, and again by a question, Judas's: 'Is it owth I, lord?', confirmed by Christ's reply: 'Judas, þu seyst þat word'. The change to question allows Judas verbally to isolate himself as previously Christ has isolated him by a question (I. 765). A further couplet emphasises Judas's guilt. The last couplet is, expectedly, Christ's words for the administering of the consecrated wine, which, Judas having departed, is repeated without interruption.

It is best to divide *Passion* II into two sections (a) and (b). Before l. 880, *Passion* II(a), the dominant forms are the quatrain (139 examples) and the couplet (67); after that line, *Passion* II(b), the romance stanza predominates (an eight-line stanza, usually rhyming *aaabcccb* and with variation in number of stresses between the *b* lines and the others). There are octaves in both sections, 15 before l. 880 and 31 after, but in *Passion* II(b) they mainly form an almost continuous series at the end of the play. There are no romance stanzas before l. 880 and no couplets after it.

The formal and specific use of the couplet in *Passion* I is quite unlike its use in *Passion* II(a). From II. 177 until 879 the couplet is one of the commonest stanza forms and is used primarily for its flexibility in moving quickly from character to character and allowing the impression, within limits, of everyday speech. It is particularly associated with Pilate who has more lines in couplets than in any other stanza form, which perhaps helps to suggest the view of him as an ordinary, well-meaning official, characteristic of *Passion* II(a). The use of the couplet is particularly sustained in II. 182–209, 314–37, 390–9, 639–74 and 683–97. Something of the isolating effect of the single couplet appears in its first use in *Passion* II where it appears as the culmination of a speech by Caiaphas. In the first part of the speech, marked by broken lines, exclamation and question, he is shown blustering. A single line (II. 166) indicates a return to a more reasonable approach and the couplet, marked by a more regular rhythm, is used as a containing vehicle for the oath with which Caiaphas finally makes his demands of Christ. The breaking up of the speech between quatrain, single line and couplet partly echoes the broken nature of Caiaphas's attack – his pauses for the demanded reply – but it also echoes the changing nature of his attack, from anger to adjuration.

In a culture where verse is the normal literary form, it is not surprising to find some that is rhythmically little different from prose. The verse in these plays has neither the regularity of syllabic rhymed metre nor the sustained cohesiveness of good alliterative verse. But nor is it merely rhymed prose. It moves between regularity of rhythm and freedom with considerable skill and dramatic aptness. What any performer is struck by in the early part of *Passion* II is the freedom and naturalness of the language and rhythm. In *Passion* I, however, there is a greater sense of form and formality in, for example, the opening speeches of Annas and Caiaphas, Peter's sermon or, most particularly, Christ's exposition of the meaning of the Passover.

There is clearly a reluctance on the part of the playwright to break stanza forms and therefore where quick exchanges are required the couplet is useful. In only a small number of cases is a stanza divided between speakers. This leads to a certain appearance of formality on the page, but it is only occasionally noticeable in performance. Oddly, though the *Mary Play* is more formal in tone its playwright divides the stanzas between speakers far more freely, and not just by making, as it were, an octave into two quatrains, but by giving the first or last one or two lines to another speaker.

In both parts extra-metrical lines appear. In *Passion* I there are only two (I. 341–2) unless 'Lord, it is not I' (I. 775) is taken as a separate rather than a half line. In *Passion* II the single lines are mainly used to allow for a natural response by the crowd at Christ's trials (e.g. '3a,

3a, 3a!' at II. 179, 345sd, 646sd, 672sd), but there is also the repetition
of 'Ho was þat?' in the game refrain (II. 188 and 193), Longeus's cry
for mercy (II. 1155) reminiscent of the use of the extra-metrical lines
in the *Mary Play*, and the line already referred to added to Caiaphas's
emotional cross-questioning of Christ (II. 166).

There is some freedom of rhyme in the *Passion Play*: rhyming *-n*
with *-m*, e.g. *cam/Satan* (I. 1/3), *on/lom* (II. 109/111), *com/everychon*
(II. 135/137); other assonances, e.g. *everychon/wrong* (I. 809/811),
not/fop (II. 162/163), *vnqwyt/skyp* (II. 507/509); variation of vowel,
e.g. *God/good* (II. 5/7), *trespas/crosse* (II. 671/673). Rhymes of this
kind make it just possible that I. 341–2 (*reson/same*) is a couplet,
though the diversity is a bit more extreme. Some rhymes depend
upon stressed or unstressed forms of the same word: e.g. unstressed
sertayn rhyming with *woman* (II. 1862/1864) and stressed *sertayn* with
peyn (I. 310/312). There are also a few rhymes that depend upon the
stressing of inflections: e.g. *awntys/grawnt us* (II. 1699/1701), and
most notable, since it seems to be a deliberate playing with the
device, *þis/Jewys* (II. 875/876) next to *þus/Jewus* (II. 877/878).

The *Passion Play* is not characterised by a rich literary language.
Aureate diction is not a special feature of the play and alliteration is
not used to an extent sufficient to produce a wide range of alliterative
words. Two words *obeycon* (II. 306) and *perdure* (I. 368) are according
to the *MED* unique to this play, and *sorwatorie* (II. 947), apparently a
combination of *sorwe* and 'purgatory', is not recorded in *OED*.
Hoberd (II. 897 and 905) appears only here and in the *N. town* Herod
pageant (Block, p. 169). For *eternalyté* (3A5), *seryattly* (I. 754), and
ouerest (II. 486sd) this is *MED*'s first recorded use; *brace* (2A44) and
batte (II. 184) are recorded here first with this meaning, and *vnete* (I.
727) and *vnlosne* (1A9) are recorded here first with these forms.

Alliteration and learned language, rhetorical balance and repetition do play some part in the play, however, though in general the
language tends towards the straightforward and plain. Alliteration is
used scantily: Annas and Caiaphas both introduce themselves (I.
165ff. and 209ff) with an alliterative line (both alliterating on *pr-*,
stemming from *prelat* and *primat*) but only Satan in *Passion* II (ll.
487ff.) appears with a heavy burst of alliteration. The use of a learned
Latinate vocabulary depends upon the needs of character and cir-
cumstance. Caiaphas employs a learned vocabulary (I. 209–16) because he is a bishop and because he is pompous, as well as because he
is making his first appearance. Appropriateness of language register
is often true of the use of language generally; that it reflects the

character, the state of mind or the situation from which the speech springs relatively naturally: e.g. the First Doctor's careful approach to Caiaphas (I. 225 ff.) allowing the Second a more open attack (I. 233ff.) – cf. Annas's two doctors (I. 185–96); the blustering incoherence of Annas's speech (II. 338–45) and Caiaphas's laborious emphasis upon the evident 'truth' of an irrelevant fact (II. 354–61); the politely veiled threat of the approach to Symon of Cyrene (II. 719–26); and the chanted game of the first mocking (II. 186–93). The language clearly remains more formal than ordinary speech, and characters often say too much about what they are doing or throw in too many conventional tags, but nevertheless it often embodies rather than simply conveying natural emotions and reactions.

The more elaborately-worked rhetorical speeches are also more integral and less decorative than for example those in the *Mary Play*. Christ's exposition of the meaning of the Passover feast is the clearest example. Repetition and balance are again the main devices used:

> And as we stodyn, so dede þei stond . . .   (I. 671)
> And as we ete it, so dede þei, hastyly . . .   (I. 674)

Sometimes this is linked with word-play or alliteration:

> Weche xal be of my body, þat am ȝour hed . . .   (I. 676)
> Of my flesch and blood in forme of bred.   (I. 678);

or reversal of order:

> For mannys love I may do no mo,
> Þan for love of man to be ded.   (I. 807–8).

Balanced phrases end Peter's first stanza of preaching:

> He xal cawse þe blynde þat þei xal se,
> Þe def to here, þe dome for to speke.   (I. 349–50)

There is also a deliberate rounding-off of Christ's speech over Jerusalem by a return to the first line:

> O, Jherusalem, woful is þe ordenawnce . . .
> O, ceté, ful woful is þin ordenawns!   (I. 443/458).

DRAMATIC AND SOCIAL CONTEXT

For an area so rich in drama in the fifteenth and early sixteenth century, East Anglia is sadly lacking in records of performance, and we are fortunate that, for example, the texts of *Mary Magdalen*, the

Castle of Perseverance and the *N. town* plays contain so much in the
way of staging information. Norwich remains, however, the only
place where records and text (unfortunately very brief) coincide. In
the search for a context of performance for the *Passion Play*, one of
the further difficulties is the sparsity of records from the fifteenth
century and earlier.[13]

The East Harling 'Interlude' reference simply establishes the existence of a play of some sort there in 1452; the 'game' references add a
few more tantalising hints for 1457 and 1463. The noting of rewards
to *jucelaris*, *mimis*, *menstrellis* and *lusoribus* at Thetford Priory exists
but tells us nothing that can be related to any of the extant plays.
Going beyond the immediate area of the main scribe's likely place of
origin, there are in the fifteenth-century Norfolk and Suffolk records
still only the merest hints of relevant performance. East Dereham in
central Norfolk has a 'frame that the monstyr is set on on Corpus
Cristi day' sometime in 1491–3, but this, which at first sight looks as
though it might be a hell-mouth, is probably in view of its cost of 4*d.*
a portable framework for a processional giant or beast. In Yar-
mouth's well-known 'game-place' performances of some kind clearly took place; the lessee is to 'permitt & suffre all suche players as ther
audiens [as well as their audience] to haue the plesure & ese of the seid
hous and Gameplace at all suche tyme & tymes as eny interludes or
pleyes ther shal be ministred or played at eny tyme withought eny
profight thereof by hym or by his assignes to be taken'. Unfortunately the earliest mention is 1531. It provides a possible later setting
but does not help with the original or with early performance. Only
King's Lynn has anything like a series of early records and they
provide only exciting but ultimately frustrating glimpses of plays at
Christmas 'coram domino de Scales' (1445/6) (with a Mary and
Gabriel in the cast, who also had to learn to sing), or a play in
Tuesday Market-place on Corpus Christi day watched by the mayor
and several of his brothers in the house of Arnulph Tixony (but only
if we put together the records for 1447/8, 1457/8 and 1461/2). There
are also the interesting groupings of places that are revealed in the
records, though these probably tell us more about financial support
for plays than about travelling performers (see, for example, Snet-
tisham and Boxford), and the evidence of the banns-criers that
comes from south Lincolnshire on the borders of Norfolk where
there is clearly interaction between a number of small towns and
villages with banns-criers travelling considerable distances to collect
money towards their plays (see, for example, Long Sutton). Again it

looks more like evidence for gathering financial support than for performance, but it does at least give a record context, and to some extent a living one, for the *N. town* banns.

To get some idea of a possible organisational context for the play it is necessary to go later in time, and in the end further afield. Bungay and Boxford in Suffolk in the sixteenth century both provide some evidence. The church wardens of Holy Trinity, Bungay, have lengthy accounts in 1566 for a 'church ale & game on Trinyté sondaie' (though two days are later referred to). A scaffold was made in the churchyard for the 'Interlude' (presumably but not necessarily the same entertainment), apparel was borrowed from Norwich, cloths were stained, masks and wigs were prepared, and 'Kelsaye the vyce' was paid 2s. for his 'pastyme before the plaie and after the playe, bothe daies'. The receipts, presumably towards church funds, were £17. 1s. 1d., and the named expenses 13s. 2d. The 1568 'game' in the 'castleyard' provides a few more pieces of evidence, when wives made the collection amounting to £22. 5s. 6½d. Booths were set up for the selling of food and drink, a stage erected and afterwards taken down, apparel borrowed (this time from Wymondham in Norfolk) and six pounds of gunpowder bought. In 1558 and 1567, other 'game' years, there are payments for writing out parts but nowhere is there an indication of the subject of the 'game'.

The play of 1535 at Boxford in south Suffolk seems to have been performed at least in part by non-local players, since not only is there 30s. paid to the 'propyrté pleyer' but also 15s. to 'dyuerse pleyers which cam owt of strange placys'. It seems to have had a similar purpose to that of the 'game' at Bungay, the increase of church funds, but it illustrates more clearly the collecting of money from neighbouring towns and villages.

To find full evidence for a local community putting on a stationary play it is necessary, however, to go to New Romney in Kent.[14] Once again unfortunately the records are late, 1555 and 1560, but they are all that survive in detail of a play that seems to have been first performed in the early fifteenth century. It had a large cast (if the 1555 lists can be taken as typical) and considerable care (in the form of legal recognizances) was taken to ensure that actors knew their parts. There is very little sign of doubling of parts: Caiaphas's and Pilate's messengers, Annas and the second devil, Philip and the blind man's mother, and one of the neighbours and one of the Jews, are the only ones named. All the parts (including five women) were played by men but their ages are not given. Judging by the cast and set it was a Passion Play and the scaffolds, built by or at the cost of individuals of the town, consisted of one for Pilate and the princes, one for Annas and the tormentors, one for the Pharisees, and one for Herod. There was also a heaven, a hell and a cave and three crosses set in mortices. Very considerable sums of money were spent on costumes, properties and sets, and the play apparently brought in over £25. The largest single payment was to Gover Martyn 'our devysour, for his seruyce at our playe'. Some costumes were hired from nearby Lydd, some made. The play-book seems to have been written once and then copied out again 'in parchement'. The whole bears witness to a remarkable community enterprise.

The New Romney play is the fullest account of a production of this kind surviving from England and seems to me to provide the best insight into the organisation and staging of the *Passion Play*. Much is, of course, unlike. It is late; it comes from Kent, and near enough to London to be constantly sending there for necessaries; it was apparently performed over four days – though the evidence here is not entirely clear. Besides this it is unhelpful in that there is no indication of where in New Romney it was performed.

Coming nearer in time and place, and looking not for organisational or performance but for human context, we come back to Robert Reynes's *Commonplace Book*. His copying-out or writing-up of four dramatic pieces makes him an important representative of a group which is often difficult to discover, the involved lay person. His book is also interesting for the nature and range of the dramatic pieces it contains: two Nine Worthies pieces, a speech from what looks as though it may have been a morality play, and a fund-raising epilogue.[15] What Reynes's relationship was with these pieces we do not know. That he took the trouble to write down what in three cases were fragmentary texts argues a more than passing interest in the drama. Are they 'parcels', perhaps, that he or some of his family learnt or performed? One interesting connection with the *Passion Play* should be noted, the similarity between the names of the knights that watched the sepulchre in the play and those listed in the *Commonplace Book*:

The iiij knyghtis þat wechyd sepulc[re]
   Syr jheraunt
   Syr Cosdran
   Syr Ameraunt
   Syr Arfaxat   (f. 39v)

The names are not unknown elsewhere, however. They occur in Bodleian Library MS Laud misc 23 (f. 114v) and in a slightly different form in Ashmole 61 in a poem on the Resurrection (ff. 138v–44v). Besides which the lists differ: Reynes has 'jheraunt', Laud 'gerrant', where the play has 'Affraunt', and anyway a mere coincidence of names is not enough to establish a place of composition or performance. Nevertheless, as with the *Mary Play* (and indeed taken in conjunction with the connections between *Mary Play* and *Commonplace Book*) it does help to establish an individual Norfolk association and to give some evidence for a possible member of the audience.

SOURCES

Passion I

Behind the play lie the gospel narratives, but the order of events, the attention given to certain incidents, and in some cases the incidents themselves seem often to be a result of the playwright's own development of his biblical sources and the commentaries on them.

The Last Supper is in some ways the most complicated example. All the gospels give some account of it and all except Matthew and Mark differ quite radically, so that to some extent even the basic form of the narrative was not fixed. In Matthew and Mark the Supper is immediately preceded by the conspiracy, the feast at Simon the Leper's and Judas's selling of Christ. The Supper itself consists of Christ's foretelling of his betrayal ('he that dippeth his hand with me into the dish') and his institution of the sacrament. In Luke the episode is preceded by the conspiracy and Judas's betrayal but not by the feast at Simon the Leper's. The account of the Supper is longer than in the previous gospels. First comes the sharing of drink with the disciples, then the institution of the sacrament and the foretelling of the betrayal ('the hand of him that betrayeth me is with me on the table'), next the discussion of precedence, Peter's boasts of his own fortitude and the statement of the need for swords. John's gospel, as is so often the case, diverges most. The episode is preceded in the previous chapter by Christ's sayings after the Entry into Jerusalem. The eating of the Supper is told in a single verse and the washing of feet and the explanation of it follow. The foretelling of the betrayal is accompanied by the incident of Peter asking John to find out who it is, and that of John sleeping on Christ's breast. The indication of the traitor is expressed more directly ('He it is to whom

I shall reach bread dipped. And when he had dipped the bread, he gave it to Judas Iscariot, the son of Simon'). This is followed by the words, quoted in *York* pageant XXVII, 'Quod facis, fac citius' ('That which thou doest, do quickly'). John is the only one to note the departure of Judas. Judas's departure is followed by a number of Christ's words to his disciples and by Peter's boasts. The next four chapters contain the rest of Christ's words at the Supper. Besides the gospel accounts there were numerous re-tellings and commentaries in English and Latin which harmonised the gospel versions, or followed one, or selectively used details from them all.

Faced with this variety the *Pepysian Gospel Harmony* has: Judas's selling of Christ, the preparation of the Passover, the sharing of drink, the first foretelling of the betrayal, the institution of the Sacrament, the discussion of precedence, Peter's boasts, the swords, washing of feet, the second foretelling of the betrayal, and then it continues as in John. *Meditationes* has no strict narrative order but draws particular attention to Judas's presence throughout the washing of feet and comments on his presence at the taking of the sacrament. Peter Comestor places the washing of feet before the foretelling and has Judas leaving before the institution of the Sacrament. Like *Meditationes* he comments on Judas but stresses that he was not present. Ludolph of Saxony in his *Vita Christi* follows the same order and stresses Judas's presence at the washing of feet. Judging by the variety of the vernacular accounts a wide variety of orders and emphases was subsequently possible.

None that I have found, however, adopts the N. town order. In no account does Judas slip out from the Last Supper to initiate the betrayal of Christ, but it is a striking way of emphasising the enormity of the treachery and also a striking theatrical device. More surprising an individual development than this, however, is the institution of the Sacrament. At the very beginning of the episode Christ indicates that they have already eaten the Paschal Lamb in precisely the way laid down in the Old Testament. It has to be remembered that this has been happening behind closed curtains while the bishops and judges plot Christ's downfall. When the curtains open we see them after the meal. Having fulfilled the Old Law, the New is to be inaugurated (I. 675). Ludolph stresses that Christ's great desire was to end the Old and begin the New. The playwright now interweaves in Christ's speech the eating of the Eucharistic wafer with the eating of the Paschal Lamb, by means of a spiritual interpretation of the Passover meal. Both the *Legenda* and Ludolph contain this kind of exposition but not presented dramatically. The one celebration has now merged with the other and the consecration of the bread follows. Not only does this effectively demonstrate the beginning of the New Law in fulfilment of the Old and act as a commentary on the meaning of the mass, but it also has a dramatic significance in the play. The disciples receive the host worthily (demonstrated by Peter's words of contrition; I. 761–2) but Judas has just sold Christ, as the audience has seen, his sin is deadly and yet, as the devil later points out, he takes the sacrament. To do so was to receive his own damnation, as endless commentators and as here Christ himself says:

> Yt xal be þi dampnacyon verylye,
> I ȝeve þe warnyng now beforn.

It is interesting that the foretelling of the betrayal should follow immediately after Judas's taking of the sacrament. His taking of it is partly to conceal his treachery, yet immediately afterwards it is revealed that Christ already knew.

The most unusual development in the institution of the sacrament is the dividing of it into two by the departure of Judas. The effect of this is to remove the uneasiness of the receiving of the bread as it approaches nearer and nearer to Judas and his damnation, and provide a receiving of the sacrament which is wholly an act of love. It also leads naturally into Christ's words entrusting the disciples, through the administration of the sacrament, with the future welfare of mankind. There is no suggestion of this order in the gospels or in any other version that I have come across.

One vernacular version that is much stressed as a source of the passion sequences in the plays and in N. town in particular is the *Northern Passion*, yet there is very little that the two have in common that is not common elsewhere. On the whole where *Passion* I is unusual it is not following the *Northern Passion*. There is no elaborated Last Supper and even the details that there are are different. In the *Northern Passion* it does not take place in the house of Simon the Leper, the accusation is different, a child is brought in, and the conversation about swords is included. On the other hand there are undoubted verbal reminiscences in N. town. Those that seem to me the most convincing I have included in the notes. They do not affect the conspiracy at all because it is dealt with summarily in the *Northern Passion*, there are one or two scattered ones in Judas's betrayal of Christ, a cluster of them at the end of and just after the washing of the feet, and another scattering in the Agony in the Garden and the

Taking of Christ. They are clearly not a sign of a deep underlying influence, but rather seem to be recollections (perhaps sometimes adoptions) of the text.

Passion II

To a greater extent than the first, the second part of the *Passion Play* depends ultimately, and sometimes it seems immediately, upon the gospels. There is little apocryphal material; the Harrowing of Hell is treated briefly (though strikingly) and shows little dependence on the *Gospel of Nicodemus*. More than in any of the cycles it arises from a traditional understanding of the incident. The other additions to the gospel accounts are the preparation by Satan for the dream of Pilate's wife (a traditional expansion), the Veronica episode (a less frequent but still well-known incident), Mary's laments at the cross (familiar from liturgy and vernacular poetry), the appearance of Christ to his mother after the Resurrection, and the opening appearance of Herod. This last has no source in any of the treatments, Latin or English, of the gospel accounts but it is a commonplace device of the pageants. There, however, the opening rant introduces the chief character of a brief episode whereas here it acts as a preparation for a character who appears long after.

Like the Harrowing of Hell, the episode of Christ's visit to his mother owes very little to what is probably its ultimate source, the *Meditationes*, or to any account derived from it. In this it is unlike the only other dramatic occurrence of the episode in England, the Cornish *Ordinalia*, where the *Meditationes* is followed closely.

Once again there are signs, similar to those in *Passion* I, of the playwright's familiarity with the *Northern Passion*. It does not in any way play a dominant part, but it may have had an effect on the general order of events in *Passion* II, and there is one incident in particular which, as Foster has pointed out, may owe its positioning to the *Northern Passion* (II, p. 96). This is the placing of Longeus's piercing of Christ's side after Joseph of Arimathea's request to Pilate for Christ's body. The connection with the poem is perhaps underlined by the fact that the playwright uses words from it to introduce an incident which is an essential part of that order, namely the necessity of knowing that Christ is dead:

> But fyrst I wole wete þat he ded be
>
> (II. 1101; *NP* 1854)

There is also the incident of the beating of Christ at Herod's court, which occurs in both but not in the gospels. Most of the lines from the poem that are used are in the same position in the play that they are in the poem, but there are occasional changes. II. 284–5 and 295–7, for example, though spoken by Pilate and Christ as in the poem are there placed very much earlier in the trials. As in *Passion* I these lines may be recollections of the poem but they remain a small influence. Even smaller and just as undoubted is the quotation from the Middle English *Harrowing of Hell* in the words of the risen Christ (II. 1440–1); though there are signs that at least the first line had an independent currency since it appears in John of Grimstone's preaching book, another Norfolk text (see note to II. 1440–3).

In both parts of the *Passion Play* there are occasional signs of closer reliance upon the bible or the liturgy in quotation (usually of a commonplace kind, like *Crucifigatur* at II. 597 and 599), or through the Latin affecting the English wording. In *Passion* I there are two quite striking examples of this in the Last Supper section: at I. 679–82,

> And with fervent desyre of hertys affecyon
> I have enterly desyryd to kepe my mawndé
> Among ʒow er þan I suffre my passyon.

Cf. 'Desiderio desideraui hoc Pascha manducare uobiscum ante quam patiar' (lit. 'With desire I have desired to eat this Passover with you before I suffer', Luke xxii, 15); and at I. 791–2,

> Now þe sone of God claryfyed is
> And God in hym is claryfyed also.

Cf. 'Nunc clarificatus est Filius hominis et Deus clarificatus est in eo' ('Now is the Son of man glorified and God is glorified in him', John xiii, 31).

STAGING

It is very seldom that we possess information both about how the staging of a play was envisaged and also about how it was actually performed. The wealth of textual and documentary evidence for the staging at Lucerne or Mons reveals just how lacking the English evidence is. In Lucerne not only do we have texts, plans, descriptions, but we also have an idea of when and why many of the documents were drawn up. The plans of the square in which the

Easter Play was performed, for example, were made by Cysat, the
director, at the time of the 1583 performance, and the description of
the layout of the play was made by Hardmeyer, the city clerk of
works, after the 1583 performance in readiness for the next.[16] A
stage plan of the *Castle of Perseverance* exists, but who drew it up and
for what purpose? Is it the playwright's ideal of how the play should
be staged? Or is it a plan, like Hardmeyer's, of the way in which it
had already been staged – successfully enough to make it worth
while recording? Even though its purpose and origin are not as clear
as the Lucerne plans, however, it is plain that it is concerned with
practical matters of staging, and that it is unlikely to have sprung out
of a theatrical vacuum – staging of this kind must have existed. Much
the same can be said of most stage directions; they are also concerned
with practical matters of staging and should tell us something about
contemporary methods, but, like the plan of the *Castle*, they should
not automatically be treated as though they were descriptions of an
actual performance.[17]

Most important of all for staging is *Passion* I, since here we are
dealing with what is known to be a self-contained play; but even here
evidence for the overall layout is lacking. Two stage structures are
specifically mentioned, a 'stage' for Annas (I. 164sd) and a 'scaffold'
for Caiaphas (I. 208sd), and two others are described in such a way as
to show that they are similar structures, *a lytil oratory* (I. 288sd) and
the *hous* of Symon Leprows (referred to in I. 494sd, 510sd, 518sd and
662sd). Besides these there is frequent mention of the 'place' and also
reference to what appears to be a part of the 'place' separated off,
Mount Olivet and *a place lych to a park* (I. 900sd). The likelihood of a
separate scaffold for Mary for the short scene right at the end of the
play seems to me doubtful but not impossible. The *lytil oratory* has
been vacant for some time and it may even be that its description as
an oratory derives from its use as such by Mary.

Not only are the scaffolds mentioned but to a certain extent their
appearances are described. The *lytil oratory* is neatly laid out with
stolys and cusshonys . . . lych as it were a cownsel hous (I. 288sd). Later the
appearance of the actors sitting in it *in astat* is said to be *lych as it were a
convocacyon* (I. 518sd), underlining the legal solemnity of what the
Jews are doing and contrasting with their frequently thuggish language and methods. Importantly there is also mention of curtaining.
Both the *lytil oratory* and the *hous* of Symon *sodeynly onclose* (I. 518sd
and 662sd); the latter unclosing *rownd abowtyn* and thus suggesting
more than merely a front curtain. The garden of Gethsemane is not

mentioned by name but is the *place lych to a park* (I. 900sd) and presumably therefore fenced off from the main 'place'. The *mount of Olyvet*, mentioned three times (I. 900sd, 908sd and 920sd), is not described but a raised area not a scaffold seems likely. The only other possible scaffold is a heaven. It is only the phrase *ascendyth aʒeyn sodeynly* (I. 948sd) which really suggests any necessity for such a thing, since it could imply some form of raising mechanism; but given the total absence of any other action connected with heaven, and the apparent unimportance of this direction, it seems unnecessary to add this scaffold to the total layout. The problem is really part of a much larger one, namely that the physical context of the play is unknown. If this were being performed somewhere where access to the necessary mechanism was easy, it would be foolish not to use it. By itself, however, the stage direction is not sufficient to build a scaffold on.

What appears from the stage directions and from the text are four scaffolds, a 'place' and a part separated off perhaps with a raised area. The possibilities of layout for these scaffolds are numerous. The circle and the semi-circle are possibilities but by no means the only ones; their advantage is that they automatically define the area of the 'place'. Preference is often given to the circle because of the layout in the *Castle* plan, supported as it is by the Cornish *Ordinalia* and *Meriasek*. These are excellent evidence for the existence of such a layout but there are a very large number of plays recorded for which evidence of stage layout is lacking and it would be wrong just because of the existence of one plan to impose circularity on all non-processional plays.

One of the most striking aspects of the staging of this play is the use of movement. Not simply processions, though they do exist, but of individuals. Annas and Caiaphas do not appear on the same scaffold to discuss the taking of Christ, as they well might, nor does one arrive at the other's scaffold. Instead a messenger is sent to arrange the meeting, and spends thirty-five lines getting from one place to the other. He is then sent back with a reply, and meets the two judges, Rewfyn and Leyon, who are already moving across the 'place'. The messenger goes ahead of them to report, at which Annas decides to go to meet Caiaphas, who in turn decides to go and meet Annas. All meet in the *myd place*. This kind of movement is partly an inevitable result of 'place and scaffold' staging, but that alone does not explain the deliberate exploitation of it. It has much to do with the defining of space. An audience is aware of the space between the scaffolds as dead ground, a gap which has no meaning. The move-ments of the messenger, and later other figures, give a sense of identity to the space, 'a local habitation', as a bounded area in which events will take place. Indeed it becomes Jerusalem, *þis ceté* (I. 392), *þis cyté* (I. 400), over which Christ will weep, and along the streets of which he will walk – *þis path is cald Syon* (I. 495) – and through which he will finally be dragged. Movement in, around, across the space therefore reduces the distancing effect that 'place and scaffold' stag-ing can have by giving what appears to be merely a gap, an existence of its own.

Movement also is connected with one of the most important theatrical devices used in the *Passion Play*, overlapping action. As the messenger runs towards him, so Caiaphas's scaffold uncloses; as the conspiracy builds against Christ, the eating of the Passover is taking place; as Christ prays on Mount Olivet, his disciples sleep and the crowd approaches to seize him. The stage directions only occa-sionally emphasise this overlapping, yet it is inevitable when there is physical space to be covered by actor or actors. No entry is sudden in this kind of staging, unless through the sudden unclosing of the curtains of a scaffold.

One of the most important elements in the stage directions of *Passion* I is that relating to costume. They are not full descriptions of costumes but tantalising, though to a considerable extent informa-tive, hints. When Annas is described as *beseyn after a busshop of þe hoold lawe* (I. 164sd), he was clearly not being visualised as wearing a contemporary bishop's regalia but rather that described in Exodus and Leviticus. That some at least in the fifteenth century were familiar with this idea is clear from the variety of attempts to repro-duce it pictorially (see note to I. 164sd). In the sixteenth-century Lucerne Easter play Aaron is described as dressed like an Old Testa-ment priest 'mitt der Alb, Leuiten Rock oder yberkleid vmbhenckt, vnden mitt Cimbalen; item das brusttaffel, yffeln vnd anderm', presumably the linen garment, the tunic with the bells at the hem, the rational and the mitre of the bible. Though the identification of the N. town Annas and Caiaphas costumes with the Old Testament vestments is certain, the embodying of this idea is left to the indi-vidual director in performance. Annas is said to be wearing a scarlet gown and over that a blue tabard edged with white fur; Caiaphas is like Annas except that his tabard is red with white fur – red on red? Their mitres (Annas's certainly, Caiaphas's presumably) are of the Old Testament – there is considerable room for variety in the interpretation of this (see note to I. 164sd). None of these descriptions exactly calls for the linen garment, the violet tunic (with bells and pomegranates at the hem), the ephod (with onyx stones on the shoulders) on which was fitted the breastplate or rational, or the mitre with the plate of gold attached to it. It seems to me that the two high priests are intended to be wearing costumes that will definitely not remind anyone of contemporary bishops but that will rather create an air of strangeness – in this case ecclesiastical strangeness – rather than that of a precise Jewish past. But clearly the final effect will depend on the knowledge and resources of the director and performers. This same sense of the exotic is called for in the Jewish caps *with a gret knop in þe crowne* of the doctors and the 'Saracen-ness' of the messenger (I. 164sd). The judges in their *ray tabardys* and *ray hodys abouth here neckys* (I. 244sd) are rather different; reminiscent of the real world but (apparently) intensifications of it. What is striking is the care that is taken to describe the costumes in *Passion* I, a concern nearer to Mons or Lucerne than to the other English plays.

Three other costume details help to bring the play visually alive. At the entry into Jerusalem a stage direction describes how the citizens, in a strangely penitential scene, stand barelegged in their shirts, with their gowns slung round their shoulders or tied round their waists, ready to be spread at Christ's feet as he dismounts from the ass. At I. 406sd the citizens *makyn hem redy*, presumably by taking off shoes and gowns, to meet Christ. It is difficult to imagine a more striking way of emphasising the contrast between this 'Royal Entry' and a worldly one. Moreover the penitential aspect of the scene is conveyed solely in the stage direction. In the taking of Christ there are also a number of costume details (I. 964sd), not only the expected armed guards with their combination of rigid and flexible armour (*white arneys and breganderys*) but also the implied strangeness of the others *dysgysyd in odyr garmentys* – why mention the fact that they are dressed in *odyr garmentys* unless they are in some way unusual? There is finally the reference in the text to the Jews' difficulty in distinguishing Christ from his disciples because of their similarity of dress (I. 637), which implies the still traditional costuming of the disciples and Christ in cloak and robe.

Moments of action are often realised visually in the stage directions. The entry with men and children welcoming Christ has already been mentioned. The silent departure of the conspirators (I. 662sd) and their silent approach to take Christ (I. 964sd) are strikingly conveyed. But most important of all is the Last Supper, where the stage directions not only convey an image of the scene but also in many cases suggest, if not actually indicate moves. There is first the tableau with the disciples seated in order (*in ere degré* I. 662sd) at the table with Christ in their midst. Then the blessing of the host and, after Christ's long explanatory sermon, the slow movements of the disciples taking the sacrament until the pause over Judas. Then the dismay at the announcement of the betrayal, the repeated denials, again the pause and Judas's hasty departure. Then the re-establishment of order with the slow taking of the wine echoing the taking of the host.

The stage layout of *Passion* II(a) was presumably envisaged as in general similar to that of *Passion* I. The first stage direction describes the opening procession with Herod, Pilate and Annas and Caiaphas taking up their positions on their scaffolds. Later Herod's scaffold *xal vnclose shewyng Herowdys in astat* (II. 377sd) – again the use of curtaining and of the set tableau. Pilate's wife runs off her scaffold to Pilate (II. 543sd) – the scaffold previously having been closed for the scene with Satan? Later stage directions, however, in *Passion* II(b), refer variously to scaffolds and to locations like *templum*, *sepulcrum*, *monumentum* as pageants and play material are merged, and it becomes impossible to recover the staging pattern in any satisfactory sense. This uncertainty and also in some cases the total absence of stage directions means that the staging of some of the most interesting effects of *Passion* II – the appearance of Anima Christi after Christ's death on the cross, the entry into the sepulchre and the Resurrection – are lost.

Altogether five scaffolds seem to be required: Pilate and his wife, Annas and Caiaphas, Herod, the Council House and Hell. There is no evidence for a heaven scaffold. Of these Herod's, Annas and Caiaphas's, the Council House and Hell have a considerable amount of action taking place on or around them. It is possible that for all but the Council House the action takes place off the scaffold. Herod's scourging of Christ, the first mockery and Peter's denial could all occur in the 'place'. Hell is rather more difficult to deal with since for its main action it falls outside the continuous play and is not described. It is however clear from the text that no action takes place inside Hell. With the Council House the case is different. It first enters the action when Pilate arrives at it and Christ is brought up to him. Annas and Caiaphas too almost certainly go up to him and the crowd is left below in the 'place'. Pilate remains there until the return of Christ from Herod (there is no reason for him to move) and it is there that his wife finds him to tell him of her dream. During the next examination of Christ, Pilate *ledyth hym into þe cowncel hous*. Since this conversation is intended to be heard there must be an inner area where this action is clearly visible and from which the dialogue is clearly audible to the audience. As Pilate moves backwards and forwards between the Jews and Christ at this point, it seems almost certain that this was a scaffold with a forestage as well as a curtained inner stage. At the judgement, Pilate formally sits and again perhaps the inner area is used. Annas and Caiaphas go in with him (II. 656sd) and the prisoners are brought to the bar. This is no large structure. It may already be in position on the forestage or it may be set up at this moment. With the departure of Annas and Caiaphas after the judgement, it would be possible for the action to move up onto the scaffold – brutality taking over from law – for the carefully described second mocking and scourging of Christ, especially since Christ is seated for much of this. If this is a reasonably accurate reconstruction of the action then it is clear that the Council House needs to be a largish structure.

Calvary is fully described except for its relationship with the scaffolds and its position in the 'place'. It should be remembered that once the judgement is over the identity of the Council House need no longer be maintained. With the departure of Christ on the road to Calvary the Council House scaffold could very well become the mount to which they are journeying – and later too perhaps the sepulchre. Comparison with Lucerne is useful here. The Cysat plans seem to suggest a whole series of chronologically disparate scenes in position at the same time. In fact it is clear from his notes that the stage staff are constantly on call to move one stage prop off, turn it round, alter its position, as scene gave way to scene.[18] The movement around the place gives the opportunity for the transformation of the Council House or simply for a stripping of its identity.

Movement and overlapping action are as important here as in *Passion* I. The only additional kind of movement is the opening procession, which raises the question of who was in it. All the characters? If Lucerne is anything to go by it would not include the Anima Christi since those who were concealed in the 'place' took up their positions in advance.[19] The idea of overlapping action also raises a number of questions. Does the 'game' of the mocking go on behind Peter's denials? Does the hanged Judas remain visible, and for how long? Do the women, Simon of Cyrene and Veronica only appear when they are needed? The only overlap to which attention is drawn is the episode of Pilate's wife's dream and the processional return of Christ from Herod (II. 486sd), which could be quite a difficult piece of timing.

Costume description centres on Christ but goes little further than the biblical accounts: the white cloth at Herod's scaffold – unmentioned in the text – (II. 486sd), the purple cloth of silk at the second mocking (II. 698sd), and the putting on and off of Christ's clothes (II. 461sd, 486sd, 696sd, 698sd, 746sd). Satan is merely described as appearing in *most orryble wyse* (II. 486sd). Only the description of Pilate's wife in her shirt and carrying her *kyrtyl* (II. 543sd), and the thieves, bare-legged and in their shirts, provide a kind of theatrical reality (II. 656sd).

Properties too are largely those which are a necessary part of the story or of the tradition. The sitting of Christ at both the mockings is a part of the tradition, as is the forcing on of the crown of thorns with *forkys* (II. 698sd) and the ropes used to make Christ's body fit the nail holes on the cross. The one simple device which is described is the board with the inscription already on it which Pilate pretends to write (II. 874sd).

Despite the later difficulties and the gaps, the stage directions in *Passion* II(a) are especially important for the picturing of the action which takes place without dialogue: the entry of the messenger – a master-stroke of 'place and scaffold' staging – (II. 89sd), the first mocking (II. 181sd), the hanging of Judas (II. 257sd), Pilate's wife's dream (II. 543sd), the second mocking (II. 696sd and 698sd) and the elaborate scenes which take place around the cross (II. 774sd, 786sd, 790sd, 798sd, 854sd).

TEACHING AND MEANING

Passion I is about law and judgment, love and mercy, but many other elements of Christian teaching are touched on in the course of the play. Many are direct teaching. John the Baptist in his Prologue preaches the importance of balancing dread of God's judgment with hope in his mercy. When Peter preaches to Jerusalem (and to the audience) he teaches the importance of the two New Testament commandments of 'love God' and 'love þi neybore' (I. 363–4).[20] He also encourages contrition and confession (I. 369) and keeping the commandments (I. 357). Christ himself teaches directly as well: those who receive the sacrament will be saved, but those who do not will die (I. 817–22). It is likely that some at least of the direct teaching is a response to Lollard criticisms of matters such as eucharistic belief and oral confession.[21] This is particularly noticeable in the stress laid on the transubstantiation of the bread and wine into Christ's body and blood (I. 696–8), on Peter's demonstration of the reverence due to the host (I. 755–8), and perhaps too on the assurance that those who do not fully understand the mystery should simply put their faith in God and believe (I. 729–30). In general, however, it seems to me that the complexity of the presentation of the eucharist here must have got in the way of such specific teaching.

The power of direct teaching, coming from a figure of biblical distance and authority, must not be under-estimated, but it is not the only kind of teaching. Christ's life has always been seen as a source of exemplary teaching and there is an element of that here, particularly in his submission to the will of God. Peter, too, is an exemplary figure in his honest ordinariness. His goodness, as seen in his attitude to the sacrament (I. 755–62), his human limitations, as seen in his precipitate responses: his refusal at first to allow Christ to wash his feet (I. 829–32), his instant denial that he will run away (I. 869–72), his eagerness to defend Christ (I. 989–90sd). Opposed to him is Judas: receiving the sacrament in deadly sin, lying, cheating, deliberately selling his master.

There is, however, more to the play than this. Central to its story is the Last Supper. In no other English play is this episode so dominant. It is used, as has already been said, for direct teaching about the eucharist but it is also being used to give a sense of human reality to what to many people must have been simply an esoteric mystery.[22] As the *Mary Play* might be called 'How the *Ave* was made', in as much as one of its purposes is to give a human solidity and clarity to a muttered prayer, so *Passion* I might be called 'How the mass was made', and in the same way anchors something distant down in a local time and place, a historic narrative of recognisable human emotion.

The Last Supper is, however, even more central than this. As I have said, the play is about law and judgment, love and mercy. The Demon's opening speech establishes the law for mankind: 'Sin, and go to hell, where there is no getting out'. Humanity cannot escape the fall of Adam. John the Baptist modifies this, but obliquely: 'Tread the path between over-hope in God's mercy and over-dread of his judgment and you will be saved'. But is John talking within the time-scheme of the play or outside it? If he is inside, then this is still a pious hope rather than a fact. *Quia in inferno nulla est redempcio* (I. 48)

still reigns. The insistence on the law returns with Annas and
Caiaphas, Rewfyn and Leyon, the judges spiritual and temporal, and
their hangers-on. The law is embodied in them as they make clear (I.
165–72 and 209–16) and consequently a threat to the law is a threat to
them. Christ is seen as overthrowing that law and so must be done
away with – not according to the law, but anyhow. If nothing can be
found against him, fabricate it, and if that does not work, kill him
anyway.

Christ, however, comes not to overthrow but to fulfil the law. He
is the embodiment of numerous prophecies, his mission, the salvation of man, is clearly seen and stated. It is at this point that the
extended Last Supper is absorbed into the theme. Christ's exposition
of the Passover in spiritual terms is an exposition of how the Old
Law is fulfilled and brought to fruition in the New (I. 675–8). It is
interesting to note that there is here no suggestion of the wrongness
of the Old Law. It is the practitioners of it who are corrupt. Instead
there is a sense of solemnity at the passing of a great and ancient
wonder. As Christ shows, they have all fulfilled to the letter the law
of the Passover (I. 663–74), and he goes on to explain how that is to
give way to the new law of the eucharist (I. 683–6). The trappings of
the old Passover become spiritual instruction for the living of the
new (I. 707–50). But the sacrament has no meaning without the final
fulfilling of the law: *Man for man an hende must make* (I. 502).

In the play more is made of Christ's manhood than is usually the
case. He prays to his Father for the power to consecrate the bread (I.
687–94), for

> . . . be my manhood I am of lesse degré.   (I. 690)

It seems to involve a different power from that of giving sight to the
blind or overthrowing those who come to take him. It is God the
Father who has the power to create the mystery of the sacrament.
Emphasis upon Christ's manhood here gives a greater reality to his
human reactions to events, his grief at his betrayal, for example:

> Me þu ast solde þat was þi frende
> Þat þu hast begonne brenge to an ende.   (I. 777–8)

And underlines his affection for his disciples, previously expressed in
the words of the gospel:

> And with fervent desyre of hertys affeccyon
> I have enterly desyryd to kepe my mawndé
> Among ȝow er þan I suffre my passyon.   (I. 679–81)

The emphasis upon his manhood also gives additional meaning to Christ's promises for the future; his body 'þat for þe xal dey' (I. 764), his blood 'wheche xal be xad for mannys love' (I. 798), 'outh of myn herte it xal renne' (I. 804). The power to create the mystery of the sacrament resided outside him in his Father, the power to give meaning to the sacrament, i.e. the salvation of man, in one way also lies outside him, in the future. But in another way it is inside him: until he has died, nothing of what he is saying has any meaning.

> For mannys love I may do no mo
> Þan for love of man to be ded.   (I. 807–8)

Without that death, however, he will have done nothing. This becomes more apparent when instead of the confident assurance of the Entry into Jerusalem,

> Frendys, beholde þe tyme of mercy,
> Þe wich is come now withowtyn dowth;
> Mannys sowle in blysse now xal edyfy,
> And þe prynce of þe werd is cast owth.   (I. 415–18)

we come to the repeated threats of his coming death, the pressure of prophecy:

> Þe day is come I must procede
> For to fulfylle þe prophecy.   (I. 853–4; and cf. I. 881–2, 887–8)

The statement of his rising again at I. 865–8, set in this context, does not sound so certain, especially when a few lines further on:

> My flesch for fere is qwakyng fast.   (I. 884)

Remarkably in the agony in the garden, the play reverses the direction of the three prayers of Matthew's gospel (xxvi, 39–44). Instead of fear giving way to acceptance and then twice-repeated fearful acceptance of his passion, we have fear giving way to acceptance and then changing back to a twice-repeated fear (I. 909–16, 921–18, 929–36). It is only the sight of the meaningless chalice and wafer (I. 936sd), meaningless, that is, without his death, that brings Christ back to an acceptance of his destiny (I. 949–52).

As with the *Mary Play*, when Mary hesitates before agreeing to the initiating act of salvation and there is a real sense that it is possible for it not to happen (1323sd), so here the playwright seems to emphasise Christ's manhood to give a real sense that it might also be possible for the completion of the act of salvation not to happen. Every

celebration of the mass then becomes for the receiver an understanding of Christ's tortured acceptance of the burden of his death for the
salvation of mankind.

The theme of the law is also present. Fulfilling the law needs more
than simply performing the rites of the Passover and moralising its
trappings to transform it into the sacrament of the Eucharist. It needs
death on the cross – it *xal be sacryd be me* (I. 685) does not merely mean
'I will bless it'. The final fulfilment of the law is satisfaction for the
sin of Adam, man for man, Christ's death for his death *as þe parlement
of hefne hath ment* (I. 941).[23]

Because of what has gone before, Mary's lament for Christ's
suffering humanity at the end of the play has a far greater pathos.
How could God allow his *owyn dere son* to *sofre al þis*, who *evyr was
obedyent*? (I. 1065–6). One does not often feel the strain of that
obedience so strongly. Mary also finally draws attention to the
absolute necessity of Christ's suffering; *May man not ellys be savyd be
non other kende?* The answer is, of course, no. His blamelessness,
which Mary sees as the reason why he should not suffer, is the very
reason that he must. Mercy thereby has triumphed, the law has been
fulfilled, but we have been made humanly aware of the cost.

The tight organisation of *Passion* I may once have existed in *Passion*
II, but it is now only possible to judge it by its first part, *Passion* II(a).
This appears to be dwelling on narrative story-telling and human
characterisation. Its teaching of the story of Christ's sufferings is
consequently direct and theatrically effective, but it does not seem to
be trying to go beyond that. As with *Passion* I, there is a measure of
direct teaching; for example, Christ's prophecy of the power of
Veronica's kerchief (II. 745–6), Mary's emphasising of Christ's great
mercy (II. 835–8); and also exemplary teaching in, for example,
Peter's repentance (II. 214–25), but what is primarily striking is the
power of the story. That this is a result of a carefully controlled
simple language in an easy metre is clear when one turns to *Passion*
II(b). This is not without some effective passages, e.g. the rising of
Anima Christi (II. 1005–8), the setting of the watch (II. 1304–67),
the characterising of the easy confidence of Annas (II. 1628–31),
though many of the most effective episodes are almost certainly the
remnants of the old *Passion Play*, such as the restoring of Longeus's
sight (II. 1123–55). Too often the thinness of the language is revealed
by the demands of the metre. There is a pleasure, it is true, in the
greater regularity of the metre but it often cannot make up for the
commonplace nature of the thought, the tags and the empty repeti-

tions. It is at its most bathetic in one of Mary Salome's speeches on the way to the sepulchre:

> My name is Mary Salomé,
> His modyr and I, systerys we be,
> Annys dowterys we be all thre;
> Jhesu, we be þin awntys.

Teaching and meaning come together in *Passion* I. It may still have been in the process of development as a play – something which could be said of most medieval English plays – but it has already become a very powerful medium for a striking Christian and human message.

NOTES

1. The thirteeners are described below (see 'Metre, language and style') and in the *Mary Play*, Introduction, p. 7. For a more detailed discussion of the form see Stephen Spector, 'The Composition and Development of an Eclectic Manuscript: Cotton Vespasian D VIII', *Leeds Studies in English* ns 9 (1977) pp. 62–83, especially 63–9.
2. This re-numbering, which is caused by the intrusion of the *Mary Play*, is discussed there, pp. 1–2, and in Block, pp. xix–xxv.
3. For the layout of the manuscript see *The N-Town Plays*, eds Peter Meredith and Stanley J. Kahrl, Leeds Texts and Monographs, Medieval Drama Facsimiles 4 (Leeds 1977).
4. See further Spector (1977). Though sometimes differing in approach and in matters of detail, our parallel investigations of the manuscript have led to broadly similar conclusions, which in turn generally confirm and a little extend those of Miss K. S. Block, briefly expressed in the introduction to her edition.
5. These alterations are discussed in 'A Reconsideration of Some Textual Problems in the N-Town Manuscript (BL Cotton Vespasian D VIII)', *Leeds Studies in English* ns 9 (1977) pp. 42–7. See also W. W. Greg, *The Assumption of the Virgin. A miracle play from the N-town Cycle* (Oxford 1915).
6. *Staging of Religious Drama*, pp. 47–8; and see the references under 'Reference Titles', s.v. Mons (p. 26) and Romans (p. 28).
7. For a discussion of the 'property player', see John C. Coldewey, 'That Enterprising Property Player: Semi-Professional Drama in Sixteenth-Century England', *Theatre Notebook* 31 (1977) pp. 5–12. For Richard Gibson, see W. R. Streitberger, 'The Development of Henry VIII's Revels Establishment', *Medieval English Theatre* 7 (1985) pp. 83–100; and for Gover Martyn, see below 'Dramatic and social context', and the New Romney accounts in Malone Society Collections Volume VII, *Records of Plays and Players in Kent, 1450–1642*, ed. Giles E. Dawson (Oxford 1965) pp. 207–11.
8. Peter Lucas discusses such copy in 'A Fifteenth-Century Copyist at Work under Authorial Scrutiny: An Incident from John Capgrave's Scriptorium', *Studies in Bibliography* 34 (1981) p. 67 (and see note 3).
9. For examples of these hands, see *Paston Letters and Papers*, ed. Norman Davis, 2 vols (Oxford 1971 and 1976) I, plates I–XII, and II, plates XIII–XXIV; and for the Northampton *Abraham and Isaac* and the Reynes Fragments, see *Non-Cycle Plays*

and the Winchester Dialogues, ed. Norman Davis, Leeds Texts and Monographs, Medieval Drama Facsimiles 5 (Leeds 1979) pp. 36–45 and 87–90; and for *Mary Magdalen* see, *The Digby Plays*, ed. Donald C. Baker and J. L. Murphy, Leeds Texts and Monographs, Medieval Drama Facsimiles 3 (Leeds 1976) ff. 95–145.

10. See for example, Block, p. xxxvii, and A. J. Fletcher (in support of Block) 'Marginal Glosses in the N-town Manuscript, British Library, MS Cotton Vespasian D. VIII', *Manuscripta* 25 (1981) pp. 113–17.

11. *The Commonplace Book of Robert Reynes of Acle*, an edition of Tanner MS 407, ed. Cameron Louis (New York and London 1980).

12. The Linguistic Profile (LP) for the N. Town manuscript (LP 4280) is given in III, pp. 339–40. Its plotting can be seen in the item maps in volume III. It should be noted that the LP is drawn only from ff. 1–106 and does not therefore cover evidence from the *Passion Play*.

13. References to records are to those printed in Malone Society Collections Volume XI, *Records of Plays and Players in Norfolk and Suffolk, 1330–1642*, eds David Galloway and John Wasson (Oxford 1980), and Volume VIII, *Records of Plays and Players in Lincolnshire, 1300–1585*, ed. Stanley J. Kahrl (Oxford 1974).

14. For the New Romney records see note 7 above.

15. The dramatic pieces are items 51 (3 Worthies), 53 (9 Worthies), 85 (Speech of Delight) and 86 (Epilogue). The last two items are reproduced in facsimile in Davis, *Non-Cycle Plays* (see note 9 above).

16. For the stage plans and translations of the text on them, see *Staging of Religious Drama*, endpiece, and for Hardmeyer's description (again in translation), pp. 81–5. For the originals, see 'Reference Titles' in *Staging*, pp. 24–6.

17. For some discussion of the nature of stage directions, see 'Stage Directions and the Editing of Early English Drama', in *Editing Early English Drama: Special Problems and New Directions*, ed. A. F. Johnston (New York 1987) pp. 65–94.

18. See John E. Tailby, 'The Role of Director in the Lucerne Passion Play', *Medieval English Theatre* 9 (1987) pp. 80–92, especially 91–2.

19. For the concealment of Adam and Eve, see *Staging of Religious Drama*, p. 130.

20. Cf. *Mary Play*, ll. 453–7 and note to ll. 453–68.

21. See notes I. 367–70 and 711–50.

22. The *Lay Folk's Mass Book* makes clear the kind of distance that must have existed between the mass and its historical meaning for most people; see e.g. Text B ll. 399–427.

23. The reference here to what appears to be an event of the *Mary Play* makes the likelihood of their composition in a similar place and context greater. It also makes understanding of *Passion* I by way of the *Mary Play* a more acceptable approach.

BIBLIOGRAPHY

The following list is mainly of books and articles referred to in the introduction and notes, but also included is some work relating directly to the *Passion Play* and to staging matters. For more general work on the N. Town plays, see *Annual Bibliography of English Language and Literature*, *New Cambridge Bibliography of English Literature*, *International Medieval Bibliography*, *Year's work in English Studies*, and the specialised *Bibliography of Medieval Drama* (Carl J. Stratman, 2 vols, New York 1972) and *A Manual of the Writings in Middle English 1050–1500* (J. Burke Severs *et al.*, New Haven 1967–). There is also a useful series of annotated bibliographies covering the years 1978–83 by Ian Lancashire in *REED Newsletter* 5 (1980: 1), 7 (1982: 1) and 9 (1984: 2). The works referred to in the notes are listed under the authors or short titles used there.

References to the Bible are to the Douay-Rheims (English) and the Vulgate (Latin). For the Vulgate New Testament the edition by John Wordsworth and Henry Julian White (Oxford 1911, corrected 1920) has been used.

Abraham and Isaac (Northampton), see under Davis
Anderson, see M. D. Anderson, *Drama and Imagery in English Medieval Churches* (Cambridge 1963)
Aspects, see *Aspects of Early English Drama*, ed. Paula Neuss (Cambridge 1983)
Assembly of the Gods, see *The Assembly of the Gods by John Lydgate*, ed. Oscar Lovell Triggs, EETS ES 69 (London 1895)
Augustine, *De Civitate Dei*, see Saint Augustine, *The City of God*, trans. John Healey, ed. R. V. G. Tasker, 2 vols, Everyman's Library (London 1945) [*The City of God Against the Pagans*, ed. and trans. George E. McCracken *et al.*, 7 vols, Loeb Classical Library (London and Cambridge, Mass 1957–72)]
Augustine on the Psalms, see *Expositions on the Book of Psalms by St Augustine*, trans. J. Tweed *et al.*, 6 vols, A Library of Fathers of the Holy

Catholic Church (Oxford 1847–57) [*Enarrationes in Psalmos*, PL 36–7 (Paris 1861 and 1865)]

Ayenbite of Inwyt, see *Dan Michel's Ayenbite of Inwyt*, ed. Pamela Gradon, 2 vols, vol. I, EETS OS 23 (London 1866, re-issued 1965)

Bakere, Jane, *The Cornish Ordinalia: a Critical Study* (Cardiff 1980)

Beadle, H. R. L., *The Medieval Drama of East Anglia: studies in dialect, documentary records and stagecraft* (unpublished D.Phil thesis, York 1978)

Beadle, Richard, 'The East Anglian "game-place": a possibility for further research', *REED Newsletter* 3 (1978: 1), pp. 2–4

Beadle, Richard, 'Plays and Playing at Thetford and nearby 1448–1540', *Theatre Notebook* 32 (1978), pp. 4–11

Bede on Exodus, see *Commentarii in Pentateuchum*, PL 91 (Paris 1862)

Benkovitz, Miriam J., 'Some Notes on the "Prologue of Demon" of *Ludus Coventriae*', *Modern Language Notes* 60 (1945), pp. 78–85

Bennett, H. E., *The Pastons and their England* (Cambridge 1922)

Bevington, see *Medieval Drama*, ed. David Bevington (Boston 1975)

Biblia Pauperum, see *Biblia Pauperum* a facsimile and edition, ed. Avril Henry (London 1987)

Blickling Homilies, see *Blickling Homilies*, ed. Richard Morris, EETS OS 58 (London 1874)

Block, see *Ludus Coventriae or the Plaie called Corpus Christi*, ed. K. S. Block, EETS ES 120 (London 1922)

Bodley *Burial/Resurrection* see *The Late Medieval Religious Plays of Bodleian MSS. Digby 133 and E. Museo 160*, eds Donald C. Baker, John L. Murphy and Louis B. Hall Jr., EETS 283 (London 1982)

Breviary, see *Breviarium ad Usum . . . Sarum*, eds Francis Proctor and Christopher Wordsworth, 3 vols (Cambridge 1882–6)

Brown *Lyrics XIII/XIV/XV*, see *English Lyrics of the XIIIth Century*, ed. Carleton Brown (Oxford 1932); *Religious Lyrics of the XIVth Century*, ed. Carleton Brown (Oxford 1924); *Religious Lyrics of the XVth Century*, ed. Carleton Brown (Oxford 1939)

Capgrave's *Abbreuiacion of Chronicles* see *John Capgrave's Abbreuiacion of Chronicles*, ed. Peter J. Lucas, EETS 285 (London 1983)

Canterbury Tales, see under Chaucer

Castle of Perseverance, see *The Macro Plays*, ed. Mark Eccles, EETS 262 (London 1969)

Catholicon Anglicum, see *Catholicon Anglicum*, ed. Sidney J. Herrtage, EETS OS 75 (London 1881)

Cave, see C. J. P. Cave, *Roof Bosses in Medieval Churches* (Cambridge 1948)

Cawley, A. C., Marion Jones, Peter F. McDonald and David Mills, *Medieval Drama*, The Revels History of Drama in English 1 (London and New York 1983)

Chaucer, see *The Riverside Chaucer*, ed. Larry D. Benson *et al.*, 3rd edition (Oxford 1988)

Chester, see *The Chester Mystery Cyrcle*, eds R. M. Lumiansky and David Mills, 2 vols, EETS SS 3 and 9 (London 1974 and 1986)

Child Jesus, see Adey Horton, *The Child Jesus* (New York 1975)

Coldewey, John C., 'That Enterprising Property Player: Semi-Professional Drama in Sixteenth-Century England', *Theatre Notebook* 31 (1977), pp. 5–12

Coletti, Theresa, 'Sacrament and Sacrifice in the N-Town Passion', *Mediaevalia* 7 (1981), pp. 239–64

Coletti, Theresa and Kathleen M. Ashley, 'The N-Town Passion at Toronto and Late Medieval Passion Iconography', (Supplement on sources by Theodore de Welles), *Research Opportunities in Renaissance Drama* 24 (1981), pp. 181–92

Comestor, see Petrus Comestor, *Historia Scholastica*, PL 198 (Paris 1855)

Cornish *Ordinalia*, see under *Ordinalia*

Croxton *Play of the Sacrament*, see under Davis

Cunnington, see C. Willett and Phillis Cunnington, *Handbook of English Medieval Costume* (London 1952)

Cursor Mundi, see *Cursor Mundi*, ed. Richard Morris, 7 vols, EETS OS 57, 59, 62, etc., (London 1874–93)

Davenport, Tony, '"Lusty fresch galaunts"', in *Aspects*, pp. 111–28

Davies, see *The Corpus Christi Play of the English Middle Ages*, ed. R. T. Davies (London 1972)

Davis, see *Non-Cycle Plays and Fragments*, ed. Norman Davis, EETS SS 1 (London 1970)

Denny, Neville, 'Arena Staging and Dramatic Quality in the Cornish Passion Play', in *Medieval Drama*, Stratford-upon-Avon Studies 16 (London 1973), pp. 124–53

Early Dutch Painting, see Albert Châtelet, *Early Dutch Painting in the Northern Netherlands in the Fifteenth Century*, trans Christopher Brown and Anthony Turner (Oxford 1981)

Eusebius, see Eusebius, *The History of the Church from Christ to Constantine*, trans. G. A. Williamson (Penguin Books 1965) [Eusebius, *Historia Ecclesiastica*, ed. K. Lake, 2 vols (London 1927)]

Fabri, see *The Wanderings of Felix Fabri*, trans. Aubrey Stewart, 2 vols, Palestine Pilgrim Text Society (London 1887–97) [Fratris Felicis Fabri, *Evagatorium in Terrae Sanctae, Arabiae et Aegypti*, ed. Conrad Dietrich Hassler, 3 vols, Bibliothek des literarischen Vereins in Stuttgart (Stuttgart 1843–9)]

Fletcher, Alan J., 'Marginal Glosses in the N-Town Manuscript, British Library MS Cotton Vespasian D VIII', *Manuscripta* 25 (1981), pp. 113–17

Flutre *Tables des noms propres*, see Louis-Fernand Flutre, *Table des noms propres avec toutes leurs variantes figurant dans les Romans du Moyen Age écrits en français ou en provençal et actuellement publiés ou analysés* (Poitiers 1962)

Fulgens and Lucres, see under Medwall

Galloway, David, 'Comment: The East Anglian "game-place": some facts and fictions', *REED Newsletter* 4 (1979: 1), pp. 24–6.

Gay, Anne Cooper, 'The "Stage" and the Staging of the N-Town Plays', *Research Opportunities in Renaissance Drama* 10 (1967), pp. 135–40

Gibson, Gail McMurray, 'Bury St Edmunds, Lydgate, and the *N-Town Cycle*', *Speculum* 56 (1981), pp. 56–90

Glass at All Souls, see F. E. Hutchinson, *Medieval Glass at All Souls College*, a history and description, based on the notes of G. M. Rushforth (London 1949)

Glossa Ordinaria, PL 113–14 (Paris 1879)

Golden Age, see Richard Marks and Nigel Morgan, *The Golden Age of English Manuscript Painting, 1250–1500* (London 1981)

Golden Legend, see *The Golden Legend or Lives of the Saints*, as Englished by William Caxton, ed. F. S. Ellis, Temple Classics, 7 vols (London 1900)

Gospel of Nicodemus, see *Apocryphal Gospels, Acts and Revelations*, trans. Alexander Walker, Ante-Nicene Library 16 (Edinburgh 1890) [*Evangelia Apocrypha*, ed. Constantin Tischendorff (Leipzig 1853)]

Gospel of Peter, see under James

Gray, *Lyrics*, see *A Selection of Religious Lyrics*, ed. Douglas Gray (Oxford 1975)

Gray, *Themes and Images*, see Douglas Gray, *Themes and Images in the Medieval English Lyric* (London and Boston 1972)

Greene, see *The Early English Carols*, ed. Richard Leighton Greene (2nd edn, Oxford 1977)

Greg, Walter W., *Bibliographical and Textual Problems in the English Mystery Cycles* (London 1914)

Griffith, John R., 'The Hegge Pilate: A Tragic Hero?', *English Studies* 51 (1970), pp. 234–44

Guy of Warwick, see *The Romance of Guy of Warwick*, ed. Julius Zupitza, EETS ES 42, 49, 59 (London 1883, 1887, 1891; repr. as one vol. 1966)

Halliwell, see *Ludus Coventriae*, ed. James Orchard Halliwell, Shakespeare Society (London 1841)

Happé, see *English Mystery Plays*, ed. Peter Happé (Penguin Books 1975)

Harrowing of Hell, see *The Middle-English Harrowing of Hell and Gospel of Nicodemus*, ed. William Henry Hulme, EETS ES 100 (London 1907)

Higden's *Polychronicon*, see *Polychronicon Ranulphi Higden, monachi Cestrensis*, ed. Churchill Babington. Rolls Series, 9 vols (London 1865–86)

Horae, see *Horae Eboracenses, the Prymer or Hours of the Blessed Virgin Mary*, ed. Christopher Wordsworth, Surtees Society 132 (Durham 1920)

Hudson, see *Selections from English Wycliffite Writings*, ed. Anne Hudson (Cambridge 1978)

Hymns, see *Hymns to the Virgin and Christ, the Parliament of Devils and other Religious Poems*, ed. Frederick J. Furnivall, EETS OS 24 (London 1868)

Isidore, see Isidori Hispalensis Episcopi, *Etymologiarum sive Originum*, ed. W. M. Lindsay, 2 vols (Oxford 1911)

Jacob's Well, see *Jacob's Well*, ed. Arthur Brandeis, EETS OS 115 (London 1900)

James, see *The Apocryphal New Testament*, ed. and trans. Montague Rhodes James (Oxford 1924)

Josephus, *Wars of the Jews*, see *The Works of Flavius Josephus*, trans. William Whiston (Edinburgh 1867) [*The Jewish War*, vols 2 and 3 of *The Works of Flavius Josephus*, 9 vols, Loeb Classical Library (London and Cambridge, Mass. 1957–65)]

Kahrl, Stanley J., *Traditions of Medieval English Drama* (London 1974)

Kelly and Schwabe, see Francis M. Kelly and Randolph Schwabe, *A Short History of Costume and Armour*, 2 vols (London 1931)

Killing of the Children, see under Bodley *Burial/Resurrection*

Lamentacion of Oure Lady, see C. Horstmann, 'Nachträge zu den Legenden', Herrig's *Archiv* 79 (1887), pp. 411–70 (*Lamentacion* is on pp. 454–9)

Lancashire, Ian, *Dramatic Texts and Records of Britain: A Chronological Topography to 1558* (Cambridge 1984)

Lay Folk's Catechism, see *The Lay Folk's Catechism*, ed. Thomas Frederick Simmons and Henry Edward Nolloth, EETS OS 118 (London 1901)

Lay Folk's Mass Book, see *The Lay Folk's Mass Book*, ed. Thomas Frederick Simmons, EETS OS 71 (London 1879)

Legenda, see Jacobus de Voragine, *Legenda Aurea*, ed. Theodor Graesse (3rd edn Breslau 1890)

Legends of the Holy Rood, see *Legends of the Holy Rood, Symbols of the Passion and Cross-Poems*, ed. Richard Morris, EETS OS 46 (London 1881)

Linguistic Atlas of Later Middle English, A, ed. Angus McIntosh, M. L. Samuels, Michael Benskin, *et al.*, 4 vols (Aberdeen 1986)

Lucas, Peter J., 'A Fifteenth-Century Copyist at Work Under Authorial Scrutiny: An Incident from John Capgrave's Scriptorium', *Studies in Bibliography* 34 (1981), pp. 66–95

Lucerne, see M. Blakemore Evans, *The Passion Play of Lucerne* (New York 1943)

Lydgate, see *The Minor Poems of John Lydgate*, vol. 1, ed. Henry Noble McCracken, EETS ES 107 (London 1911)

Lyf of Oure Lady, see *The Lyf of Oure Lady, the Middle English Translation of Thomas of Hales' Vita Sancte Marie*, ed. Sarah M. Horrall, Middle English Texts 17 (Heidelberg 1985)

Lyrics XIII/XIV/XV, see under Brown *Lyrics*

Mankind, see under *Castle of Perseverance*

Margery Kempe, see *The Book of Margery Kempe*, ed. Sanford Brown Meech and Hope Emily Allen, EETS OS 212 (London 1940)

Marrow, James A., *Passion Iconography in Northern European Art of the Late Middle Ages and Early Renaissance*, Ars Neerlandica 1 (Kostrijk 1979)

Mary Magdalen, see under Bodley *Burial/Resurrection*

'Mary Magdalen at Durham' (1982), reviews by Meg Twycross and Peter Meredith in *Medieval English Theatre* 4 (1982), pp. 63–70

Mary Play, see *The Mary Play from the N.town Manuscript*, ed. Peter Meredith (London 1987)

Maskell, see *Monumenta Ritualia Ecclesiae Anglicanae*, ed. William Maskell, 3 vols (Oxford 1882)

Mayo, see Janet Mayo, *A History of Ecclesiastical Dress* (London 1984)

Meditationes, see 'Meditationes Vitae Christi' in *S. Bonaventurae . . . Opera Omnia*, ed. A. C. Peltier, vol. 12 (Paris 1868) [*Meditations on the Life of Christ*, trans. Isa B. Ragusa and Rosalie B. Green, Princeton Monographs in Art and Archaeology 35 (Princeton, NJ 1961)]

Meditations on the Supper, see *Meditations on the Supper of Our Lord, and the Hours of the Passion*, ed. J. Meadows Cowper, EETS OS 60 (London 1875)

Medwall, see *The Plays of Henry Medwall*, ed. Alan H. Nelson (Cambridge 1980)

Meiss, see Millard Meiss, *French Painting in the Time of Jean de Berry: The Limbourgs and their Contemporaries*, 2 vols (London 1974)

Meredith, Peter, 'Scribes, texts and performance', in *Aspects*, pp. 13–29

Meredith, Peter, 'Stage Directions and the Editing of Early English Drama', in *Editing Early English Drama: Special Problems and New Directions*, ed. A. F. Johnston (New York 1987)

Meredith, Peter and Stanley J. Kahrl, *The N-Town Plays, a facsimile of BL MS Cotton Vespasian D VIII*, Leeds Texts and Monographs, Medieval Drama Facsimiles 4 (Leeds 1977)

Meriasek, see *Beunans Meriasek: The Life of St Meriasek, A Cornish Drama*, ed. Whitley Stokes (London 1872)

Metrical Life, see *The Metrical Life of Christ*, ed. Walter Sauer, Middle English Texts 5 (Heidelberg 1977)

Michel's *Passion*, see Jean Michel, *Le Mystère de la Passion (Angers, 1486)*, ed. Omer Jodogne (Gembloux 1959)

Middle English Sermons, see *Middle English Sermons, edited from British Museum MS. Royal 18 B. xxiii*, ed. Woodburn O. Ross, EETS OS 209 (London 1940)

Mills, David, 'The Stage Directions in the MSS of the Chester Mystery Cycle', *Medieval English Theatre* 3 (1981), pp. 45–51

Ministry and Passion, see *The South English Ministry and Passion*, ed. O. S. Pickering, Middle English Texts 16 (Heidelberg 1984)

Minor Poems, see *The Minor Poems of the Vernon MS.*, ed. Carl Horstmann (vol. 1), and F. J. Furnivall (vol. 2), 2 vols, EETS OS 98 and 117 (London 1892 and 1901)

Mirk, see *Mirk's Festial*, ed. Theodor Erbe, EETS ES 96 (London 1905)

Missal, see *Missale ad Usum . . . Sarum*, ed. Francis Henry Dickinson (Burntisland 1861–83)

Mons *Livre de Conduite*, see *Le Livre de Conduite du Régisseur et le Compte des Dépenses pour le Mystère de la Passion joué à Mons en 1501*, ed. Gustave Cohen (Paris 1925)

Myrc's *Instructions*, see *Instructions for Parish Priests by John Myrc*, ed. Edward Peacock, EETS OS 31 (London 1902)

Mystères, see L. Petit de Julleville, *Les Mystères*, 2 vols (Paris 1880)

N. town, see under Block

Nature, see under Medwall

Nelson, Alan, 'Some Configurations of Staging in Medieval English Drama', in *Medieval English Drama: Essays Critical and Contextual*, ed. Jerome Taylor and Alan H. Nelson (Chicago 1972)

New Romney, see under *Records of Plays and Players in Kent*

Newton, Stella Mary, *Renaissance Theatre Costume and the Sense of the Historical Past* (London 1975)

Northern Passion, see *Northern Passion*, ed. Frances A. Foster, 2 vols, EETS OS 145 and 147 (London 1913 and 1916)

Norwich text/records, see under Davis and *REED Norwich*

Norwich School, see Christopher Woodforde, *The Norwich School of Glass-Painting in the Fifteenth Century* (Oxford 1950)

Octovian Imperator, see *Octovian Imperator*, ed. Frances McSparran, Middle English Texts 11 (Heidelberg 1979)

Opies, see Iona and Peter Opie, *Children's Games in Street and Playground* (Oxford 1969)

Ordinalia: Passio/Resurrexio, see *The Ancient Cornish Drama*, ed. and trans. Edwin Norris, 2 vols (Oxford 1869); see also *The Cornish Ordinalia*, trans. Markham Harris (Washington 1969)

Owst, see G. R. Owst, *Literature and Pulpit in Medieval England* (Oxford 1933, 2nd edn 1961)

Oxford Dictionary of Saints, see David Hugh Farmer, *The Oxford Dictionary of Saints* (Oxford 1978)

Paston Letters, see *Paston Letters and Papers of the Fifteenth Century*, ed. Norman Davis, 2 vols (Oxford 1971 and 1976)

Pepysian Gospel Harmony, see *The Pepysian Gospel Harmony*, ed. Margery Goates, EETS OS 157 (London 1922)

Piers Plowman, see William Langland, *The Vision of Piers Plowman*, ed. A. V. C. Schmidt (London 1978)

Play of the Sacrament, see under Davis

Poteet, Daniel P., 'Time, Eternity, and Dramatic Form in *Ludus Coventriae* Passion Play I', in *The Drama of the Middle Ages*, ed. Clifford Davidson, *et al.* (New York 1982), pp. 232–48

Prosser, Eleanor, *Drama and Religion in the English Mystery Plays: A Re-evaluation*, Stanford Studies in Language and Literature 23 (Stanford 1961)

Pseudo-Matthew, see under *Gospel of Nicodemus*

'Reconsideration', see Peter Meredith, 'A Reconsideration of Some Textual Problems in the N-Town Manuscript (BL MS Cotton Vespasian D VIII)', *Leeds Studies in English* ns 9 (1977), pp. 35–50

Records of Plays and Players in Kent, 1450–1642, ed. Giles E. Dawson, Malone Society Collections Volume VII (Oxford 1965)

Records of Plays and Players in Lincolnshire, 1300–1585, ed. Stanley J. Kahrl, Malone Society Collections Volume VIII (Oxford 1974)

Records of Plays and Players in Norfolk and Suffolk, 1330–1642, eds David Galloway and John Wasson, Malone Society Collections Volume X (Oxford 1980)

REED *Coventry*, see *Coventry*, ed. R. W. Ingram, Records of Early English Drama (Toronto 1981)

REED *Norwich*, see *Norwich, 1540–1642*, ed. David Galloway, Records of Early English Drama (Toronto 1984)

REED *York*, see *York*, ed. Alexandra F. Johnston and Margaret Rogerson, 2 vols, Records of Early English Drama (Toronto 1979)

Religious Pieces, see *Religious Pieces in Prose and Verse*, ed. George G. Perry, EETS OS 26 (London 1867, 1914)

Reynes *Commonplace Book*, see *The Commonplace Book of Robert Reynes of Acle*, an edition of Tanner MS 407, ed. Cameron Louis (New York and London 1980)

Richard Hill, see *Songs, Carols, and Miscellaneous Poems, from the Balliol MS 354, Richard Hill's Commonplace-book*, ed. Roman Dyboski, EETS ES 101 (London 1908)

Rose, Martial, 'The Staging of the Hegge Plays', in *Medieval Drama* (see under Denny), pp. 196–221

Rushforth, see G. McN. Rushforth, *Medieval Christian Imagery* (Oxford 1936)

Sarum Processional, see Richard Pynson, *Processionale ad Usum Sarum, 1502*, photographic reprint, Musical Sources 16 (Boethius Press, Clifden 1980)

Schiller, see Gertrud Schiller, *Iconography of Christian Art*, trans. Janet Seligman, 2 vols (London 1971)

Southern, Richard, *The Medieval Theatre in the Round* (London 1957)

Spector, Stephen, 'The Composition and Development of an Eclectic Manuscript: Cotton Vespasian D VIII', *Leeds Studies in English* ns 9 (1977), pp. 62–83

Spector, Stephen, 'Symmetry in Watermark Sequences', *Studies in Bibliography* 31 (1978), pp. 162–78

Speculum Christiani, see *Speculum Christiani*, ed. Gustaf Holmstedt, EETS OS 182 (London 1933)

Squires, Lynn, 'Law and Disorder in *Ludus Coventriae*', in *The Drama of the Middle Ages* (see under Poteet), pp. 272–85 [In the copies that I have seen p. 280 is duplicated and p. 279 missing.]

Staging of Religious Drama, see Peter Meredith and John E. Tailby, *The*

Staging of Religious Drama in Europe in the Later Middle Ages: Texts and Documents in English Translation (Kalamazoo 1983)

Stanzaic Life, see *A Stanzaic Life of Christ*, Frances A. Foster, EETS OS 166 (London 1926)

Statutes of the Realm, The, 9 vols + 2 of Appendices (London 1810–24)

Stevens, Martin, *Four Middle English Mystery Cycles: Textual, Contextual, and Critical Interpretations* (Princeton 1987)

Streitberger, W. R., 'The Development of Henry VIII's Revels Establishment', *Medieval English Theatre* 7 (1985), pp. 83–100

Towneley, see *The Towneley Plays*, eds George England and Alfred W. Pollard, EETS ES 71 (London 1897)

Twenty-Six Political Poems, see *Twenty-Six Political and Other Poems*, ed. Dr J. Kail, EETS OS 124 (London 1904)

Twycross, Meg, 'Apparel comelye', in *Aspects*, pp. 30–49

Twycross, Meg, review of 'The Toronto [N. town] Passion Play', in *Medieval English Theatre* 3 (1981), pp. 122–31

Tydeman, Bill, 'Stanislavski in the Garden of Gethsemane: an Interlude', *Medieval English Theatre* 5 (1983), pp. 53–7

Vita Christi, see *Vita Jesu Christi . . . Ludolphum de Saxonia*, ed. A-C. Bolard, L-M. Rigollot and J. Carnandet (Paris and Rome 1865)

Whiting, see Bartlett Jere Whiting, *Proverbs, Sentences, and Proverbial Phrases from English Writings mainly before 1500* (Cambridge, Mass. 1968)

Wisdom, see under *Castle of Perseverance*

Woodforde, see under *Norwich School*

Woolf *Lyrics*, see Rosemary Woolf, *The English Religious Lyric in the Middle Ages* (Oxford 1968)

Woolf *Mystery Plays*, see Rosemary Woolf, *The English Mystery Plays* (London 1972)

Wright, Michael, '*Ludus Coventriae* Passion Play I: Action and Interpretation', *Neuphilologische Mitteilungen* 86 (1985), pp. 70–7

York, see *The York Plays*, ed. Richard Beadle (London 1982)

Young, see Karl Young, *The Drama of the Medieval Church*, 2 vols (Oxford 1933)

EDITORIAL PROCEDURES

1. Capitalisation, word division and punctuation are editorial.
2. The manuscript distinction between *u* and *v* has been retained. Manuscript *ff* and *ss* have been simplified to *f/F* and *s* when initial. In the manuscript þ and y are written as y. For the sake of clarity I have distinguished between them.
3. For the convenience of the reader, stressed final *-e* has been marked with an acute accent.
4. All abbreviations have been silently expanded. Among suspensions, only that of final *-r* has been regularly expanded since the others appear in most cases to be merely final flourishes.
5. The form *þu* is used throughout for the expansion of the abbreviation in the manuscript. Though forms with *-ou/-ow* occur when the word is written in full, they are less common than those with *-u*.
6. The scribe uses a wide variety of spellings, especially for final *-th/-t*. These have been retained except where indicated in the textual notes.
7. Speakers' names in the manuscript are most commonly in the right margin. Stage directions in the manuscript are usually underlined in red and centred on the page. Attention is drawn in the textual notes to any divergence from these patterns.
8. Roman numerals in text and stage directions have normally been replaced by the forms appearing most commonly elsewhere. In the case of *five* and *twelve*, which occur only as roman numerals, the modern forms have been used. All roman numerals in speakers' names when followed by an appropriate sign of abbreviation have been silently expanded using the required Latin form.
9. Editorial emendations or additions are enclosed within square brackets in the text only when the emendation or addition results in a new word. All emendations or additions are noted in the textual notes.
10. Stanza division in the manuscript is normally indicated by a *paragraphus*, ¶ (or in the case of the couplets in *Passion* II normally by a *capitulum*, ⁊) preceding the first line of a new stanza, and sometimes also by a space. The scribe has occasionally failed to indicate a new stanza and in a very few cases has indicated one wrongly. I have followed his stanza division except where it seems to be wrong or inadequate.

PASSION PLAY I

f. 136 *Demon*

I am ȝour lord, Lucifer, þat out of helle cam,
Prince of þis werd and gret duke of helle;
Wherefore my name is clepyd Sere Satan,
Whech aperyth among ȝow a matere to spelle.
I am norsshere of synne, to þe confusyon of man,   5
To bryng hym to my dongeon, þer in fyre to dwelle;
Hosoevyr serve me, so reward hym I kan,
Þat he xal syng wellaway ever in peynes felle.

Lo! þus bountevous a lord þan now am I,
To reward so synners as my kend is;   10
Whoso wole folwe my lore and serve me dayly,
Of sorwe and peyne anow he xal nevyr mys.

For I began in hefne synne for to sowe,
Among all þe angellys þat weryn þere so bryth;
And þerfore was I cast out into helle ful lowe,   15
Notwithstandyng I was þe fayrest and berere of lyth.
Ȝet I drowe in my tayle of þo angelys bryth,
With me into helle – takyth good hed what I say! –
I lefte but tweyn aȝens on to abyde þere in lyth,
But þe thryde part come with me – þis may not be
                                        seyd nay.   20

Takyth hed to ȝour prince, þan, my pepyl euerychon,
And seyth what maystryes in hefne I gan þer do play.
To gete a thowsand sowlys in an houre methynkyth
                                        it but skorn,
Syth I wan Adam and Eve on þe fyrst day.

3–6] *large red numeral 26 in right margin*   20 thryde] *MS.* iij^de

But now mervelous mendys rennyn in myn
                                    rememberawns   25
Of on, Cryst, wiche is clepyd Joseph and Maryes
                                    sone.
Thryes I tempte hym, be ryth sotylle instawnce,
Aftyr he fast fourty days ageyns sensual myth or
                                    reson:

f. 136v   For of þe stonys to a mad bred – but sone I had
                                    conclusyon;
Pan upon a pynnacle – but angelys were to hym
                                    assystent,   30
His answerys were mervelous, I knew not his
                                    intencyon;
And at þe last to veynglory – but nevyr I had myn
                                    intent.

And now hath he twelve dysypulys to his attendauns;
To eche town and cety he sendyth hem as bedellys,
In dyverce place to make for hym puruyauns.   35
The pepyl of hese werkys ful grettly merveyllys.
To þe crokyd, blynd and dowm, his werkys
                                    provaylys;
Lazare, þat foure days lay ded, his lyff recuryd.
And where I purpose me to tempt, anon he me
                                    asaylys;
Mawdelyn, playn remyssyon also he hath ensuryd.   40

Goddys son he pretendyth and to be born of a mayde,
And seyth he xal dey for mannys saluacyon.
Pan xal þe trewth be tryed and no fordere be delayd,
Whan þe soule fro þe body xal make separacyon.
And as for hem þat be vndre my grett domynacyon, 45
He xal fayle of hese intent and purpose also
Be þis tyxt of holde, remembryd to myn intencyon:
Quia in inferno nulla est redempcio.

But whan þe tyme xal neyth of his persecucyon,
I xal arere new engynes of malycyous conspiracy;   50
Plenté of reprevys I xal provide to his confusyon.
Pus xal I false þe wordys þat his pepyl doth testefy,

---

33 twelve] *MS.* xij   46 purpose] *MS.* puurpose   52 testefy] *MS.* testefyn

His discipulis xal forsake hym, and here mayster
                              denye.
Innovmberabyl xal hese woundys be, of woful
                              grevauns;
A tretowre xal countyrfe his deth to fortyfye;   55
Þe rebukys þat he gyf me xal turne to his displesauns.

Some of hese dyscypulys xal be chef of þis ordenawns,
Þat xal fortefye þis term, þat in trost is treson.
Þus xal I venge be sotylté al my malycyous grevauns,
For nothyng may excede my prudens and
                              dyscrecyon.   60
Gyff me ȝour love, grawnt me myn affeccyon,
And I wyl vnclose þe tresour of lovys alyawns
And gyff ȝow ȝoure desyrys afftere ȝoure intencyon;
No poverté xal aproche ȝow fro plentévous
                              abundauns.

Byholde þe dyvercyté of my dysgysyd varyauns;   65
Eche thyng sett of dewe naterall dysposycyon,
And eche parte acordynge to his resemblauns,
Fro þe sool of þe foot to þe hyest asencyon.
Off fyne cordewan, a goodly peyre of long pekyd
                              schon;
Hosyn enclosyd of þe most costyous cloth of
                              crenseyn –   70
Þus a bey to a jentylman to make comparycyon –
With two doseyn poyntys of cheverelle, þe aglottys
                              of syluer feyn.

A shert of feyn holond, but care not for þe payment,
A stomachere of clere reynes, þe best may be bowth.
Þow poverté be chef, lete pride þer be present,   75
And all þo þat repreff pride, þu sette hem at nowth.
Cadace, wolle, or flokkys, where it may be sowth,
To stuffe withal þi dobbelet and make þe of
                              proporcyon:
Two smale legges and a gret body, þow it ryme
                              nowth,
Ȝet loke þat þu desyre, to an þe newe faccyon.   80

---

68 Fro]-r- *written over an* o   72 syluer] s- *written over a* y   73 holond] cloth *deleted*
after holond

A gowne of thre ȝerdys – loke þu make comparison
Vnto all degrees dayly þat passe þin astat.
A purse withoutyn mony, a daggere for devoscyon;
And þere repref is of synne, loke þu make debat.

f. 137v   With syde lokkys i-schrewe þin here, to þi colere
                                    hangyng down,   85
To herborwe qweke bestys þat tekele men o nyth;
An hey smal bonet for curyng of þe crowne;
And all beggerys and pore pepyll haue hem on
                                    dyspyte.
Onto þe grete othys and lycherye gyf þi delyte;
To maynteyn þin astate lete brybory be present,   90
And yf þe lawe repreve þe, say þu wylt fyth,
And gadere þe a felachep after þin entent.

Loke þu sett not be precept nor be comawndement;
Both sevyle and canoun sett þu at nowth.
Lette no membre of God but with othys be rent –   95
Lo! þus þis werd at þis tyme to myn intent is browth.
I, Sathan, with my felawus þis werd hath sowth,
And now we han it at houre plesawns;
For synne is not shamfast but boldnes hath bowth,
Þat xal cause hem in helle to han inerytawns.   100

A beggerys dowtere to make gret purvyauns
To cownterfete a jentylwoman, dysgeysyd as she can;
And yf mony lakke, þis is þe newe chevesauns,
With here prevy plesawns to gett it of sum man.
Here colere splayed, and furryd with ermyn,
                                    calabere or satan – 105
A seyn to selle lechory to hem þat wyl bey.
And þei þat wyl not by it, yet inow xal þei han,
And telle hem it is for love – she may it not deney.

I haue browth ȝow newe namys, and wyl ȝe se why?
For synne is so plesaunt to ech mannys intent.   110
f. 138   Ȝe xal kalle pride, onesté, and naterall kend, lechory;
And covetyse, wysdam there tresure is present;

---

85 i-schrewe þin here] ouer þin eyn and þin herys *written above line*;   i-schrewe] *MS.*
j schrewe   91 lawe] ll *deleted after* lawe   101] *in left margin, a small capitulum deleted*
between paragraph mark and beginning of line   103 is þe] ll *deleted after* þe

Wreth, manhod, and envye callyd chastément.
Seyse nere sessyon, lete periory be chef;
Glotenye rest, let abstynawnce beyn absent.   115
And he þat wole exorte þe to vertu, put hem to repreff.

To rehers al my servauntys my matere is to breff,
But all þese xal eneryth þe dyvicyon eternal.
Þow Cryst by his sotylté many materys meef,
In evyrlastynge peyne with me dwellyn þei xal.   120
Remembre, oure seruauntys, whoys sowlys ben
                                                    mortall,
For I must remeffe for more materys to provyde;
I am with ȝow at all tymes whan ȝe to councel me call,
But for a short tyme myself I devoyde.

Johannes Baptista
I, John Baptyst, to ȝow þus prophesye   125
Þat on xal come aftyr me and not tary longe,
In many folde more strengere þan I,
Of whose shon I am not worthy to lose þe thonge.
Wherefore I councel [þat] ȝe reforme all wronge
In ȝour concyens of þe mortall dedys sevyn;   130
And for to do penawns loke þat ȝe fonge,
For now xal come þe kyngdham of hevyn.

Þe weys of Oure Lord cast ȝow to aray,
And þerin to walk loke ȝe be applyande.
And make his pathys as ryth as ȝe may,   135
Kepyng ryth forth; and be not declinande
f. 138v   Neyther to fele on ryth nor on lefte hande;
But in þe myddys purpose ȝow to holde,
For þat in all wyse is most plesande –
As ȝe xal here whan I have tolde.   140

Of þis wey for to make moralysacyon:
Be þe ryth syde ȝe xal vndyrstonde mercy,
And on þe lefte syde, lykkenyd dysperacyon;
And þe patthe betwyn bothyn, þat may not wry,
Schal be hope and drede, to walk in perfectly,   145
Declynyng not to fele for no maner nede.

125 *sn Baptista*] *MS.* baptis *the rest lost at edge of leaf*   129 þat] *MS.* þe   137 lefte]
syde *deleted after* lefte   141–2] be þe ryth syde lyknyd dysperacyon/and þe patthe
betwyn bothyn *deleted between lines 141 and 142*

Grete cawsys I xal shove ʒow why
Þat ʒe xal sewe þe patthe of hope and drede.

On þe mercy of God, to meche ʒe xal not holde;
As in þis wyse – beheld what I mene! –   150
For to do synne be þu no more bolde
In trost þat God wole mercyful bene.
And yf be sensualyté, as it is ofte sene,
Synnyst dedly, þu xalt not þerfore dyspeyre,
But þerfore do penawns and confesse þe clene,   155
And of hevyn þu mayst trost to ben eyre.

Þe pathe þat lyth to þis blyssyd enherytawns
Is hope and drede, copelyd be coniunccyon.
Betwyx þese tweyn may be no dysseuerawns,
For hope withoutyn drede is maner of
                              presumpcyon,   160
f. 139   And drede withowtyn hope is maner of dysperacyon;
So these tweyn must be knyt be on acorde.
How ʒe xal aray þe wey, I haue made declaracyon,
Also þe ryth patthis aʒens þe comyng of Oure Lord.

*Here xal Annas shewyn hymself in his stage, beseyn after a busshop
of þe hoold lawe in a skarlet gowne and ouer þat a blew tabbard
furryd with whyte, and a mytere on his hed after þe hoold lawe; two
doctorys stondyng by hym in furryd hodys, and on beforn hem with
his staff of astat, and eche of hem on here hedys a furryd cappe with a
gret knop in þe crowne; and on stondyng beforn as a Sarazyn, þe
wich xal be his masangere; Annas þus seyng:*

Annas

As a prelat am I properyd to provyde pes,   165
And of Jewys jewge, þe lawe to fortefye.
I, Annas, be my powere xal comawnde dowteles
Þe lawys of Moyses, no man xal denye.
Hoo excede my comawndement, anon ʒe certefye;
Yf any eretyk here reyn, to me ʒe compleyn;   170
For in me lyth þe powere all trewthis to trye,
And pryncypaly oure lawys, þo must I susteyn.

163 declaracyon] *MS.* declararacyon   164 *sd* two] *MS.* ij

Зef I may aspey þe contrary, no wheyle xal þei reyn,
But anon to me be browth and stonde present
Before here jewge, wich xal not feyn   175
But aftere here trespace to gef hem jugement.
Now, serys, for a prose heryth myn intent:
There is on Jhesus of Nazareth þat oure lawys doth
                                                    excede;
Yf he procede thus, we xal us all repent,
For oure lawys he dystroyt dayly with his dede.   180

f. 139v   Therefore be зour cowncel we must take hede
What is best to provyde or do in þis case;
For yf we let hym þus go and ferdere prosede,
Ageyn Sesare and oure lawe we do trespace.

Primus doctor
Sere, þis is myn avyse þat зe xal do: 185
Send to Cayphas for cowncel, knowe his intent;
For yf Jhesu procede and þus forth go,
Oure lawys xal be dystroyd; thes se we present.

Secundus doctor
Sere, remembre þe gret charge þat on зow is leyd,
Þe lawe to kepe which may not fayle.   190
Yf any defawth prevyd of зow be seyd,
Þe Jewys with trewth wyl зow asayl.
Tak hed whath cownsayl may best provayl.
After Rewfyn and Leyon I rede þat зe sende,
They arn temperal jewgys þat knowyth þe parayl,   195
With зoure cosyn, Cayphas, þis matere to amende.

Annas
Now surely þis cowncel revyfe myn herte;
Зoure cowncel is best as I can se.
Arfexe, in hast loke þat þu styrte,
And pray Cayphas, my cosyn, come speke with me.   200

173 contrary] *MS.* contraly; -r- *first written, 'corrected' to* -l-?   182 best to] *MS.* be
to   185 *sn*] Annas *added on line beneath by later hand*   187 procede] *MS.* proce
189 *sn*] Annas *added as at 185*   190 kepe] *MS.* ke;   fayle] fay *written over other letters*

To Rewfyn and Leon þu go also,
And pray hem þei speke with me in hast
For a pryncipal matere þat haue to do,
Wich must be knowe or þis day be past.

Arfexe
My souereyn, at ȝour intent I xal gon   205
In al þe hast þat I kan hy
Onto Cayphas, Rewfyn and Lyon,
And charge ȝoure intent þat þei xal ply.

f. 140 *Here goth þe masangere forth; and in þe mene tyme Cayphas*
        shewyth himself in his skafhald, arayd lych to Annas savyng his
        tabbard xal be red furryd with white; two doctorys with hym, arayd
        with pellys aftyr þe old gyse and furryd cappys on here hedys;
        Cayphas þus seyng:

Cayphas
As a primat most preudent, I present here sensyble,
Buschopys of þe lawe, with al þe cyrcumstawns.   210
I, Cayphas, am jewge with powerys possyble
To distroye all errouris þat in oure lawys make
                                        varyawns.
All thyngys I convey be reson and temperawnce,
And all materis possyble to me ben palpable.
Of þe lawe of Moyses I haue a chef governawns,   215
To seuere ryth and wrong in me is termynable.

But þer is on Cryst þat [in] oure lawys is varyable;
He perverte þe pepyl with his prechyng ill.
We must seke a mene onto hym reprevable,
For yf he procede oure lawys he wyl spyll.   220

We must take good cowncel in þis case,
Of þe wysest of þe lawe þat kan þe trewthe telle,
Of þe jewgys of Pharasy, and of my cosyn, Annas;
For yf he procede be prossesse, oure lawys he wyl
                                        felle.

208 sd two] MS. ij   216 To] deuere *deleted after* To   217 in] *omitted in*
MS.   222 lawe] ll *deleted before* lawe   224 he wyl] ll *deleted before* he

Primus doctor

Myn lord, plesyt ʒow to pardon me for to say   225
Þe blame in ʒow is, as we fynde,
To lete Cryst contenue þus day be day,
With his fals wichcraft þe pepyl to blynde.

f. 140v He werkyth fals meraclis ageyns all kende,
And makyth our pepyl to leve hem in.   230
It is ʒour part to take hym and do hym bynde,
And gyf hym jugement for his gret syn.

Secundus doctor

Forsothe, sere, of trewth this is þe case:
Onto our lawe ʒe don oppressyon
Þat ʒe let Cryst from ʒou pace   235
And wyl not don on hym correxion.
Let Annas knowe ʒour intencyon,
With prestys and jewgys of þe lawe,
And do Cryst forsake his fals oppynyon,
Or into a preson lete hem be thrawe.   240

Cayphas

Wel, serys, ʒe xal se withinne short whyle
I xal correcte hym for his trespas.
He xal no lenger oure pepyl begyle;
Out of myn dawngere he xal not pas.

*Here comyth þe masangere to Cayphas; and in þe mene tyme
Rewfyn and Lyon schewyn hem in þe place in ray tabardys furryd
and ray hodys abouth here neckys furryd; þe masangere seyng:*

Masangere

Myn reverent souereyn, and it do ʒow plese,   245
Sere Annas, my lord, hath to ʒou sent.
He prayt ʒou þat ʒe xal not sese
Tyl þat ʒe bèn with hym present.

---

225 *sn*] Cayfas *added on line beneath in a later hand*   226 fynde] haue fow *deleted before*
fynde   229 meraclis] all kende *deleted after* meraclis   233 *sn*] Cayphas *added as at*
225   240 lete hem] h *deleted after* hem

Cayphas
　　Sere, telle myn cosyn I xal not fayl.
　　It was my purpose hym for to se,　　　　　　　　　　250
　　For serteyn materys þat wyl provayle,
　　Þow he had notwth a sent to me.
Masager
f. 141　　I recomende me to ȝour hey degré,
　　On more massagys I must wende.
Cayphas
　　Farewel, sere, and wel ȝe be,　　　　　　　　　　255
　　Gret wel my cosyn and my frende.

Here þe masager metyth with þe jewgys sayng:

Masager
　　Heyl, jewgys of Jewry, of reson most prudent,
　　Of my massage to ȝou I make relacyon.
　　My lord, sere Annas, hath for ȝou sent
　　To se his presens withowth delacyon.　　　　　　　260

Rewfyn
　　Sere, we are redy at his comawndement
　　To se sere Annas in his place.
　　It was oure purpose and oure intent
　　To a be with hym withinne short space.

Leyon
　　We are ful glad his presence to se.　　　　　　　265
　　Sere, telle hym we xal come in hast;
　　No delacyon þerin xal be,
　　But to his presens hye us fast.

Masager
　　I xal telle my lord, seris, as ȝe say,
　　Ȝe wyl fulfylle al his plesawns.　　　　　　　　270
Rewfyn
　　Sere, telle hym we xal make no delay,
　　But come in hast at his instawns.

251 wyl] -l *inserted later, probably by main scribe*　　256 frende] *MS.* frede

Here þe masangere comyth to Annas þus seyng:

Masanger

My lord, and it plese ȝou to haue intellygens,
Ser Cayphas comyth to ȝou in hast;
Rewfyn and Lyon wyl se ȝour presens   275
And se ȝow here or þis day be past.

Annas

f. 141v   Sere, I kan þe thank of þi dyligens.
Now ageyn my cosyn I wole walk.
Serys, folwyth me onto his presens,
For of these materys we must talk.   280

Here Annas goth down to mete with Cayphas; and in þe mene tyme
þus seyng

Cayphas

Now onto Annas let us wende,
Ech of vs to knowe otherys intent.
Many materys I haue in mende,
Þe wich to hym I xal present.

Primus doctor C

Sere, of all othere thyng remembre þis case;   285
Loke þat Jhesus be put to schame.

Secundus doctor C

Whan we come present beforn Annas,
Whe xal rehers all his gret blame.

Here þe buschopys with here clerkys and þe Pharaseus mett [in] þe
myd place; and þer xal be a lytil oratory with stolys and cusshonys
clenly beseyn, lych as it were a cownsel hous; Annas þus seyng:

Annas

Welcome, ser Cayphas and ȝe jewgys alle,
Now xal ȝe knowe all myn entent.   290

---

273 *sn Masanger*] MS. Masan *the rest lost at edge of leaf;   sn precedes sd*   282 vs] MS.
ovs *the* o *partly covered by the* v–   288 *sd* in] MS. and;   beseyn] MS. benseyn   289
jewgys] -g- *added by main scribe above line*

A wondyr case, serys, here is befalle
On wich we must gyf jewgement –
Lyst þat we aftere þe case repent –
Of on, Cryst, þat Goddys sone som doth hym calle.
He shewyth meraclys and sythe present   295
Þat he is prynce of pryncys allé.

The pepyl so fast to hym doth falle,
Be prevy menys as we aspye,
Ʒyf he procede son sen ȝe xalle
Þat oure lawys he wyl dystrye.   300

f. 142   It is oure part þis to deny.
What is ȝour cowncell in þis cas?
Cayphas
Be reson þe trewth here may we try.
I cannot dem hym withouth trespace;
Because he seyth in every a place   305
Þat he [is] kyng of Jewys in every degré,
Þerfore he is fals, knowe wel þe case,
Sesar is kyng and non but he.

Rewfyn
He is an eretyk and a tretour bolde
To Sesare and to oure lawe sertayn,   310
Bothe in word and in werke, and ȝe beholde;
He is worthy to dey with mekyl peyn.

Leon
Þe cawse þat we been here present,
To fortefye þe lawe and trewth to say;
Jhesus ful nere oure lawys hath shent,   315
Þerfore he is worthy for to day.

Primus doctor Annas
Serys, ȝe þat ben rewelerys of þe lawe,
On Jhesu ȝe must gyf jugement.
Let hym fyrst ben hangyn and drawe,
And þanne his body in fyre be brent.   320

---

292 jewgement] alle *deleted after* jewgement   301 þis] *MS. possibly* þes   306 he is]
is *omitted in MS.*   317 *sn* Annas] *MS.* An *the rest lost at edge of leaf*

Secundus doctor Annas
  Now xal 3e here þe intent of me:
  Take Jhesu þat werke us all gret schame,
  Put hym to deth; let hym not fle,
  For than þe comownys þei wyl 3ow blame.

Primus doctor Cayphas
f. 142v   He werke with wechecrafte in eche place,   325
  And drawyth þe pepyl to hese intent.
  Be whare, 3e jewgys, let hym not passe,
  Þan, be my trewthe, 3e xal repent.

Secundus doctor Cayphas
  Serys, takyth hede onto þis case,
  And in 3our jewgement be not slawe;   330
  Þer was nevyr man dyd so gret trespace
  As Jhesu hath don ageyn oure lawe.

Annas
  Now, bretheryn, þan wyl 3e here myn intent:
  These nyn days let us abyde,
  We may not gyf so hasty jugement;   335
  But eche man inqwere on his syde,
  Send spyes abouth þe countré wyde
  To se and recorde and testymonye,
  And þan hese werkys he xal not hyde
  Nor haue no power hem to denye.   340

Cayphas
  This cowncell acordyth to my reson.

[Omnes]
  And we all to þe same.

Here enteryth þe apostyl Petyr and John þe Euangelyst with hym;
Petyr seyng:

---

321 *sn Annas*] MS. *as at 317*   324 comownys] w *erased after* co-   325 *sn Cayphas*]
MS. Cayp *the rest lost at edge of leaf;*   wechecrafte] f(?) *deleted after* weche-   328
repent] MS. repepent; *first* -pe- *dotted for deletion and blotted*   329 *sn Cayphas*] -p-
apparently written over an f   334 nyn] MS. ix   342 *sn Omnes*] MS. Annas   342
sd – 348] *deleted in MS.;* vacat + *red bracket in left margin. See notes*

[*Petrus*]

    O, ȝe pepyl dyspeyryng, be glad!
    A gret cause ȝe haue and ȝe kan se:
    Þe Lord þat all þing of nowth mad   345
    Is comyng, ȝour comfort to be.
    All ȝour langorys salvyn xal he,
    Ȝour helthe is more þan ȝe kan wete;

f. 144   He xal cawse þe blynde þat þei xal se,
    Þe def to here, þe dome for to speke.   350

    Þei þat be crokyd, he xal cause hem to goo
    In þe wey þat John Baptyst of prophecyed.
    Sweche a leche kam ȝow nevyr non too;
    Wherfore what he comawndyth loke ȝe applyed.
    Þat som of ȝow be blynd, ȝe may not deny it.   355
    For hym þat is ȝour makere with ȝour gostly ey ȝe
                                 xal not knowe.
    Of his comaundementys, in ȝow gret necglygens is
                                 aspyed,
    Wherefore def fro gostly heryng clepe ȝow I howe.

    And some of ȝow may not go, ȝe be so crokyd,
    For of good werkyng in ȝow is lytyl habundawns.   360
    Tweyn fete heuery man xuld haue, and it were
                                   lokyd,
    Wyche xuld bere þe body gostly, most of substawns:
    Fyrst is to love God above all other plesawns,
    Þe secunde is to love þi neybore as þin owyn persone.
    And yf þese tweyn be kepte in perseverawns,   365
    Into þe celestyal habytacyon ȝe arn habyl to gone.

    Many of ȝow be dome. Why? For ȝe wole not
                                   redresse
    Be mowthe ȝour dedys mortal, but þerin don perdure.
    Of þe wych, but ȝe haue contrycyon and ȝow
                                  confesse,
    Ȝe may not inheryte hevyn, þis I ȝow ensure.   370

---

343 *sn Petrus*] *omitted in MS.*   345 þat] *MS.* of; þat *supplied from parallel passage on f.*
143v   348 ȝe kan] ȝe *omitted in MS.; supplied from f. 143v; for passage omitted here*
see Appendix 1   355 ȝe may not] it *heavily written over erased* ȝe; be *added above line +*
caret after not;   deny it] dey *deleted before* deny; -id *joined to* deny *by double hyphen and*
written over original it; *see notes*   361 Tweyn] *suspension mark above* y *blotted*

And of all þese maladyes ȝe may haue gostly cure,
For þe hevynly leche is comyng ȝow for to vicyte.
And as for payment, he wole shewe ȝow no redrure,
For with þe love of ȝowre hertys he wole be aqwhyte.

Johannes apostolus

f. 144v Onto my brotherys forseyd rehersall 375
 Þat ȝe xuld ȝeve þe more veray confydens,
 I come with hym as testymonyall
 For to conferme and fortefye his sentens.
 Þis lord xal come without resystens;
 Onto þe cetyward he is now comyng. 380
 Wherefore dresse ȝow with all dew dylygens
 To honowre hym as ȝour makere and kyng.

 And to fulfylle þe prophetys prophesé,
 Vpon an asse he wole hedyr ryde;
 Shewyng ȝow exawmple of humylyté, 385
 Devoydyng þe abhomynable synne of pryde
 Whech hath ny conqweryd all þe werd wyde,
 Grettest cause of all ȝour trybulacyon.
 Vse it hoso wole, for it is þe best gyde
 Þat ȝe may haue to þe place of dampnacyon. 390

 Now, brothyr in God, syth we have intellygens
 Þat oure lord is ny come to þis ceté,
 To attend upon his precyous presens
 It syttyth to us, as semyth me.
 Wherfore to mete whit hym now go we, 395
 I wold fore nothyng we where to late.
 To þe cetéward fast drawyth he,
 Mesemyth he is ny at þe gate.

Here spekyth þe foure ceteseynys; þe fyrst þus seyng:

Primus ciues de Jherusalem

f. 145 Neyborys, gret joye in oure herte we may make
 Þat þis hefly kyng wole vycyte þis cyté. 400

---

375 *sn*] *also* Apostolus Johannes *in centre at head of f. 144v* 377 testymonyall] *second* -l
written over an e 396 where] -h- *written over an* e 398 gate] g- *written over earlier* ȝ
in a later hand 398 *sd* foure] MS. iiij; *in left margin the addition* here entrith þe fyrst
prophete

Secundus ciues

Yf oure eerly kyng swech a jorné xuld take,
To don hym honour and worchepe besy xuld we be.

Tertius ciues

Meche more þan to þe hevynly kyng bownd are we
For to do þat xuld be to his persone reuerens.

Quartus ciues

Late vs þan welcome hym with flowrys and
                              brawnchis of þe tre,   405
For he wole take þat to plesawns becawse of redolens.

*Here þe foure ceteseynys makyn hem redy for to mete with Oure
Lord, goyng barfot and barelegged and in here shyrtys savyng þei
xal have here gownys cast abouth them; and qwan þei seen Oure
Lord, þei xal sprede þer clothis beforn hym and he xal lyth and go
þerupon; and þei xal falle downe upon þer knes all at onys; þe fyrst
þus seyng:*

Primus ciues

Now blyssyd he be þat in oure Lordys name
To us in any wyse wole resorte:
And we beleve veryly þat þu dost þe same,
For be þi mercy xal spryng mannys comforte.   410

*Here Cryst passyth forth; þer metyth with hym a serteyn of
chylderyn with flowrys and cast beforn hym; and they synggyn,*
Gloria laus, *and beforn on seyth:*

[Secundus ciues]

Thow sone of Davyd, þu be oure supporte
At oure last day whan we xal dye;
Wherefore we alle at onys to þe exorte,
Cryeng, mercy, mercy, mercye!

Jhesu

f. 145v   Frendys, beholde þe tyme of mercy,   415
            Þe wich is come now withowtyn dowth;

---

405 sn ciues] MS. ci *the rest lost at edge of leaf*   406 sd foure] MS. iiij   410 sd seyth]
MS. seyt *the rest lost at edge of leaf*   411 sn Secundus ciues] *omitted in MS.*   414]
added below the line at foot of page here entreth þe parte off þe ij^de prophete + *caret
indicating position after* 414   415 sn] *repeated in centre at head of* f. 145v

Mannys sowle in blysse now xal edyfy,
And þe prynce of þe werd is cast owth.
As I haue prechyd in placys abowth,
And shewyd experyence to man and wyf,   420
Into þis werd Goddys sone hath sowth
For veray loue man to revyfe.

The trewthe of trewthis xal now be tryede,
And a perfyth of-corde betwyn God and man;
Wich trewth xal nevyr be dyvide –   425
Confusyon onto þe fynd, Sathan!

Primus pauper homo
Þu sone of Davyd, on vs haue mercye,
As we must stedfast belevyn in þe.
Þi goodnesse, lord, lete us be nye,
Whech lyth blynd here and may not se.   430

Secundus pauper homo
Lord, lete þi mercy to us be sewre,
And restore to us oure bodyly syth;
We know þu may us wel recure
With þe lest poynt of þi gret myth.

Jhesu
Зowre beleve hath mad зou for to se,   435
And delyveryd зou fro all mortal peyn.
Blyssyd be all þo þat beleve on me
And se me not with here bodyly eyn.

Here Cryst blyssyth here eyn and þei may se; þe fryst seyng:

f. 146   *Primus pauper homo*
Gromercy, lord, of þi gret grace,
I þat was blynd, now may se.   440
Secundus pauper homo
Here I forsake al my trespace
And stedfastly wyl belevyn on þe.

438–45] *large sign in dark ink in left margin*

Here Cryst procedyth on fote with his dyscipulys after hym; Cryst wepyng upon þe cyté, sayng þus:

Jhesu

O, Jherusalem, woful is þe ordenawnce
Of þe day of þi gret persecucyon!
Þu xalt be dystroy with woful grevans,   445
And þi ryalté browth to trew confusyon.
3e þat in þe ceté han habytacyon,
Þei xal course þe tyme þat þei were born,
So gret advercyté and trybulacyon
Xal falle on hem both evyn and morwyn.   450

Þei þat han most chylderyn sonest xal wayle
And seyn, "Alas, what may þis meen?"
Both mete and drynk sodeynly xal fayle;
Þe vengeance of God þer xal be seen.
Þe tyme is comyng hes woo xal ben,   455
Þe day of trobyl and gret grevauns;
Bothe templys and towrys they xal down cleen –
O, ceté, ful woful is þin ordenawns!

Petrus

Lord, where wolte þu kepe þi maundé?
I pray þe now lete us haue knowyng,   460
Þat we may make redy for þe,
Þe to serve withowte latyng;

Johannes

f. 146v   To provyde, lord, for þi comyng
With all þe obedyens we kan atende,
And make redy for þe in al thyng   465
Into what place þu wylt us send.

Jhesu

Serys, goth to Syon and 3e xal mete
A pore man in sympyl aray
Beryng watyr in þe strete;
Telle hym I xal come þat way.   470

446–9] *large red numeral 27 in right margin*   466 wylt] *MS.* wytl

Onto hym mekely loke þat ȝe say
Þat hese hous I wele come tylle.
He wele not onys to ȝow sey nay,
But sofre to haue all ȝour wylle.

Petrus
    At þi wyl, lord, it xal be don,   475
    To seke þat place we xal us hye,
Johannes
    In all þe hast þat we may go,
    Þin comawndement nevyr to denye.

*Here Petyr and John gon forth metyng with Symon Leprows
beryng a kan with watyr; Petyr þus seyng:*

Petrus
    Good man, þe prophete, oure lord Jhesus,
    Þis nyth wyl rest wythin þin halle.   480
    On massage to þe he hath sent vs,
    Þat for his sopere ordeyn þu xalle.
Johannes
    ȝa, for hym and his dyscipulys alle,
    Ordeyn þu for his maundé
    A Paschall lomb, whatso befalle,   485
    For he wyl kepe his Pasch with the.

Symon
f. 147   What, wyl my lord vesyte my plase?
    Blyssyd be þe tyme of his comyng!
    I xal ordeyn withinne short space
    For my good lordys welcomyng.   490
    Serys, walkyth in at þe begynnyng
    And se what vetaylys þat I xal take.
    I am so glad of þis tydyng
    I wot nevyr what joye þat I may make.

*Here þe dyscypulys gon in with Symon to se þe ordenawns; and
Cryst comyng thedyrward þus seyng:*

478 comawndement] *MS.* comawdement

Jhesus
    Þis path is [cald Syon], be goostly ordenawns,   495
    Wech xal conuey us wher we xal be.
    I knowe ful redy is þe purvyaunce
    Of my frendys þat lovyn me.
    Contewnyng in pees now procede we;
    For mannys love þis wey I take,   500
    With gostly ey I veryly se
    Þat man for man an hende must make.

Here þe dysciplys com ageyn to Cryst; Petyr þus seyng:

Petrus
    All redy, lord, is oure ordenawns,
    As I hope to ȝow plesyng xal be.
    Seymon hath don at ȝoure instawns;   505
    He is ful glad ȝour presens to se.

Johannes
    All thyng we haue, lord, at oure plesyng
    Þat longyth to ȝoure mawndé with ful glad chere.
    Whan he herd telle of ȝour comyng,
    Gret joye in hym þan dyd appere.   510

f. 147v *Here comyth Symon owt of his hous to welcome Cryst.*

Symon
    Gracyous lord, welcome þu be!
    Reverens be to þe, both God and man,
    My poer hous þat þu wylt se,
    Weche am þi servaunt as I kan.

Jhesu
    There joye of all joyis to þe is sewre.   515
    Symon, I knowe þi trewe intent,
    Þe blysse of hefne þu xalt recure;
    Þis rewarde I xal þe grawnt present.

---

495 cald Syon] *MS.* calsydon   510 *sd* owt) -t *added just above the line*

Here Cryst enteryth into þe hous with his disciplis and ete þe
Paschal lomb. And in þe mene tyme þe cownsel hous befornseyd xal
sodeynly onclose schewyng þe buschopys, prestys and jewgys syt-
tyng in here astat lych as it were a convocacyon; Annas seyng þus:

Annas

    Behold it is nowth, al þat we do,
    In alle houre materys we prophete nowth.   520
    Wole ȝe se wech peusawns of pepyl drawyth hym
                                   to,
    For þe mervaylys þat he hath wrowth.

    Some othyr sotylté must be sowth,
    For in no wyse we may not þus hym leve;
    Than to a schrewde conclusyon we xal be browth.   525
    For þe Romaynes þan wyl us myscheve,
    And take oure astat, and put us to repreve,
    And convey all þe pepyl at here owyn request;
    And þus all þe pepyl in hym xal beleve.
    Þerfore I pray ȝow, cosyn, say what is þe best.   530

Cayphas

f. 148   Attende now, serys, to þat I xal seye:
    Onto us all it is most expedyent
    Þat o man for þe pepyl xuld deye
    Þan all þe pepyl xuld perysch and be shent.

    Þerfor late us werk wysely þat we us not repent.   535
    We must nedys put on hym som fals dede;
    I sey for me I had levyr he were brent
    Þan he xuld us alle þus ouyrlede.
    Þerfore every man on his party help at þis nede
    And cowntyrfete all þe sotyltés þat ȝe kan.   540
    Now late se ho kan ȝeve best rede
    To ordeyn sum dystruccyon for þis man.

Gamalyel

    Late us no lenger make delacyon,
    But do Jhesu be takyn in hondys fast,

---

523 must be] wrowth *deleted after* be

And all [hese] folwerys to here confusyon,   545
And into a preson do hem be cast.
Ley on hem yron þat wol last,
For he hath wrouth aȝens þe ryth;
And sythyn aftyr we xal in hast
Jewge hym to deth with gret dyspyth.   550

Rewfyn
For he hath trespacyd aȝens oure lawe,
Mesemyth þis were best jewgement:
With wyld hors lete hym be drawe
And afftyr in fyre he xal be brent.

Leyon
Serys, o thyng myself herd hym sey,   555
Þat he was kyng of Jewys alle;
Þat is anow to do hym dey,
For treson to Sezar we must it calle.

f. 148v   He seyd also to personys þat I know,
Þat he xuld and myth, serteyn,   560
Þe gret tempyl mythtyly ovyrthrow,
And þe thrydde day reysynt ageyn.
Seche materys þe pepyl doth [constreyn]
To ȝeve credens to his werkys alle;
In hefne he seyth xal be his reyn,   565
Bothe God and man he doth hym calle.

Rewfyn
And all þis day we xuld contryve
What shameful deth Jhesu xuld haue;
We may not do hym to meche myscheve,
Þe worchep of oure lawe to save.   570

Leyon
Vpon a jebet lete hym hongyn be,
Þis jugement mesemyth it is reson;
Þat all þe countré may hym se
And be ware be his gret treson.

---

545 hese] *MS.* here   563 constreyn] *MS.* conseyve   572 mesemyth] is i *deleted*
after mesemyth

Rewfyn
>3et o thyng, serys, 3e must aspye,					575
>And make a ryth sotyl ordenawns
>Be what menys 3e may come hym bye;
>For he hath many folwerys at his instawns.

Annas
>Serys, þerof we must have avysement,
>And ben acordyd or þan we go					580
>How we xal han hym at oure entent;
>Som wey we xal fynd þerto.

Here Judas Caryoth comyth into þe place.

f. 152	*Judas*
>Now cowntyrfetyd I haue a prevy treson
>My maysterys power for to felle.
>I, Judas, xal asay be some encheson					585
>Onto þe Jewys hym for to selle.
>Som mony for hym 3et wold I telle –
>Be prevy menys I xal asay.
>Myn intent I xal fulfylle,
>No lenger I wole make delay.					590

>Þe princys of prestys now be present,
>Vnto hem now my way I take;
>I wyl go tellyn hem myn entent –
>I trow ful mery I xal hem make.
>Mony I wyl non forsake,					595
>And þei profyr to my plesyng;
>For covetyse I wyl with hem wake,
>And onto my maystyr I xal hem bryng.

>Heyl, prynsesse and prestys þat ben present!
>New tydyngys to 3ow I come to telle.					600
>3yf 3e wole folwe myn intent,
>My mayster, Jhesu, I wele 3ow selle,
>Hese intent and purpose for to felle;
>For I wole no lenger folwyn his lawe.

---

582 *sd*] *deleted in MS.   after* 582 *sd*] *for omission of quire O and for text see Appendix*
2	585 encheson] j *deleted before* encheson

Late sen what mony þat I xal telle,   605
And late Jhesu, my maystyr, ben hangyn and
                                                    drawe.

Gamalyel
Now welcome, Judas, oure owyn frende –
Take hym in, serys, be þe honde.
We xal þe both geve and lende,
And in every qwarel by þe stonde.   610

Rewfyn
f. 152v   Judas, what xal we for þi mayster pay?
Þi sylver is redy and we acorde;
Þe payment xal haue no delay
But be leyde down here at a worde.

Judas
Late þe mony here down be layde   615
And I xal telle ȝow as I kan;
In old termys I haue herd seyde
Þat mony makyth schapman.

Rewfyn
Here is thretty platys of sylver bryth,
Fast knyth withinne þis glove;   620
And we may have þi mayster þis nyth,
Þis xalt þu haue and all oure love.

Judas
Ȝe are resonable chapmen to bye and selle;
Þis bargany with ȝow now xal I make.
Smyth up, ȝe xal haue al ȝour wylle,   625
For mony wyl I non forsake.

Leyon
Now þis bargany is mad ful and fast,
Noyther part may it forsake;
But, Judas, þu must telle us in hast
Be what menys we xal hym take.   630

---

607 sn *Gamalyel*] MS. Gamalye *the rest lost at edge of leaf*

Rewfyn

    3a, þer be many þat hym nevyr sowe
    Weche we wyl sende to hym in fere;
    Perfor be a tokyn we must hym knowe,
    Þat must be prevy betwyx us here.

Leyon

    3a, be ware of þat for onythynge,   635
    For o dyscypil is lyche þi mayster in al parayl;
f. 153   And 3e go lyche in all clothyng,
    So myth we of oure purpose fayl.

Judas

    As for þat, serys, haue 3e no dowth,
    I xal ordeyn so 3e xal not mysse: 640
    Whan þat 3e cvm hym all abowth,
    Take þe man þat I xal kysse.

    I must go to my maystyr ageyn.
    Dowth not, serys, þis matere is sure inow.
Gamalyel

    Farewel, Judas, oure frend serteyn,   645
    Þi labour we xal ryth wel alow.

Judas

    Now wyl I sotely go seke my mayster ageyn
    And make good face as I nowth knew.
    I haue hym solde to wo and peyn,
    I trowe ful sore he xal it rew.   650

Here Judas goth in sotylly wher-as he cam fro.

Annas

    Lo, serys, a part we haue of oure entent.
    For to take Jhesu now we must provyde
    A sotyl meny to be present,
    Þat dare fyth and wele abyde.

Gamalyel

    Ordeyn eche man on his party,   655

655 *sn* Gamalyel] MS. Gamalye *the rest lost at edge of leaf*

Cressetys, lanternys and torchys lyth,
And þis nyth to be þer redy
With exys, gleyvis and swerdys bryth.

Cayphas
No lenger þan make we teryeng,
But eche man to his place hym dyth   660
And ordeyn preuély for þis thyng,
Þat it be don þis same nyth.

f. 153v *Here the buschopys partyn in þe place, and eche of hem takyn*
here leve be contenawns, resortyng eche man to his place with
here meny to make redy to take Cryst; and þan xal þe place þer
Cryst is in sodeynly vnclose rownd abowtyn, shewyng Cryst
syttyng at þe table and hese dyscypulys ech in ere degré; Cryst
þus seyng:

Jhesu
Brederyn, þis lambe þat was set us beforn,
Þat we alle haue etyn in þis nyth,
It was comawndyd be my Fadyr to Moyses and
                                             Aaron   665
Whan þei weryn with þe chylderyn of Israel in
                                             Egythp.

And as we with swete bredys haue it ete,
And also with þe byttyr sokelyng,
And as we take þe hed with þe fete,
So dede þei in all maner thyng.   670

And as we stodyn, so dede þei stond,
And here reynes þei gyrdyn veryly,
With schon on here fete and stavys in here hond;
And as we ete it, so dede þei, hastyly.
Þis fygure xal sesse, anothyr xal folwe þerby   675
Weche xal be of my body, þat am 30ur hed;
Weche xal be shewyd to 30w be a mystery
Of my flesch and blood in forme of bred.

---

656 torchys] bryth *deleted after* torchys   658 gleyvis] -le- *written over other*
letters   662 *sd* sodeynly] xal *repeated before* sodeynly   667 swete] *letter erased after*
swete

And with fervent desyre of hertys affeccyon
I have enterly desyryd to kepe my mawndé   680
Among ȝow er þan I suffre my passyon;
For, of þis, no more togedyr suppe xal we.

f.154 And as þe Paschal lomb etyn haue we,
In þe old lawe was vsyd for a sacryfyce,
So þe newe lomb, þat xal be sacryd be me,   685
Xal be vsyd for a sacryfyce most of price.

Here xal Jhesus take an oblé in his hand lokyng vpward into hefne
to þe Fadyr; þus seyng:

Wherefore to þe, Fadyr of hefne, þat art eternall,
Thankyng and honor I ȝeld onto þe;
To whom be þe godhed I am eqwall,
But be my manhod I am of lesse degré.   690
Wherefore I as man worchep þe deyté,
Thankyng þe, Fadyr, þat þu wylt shew þis mystery.
And þus þurwe þi myth, Fadyr, and blyssyng of me,
Of þis þat was bred is mad my body.

Here xal he spekyn ageyn to his dysciplys; þus seyng:

Bretheryn, be þe vertu of þese wordys þat rehercyd
                                              be,   695
Þis þat shewyth as bred to ȝour apparens
Is mad þe very flesche and blod of me,
To þe weche þei þat wole be savyd must ȝeve
                                        credens.

And as in þe olde lawe it was comawndyd and
                                          precepte
To ete þis lomb to þe dystruccyon of Pharao
                                      vnkende;   700
So to dystroy ȝour gostly enmye þis xal be kepte
For ȝour Paschal lombe into þe werdys ende.

695] *The whole line was omitted; written in red at foot of page, and also entered in right margin*
beside sd and 696–7 where most of vertu *and* re *of* rehercyd *lost at edge*   696 apparens]
second -a- *written above* e *dotted for deletion*   701 gostly] *an odd-shaped* g- *and a blotted*
approach stroke to -o- *give the appearance of* goostly

For þis is þe very lombe withowte spot of synne
Of weche John þe Baptyst dede prophesy,
Whan þis prophesye he dede begynne   705
Seyng: *Ecce agnus Dey.*

And how ȝe xal ete þis lombe I xal ȝeve
                        infformacyon,
In þe same forme as þe eld lawe doth specyfye,
As I shewe be gostly interpretacyon.
Þerfore to þat I xal sey, ȝour wyttys loke ȝe replye.   710

f. 154v   With no byttyr bred þis [lombe] ete xal be,
Þat is to say with no byttyrnesse of hate and envye,
But with þe suete bred of loue and charyté
Weche fortefyet þe soule gretlye.

And it schuld ben etyn with þe byttyr sokelyng;   715
Þat is to mene, ȝyf a man be of synful dysposycyon,
Hath led his lyff here with myslevyng,
Þerfore in his hert he xal haue byttyr contrycyon.

Also þe hed with þe feet ete xal ȝe;
Be þe hed ȝe xal vndyrstand my godhed,   720
And be þe feet ȝe xal take myn humanyté;
Þese tweyn ȝe xal receyve togedyr indede.

This immaculat lombe þat I xal ȝow ȝeve
Is not only þe godhed alone,
But bothe God and man, þus must ȝe beleve;   725
Þus þe hed with þe feet ȝe xal receyve echon.

Of þis lombe vnete yf owth be levyth, iwys,
Yt xuld be cast in þe clere fyre and brent;
Weche is to mene: yf þu vndyrstande nowth al þis,
Put þi feyth in God and þan þu xalt not be shent.   730

The gyrdyl þat was comawndyd here reynes to
                        sprede
Xal be þe gyrdyl of clennes and chastyté;
Þat is to sayn to be contynent in word, thought and
                        dede,
And all leccherous levyng cast ȝow for to fle.

---

710 wyttys] ȝe *deleted after* wyttys   711 lombe) *MS.* bred;   ete xal] ȝe *deleted after*
xal   716 man] *a word,* ?manbe, *deleted before* man

And þe schon þat xal be ȝour feet vpon   735
Is not ellys but exawnpyl of vertuis levyng
Of ȝour form-faderys ȝou beforn;
With þese schon my steppys ȝe xal be sewyng.

f. 155 And þe staf þat in ȝour handys ȝe xal holde
Is not ellys but þe exawmplys to other men teche.   740
Hold fast ȝour stauys in ȝour handys and beth bolde
To every creature myn precepttys for to preche.

Also ȝe must ete þis Paschall lombe hastyly;
Of weche sentens þis is þe very entent:
At every oure and tyme ȝe xal be redy   745
For to fulfylle my cowmawndement.

For þow ȝe leve þis day, ȝe are not sure
Whedyr ȝe xal leve tomorwe or nowth;
Perfor hastyly every oure do ȝoure besy cure
To kepe my preceptys and þan þar ȝe not dowth.   750

Now haue I lernyd ȝow how ȝe xal ete
Ȝour Paschal lombe þat is my precyous body.
Now I wyl fede ȝow all with awngellys mete,
Wherfore to reseyve it come forth seryattly.

Petrus
Lord, for to receyve þis gostly sustenawns   755
In dewe forme, it excedyth myn intellygens;
For no man of hymself may have substawns
To receyve it with to meche reverens.

For with more delycyous mete, lord, þu may us
                                            not fede
Þan with þin owyn precyous body.   760
Wherfore what I haue trespacyd in word, thought
                                            or dede,
With byttyr contrycyon, lord, I haske þe mercy.

*Whan Oure Lord ȝyvyth his body to his dyscypulys he xal sey to
eche of hem except to Judas:*

---

740 not ellys] I *deleted before* not   754 come] s *or* f *deleted before* come;   forth] sey
deleted after forth

f. 155v [*Jhesu*]
> This is my body, flesch and blode,
> Þat for þe xal dey upon þe rode.

And whan Judas comyth last, Oure Lord xal sey to hym:

> Judas, art þu avysyd what þu xalt take?   765
Judas
> Lord, þi body I wyl not forsake.

And sythyn Oure Lord xal sey onto Judas:

Jhesu
> Myn body to þe I wole not denye,
> Sythyn þu wylt presume þerupon.
> Yt xal be þi dampnacyon verylye,
> I ȝeve þe warnyng now beforn.   770

And aftyr þat Judas hath reseyvyd, he xal syt þer he was; Cryst seyng:

> On of ȝow hath betrayd me,
> Þat at my borde with me hath ete.
> Bettyr it hadde hym for to a be
> Bothe vnborn and vnbegete.

Than eche dyscypyl xal loke on other, and Petyr xal sey;

Petrus
> Lord, it is not I.

And so all xul seyn tyl þei comyn at Judas, wech xal sey:

Judas
> Is it owth I, lord?   775

Þan Jhesus xal sey:

---

763 sn *Jhesu*] *omitted in MS.*   765 xalt] *a letter dotted for deletion after* xalt *and erased*
775 sd] *both sds to right of text*

Jhesu

Judas, þu seyst þat word,

Me þu ast solde þat was þi frend;
Pat þu hast begonne brenge to an ende.

Pan Judas xal gon ageyn to þe Jewys, and yf men wolne [the devil]
xal mete with hym and sey þis spech folwyng – or levynt whether
þei wyl; þe devyl þus seyng:

Demon

f. 156   A, a, Judas, derlyng myn!
Pu art þe best to me þat evyr was bore.   780
Pu xalt be crownyd in helle peyn
And þerof þu xalt be sekyr for evyrmore.

Thow hast solde þi maystyr and etyn hym also,
I wolde þu kowdyst bryngyn hym to helle everydel.
But ʒet I fere he xuld do þer sum sorwe and wo,   785
Pat all helle xal crye out on me þat sel.

Sped up þi matere þat þu hast begonne,
I xal to helle for þe to mak redy.
Anon þu xalt come wher þu xalt wonne,
In fyre and stynk þu xalt sytt me by.   790

Jhesu

Now þe sone of God claryfyed is,
And God in hym is claryfyed also.
I am sory þat Judas hath lost his blysse,
Weche xal turne hym to sorwe and wo.

But now in þe memory of my passyon,   795
To ben partabyl with me in my reyn above,
ʒe xal drynk myn blood with gret devocyon,
Wheche xal be xad for mannys love.

Takyth þese chalys of þe newe testament,
And kepyth þis evyr in ʒour mende;   800
As oftyn as ʒe do þis with trewe intent
It xal defende ʒow fro þe fende.

---

778 *sd* the devil] *omitted in MS., see note*;   folwyng] -l- *written over an* r

Then xal þe dysciplys com and take þe blod; Jhesus seyng:

f. 156v   Þis is my blood þat for mannys synne
            Outh of myn herte it xal renne.

*And þe dysciplys xul sett þem aȝen þer þei wore; and Jhesus xal
seyn:*

Takyth hed now, bretheryn, what I haue do;   805
With my flesch and blood I haue ȝow fed.
For mannys love I may do no mo,
Þan for love of man to be ded.

Werfore, Petyr, and ȝe everychon,
Ȝyf ȝe loue me, fede my schep,   810
Þat for fawth of techyng þei go not wrong,
But evyr to hem takyth good kep.

Ȝevyth hem my body as I haue to ȝow,
Qweche xal be sacryd be my worde,
And evyr I xal þus abyde with ȝow   815
Into þe ende of þe werde.

Hoso etyth my body and drynkyth my blood,
Hol God and man he xal me take;
It xal hym defende from þe deuyl wood,
And at his deth I xal hym nowth forsake.   820

And hoso not ete my body nor drynke my blood,
Lyf in hym is nevyr a dele;
Kepe wel þis in mende for ȝour good,
And every man save hymself wele.

*Here Jhesus takyth a basyn with watyr and towaly gyrt abowtyn
hym and fallyth beforn Petyr on his o kne.*

f. 157 *Jhesus*
Another exawmpyl I xal ȝow shewe   825
How ȝe xal leve in charyté;
Syt here down at wordys fewe
And qwat I do ȝe sofre me.

817 drynkyth] -r- *written over a* y   *after* 824 *sd*] ?Petrus *erased at foot of right*
margin   825 *sn Jhesus*] *centred at head of* f. 157   827 wordys] fe *deleted before* wordys

Here he takyth þe basyn and þe towaly and doth as þe roberych
seyth beforn.

Petrus
> Lord, what wylt þu with me do?
> Þis servyce of þe I wyl forsake.   830
> To wassche my feet þu xal not so,
> I am not worthy it of þe to take.

Jhesu
> Petyr, and þu forsake my servyce all,
> Þe weche to ȝow þat I xal do,
> No part with me haue þu xal   835
> And nevyr com my blysse onto.

Petrus
> Þat part, lord, we wyl not forgo.
> We xal abey his comawndement.
> Wasche hed and hond, we pray þe so,
> We wyl don after þin entent.   840

Here Jhesus wasshyth his dyscipulys feet by and by and whypyth
hem and kyssyth hem mekely, and sythyn settyth hym down; þus
seyng:

Jhesu
> Frendys, þis wasshyng xal now prevayll;
> Ȝoure lord and mayster ȝe do me calle,
> And so I am withowtyn fayl,
> Ȝet I haue wasschyd ȝow alle.

f. 157v
> A memory of þis haue ȝe xall,   845
> Þat eche of ȝow xal do to othyr;
> With vmbyl hert submyt egal,
> As eche of ȝow were otherys brother.

> Nothyng, serys, so wele plesyth me,
> Nor no lyf þat man may lede,   850
> As þei þat levyn in charyté;
> In efne I xal reward here mede.

---

840 *sd* sythyn] *MS.* sythym

Þe day is come I must procede
For to fulfylle þe prophecy.
Þis nyth for me ȝe xal han drede,   855
Whan novmbyr of pepyl xal on me cry.

For þe prophetys spoke of me
And seydyn of deth þat I xuld take;
Fro whech deth I wole not fle,
But for mannys synne amendys make.   860

This nyth fro ȝow be led I xal,
And ȝe for fer fro me xal fle;
Not onys dur speke whan I ȝow call,
And some of ȝow forsake me.

For ȝow xal I dey and ryse ageyn;   865
Vn þe thrydde day ȝe xal me se
Beforn ȝow all walkyng playn
In þe lond of Galylé.

Petrus
Lord, I wyl þe nevyr forsake,
Nor for no perellys fro þe fle;   870
f. 158   I wyl rather my deth take
Þan onys, lord, forsake þe.

Jhesu
Petyr, ferthere þan þu doyst knowe,
As for þat, promese loke þu not make;
For or þe cok hath twyes crowe,   875
Thryes þu xal me forsake.

But all my frendys þat arn me dere,
Late us go, þe tyme drawyth ny;
We may no lengere abydyn here,
For I must walke to Betany.   880

Þe tyme is come, þe day drawyth nere,
Onto my deth I must in hast.
Now, Petyr, make hall þi felawys chere,
My flesch for fere is qwakyng fast.

873 ferthere] *MS.* þu ferthere *or* yn ferthere   884 qwakyng] q- *written heavily and*
-w- *unfinished*

Here Jhesus goth to Betanyward and his dyscipulys folwyng with
sad contenawns; Jhesus seyng:

Now, my dere frendys and bretheryn echon,   885
Remembyr þe wordys þat I xal sey;
Þe tyme is come þat I must gon
For to fulfylle þe prophesey
Þat is seyd of me þat I xal dey,
Þe fendys power fro зow to flem;   890
Weche deth I wole not deney,
Mannys sowle, my spovse, for to redem.

Þe oyle of mercy is grawntyd playn,
Be þis jorné þat I xal take;
Be my Fadyr I am sent sertayn,   895
Betwyx God and man an ende to make.
f. 158v   Man for my brother may I not forsake,
Nor shewe hym vnkendenesse be no wey;
In peynys for hym my body schal schake,
And for love of man, man xal dey.   900

Here Jhesus and his discipulys go toward þe mount of Olyvet; and
whan he comyth a lytyl þerbesyde, in a place lych to a park, he
byddyt his dyscipulys abyde hym þer, and seyth to Petyr or he goth:

Petyr, with þi felawys here xalt þu abyde
And weche tyl I come ageyn.
I must make my prayere here зou besyde;
My flesch qwakyth sore for fere and peyn.
Petrus
Lord, þi request doth me constreyn;   905
In þis place I xal abyde stylle,
Not remeve tyl þat þu comyst ageyn,
In confermyng, lord, of þi wylle.

Here Jhesu goth to Olyvet and settyth hym down on his knes, and
prayth to his Fadyr; þus seyng:

Jhesu
O, Fadyr, Fadyr, for my sake
Þis gret passyon þu take fro me,   910

885–8] *large red numeral 28 in right margin*

Wech arn ordeyned þat I xal take
3yf mannys sowle savyd may be.
And 3yf it behove, Fadyr, for me
To save mannys sowle þat xuld spylle,
I am redy in eche degré   915
Þe vyl of þe for to fulfylle.

Here Jhesus goth to his dysciplis and fyndyth hem sclepyng; Jhesus
þus seyng to Petyr:

f. 159   Petyr, Petyr, þu slepyst fast,
            Awake þi felawys and sclepe no more;
            Of my deth 3e are not agast,
            3e take 3our rest and I peyn sore.   920

Here Cryst goth ageyn þe second tyme to Olyvet, and seyth
knelyng:

Fadyr, in hevyn, I beseche þe,
Remeve my peynes be þi gret grace,
And lete me fro þis deth fle,
As I dede nevyr no trespace.
The watyr and blood owth of my face   925
Dystyllyth for peynes þat I xal take,
My flesche qwakyth in ferful case,
As þow þe joyntys asondre xuld schake.

Here Jhesus goth a3en to his disciplis and fyndyth hem asclepe;
Jhesus þus seyng, latyng hem lyne:

Fadyr, þe thrydde tyme I come ageyn,
Fulleche myn erdon for to spede.   930
Delyuere me, Fadyr, fro þis peyn,
Weche is reducyd with ful gret drede.
Onto þi sone, Fadyr, take hede,
Þu wotyst I dede nevyr dede but good;
It is not for me þis peyn I lede,   935
But for man I swete bothe watyr and blode.

922 Remeve] þi *deleted after* Remeve   932 gret] s *deleted after* gret

*Here an aungel descendyth to Jhesus and bryngyth to hym a chalys
with an host þerin.*

f. 159v *Angelus*

Heyl, bothe God and man indede!
The Fadyr hath sent þe þis present.
He bad þat þu xuldyst not drede,
But fulfylle his intent,   940
As þe parlement of hefne hath ment,
Þat mannys sowle xal now redemyd be.
From hefne to herd, lord, þu wore sent;
Þat dede appendyth onto the.

Þis chalys ys þi blood, þis bred is þi body,   945
For mannys synne evyr offeryd xal be
To þe Fadyr of heffne þat is almythty;
Þi dysciplis and all presthood xal offere fore the.

Here þe aungel ascendyth aȝen sodeynly.

Jhesu

Fadyr, þi wyl fulfyllyd xal be,
It is nowth to say aȝens þe case.   950
I xal fulfylle þe prophesye
And sofre deth for mannys trespace.

*Here goth Cryst ageyn to his dyscipulys and fyndyth hem sclepyng
stylle.*

Awake, Petyr! þi rest is ful long;
Of sclep þu wylt make no delay.
Judas is redy with pepyl strong   955
And doth his part me to betray.
Ryse up, serys, I ȝou pray!
Onclose ȝour eyne for my sake;
We xal walke into þe way
And sen hem come þat xul me take.   960

945 blood] -l- *written over an o*

f. 160 Petyr, whan þu seyst I am forsake
Amonge myn frendys and stond alone,
All þe cher þat þu kanst make,
Geve to þi bretheryn everychone.

*Here Jhesus with his dyscipulis goth into þe place, and þer xal come
in a ten personys weyl beseen in white arneys and breganderys, and
some dysgysed in odyr garmentys, with swerdys, gleyvys and other
straunge wepon, as cressettys with feyr and lanternys and torchis
lyth, and Judas formest of al conveyng hem to Jhesu be contenawns;
Jhesus þus seyng:*

Serys, in ȝour way ȝe haue gret hast   965
To seke hym þat wyl not fle.
Of ȝow I am ryth nowth agast,
Telle me, serys, whom seke ȝe?

Leyon
Whom we seke here I telle þe now,
A tretour is worthy to suffer deth;   970
We knowe he is here among ȝow,
His name is Jhesus of Nazareth.

Jhesu
Serys, I am here þat wyl not fle;
Do to me all þat ȝe kan.
Forsothe I telle ȝow I am he,   975
Jhesus of Nazareth, þat same man.

*Here all þe Jewys falle sodeynly to þe erde whan þei here Cryst
speke, and qwan [he] byddyth hem rysyn, þei rysyn aȝen; Cryst
þus seyng:*

Aryse, serys, whom seke ȝe? Fast haue ȝe gon;
Is howth ȝour comyng hedyr for me?
I stond beforn ȝow here echon,
Þat ȝe may me bothe knowe and se.   980

---

964 *sd* ten] *MS.* x;   wepon] *suspension mark perhaps intended to indicate* weponys; seyng]
only the descender of the s- *remains at the edge of the leaf*   965 Serys] What *deleted before*
Serys   975 *sd* he] *omitted in MS.*

Rufyne

f. 160v Jhesus of Nazareth we seke,
    And we myth hym here aspye.

Jhesu
    I told ʒow now with wordys meke
    Beforn ʒou all þat it was I.

Judas
    Welcome, Jhesu, my mayster dere,   985
    I haue þe sowth in many a place;
    I am ful glad I fynd þe here,
    For I wyst nevyr wher þu wace.

Here Judas kyssyth Jhesus and anoon all þe Jewys come abowth
hym and ley handys on hym and pullyn hym as þei were wode, and
makyn on hym a gret cry all at onys; and aftyr þis Petyr seyth:

Petrus
    I drawe my swerd now þis sel;
    Xal I smyte, mayster? Fayn wolde I wete.   990

And forthwith he smytyth of Malchus here, and he cryeth, "Help,
myn here, myn here!"; and Cryst blyssyth it and tys hol.

Jhesu
    Put þi swerd in þe shede, fayr and wel;
    For he þat smyth with swerd, with swerd xal be
                       smete.

    A, Judas, þis treson cowntyrfetyd hast þu,
    And þat þu xalt ful sore repent;
    Þu haddyst be bettyr a ben vnborn now,   995
    Þi body and sowle þu hast shent.

Gamalyel
    Lo, Jhesus, þu mayst not þe cace refuse,
    Bothe treson and eresye in þe is fownde.
    Stody now fast on þin excuse
    Whylys þat þu gost in cordys bownde.   1000

---

981 seke] and we *deleted after* seke   988 wher) -h- *added by main scribe above the line*
990 sd And forthwith] Petyr put þi s *deleted in red before* And;   Malchus] *suspension mark*
apparently preceded by a small e   991 sn Jhesus] *precedes sd*

Þu kallyst þe kyng of þis werd rownde,
Now lete me se þi gret powere,
And saue þiself here, hool and sownde,
And brynge þe out of þis dawngere.

Leyon

Bryng forth þis tretoure, spare hym nowth!   1005
Onto Cayphas þi jewge we xal þe lede.
In many a place we haue þe sowth
And to þi werkys take good hede.

Rufyne

Come on, Jhesus, and folwe me!
I am ful glad þat I þe haue;   1010
Þu xalt ben hangyn upon a tre,
A melyon of gold xal þe not save.

Leyon

Lete me leyn hand on hym in heye!
Onto his deth I xal hym bryng.
Shewe forth þi wychecrafte and nygramansye!   1015
What helpyth þe now al þi fals werkyng?

Jhesu

Frendys, take hede, ȝe don vnryth
So vnkendely with cordys to bynd me here,
And þus to falle on me be nyth
As thow I were a thevys fere.   1020
Many tyme beforn ȝow I dede apere;
Withinne þe temple sen me ȝe have,
Þe lawys of God to teche and lere
To hem þat wele here sowlys sawe.

Why dede ȝe not me dysprave,   1025
And herd me preche bothe lowd and lowe?
But now as woodmen ȝe gynne to rave,
And do thyng þat ȝe notwth knove.

1006 lede] *second -e written over partially erased* d
A   1015 Shewe] -w- *squashed in, written later*
-e *added above to change word to* þe

1012 A melyon] m *deleted before*
1022 þe] -is *dotted for deletion after* þ,

Gamalyel
>Serys, I charge 30w not o word more þis nyth,
>But onto Cayphas in hast loke 3e hym lede.   1030

f. 161v
>Have hym forth with gret dyspyte
>And to his wordys take 3e non hede.

Here þe Jewys lede Cryst outh of þe place with gret cry and noyse;
some drawyng Cryst forward and some bakward, and so ledyng
forth with here weponys alofte and lytys brennyng; and in þe mene
tyme Marye Magdalene xal rennyn to Oure Lady and telle here of
Oure Lordys takyng; þus seyng:

Maria Magdalene
>O, inmaculate modyr, of all women most meke,
>O, devowtest, in holy medytacyon evyr abydyng!
>Þe cawse, lady, þat I to 3our person seke   1035
>Is to wetyn yf 3e heryn ony tydyng

>Of 3our swete sone and my reverent lord, Jhesu,
>Þat was 3our dayly solas, 3our gostly consolacyon.

Marya
>I wold 3e xuld telle me, Mawdelyn, and 3e knew,
>For to here of hym it is all myn affeccyon.   1040

Maria Magdalene
>I would fayn telle, lady, and I myth for wepyng.
>Forsothe, lady, to þe Jewys he is solde.
>With cordys þei haue hym bownde and haue hym
>   in kepyng;
>Þei hym bety spetously and haue hym fast in holde.

Maria Uirgo
>A, a, a! How myn hert is colde!   1045
>A, hert hard as ston, how mayst þu lest
>Whan þese sorweful tydyngys are þe told?
>So wold to God, hert, þat þu mytyst brest.

>A, Jhesu, Jhesu, Jhesu, Jhesu!
>Why xuld 3e sofere þis trybulacyon and advercyté?   1050

1029 *sn Gamalyel*] MS. Gamaly *the rest lost at edge of leaf*   1041 *sn Maria Magdalene*]
MS. Maria Magd *the rest lost at edge of leaf*

How may thei fynd in here hertys ȝow to pursewe
Þat nevyr trespacyd in no maner degré?
For nevyr thyng but þat was good thowth ȝe.

Wherefore þan xuld ȝe sofer þis gret peyn?
I suppoce veryly it is for þe tresspace of me.   1055
And I wyst þat, myn hert xuld cleve on tweyn,

For þese langowrys may I susteyn?
Þe swerd of sorwe hath so thyrlyd my meende.
Alas, what may I do? Alas, what may I seyn?
Þese prongys myn herte asondyr þei do rende.   1060

O, Fadyr of hefne, wher ben al þi behestys
Þat þu promysyst me whan a modyr þu me made?
Þi blyssyd sone I bare betwyx tweyn bestys,
And now þe bryth colour of his face doth fade.

A, good Fadyr, why woldyst þat þin owyn dere
                    sone xal sofre al þis?   1065
And dede he nevyr aȝens þi precept, but evyr was
                    obedyent,
And to every creature most petyful, most jentyl and
                    benyng, iwys;
And now for all þese kendnessys is now most
                    shameful schent.

Why wolt þu, gracyous Fadyr, þat it xal be so?
May man not ellys be savyd be non other kende?   1070
Ȝet, Lord, Fadyr, þan þat xal comforte myn wo,
Whan man is savyd be my chylde and browth to a
                    good ende.

Now, dere sone, syn þu hast evyr be so ful of mercy,
Þat wylt not spare þiself for þe love þu hast to man,
On all mankend now have þu pety   1075
And also thynk on þi modyr, þat hevy woman.

1071 myn] *added above line + caret*

PASSION PLAY II

f. 165 *What tyme þat processyon is enteryd into þe place and þe*
Herowdys takyn his schaffalde and Pylat and Annas and
Cayphas here schaffaldys also, þan come þer an exposytour in
doctorys wede, þus seyng:

Contemplacio

Sofreynes and frendys, ȝe mut alle be gret with
                                        gode;
Grace, love and charyté evyr be ȝou among!
Þe maydenys sone preserve ȝou, þat for man deyd
                                        on rode;
He þat is o God in personys thre defende ȝou fro
                                        ȝour fon!

Be þe leue and soferauns of allmythty God,   5
We intendyn to procede þe matere þat we lefte þe
                                        last ȝere;
Wherefore we beseche ȝow þat ȝour wyllys be good
To kepe þe passyon in ȝour mende þat xal be
                                        shewyd here.

The last ȝere we shewyd here how Oure Lord for
                                        love of man
Cam to þe cety of Jherusalem mekely his deth to take;   10
And how he made his mawndé, his body ȝevyng þan
To his apostelys, evyr with us to abydyn for mannys
                                        sake.

---

1 sd] large red numeral 29 at head of page before sd   6 intendyn] –d– written over a t   9
last] lass deleted before last

In þat mawndé he was betrayd of Judas, þat hym
                                                solde
To þe Jewys for thretty platys to delyvyr hym þat
                                                nyth.
With swerdys and gleyvys to Jhesu they come with þe
                                    tretour bolde, 15
And toke hym amongys his apostelys about
                                mydnyth.

Now wold we procede how he was browth þan
Beforn Annas and Cayphas, and syth beforn Pylate,
And so forth in his passyon, how mekely he toke it
                                        for man;
Besekyng ʒou for mede of ʒour soulys to take good
                                    hede þeratte.   20

Here þe Herowndys xal shewe hymself and speke:

Herowdys

f. 165v   Now sees of ʒour talkyng and gevyth lordly
                                    audyence!
Not o word, I charge ʒou þat ben here present;
Noon so hardy to presume in my hey presence
To onlose hese lyppys ageyn myn intent.
I am Herowde, of Jewys kyng most reverent,   25
Þe lawys of Mahownde my powere xal fortefye.
Reverens to þat lord, of grace moost excyllent,
For be his powere all þinge doth multyplye.

ʒef ony Crystyn be so hardy his feyth to denye,
Or onys to erre ageyns his lawe,   30
On gebettys with cheynes I xal hangyn hym heye,
And with wylde hors þo traytorys xal I drawe.
To kylle a thowsand Crystyn I gyf not an hawe;
To se hem hangyn or brent, to me is very plesauns;
To dryvyn hem into doongenys, dragonys to knawe 35
And to rend here flesche and bonys onto here
                                    sustenauns.

---

13 mawndé] y *or* þ *deleted before* mawndé   14 thretty) *MS.* xxxᵗⁱ   15 to] *MS.*
toke   17 procede] *some letters erased after* procede   *before* 21] Herodes Rex *in centre*
at head of page

John þe Baptyst crystenyd Cryst, and so he dede
many on;
Þerfore myself dede hym brynge o dawe.
It is I þat dede hym kylle, I telle ȝou everychon,
For and he had go forth, he xuld a dystroyd our
lawe.   40

Where–as Crystyn apperyth, to me is gret grevauns;
It peynyth myn hert of tho tretowrys to here.
For þe lawys of Mahownde I have in governawns,
Þe which I wele kepe; þat lord hath no pere
For he is god most prudent.   45
Now I charge ȝou, my lordys þat ben here,
Yf any Crystyn doggys here doth apere,
Bryng þo tretorys to my hey powere
And þei xal haue sone jewgement.

f. 166

Primus miles
My sovereyn lord, heyest of excillens,   50
In ȝou all jewgement is termynabyle;
All Crystyn doggys þat do not here dyligens,
Ȝe put hem to peynes þat ben inportable.

Secundus miles
Noþing in ȝou may be more comendable
As to dysstroye þo traytorys þat erre   55
Ageyn oure lawys þat ben most profytable;
Be rythwysnesse þat lawe ȝe must proferre.

Rex Herowdys
Now be gloryous Mahownd, my sovereyn savyour,
These promessys I make as I am trewe knyth:
Þoo þat excede his lawys be ony errour,   60
To þe most xamefullest deth I xal hem dyth.
But o thyng is sore in my gret delyte:
Þere is on Jhesus of Nazareth, as men me tellyth,
Of þat man I desyre to han a sythte,
For with many gret wondrys oure lawe he fellyth.   65

47 here] -r + *suspension mark written over* d   58 *sn* Rex Herowdys] MS. Rex Herow *the rest lost at edge of leaf*

The son of God hymself he callyth,
And kyng of Jewys he seyth is he,
f. 166v   And many woundrys of hym befallyth;
My hert desyryth hym for to se.
Serys, yf þat he come in þis cowntré   70
With oure jurresdyccyon, loke ʒe aspye,
And anon þat he be brouth onto me,
And þe trewth myself þan xal trye.

Primus miles
Tomorwe my jorné I xal begynne
To seke Jhesus with my dew dilygens.   75
ʒyf he come ʒour provynce withinne,
He xal not askape ʒour hey presens.

Secundus miles
Myn sovereyn, þis is my cowncel þat ʒe xal take:
A man þat is bothe wyse and stronge
Thurwe all Galylé a serge to make.   80
Yf Jhesu be enteryd ʒour pepyl among,
Correcte hese dedys þat be do wronge,
For his body is vndyr ʒour baylé;
As men talkyn hem among
Þat he was born in Galylé.   85

Rex
Thanne of þese materys, serys, take hede,
For a whyle I wele me rest.
Appetyde requyryth me so indede,
And fesyk tellyth me it is þe best.

*Here xal a massanger com into þe place, rennyng and criyng,
"Tydyngys, tydyngys!", and so rownd abowth þe place,
"Jhesus of Nazareth is take! Jhesus of Nazareth is take!", and
forthwith heylyng þe prynces, þus seyng:*

Massanger
f. 167   All heyle, my lordys, princys of prestys!   90
Sere Cayphas and sere Annas, lordys of þe lawe,
Tydyngys I brynge ʒou, reseyve þem in ʒour brestys:
Jhesus of Nazareth is take, þerof ʒe may be fawe.

78 is] *omitted Block*

He xal be browth hedyr to ȝou anon,
I telle ȝou trewly, with a gret rowth. 95
Whan he was take, I was hem among,
And þer was I ner-to kachyd a clowte.

Malcus bar a lanterne and put hym in pres,
Anoon he had a towche and of went his ere.
Jhesus bad his dyscyple put up his swerd and ces, 100
And sett Malcus ere ageyn as hool as it was ere.

So moty the, methowut it was a strawnge syth.
Whan we cam fyrst to hym, he cam vs ageyn,
And haskyd whom we sowth þat tyme of nyth;
We seyd, "Jhesus of Nazareth, we wolde haue hym
fayn". 105

And he seyd, "It is I, þat am here in ȝour syth".
With þat word we ovyrthrewyn bakward everychon,
And some on here bakkys lyeng upryth,
But standing upon fote manly þer was not on.

Cryst stod on his fete, as meke as a lom, 110
And we loyn stylle lyche ded men tyl he bad vs ryse.
Whan we were up, fast handys we leyd hym upon,
But ȝet methought I was not plesyd with þe newe
gyse.

Therfore takyth now ȝour cowncel and avyse ȝou ryth
weyl,
f. 167v   And beth ryth ware þat he make ȝou not amat; 115
For, be my thryfte, I dare sweryn at þis seyl
Ȝe xal fynde hym a strawnge watt.

*Here bryng þei Jhesus beforn Annas and Cayphas; and on xal seyn
þus:*

[*Primus Judeus*]
Lo, lo, lordys, here is þe man
Þat ȝe sent vs fore!
Annas
Þerfore we cone ȝou thanke than, 120
And reward ȝe xal haue þe more.

107 ovyrthrewyn] -e- *written heavily over an ?* o   117 *sd* Cayphas] *MS.* C   118 *sn*
Primus Judeus] *omitted in MS.*

Jhesus, þu art welcome hedyr to oure presens,
Ful oftyn-tymes we han þe besyly do sowth;
We payd to þi dyscyple for þe thretty pens,
And as an ox or an hors we trewly þe bowth.   125

Þerfore now art oure, as þu standyst us before;
Sey why þu ast trobelyd us and subuertyd oure lawe.
Þu hast ofte concludyd us and so þu hast do more,
Wherefore it were ful nedful to bryng þe a dawe.

Cayphas
What arn þi dysciplys þat folwyn þe aboute?   130
And what is þi doctryne þat þu dost preche?
Telle me now somewhath and bryng us out of doute,
Þat we may to othere men þi prechyng forth teche.

Jhesus
Al tymes þat I haue prechyd, opyn it was don,
In þe synagog or in þe temple where þat all Jewys
                                             com;   135
Aske hem what I haue seyd, and also what I haue don,
Þei con telle þe my wordys, aske hem everychon.

Primus Judeus
f. 168   What, þu fela! To whom spekyst þu?
Xalt þu so speke to a buschop?
Þu xalt haue on þe cheke, I make avow,   140
And ȝet þerto a knok.

Here he xal smyte Jhesus on þe cheke.

Jhesus
Yf I haue seyd amys,
Þerof wytnesse þu mayst bere;
And yf I haue seyd but weyl in þis,
Þu dost amys me to dere.   145

Annas
Serys, takyth hed now to þis man
Þat he dystroye not oure lawe;
And brynge ȝe wytnesse aȝens hym þat ȝe can,
So þat he may be browt of dawe.

131 doctryne] *MS. possibly* dottryne   134 *sn Jhesus] final part of word blotted out*

Primus doctor
    Sere, þis I herd hym with his owyn mowth seyn,   150
    "Brekyth down þis temple without delay,
    And I xal settynt up ageyn
    As hool as it was be þe thrydde day".

Secundus doctor
    Ȝa, ser, and I herd hym seyn also
    Þat he was þe sone of God;   155
    And ȝet many a fole wenyth so,
    I durst leyn þeron myn hod.

Tertius doctor
    Ȝa, ȝa, and I herd hym preche meche þing,
    And aȝens oure lawe everydel;
    Of wheche it were longe to make rekenyng,   160
    To tellyn all at þis seel.

Cayphas
f. 168v   What seyst now, Jhesus? Whi answeryst not?
    Heryst not what is seyd aȝens þe?
    Spek, man, spek! Spek, þu fop!
    Hast þu scorn to speke to me?   165

    Heryst not in how many thyngys þei þe acuse?

    Now I charge þe and coniure be þe sonne and þe
                mone,
    Þat þu telle us and þu be Goddys sone.

Jhesus
    Goddys sone I am, I sey not nay to þe;
    And þat ȝe all xal se at domysday,   170
    Whan þe Sone xal come in gret powere and magesté
    And deme þe qweke and dede, as I þe say.

Cayphas
    A! Out, out, allas! What is this?
    Heryth ȝe not how he blasfemyth God?
    What nedyth us to haue more wytness,   175
    Here ȝe han herd all his owyn word.

157 hod] -e- *deleted after* h- *and* -o- *written in line above*

Thynk ȝe not he is worthy to dey?

Et clamabunt omnes

ȝys, ȝys, ȝys! All we seye he is worthy to dey.

ȝa, ȝa, ȝa!

Annas

Takyth hym to ȝow and betyth hym somdel   180

For hese blasfemyng at þis sel.

Here þei xal bete Jhesus about þe hed and þe body and spyttyn in his face and pullyn hym down and settyn hym on a stol and castyn a cloth ouyr his face; and þe fyrst xal seyn:

Primus Judeus

A, felawys, beware what ȝe do to þis man,

For he prophecye weyl kan.

Secundus Judeus

Þat xal be asayd be þis batte –

What þu, Jhesus, ho ȝaff þe þat?   185

Et percuciet super caput.

Tertius Judeus

f. 169   Whar, whar, now wole I

Wetyn how he can prophecy!

Ho was þat?

Quartus Judeus

A, and now wole I a newe game begynne

Þat we mon pley at, all þat arn hereinne: 190

Whele and pylle, whele and pylle,

Comyth to halle hoso wylle –

Ho was þat?

Here xal þe woman come to [þe] Jewys and seyn:

---

178 *sd/sn*] *in right margin in MS.*   185 *sd*] *in right margin and not underlined in red in MS.*   193 *sd* þe Jewys] þe *omitted in MS.*

Prima ancilla
    What, serys! How take ȝe on with þis man?
    Se ȝe not on of hese dysciplys how he beheldyth
                                    ȝou þan?   195

Here xal þe tother woman seyn to Petyr:

Secunda ancilla
    A, goodman, mesemyth be þe
    Þat þu on of hese dysciplys xulde be.

Petrus
    A, woman, I sey nevyr er þis man,
    Syn þat þis werd fyrst began.

Et cantabit gallus.

Prima ancilla
    What, þu mayst not sey nay! Þu art on of hese men.   200
    Be þi face wel we may þe ken.

Petrus
    Woman, þu seyst amys of me;
    I knowe hym not, so mote I the.

Primus Judeus
    A, fela myn, wel met!
    For my cosynys ere þu of smet.   205

    Whan we þi mayster in þe ȝerd toke,
    Þan all þi felawys hym forsoke;

    And now þu mayst not hym forsake,
    For þu art of Galylé, I vndyrtake.

Petrus
    Sere, I knowe hym not, be hym þat made me! –   210
    And ȝe wole me beleve for an oth.
f. 169v   I take record of all þis compayné,

Et cantabit gallus.
    Þat I sey to ȝow is soth.

*And þan Jhesus xal lokyn on Petyr and Petyr xal wepyn; and þan
he xal gon out and seyn:*

    A, weelaway, weelaway, fals hert, why whylt þu
                                    not brest,
    Syn þi maystyr so cowardly þu hast forsake?   215
    Alas, qwher xal I now on erthe rest,
    Tyl he of his mercy to grace wole me take?

    I haue forsake my mayster and my lord Jhesu
    Thre tymes, as he tolde me þat I xuld do þe same;
    Wherfore I may not haue sorwe anow,   220
    I, synful creature, am so mech to blame.

    Whan I herd þe cok crowyn, he kest on me a loke
    As who seyth, "Bethynke þe what I seyd before".
    Alas þe tyme þat I evyr hym forsoke!
    And so wyl I thynkyn from hens evyrmore.   225

Cayphas
    Massangere! Massangere!
Massangere
    Here, lord, here!

Cayphas
    Massanger, to Pylat in hast þu xalt gon,
    And sey hym we comawnde us in word and in dede,
    And prey hym þat he be at þe mothalle anoon;   230
    For we han a gret matere þat he must nedys spede.

    In hast now go þi way
    And loke þu tery nowth.
Massanger
    It xal be do, lord, be þis day,
    I am as whyt as thought.   235

f.170   *Here Pylat syttyth in his skaffald and þe massanger knelyth to hym,
        þus seyng:*

226–7] *large red numeral 30 in right margin*

Al heyl, sere Pylat, þat semly is to se,
Prynce of al þis Juré, and kepere of þe lawe!
My lord busshop, Cayphas, comawndyd hym to þe,
And prayd the to be at þe mothalle by þe day dawe.

Pylat

Go þi way, praty masanger, and comawnde me also;   240
I xal be þere in hast, and so þu mayst say.
Be þe oure of prime I xal comyn hem to;
I tery no lenger [ne] make no delay.

Here þe massanger comith aȝen and bryngith an ansuere, þus seyng:

Massanger

Al heyl, myn lordys and buschoppys and princys of
þe lawe!
Ser Pylat comawndyth hym to ȝou, and bad me to
ȝou say   245
He wole be at þe mothalle in hast sone after þe day
dawe.
He wold ȝe xuld be þer be prime withouth lenger
delay.

Cayphas

Now weyl mote þu fare, my good page!
Take þu þis for þi massage.

Here enteryth Judas onto þe Juwys, þus seyng:

Judas

I, Judas, haue synnyd and treson haue don,   250
For I haue betrayd þis rythful blood.
Here is ȝour mony aȝen, all and som!
For sorwe and thowth I am wax wood.

Annas

What is þat to us? Avyse þe now:
Þu dedyst with us counawnt make,   255

243 lenger] and *deleted after* lenger;   ne] *MS.* no   243 *sd* comith . . . bryngith] *MS.*
comᵗ . . . bryngᵗ;   ansuere] u *written over an* ?e   255 counawnt] *MS.* cōnawnt *or*
cōuawnt

Þu seldyst hym us as hors or kow,
Þerfore þin owyn dedys þu must take.

Pan Judas castyth down þe mony and goth and hangyth hymself.

f. 170v *Cayphas*
Now, serys, þe nyth is passyd, þe day is come,
It were tyme þis man had his jewgement;
And Pylat abydyth in þe mothalle alone   260
Tyl we xuld þis man present.

And þerfore go we now forth with hym in hast.
Primus Judeus
It xal be don and þat in short spas.
Secundus Judeus
3a, but loke yf he be bownd ryth wel and fast.
Tertius Judeus
He is saff anow! Go we ryth a good pas.   265

Here þei ledyn Jhesu abowt þe place tyl þei come to þe halle.

Cayphas
Sere Pylat, takyht hede to þis thyng;
Jhesus we han beforn þe browth
Wheche oure lawe doth down bryng,
And mekyl schame he hath us wrowth.

Annas
From þis cetye into þe lond of Galylé,   270
He hath browth oure lawys neyr into confusyon,
With hese craftys wrowth be nygramancye,
Shewyth to þe pepyl be fals symulacyon.

Primus doctor
3a, 3et, ser, another and werst of alle,
A3ens Sesare, oure emperour, þat is so fre,   275
Kyng of Jewys he doth hym calle;
So oure emperourys power nowth xulde be.

270 cetye] ceyt *deleted before* cetye

Secundus doctor
>Sere Pylat, we kannot telle half þe blame
>Þat Jhesus in oure countré hath wrowth;
>Þerfore we charge þe in þe emperorys name   280
>Þat he to þe deth in hast be browth.

Pylat
f. 171
>What seyst to these compleyntys, Jhesu?
>These pepyl hath þe sore acusyd
>Because þu bryngyst up lawys newe,
>Þat in oure days were not vsyd.   285

Jhesus
>Of here acusying me rowth nowth,
>So þat þei hurt not here soulys ne non mo.
>I haue nowth ȝet founde þat I haue sowth,
>For my Faderys wyl forth must I go.

Pylat
>Jhesus, be þis þan I trowe þu art a kyng,   290
>And þe sone of God þu art also,
>Lord of erth and of all þing –
>Telle me þe trowth if it be so.

Jhesus
>In hefne is knowyn my Faderys intent,
>And in þis werlde I was born;   295
>Be my Fadyr I was hedyr sent,
>For to seke þat was forlorn.

>Alle þat me heryn and in me belevyn,
>And kepyn here feyth stedfastly,
>Þow þei weryn dede, I xal þem recuryn,   300
>And xal þem bryng to blysse endlesly.

Pilate
>Lo, serys, now ȝe an erde þis man, how thynk ȝe?
>Thynke ȝe not all be ȝoure reson
>But as he seyth it may wel be?
>And þat xulde be be þis incheson: 305

284 newe] *beginning of* w *deleted before* newe

I fynde in hym non obecyon
Of errour nor treson, ne of no maner gylt.
f. 171v   The lawe wole in no conclusyon
Withowte defawth he xuld be spylt.

Primus doctor
Sere Pylat, þe lawe restyth in þe,   310
And we knowe, veryly, his gret trespas;
To þe emperour þis mater told xal be
Yf þu lete Jhesus þus from þe pas.

Pylat
Serys, þan telle me o thyng:
What xal be his acusyng?   315

Annas
Sere, we telle þe al togedyr,
For his evyl werkys we browth hym hedyr.

And yf he had not an evyldoere be,
We xuld not a browth hym to þe.

Pylat
Takyth hym þan aftyr ȝour sawe,   320
And demyth hym aftyr ȝour lawe.

Cayphas
It is not lefful to vs ȝe seyn,
No maner man for to slen.

Þe cawse why we bryng hym to þe,
Þat he xuld not oure kyng be;   325

Weyl þu knowyst kyng we have non
But our emperour alon.

Pylat
Jhesu, þu art kyng of Juré?
Jhesus
So þu seyst now to me.

312 emperour] *MS.* emperouur   322 ȝe] we *deleted*, ȝe *added above*

Pylat
　　Tel me þan,   330
　　Where is þi kyngham?

Jhesus
　　My kyngham is not in þis werld,
　　I telle þe at o word.

　　Yf my kyngham here had be,
　　I xuld not a be delyveryd to þe.   335

Pylat
f. 172 　　Serys, avyse ȝow as ȝe kan,
　　I can fynde no defawth in þis man.

Annas
　　Sere, here is a gret record, take hed þerto,
　　And knowyng gret myschef in þis man –
　　And not only in o day or to,   340
　　It is many ȝerys syn he began.
　　We kan telle þe tyme where and whan
　　Þat many a thowsand turnyd hath he,
　　As all þis pepyll record weyl kan,
　　From hens into þe lond of Galylé.   345

Et clamabunt: "Ȝa, ȝa, ȝa!"

Pilat
　　Serys, of o thyng than gyf me relacyon,
　　If Jhesus were outborn, in þe lond of Galelye,
　　For we han no poer ne no jurediccyon
　　Of no man of þat contré.
　　Therfore þe trewth ȝe telle me,   350
　　And another wey I xal provyde;
　　If Jhesus were born in þat countré
　　Þe jugement of Herowdys he must abyde.

---

331 is] *omitted and added above line* + *caret*   331–2] *one line in MS.*   332–5] *two lines in MS.*   345 sd] *in right margin*

Cayphas
Sere, as I am to þe lawe trewly sworn,
To telle þe trewth I haue no fer;   355
In Galelye I know þat he was born,
I can telle in what place and where.
Aȝens þis no man may answere,
For he was born in Bedlem Judé;
And þis ȝe knowe now all, and haue don, here   360
Þat it stant in þe lond of Galelye.

Pylat
f. 172v   Weyl, serys, syn þat I knowe þat it is so,
Þe trewth of þis I must nedys se.
I vndyrstand ryth now what is to do,
Þe jugement of Jhesu lyth not to me.   365
Herowde is kyng of þat countré,
To jewge þat regyon in lenth and in brede;
Þe jurysdyccyon of Jhesu now han must he,
Þerfore Jhesu in hast to hym ȝe lede.
In hall þe hast þat ȝe may spede   370
Lede hym to þe Herownde, anon present,
And sey I comawnde me with worde and dede,
And Jhesu to hym þat I haue sent.

Primus doctor
This erand in hast sped xal be,
In all þe hast þat we can do.   375
We xal not tary in no degré
Tyl þe Herowdys presens we com to.

Here þei take Jhesu and lede hym in gret hast to þe Herowde. And þe Herowdys scafald xal vnclose shewyng Herowdys in astat; all þe Jewys knelyng, except Annas and Cayphas, þei xal stondyn etc.

Primus doctor
Heyl, Herowde, most excyllent kyng!
We arn comawndyd to þin presens.
Pylat sendyth þe be us gretyng,   380
And chargyth us be oure obedyens
Secundus doctor
Þat we xuld do oure dylygens
To bryng Jhesus of Nazareth onto þe.

And chargyth us to make no resystens,
Becawse he was born in þis countré.   385

Annas

f. 173   We knowe he hath wrowth gret folé
Ageyns þe lawe shewyd present,
Therfore Pylat sent hym onto þe
Þat þu xuldyst gyf hym jugement.

Herowde Rex

Now, be Mahound, my god of grace,   390
Of Pylat þis is a dede ful kende.
I forgyf hym now his gret trespace
And schal be his frend withowtyn ende
Jhesus to me þat he wole sende.
I desyred ful sore hym for to se;   395
Gret ese in þis Pylat xal fynde –
And, Jhesus, þu art welcome to me.

Primus Judeus

My sovereyn lord, þis is þe case:
Þe gret falsnesse of Jhesu is opynly knawe,
Þer was nevyr man dede so gret trespas,   400
For he hath almost dystroyd oure lawe.

Secundus Judeus

3a, be fals crafte of soserye,
Wrowth opynly to þe pepyll alle,
And be sotyl poyntys of nygramancye,
Many thowsandys fro oure lawe be falle.   405

Cayphas

Most excellent kyng, 3e must take hede,
He wol dystroye all þis countré, both elde and 3yng,
Yf he ten monthis more procede.
Be his meraclys and fals prechyng
He bryngyth þe pepyl in gret fonnyng,   410
And seyth dayly among hem alle
f. 173v   That he is lord and of þe Jewys kyng,
And þe sone of God he doth hym calle.

406 excellent] excelyng, -yng *deleted and* -lent *added*

Rex Herowde
 Serys, alle þese materys I haue herd sayd,
 And meche more þan ʒe me telle;   415
 Alle togedyr þei xal be layde,
 And I wyl take þeron cowncelle.

 Jhesus, þu art welcome to me,
 I kan Pylat gret thank for his sendyng.
 I haue desyryd ful longe þe to se   420
 And of þi meracles to haue knowyng.
 It is told me þu dost many a wondyr thyng:
 Crokyd to gon and blynd men to sen,
 And þei þat ben dede gevyst hem levyng,
 And makyst lepers fayre and hool to ben. 425

 These arn wondyr werkys wrougth of þe,
 Be what wey I wolde knowe þe trew sentens.
 Now, Jhesu, I pray the let me se
 O meracle wrougth in my presens.
 In hast now do þi dylygens   430
 And, peraventure, I wyl shew favour to the;
 For now þu art in my presens
 Thyn lyf and deth here lyth in me.

And here Jhesus xal not speke no word to þe Herowde.

 Jhesus, why spekyst not to þi kyng?
 What is þe cawse þu stondyst so stylle? 435
 Þu knowyst I may deme all thyng,
 Thyn lyf and deth lyth at my wylle.

f. 174 What, spek, Jhesus! And telle me why
 Þis pepyl do þe so here acuse.
 Spare not but telle me now on hey 440
 How þu canst þiself excuse.

Cayphas
 Loo, serys, þis is of hym a false sotylté;
 He wyl not speke but whan he lyst.
 Þus he dysceyvyth þe pepyl in eche degré;
 He is ful fals ʒe veryly tryst. 445

414 *sn Rex Herowde*] MS. Rex Her *the rest lost at edge of leaf* 439 þe] *letter obliterated before* þe

Rex Herowde
  What, þu onhangyd harlot! Why wylt þu not speke?
  Hast þu skorne to speke onto þi kyng?
  Becawse þu dost oure lawys breke,
  I trowe þu art aferd of oure talkyng.

Annas
  Nay, he is not aferde, but of a fals wyle   450
  Becawse we xuld not hym acuse;
  If þat he answerd ʒow ontylle,
  He knowyth he kannot hymself excuse.

Rex Herowde
  What, spek I say, þu foulyng! Evyl mot þu fare!
  Loke up, þe devyl mote þe cheke!   455
  Serys, bete his body with scorgys bare,
  And asay to make hym for to speke.

Primus Judeus
  It xal be do withoutyn teryeng.
  Come on, þu tretour, evyl mot þu þe!
  Whylt þu not speke onto oure kyng?   460
  A new lesson we xal lere þe.

Here þei pulle of Jhesus clothis and betyn hym with whyppys.

Secundus Judeus
f. 174v   Jhesus, þi bonys we xal not breke,
  But we xal make þe to skyppe.
  Þu hast lost þi tonge, þu mayst not speke,
  Þu xalt asay now of þis whippe.   465

Tertius Judeus
  Serys, take þese whyppys in ʒour honde,
  And spare not whyl þei last;
  And bete þis tretoure þat here doth stonde –
  I trowe þat he wyl speke in hast.

---

453 hymself] -y- *written over an* e   454 *sn* Herowde] MS. Hero *the rest lost at edge of*
leaf

> And qwan þei han betyn hym tyl he is all blody þan þe Herownd
> seyth:

[*Rex Herowde*]
    Sees, serys, I comawnde ȝou, be name of þe
                          devyl of helle!   470
  Jhesus, thynkyst þis good game?
  Þu art strong to suffyr schame;
  Þu haddyst levyr be betyn lame
      Þan þi defawtys for to telle.

  But I wyl not þi body all spyl,   475
  Nor put it here into more peyn.
  Serys, takyth Jhesus at ȝour owyn wyl
  And lede hym to Pylat hom ageyn.
  Grete hym weyl and telle hym serteyn
  All my good frenchep xal he haue.   480
  I gyf hym powere of Jhesus, þus ȝe hym seyn,
  Whether he wole hym dampne or save.

Primus doctor
  Sere, at ȝour request it xal be do,
  We xal lede Jhesus at ȝour demawnde
  And delyver hym Pylat onto,   485
  And telle hym all as ȝe comawnde

f. 175 *Here enteryth Satan into þe place in þe most orryble wyse, and qwyl*
       þat he pleyth þei xal don on Jhesus clothis and ouerest a whyte
       clothe, and ledyn hym abowth þe place and þan to Pylat be þe tyme
       þat hese wyf hath pleyd.

Sathan
  Thus I reyne as a rochand with a rynggyng rowth,
  As a devyl most dowty dred is my dynt.
  Many a thowsand develys to me do þei lowth,
  Brennyng in flamys as fyre out of flynt.   490
  Hoso serve me, Sathan, to sorwe is he sent,
  With dragonys in doungenys and develys ful derke,
  In bras and in bronston þo brethellys be brent
  Þat wone in þis werd my wyl for to werke.

470 *sn* Rex Herowde] *omitted in MS.*   484 demawnde] *MS.* demawde   488 dynt]
dyth *deleted before* dynt   490–3 *large red numeral* 31 *in right margin*   492 ful] *MS.*
fu   493 þo] *or* þe

With myschef on moolde here membrys I merke   495
Þat japyn with Jhesus þat Judas solde;
Be he nevyr so crafty nor conyng clerke
I harry þem to helle as tretour bolde.

But þer is o thyng þat grevyth me sore,
Of a prophete þat Jhesu men calle;   500
He peynyth me every day more and more,
With his holy meraclis and werkys alle.

I had hym onys in a temptacyon,
With glotenye, with covetyse, and veynglorye.
I hasayd hym be all weys þat I cowde don,   505
And vttyrly he refusyd hem and gan me defye.

Þat rebuke þat he gaf me xal not be vnqwyt.
Somwhat I haue begonne and more xal be do;
f. 175v   For all his barfot-goyng fro me xal he not skyp,
But my dark dongeon I xal bryngyn hym to.   510

I haue do made redy his cros þat he xal dye upon,
And thre nayles to takke hym with, þat he xal not
        styrte.
Be he nevyr so holy he xal not fro me gon,
But with a sharpe spere he xal be smet to þe herte.

And sythyn he xal come to helle, be he nevyr so
        stowte;   515
And ȝet I am aferd and he come he wole do som
        wrake.
Þerfore I xal go warnyn helle þat þei loke abowte,
Þat þei make redy chenys to bynd hym with in lake.

Helle, helle, make redy! For here xal come a gest,
Hedyr xal come Jhesus þat is clepyd Goddys sone;   520
And he xal ben here be þe oure of none,
And with þe here he xal wone
    And han ful shrewyd rest.

Here xal a devyl spekyn in helle.

499 me sore] myn hert *deleted before* me   505 cowde] *MS.* cownde *or* cowude

Demon

    Out upon þe! We coniure þe
    Þat nevyr in helle we may hym se;   525
    For and he onys in helle be
        He xal oure power brest.

Sathan

    A, a, than haue I go to ferre!
    But som wyle help, I have a shrewde torne,
    My game is wers þan I wend here –   530
    I may seyn my game is lorne.

    Lo, a wyle ȝet haue I kast:
    If I myth Jhesus lyf save,
    Helle gatys xal be sperd fast
    And kepe stylle all þo I haue.   535

    To Pylatys wyff I wele now go,
f. 176   And sche is aslepe abed ful fast,
    And byd here withowtyn wordys mo
    To Pylat þat sche send in hast.

    I xal asay, and þis wol be,   540
    To bryng Pylat in belef.
    Withinne a whyle ȝe xal se
    How my craft I wole go pref.

*Here xal þe devyl gon to Pylatys wyf, þe corteyn drawyn as she lyth
in bedde, and he xal no dene make. But she xal sone after þat he is
come in makyn a rewly noyse, comyng and rennyng of þe schaffald
[in] here shert, and here kyrtyl in here hand. And sche xal come
beforn Pylat leke a mad woman, seyng þus:*

Vxor Pilaty

    Pylat, I charge þe þat þu take hede;
    Deme not Jhesu but be his frende.   545
    Ȝyf þu jewge hym to be dede
    Þu art dampnyd withowtyn ende.

    A fend aperyd me beforn,
    As I lay in my bed slepyng fast;

543 *sd* in³] *MS.* and

Sethyn þe tyme þat I was born   550
Was I nevyr so sore agast.

As wylde fyre and thondyr–blast
He cam cryeng onto me.
He seyd þei þat bete Jhesu or bownd hym fast
Withowtyn ende dampnyd xal be.   555

Þerfore a wey herein þu se
And lete Jhesu from þe clere pace;
Þe Jewys þei wole begyle þe
And put on þe all þe trespace.

Pylat
f. 176v   Gramercy, myn wyf, forevyr ʒe be trewe;   560
ʒour cowncel is good and evyr hath be.
Now to ʒour chawmer ʒe do sewe,
And all xal be weyl, dame, as ʒe xal se.

Here þe Jewys bryng Jhesus aʒen to Pylat.

Primus doctor
Sere Pylat, gode tydandys þu here of me:
Of Herowd þe kyng þu hast good wyl,   565
And Jhesus he sendyth aʒen to the
And byddyth þe chese hym to save or spylle.

Secundus doctor
ʒa, ser, all þe poer lyth now in þe,
And þu knowyst oure feyth he hath ner schent;
Þu knowyst what myschef þeerof may be;   570
We charge þe to gyf hym jwgement.

Pylat
Serys, trewly ʒe be to blame,
Jhesus þus to bete, dyspoyle or bynde,
Or put hym to so gret schame;
For no defawth in hym I fynde.   575

569 knowyst] h *deleted before* knowyst

Ne Herowdys nother, to whom I sent ȝow,
Defawte in hym cowde fynde ryth non;
But sent hym aȝen to me be ȝow,
As ȝe knowe wel everychon.

Therfore vndyrstande what I xal say: 580
ȝe knowe þe custom is in þis londe
Of ȝour Pasche day þat is nerhonde;
What þeff or tretore be in bonde
    For worchep of þat day xal go fre away

Without any price.   585
f. 177   Now þan methynkyth it were ryth
To lete Jhesus now go qwyte
And do to hym no mo dyspyte;
    Serys, þis is myn avyse.

I wolde wete what ȝe say.   590

Here all þei xul cryen:

[*Omnes*]
    Nay, nay, nay!

Primus doctor
    Delyvere us þe þeff, Barabas,
    Þat for mansclawth presonde was.

Pylat
    What xal I þan with Jhesu do?
    Whethyr xal he abyde or go?   595

Secundus doctor
    Jhesus xal on þe cros be don,
    "*Crucifigatur*" we crye echon.

Pylat
    Serys, what hath Jhesus don amys?

Populus clamabit:

---

584 xal go] *letters, ?ff , deleted before* xal   591 *sn* Omnes] *omitted in MS.*   598 *sd*] *in*
right margin

[*Omnes*]
"*Crucifigatur*" we sey at onys.

Pylat

Serys, syn algatys ʒe wolyn so   600
Puttyn Jhesu to wo and peyn,
Jhesus a wyle with me xal go,
I wole hym examyne betwyx us tweyn.

Here Pylat takyth Jhesu and ledyth hym into þe cowncel hous and seyth:

Jhesus, what seyst now, lete se?
This matere now þu vndyrstonde;   605
In pes þu myth be for me,
But for þi pepyl of þi londe.

Busshoppys and prestys of þe lawe,
Þei love þe not, as þu mayst se,
And þe comoun pepyl aʒens þe drawe.   610
In pes þu myth a be for me,

Þis I telle þe pleyn.
f. 177v   What seyst, Jhesus? Whi spekyst not me to?
Knowyst not I haue power on þe cros þe to do?
And also I haue power to lete þe forth go;   615
What kanst þu hereto seyn?

Jhesus

On me poer þu hast ryth non
But þat my Fadyr hath grawntyd beforn.

I cam my Faderys wyl to fullfylle,
Þat mankynd xuld not spylle.   620

He þat hath betrayd me to þe at þis tyme,
His trespas is more þan is þine.

---

599 *sn Omnes*] *deleted in right margin*   613 *not*] not *followed by* spekyst not to me to
deleted in red; me to *added above* + *carets and red rhyme link*   619] *large decorated* n *in left
margin at beginning of line*   621] *large decorated* m *in left margin at beginning of line*

Primus doctor
> Ʒe pryncys and maysterys, takyth hed and se
> How Pylat in þis matere is favorabyl;
> And þus oure lawys dystroyd myth be,   625
> And to vs alle vnrecurabyl.

Here Pylat letyth Jhesus alone and goth in to þe Jewys and seyth:

Pylat
> Serys, what wele ʒe now with Jhesu do?
> I can fynde in hym but good.
> It is my cowncel ʒe let hym go;
> It is rewthe to spylle his blood.   630

Cayphas
> Pylat, methynkyth þu dost gret wrong
> Aʒens oure lawe þus to fortefye;
> And þe pepyl here is so strong
> Bryngyng þe lawful testymonye.

Annas
> Ʒa, and þu lete Jhesu fro us pace,   635
> Þis we welyn upholdyn alle;
> Þu xalt answere for his trespas
> And tretour to þe emperour we xal þe kalle.

Pylat
f. 178
> Now þan, syn ʒe wolne non other weye
> But in al wyse þat Jhesus must deye;   640
>
> Artyse, bryng me watyr I pray þe,
> And what I wole do ʒe xal se.

Hic vnus afferet aquam.

> As I wasche with watyr my handys clene,
> So gyltles of hese deth I mut ben.

Primus doctor
> Þe blod of hym mut ben on vs   645
> And on oure chyldyr aftyr vs.

627 *sn* Pylat] *written above sd*   629 cowncel] *MS.* cownce   642 *sd*] *in right margin*   646 *sd*] Et . . . ʒa! *in right margin;*   bryngith] *in MS. the word combines suspension mark for* –ys *and* –ith

Et clamabunt: "3a, 3a, 3a!" Þan Pylat goth a3en to Jhesu and
bryngith hym; þus seyng:

Pylat

Lo, serys, I bryng hym here to 3our presens
Þat 3e may knowe I fynde in hym non offens.

Secundus doctor

Dylyuere hym, delyvere hym, and lete us go,
On þe crosse þat he were do!   650

Pilat

Serys, wolde 3e 3our kyng I xulde on þe cros don?
Tertius doctor

Sere, we seyn þat we haue no kyng but þe
                                            emperour alon.

Pilat

Serys, syn algatys it must be so,
We must syt and our offyce do.

Brynge forth to þe barre þat arn to be dempt,   655
And þei xal haue here jugement.

Here þei xal brynge Barabas to þe barre, and Jhesu, and two þewys
in here shertys, bareleggyd; and Jhesus standyng at þe barre betwyx
them. And Annas and Cayphas xal gon into þe cowncell hous qwan
Pylat syttyth.

Pylat

Barabas, hold up þi hond,
For here at þi delyveré dost þu stond.

And he halt up his hond.

f. 178v   Serys, qwhat sey 3e of Barabas, thef and tretour
                                            bold?
           Xal he go fre or xal he be kept in holde?   660

---

656 sd two] MS. ij;   syttyth] *end of word lost at edge of leaf*   658 dost] he *erased before*
dost   658 sd] *in right margin*   660 xal he] MS. he xal

Primus doctor
 Sere, for þe solemnyté of oure Pasche day,
 Be oure lawe he xal go fre away.

Pylat
 Barabas, þan I dymysse þe
 And ȝeve þe lycens to go fre.

Et curret.

 Dysmas and Jesmas, ther as ȝe stondys,   665
 Þe lawe comawndyth ȝou to hald up ȝour hondys.

 Sere, what say ȝe of þese thevys tweyn?
Secundus doctor
 Sere, þei ben both gylty we seyn.

Pylat
 And what sey ȝe of Jhesu of Nazareth?
Primus doctor
 Sere, we say he xal be put to deth.   670

Pylat
 And kone ȝe put aȝens hym no trespas?
Secundus doctor
 Sere, we wyl all þat he xal be put upon þe crosse.

Et clamabunt omnes, voce magna, dicentes: "ȝa, ȝa, ȝa!"

Pylat
 Jhesu, þin owyn pepyl han dysprevyd
 Al þat I haue for þe seyd or mevyd.

 I charge ȝou all at þe begynnyng,   675
 As ȝe wole answere me beforn,
 Þat þer be no man xal towch ȝour kyng,
 But yf he be knyght or jentylman born.

661 solemnyté] *first minim of -m- merges with -e-* 664 sd] *in right margin and not underlined* 668 ben] *erased letter after* ben 672] *line underlined in red in error*

Fyrst his clothis ȝe xal of don
And maken hym nakyd for to be.   680
Bynde hym to a pelere, as sore as ȝe mon,
Þan skorge hym with qwyppys þat al men may se.

f. 179   Whan he is betyn, crowne hym for ȝour kyng,
And þan to þe cros ȝe xal hym bryng.

And to þe crosse þu xalt be fest,   685
And on thre naylys þi body xal rest:

On xal thorwe þi ryth hand go,
Anothyr thorwe þi lyfte hand also;

Þe thred xal be smet þour bothe þi feet,
Whech nayl þerto be mad ful mete.   690

And ȝet þu xalt not hange alone,
But on eyther syde of þe xal be on;

Dysmas, now I deme þe
Þat on hese ryth hand þu xalt be;

And Jesmas on þe left hand hangyd xal ben   695
On þe mownth of Caluerye, þat men may sen.

Here Pylat xal rysyn and gon to his schaffald and þe busshoppys
with hym. And þe Jewys xul crye for joy with a gret voys, and
arryn hym and pullyn of his clothis and byndyn hym to a pelere and
skorgyn hym; on seyng þus:

Primus Judeus
    Doth gladly oure kyng,
    For þis is ȝour fyrst begynnyng.

And qwan he is skorgyd, þei put upon hym a cloth of sylk and settyn
hym on a stol and puttyn a kroune of þornys on hese hed with
forkys, and þe Jewys knelyng to Cryst, takyng hym a septer, and
skornyng hym. And þan þei xal pullyn of þe purpyl cloth and don
on ageyn his owyn clothis and leyn þe crosse in hese necke to berynt,
and drawyn hym forth with ropys. And þan xal come to women
wepyng and with here handys wryngyn, seyng þus:

696 mownth] *MS.* mowth *with abbreviation mark through ascenders of* th

Prima mulier

f. 179v   Allas, Jhesus! Allas, Jhesus! Wo is me
     Þat þu art þus dyspoylyd, allas!   700
     And ȝet nevyr defawth was fownd in the,
     But evyr þu hast be fole of grace.

Secunda mulier

     A, here is a rewful syth of Jhesu so good,
     Þat he xal þus dye aȝens þe ryth.
     A, wykkyd men, ȝe be more þan wood   705
     To do þat good lord so gret dyspyte.

Here Jhesus turnyth aȝen to þe women with his crosse, þus seyng:

Jhesus

     Dowterys of Hierusalem, for me wepyth nowth,
     But for ȝourself wepyth and for ȝour chyldyr also;
     For þe days xal come þat þei han aftyr sowth,
     Here synne and here blyndnesse xal turne hem to
                  wo.   710

     Þan xal be sayd, "Blyssyd be þe wombys þat bareyn
              be,
     And wo to þe tetys tho days þat do ȝevyn sokyng!"
     And to here faderys þei xul seyn, "Wo to þe tyme þat
              þu begat me!";
     And to here moderys, "Allas, wher xal be oure
              dwellyng?"

     Þan to þe hyllys and mownteynes they xal crye and
              calle, 715
     "Oppyn and hyde us from þe face of Hym syttyng
              in trone!
     Or ellys ovyrthrowyth and on us now come falle
     Þat we may be hyd from oure sorweful mone".

Here Jhesus turnyth fro þe women and goth forth. And þer þei metyn with Symone in þe place, þe Jewys seyng to hym:

---

699 *sn Prima mulier*] MS. I^us   699–705 *large red numeral 32 in right margin*   703 *sn Secunda*] MS. ij^us   718 *sd Symone*] MS. Symone

Primus Judeus
 Sere, to þe a word of good:
 A man is here þu mayst se,   720
 Beryth hevy of a rode
 Whereon he xal hangyd be;

f. 180 Therfore we prey all the,
 Þu take þe crosse of þe man.
 Bere it with vs to Kalvarye   725
 And ryth gret thank þu xalt han.

Symon
 Serys, I may not in no degré;
 I haue gret errandys for to do.
 Þerfore I pray ȝow excuse me,
 And on my herand lete me go.   730

Secundus Judeus
 What, harlot! Hast þu skorne
 To bere þe tre whan we þe preye?
 Þu xalt berynt haddyst þu sworn,
 And yt were ten tyme þe weye.

Symon
 Serys, I prey ȝou dysplese ȝou nowth; 735
 I wole help to bere þe tre.
 Into þe place it xal be browth
 Where ȝe wole comawnde me.

Here Symon takyth þe cros of Jhesus and beryth it forth.

Veronica
 A, ȝe synful pepyl, why fare [ȝe] þus?
 For swet and blood he may not se. 740
 Allas, holy prophete, Cryst Jhesus,
 Careful is myn hert for the!

And sche whypyth his face with here kerchy.

---

after 722] *catch words for quire* T þerfore we prey 739 ȝe] *omitted in MS.* 742 *sd*] *in right margin*

Jhesus

    Veronyca, þi whipyng doth me ese;

    My face is clene þat was blak to se.

    I xal þem kepe from all mysese   745

    Þat lokyn on þi kerchy and remembyr me.

f. 180v *Þan xul þei pulle Jhesu out of his clothis and leyn them togedyr.*
And þer þei xul pullyn hym down and leyn hym along on þe cros
and after þat naylyn hym þeron.

Primus Judeus

    Come on now, here we xal asay

    Yf þe cros for þe be mete.

    Cast hym down here, in þe devyl way!

    How long xal he standyn on his fete?   750

Secundus Judeus

    Pul hym down, evyl mote he the!

    And gyf me his arm in hast!

    And anon we xal se

    Hese good days þei xul be past.

Tertius Judeus

    Gef hese other arm to me!   755

    Another take hed to hese feet!

    And anon we xal se

    Yf þe borys be for hym meet.

Quartus Judeus

    Þis is mete, take good hede!

    Pulle out þat arm to þe, sore!   760

Primus Judeus

    Þis is short, þe deuyl hym sped,

    Be a large fote and more!

Secundus Judeus

    Fest on a rop and pulle hym long,

    And I xal drawe þe ageyn.

    Spare we not þese ropys strong,   765

    Þow we brest both flesch and veyn.

743 *sn*] Jh *written over* ve   761 þe] þ *written over a* d

Tertius Judeus
 Dryve in þe nayl, anon lete se!
 And loke and þe flesch and senues well last.
Quartus Judeus
 Þat I graunt, so mote I the!
 Lo, þis nayl is dreve ryth wel and fast.   770

Primus Judeus
f. 181 Fest a rop þan to his feet,
 And drawe hym down long anow.
Secundus Judeus
 Here is a nayl for both, good and greet;
 I xal dryve it thorwe, I make avow!

Here xule þei leve of, and dawncyn abowte þe cros shortly.

Tertius Judeus
 Lo, fela! Here alythe, takkyd on a tre! 775
Quartus Judeus
 3a, and I trowe þu art a worthy kyng.
Primus Judeus
 A, good sere, telle me now what helpyth þi prophecy
              þe?
Secundus Judeus
 3a, or any of þi fals prechyng?

Tertius Judeus
 Serys, set up þe cros on þe hende
 Þat we may loke hym in þe face. 780
Quartus Judeus
 3a, and we xal knelyn onto oure kyng so kend,
 And preyn hym of his gret grace.

Here qwan þei han set hym up þei xuln gon before hym seyng eche affter other þus:

Primus Judeus
 Heyl, kyng of Jewys, yf þu be!

773 greet] g- *written over an t* 774 dryve] -r- *written over a y* 776 sn Judeus] MS.
Ju *end of word lost in tear at edge of leaf* 782 sd hym] MS. hyn + *suspension mark*

Secundus Judeus
   3a, 3a, sere, as þu hangyst þere flesche and bonys;
Tertius Judeus
   Com now down of þat tre   785
Quartus Judeus
   And we wole worchepe þe all at onys.

*Here xul poer comonys stand and loke upon þe Jewys, foure or five;
and þe Jewys xul come to them and do them hange þe þevys.*

Primus Judeus
   Come on, 3e knavys, and set up þese two crosses
                                                   ryth,
   And hange up þese to thevys anon!
Secundus Judeus
f. 181v   3a, and in þe worchep of þis worthy knyth,
   On eche syde of hym xal hangyn on.   790

*Here þe sympyl men xul settyn up þese two crossys and hangyn up
þe thevys be þe armys. And þerwhylys xal þe Jewys cast dyce for his
clothis, and fytyn and stryvyn. And in þe mene tyme xal Oure
Lady come with thre Maryes with here and sen John with hem,
settyng hem down asyde afore þe cros, Oure Lady swuonyng and
mornyng and leysere seyng:*

Maria
   A, my good lord, my sone so swete!
   What hast þu don? Why hangyst now þus here?
   Is þer non other deth to þe now mete,
   But þe most shamful deth among þese thevys fere?

   A, out on my hert, whi brest þu nowth?   795
   And þu art maydyn and modyr, and seyst þus þi
                                       childe spylle?
   How mayst þu abyde þis sorwe and þis woful
                                       þowth?
   A, deth, deth, deth, why wylt þu not me kylle?

Here Oure Lady xal swonge a3en and Oure Lord xal seyn þus:

786 *sd* foure or five] *MS.* iiij or v   787 þese] *MS. perhaps originally* þise *altered to*
þese   two] *MS.* ij   789 *sn* Judeus] *MS.* Jud *end of word lost at edge of leaf*   790 *sd*
two] *MS.* ij;   thre] *MS.* iiij   798 *sd* Oure²] *MS.* or + *suspension mark*

Jhesus
   O, Fadyr almythy, makere of man,
   Forgyff þese Jewys þat don me wo!   800
   Forgeve hem, Fadyr, forgeve hem þan!
   For thei wete nowth what þei do.

Primus Judeus
   3a, vath, vath! Now here is he
   Þat bad us dystroye oure tempyl on a day,
   And withinne days thre   805
   He xulde reysynt aзen in good aray.

Secundus Judeus
f. 182   Now, and þu kan do swech a dede,
   Help now þiself yf þat þu kan,
   And we xal belevyn on þe withoutyn drede
   And seyn þu art a mythty man.   810

Tertius Judeus
   3a, yf þu be Goddys sone as þu dedyst teche,
   From þe cros come now down;
   Þan of mercy we xal þe beseche
   And seyn þu art a lord of gret renown.

Jestes
   Yf þu be Goddys sone as þu dedyst seye,   815
   Helpe here now both þe and vs;
   But I fynde it not al in my feye
   Þat þu xuldyst be Cryst, Goddys sone Jhesus.

Dysmas
   Do wey, fool, why seyst þu so?
   He is þe sone of God, I beleve it wel;   820
   And synne dede he nevyr, lo,
   Þat he xuld be put þis deth tyl.

   But we ful mech wrong han wrowth;
   He dede nevyr þing amys.
   Now, mercy, good lord, mercy! And forgete me
                             nowth   825
   Whan þu comyst to þi kyngham and to þi blysse.

800 wo] wo *written twice, the first deleted*   802 nowth] *MS.* notwh   803 3a] w
obliterated after 3a   824 dede] *erasure before* dede; he *to left of erasure in margin*

Jhesus

    Amen, amen! Þu art ful wyse,
    Þat þu hast askyd I grawnt þe;
    Þis same day in paradyse
    With me, þi God, þu xalt þer be.   830

Maria

f. 182v   O my sone, my sone, my derlyng dere!
    What haue I defendyd þe?
    Þu hast spoke to alle þo þat ben here
    And not o word þu spekyst to me.

    To þe Jewys þu art ful kende,   835
    Þu hast forgove al here mysdede;
    And þe thef þu hast in mende,
    For onys haskyng mercy, hefne is his mede.

    A, my sovereyn lord, why whylt þu not speke
    To me þat am þi modyr, in peyn for þi wrong?   840
    A, hert, hert, why whylt þu not breke
    Þat I wore out of þis sorwe so stronge?

Jhesus

    A, woman, woman, beheld þer þi sone!
    And þu, Jon, take her for þi modyr.
    I charge þe to kepe here as besyly as þu kone –   845
    Þu a clene mayde xal kepe another.

    And, woman, þu knowyst þat my Fadyr of hefne me
                             sent
    To take þis manhod of þe, Adamys rawnsom to
                             pay;
    For þis is þe wyl and my Faderys intent,
    Þat I xal þus deye to delyuere man fro þe develys
                           pray.   850

    Now syn it is þe wyl of my Fadyr it xuld þus be,
    Why xuld it dysplese þe, modyr, now my deth so
                             sore?
    And for to suffre al þis for man I was born of the;
    To þe blys þat man had lost, man aȝen to restore.

850 develys] l *written over an* r

Here Oure Lady xal ryse and renne and halse þe crosse.

Maria Magdalene

f. 183   A, good lady, why do ȝe þus?   855
          Ȝour dolfol cher now cheuith us sore.
          And for þe peyne of my swete lord, Jhesus,
          Þat he seyth in ȝou, it peyneth hym more.

Maria Virgo

          I pray ȝow alle let me ben here,
          And hang me up here on þis tre   860
          Be my frend and sone þat me is so dere;
          For þer he is, þer wold I be.

Johannes

          Jentyl lady, now leve ȝour mornyng,
          And go with us now we ȝou pray,
          And comfort oure lord at hese departyng,   865
          For he is almost redy to go his way.

*Here þei xal take Oure Lady from þe crosse. And here xal Pylat
come down from his shaffald with Cayphas and Annas and all here
mené, and xul come and lokyn on Cryst; and Annas and Cayphas
xul skornfully seyn:*

Cayphas

          Lo, serys, lo! Beheldyth and se!
          Here hangyth he þat halpe many a man;
          And now yf he Goddys sone be,
          Helpe now hymself yf þat he kan.   870

Annas

          Ȝa, and yf þu kyng of Israel be,
          Come down of þe cros among us alle!
          And lete þi God now delyuere the,
          And þan oure kyng we wole þe calle.

---

856 cheuith] *see 243sd*   866 sd seyn] *end of word lost at edge of leaf*

Here xal Pylat askyn penne and inke, and a tabyl xal be take hym
f. 183v *wretyn afore, "Hic est Jhesus Nazarenus rex Judeorum". And he*
xal make hym to wryte and þan gon up on a leddere and settyn þe
tabyl abovyn Crystys hed; and þan Cayphas xal makyn hym to
redyn and seyn:

Cayphas
    Sere Pylat, we merveylyth of þis   875
    Þat ȝe wryte hym to be kyng of Jewys.

    Þerfore we wolde þat ȝe xuld wryte þus,
    Þat he namyd hymself kyng of Jewus.

Pylat
    Þat I haue wretyn, wretyn it is,
    And so it xal be for me, iwys.   880

And so forth all þei xal gon aȝen to þe skaffald. And Jhesus xal
cryen:

[Jhesus]
    Heloy, heloy,
    Lamazabathany!
    My Fadyr in hevyn on hy,
        Why dost þu me forsake?
    The frelté of my mankende   885
    With stronge peyn yt gynnyth to peynde.
    Ha, dere Fadyr, haue me in mende
        And lete deth my sorwe slake!

Secundus Judeus
    Methynkyth he this doth calle, "Hely".
    Lete us go nere and aspy   890
    And loke yf he come preuély,
        From cros hym down to reve.
Jhesus
    So grett a thrust dede nevyr man take,
    As I haue, man, now for þi sake.
    For thrust asundyr my lyppys gyn crake,   895
        For drynes þei do cleve.

881 *sn Jhesus] omitted in MS.; Jhesus in sd underlined as sn*   892 cros] -r- *written over*
an o

Tertius Judeus
   3our thrust, sere hoberd, for to slake,
   Eyzil and galle here I þe take.
   What! Methynkyth a mowe 3e make;
      Is not þis good drynk?   900
   To crye for drynke 3e had gret hast
   And now it semyth it is but wast.
   Is not þis drynk of good tast?
      Now telle me how 3e thynk!

Quartus Judeus
   On lofte, sere hoberd, now 3e be sett,   905
   We wyll no lenger with 3ou lett.
   We grete 3ou wel on þe newe gett,
     And make on 3ou a mowe.
Primus Judeus
   We grete 3ou wel with a scorn,
   And pray 3ou bothe evyn and morn,   910
   Take good eyd to oure corn
     And chare awey þe crowe.

Jhesus
f. 184   *In manus tuas, domine* –
   Holy Fadyr, in hefly se,
   I comende my spyryte to þe,   915
     For here now hendyth my fest.
   I xal go sle þe fende, þat freke,
   For now myn herte begynnyth to breke,
   Wurdys mo xal I non speke –
     Nunc consummatum est.   920

Maria
   Alas, alas, I leve to longe,
   To se my swete sone with peynes stronge
   As a theff on cros doth honge,
     And nevyr 3et dede he synne.
   Alas, my dere chyld to deth is dressyd!   925
   Now is my care wel more incressyd;
   A, myn herte with peyn is pressyd,
     For sorwe myn herte doth twynne.

905 sn *Quartus*] *Arabic instead of the usual Roman numeral*   913–1034] *This section of
the text is contained in an interpolated bifolium, ff. 184–5*

Johannes

   A, blyssyd mayde, chaunge ʒour thought;
   For þow ʒour sone with sorwe be sought,   930
   ʒitt by his owyn wyl þis werk is wrought,
     And wylfully his deth to take.
   ʒow to kepe, he chargyd me here,
   I am ʒour servaunt, my lady dere;
   Wherfore I pray ʒow be of good chere,   935
     And merthis þat ʒe make.

Maria

   Thow he had nevyr of me be born,
   And I sey his flesch þus al to-torn,
   On bak behyndyn, on brest beforn,
     Rent with woundys wyde;   940
   Nedys I must wonyn in woo

f. 184v

   To se my frende with many a fo
   All to-rent from top to too,
     His flesch withowtyn hyde.

Johannes

   A, blyssyd lady, as I ʒow telle,   945
   Had he not deyd we xuld to helle,
   Amongys fendys þer evyr to dwelle
     In peynes þat ben smert.
   He sufferyth deth for our trespace,
   And thorwe his deth we xal haue grace   950
   To dwelle with hym in hevyn place;
     Þerfore beth mery in hert.

Maria

   A, dere frende, weel woot I this,
   Þat he doth bye us to his blys,
   But ʒitt of myrth evyrmor I mys   955
     Whan I se þis syght.

Johannes

   Now, dere lady, þerfore I ʒow pray,
   Fro þis dolful dolour wende we oure way;
   For whan þis syght ʒe se nought may,
     ʒoure care may waxe more lyght.   960

955 myrth] -y- *written over an* r

Maria
  Now, sythe I must parte hym fro,
  3it lete my kysse, or þat I go,
  His blyssyd feyt þat sufferyn wo
    Naylid on þis tre.
  So cruelly with grett dyspyte,   965
  Þus shamfully was nevyr man dyghte,
  Þerfore in peyn myn hert is pyghte,
    Al joye departyth fro me.

Hic quasi semi-mortua cadat prona in terram; et dicit Johannes:

f. 185 *Johannes*
  Now, blyssyd mayd, com forthe with me,
  No lengere þis syght þat 3e se;   970
  I xal 3ow gyde in þis countré
    Where þat it plesyth 3ow best.
Maria
  Now, jentyl John, my sonys derlyng,
  To Goddys temple þu me brynge,
  Þat I may prey God with sore wepynge   975
    And mornynge þat is prest.

Johannes
  All 3our desyre xal be wrought,
  With herty wyll I werke 3our thought.
  Now, blyssyd mayde, taryeth nowth
    In þe temple þat 3e ware.   980
  For holy prayere may chaunge 3our mood,
  And cawse 3our chere to be more good,
  Whan 3e se no3t 3our childys blood
    Þe lasse may be 3our care.

Tunc transiet Maria ad templum cum Johanne, et cetera.

Maria
  Here in þis temple my lyff I lede   985
  And serue my lord God with hertyly drede.
  Now xal wepynge me fode and fede
    Som comforte tyll God sende.

968 sd semi-mortua] *MS.* seminor tua   983 no3t] *MS.* not3;   3our] *letter deleted*
after 3our

A, my lord God, I þe pray,
Whan my childe ryseth þe thrydde day   990
Comforte thanne, thyn handmay,
    My care for to amende.

Anima Christi
Now all mankende in herte be glad
With all merthis þat may be had,
For mannys sowle þat was bestad   995
    In þe logge of helle.
f. 185v   Now xal I ryse to lyve agayn,
From peyn to pleys of paradyse pleyn;
Þerfore, man, in hert be fayn,
    In merthe now xalt þu dwelle.   1000

I am þe sowle of Cryst Jhesu,
Þe which is kynge of all vertu;
My body is ded, þe Jewys it slew,
    Þat hangyth ȝitt on þe rode.
Rent and torn, al blody red,   1005
For mannys sake my body is deed,
For mannys helpe my body is bred,
    And sowle-drynk my bodyes blode.

Þow my body be now sclayn,
Þe thrydde day, þis is certayn,   1010
I xal reyse my body agayn
    To lyve, as I ȝow say.
Now wole I go streyth to helle,
And feche from þe fendys felle
All my frendys þat þerin dwelle   1015
    To blysse þat lestyth ay.

The sowle goth to helle gatys and seyth:

Attollite portas, principes, vestras et eleuamini porte
    eternales, et introibit rex glorie.

---

990 thrydde] *MS.* iij^{de}   990–3] *large red numeral* 33 *in right margin*   1016 *sd* -1017]
nota anima latronis *added in left margin (scribe B)*   1017] *line preceded in left margin by a
red abbreviation mark for* versus

Ondothe ȝoure ȝatys of sorwatorie!
On mannys sowle I haue memorie;   1020
Here comyth now þe kynge of glorye
    These gatys for to breke.
Ȝe develys þat arn here withinne,
Helle gatys ȝe xal vnpynne,
I xal delyvere mannys kynne,   1025
    From wo I wole hem wreke.

Belyall
    Alas, alas, out and harrow!
    Onto þi byddynge must we bow;
    Þat þu art God, now do we know,
       Of þe had we grett dowte.   1030
    Aȝens þe may nothynge stonde,
    All thynge obeyth to thyn honde,
    Both hevyn and helle, watyr and londe,
       All thynge must to þe lowte.

Anima Christi
f. 186   Aȝens me it wore but wast   1035
    To holdyn or to stondyn fast;
    Helle logge may not last
       Aȝens þe kynge of glorye.
    Þi derke dore down I throwe,
    My fayr frendys now wele I knowe,   1040
    I xal hem brynge, reknyd be rowe,
       Out of here purcatorye.

Centurio
    In trewth now I knowe with ful opyn syght
    That Goddys dere sone is naylid on tre;
    These wundyrful tokenys aprevyn ful ryght   1045
    Quod vere filius dei erat iste.
Alius miles 2
    The very childe of God, I suppose þat he be,
    And so it semyth wele be his wundyrful werk;
    Þe erth sore qwakyth, and þat agresyth me,
    With myst and grett wedyr it is woundyr dyrk.   1050

1047–50] *large red numeral* 34 *in right margin*

Alius miles 3
 Soch merveylis shewe may non ertheley man;
 Þe eyr is ryght derke, þat fyrst was ryght clere,
 The erthqwave is grett, þe clowdys waxe whan –
 These tokenys preue hym a lorde without any pere.
Centurio
 His fadyr is pereles kyng of most empere,   1055
 Bothe lorde of þis world and kynge of hevyn hyȝe;
 Ȝit out of all synne, to brynge us owt of daungere,
 He soferyth his dere sone for us all to dye.

Nichodemus
 Alas, alas, what syght is this?
 To se þe lorde and kynge of blys   1060
 Þat nevyr synnyd ne dede amys
    Þus naylid vpon a rode.
 Alas, Jewys, what haue ȝe wrought?
 A, ȝe wyckyd wytys, what was ȝour thought?
 Why haue ȝe bobbyd and þus betyn owth   1065
    All his blyssyd blood?

f. 186v *Senturyo*
 A, now trewly telle weyl I kan,
 Þat þis was Goddys own sone.
 I knowe he is both God and man
 Be þis wark þat here is done.   1070

 Þer was nevyr man but God þat cowden make þis werk
 Þat evyr was of woman born;
 Were he nevyr so gret a clerk,
 It passeth hem all þow þei had sworn.

 Hese lawe was trewe, I dare wel saye,   1075
 Þat he tawth us here amonge,
 Þerfore I rede ȝe turne ȝour faye
 And amende þat ȝe han do wronge.

Joseph of Aramathia
 O, good lord Jhesu, þat deyst now here on rode,
 Haue mercy on me and forgyf me my mys!   1080

I wold þe worchep here with my good,
Þat I may come to þi blysse.

To Pylat now wole I goon
And aske þe body of my lord Jhesu.
To bery þat now wold I soon   1085
In my grave þat is so new.

Heyl, sere Pylat, þat syttyth in sete!
Heyl, justyce of Jewys, men do þe calle!
Heyl, with helthe I do þe grete!
I pray þe of a bone, whatso befalle.   1090

To bery Jhesu-is body, I wole þe pray,
Þat he were out of mennys syth;
For tomorwyn xal be oure holyday
Þan wole no man hym bery, I þe plyth.

f. 187   And yf we lete hym hange þer stylle,   1095
Some wolde seyn þerof anow,
Þe pepyl þerof wold seyn ful ylle,
Þat nother xuld be ȝour worchep nor prow.

Pylat
Sere Joseph of Baramathie, I graunt þe
With Jhesu-is body do þin intent.   1100
But fyrst I wole wete þat he ded be,
As it was his jugement.

Sere knytys, I comawnd ȝow þat ȝe go
In hast with Joseph of Baramathie,
And loke ȝe take good hede þerto   1105
Þat Jhesu suerly ded be.

Se þat þis comawndement ȝe fulfylle
Without wordys ony mo;
And þan lete Joseph do his wylle,
What þat he wyl with Jhesu do.   1110

Here come to knytys beforn Pylat at onys, þus seyng:

1083 goon] god *deleted before* goon   1084 And aske] *MS. possibly* taske *(= to ask)*   1091 Jhesu-is] *written as two words in MS.; see also 1100, 1120, 1228*   1104 Joseph] *MS.* Josepht

Primus miles
    Sere, we xal do oure dylygens
    With Joseph goyng to Caluerye.
    Be we out of þi presens
    Sone þe trewth we xal aspye.

Joseph ab [Aramathia]
    Gramercy, Pylat, of ȝour jentylnesse   1115
    Þat ȝe han grawntyd me my lyst.
    Anythyng in my province
    ȝe xal haue at ȝour request.

Pylat
f. 187v   Sere, all ȝour lest ȝe xal haue,
    With Jhesu–is body do ȝour intent.   1120
    Whethyr ȝe bery hym in pyt or grave,
    Þe powere I grawnt ȝow here present.

The two knygtys go with Joseph to Jhesus and stande and heldyn
hym in þe face.

Secundus miles
    Methynkyth Jhesu is sewre anow,
    It is no ned his bonys to breke,
    He is ded. How þinkyth ȝow?   1125
    He xal nevyr go nor speke.

Primus miles
    We wyl be sure or þan we go.
    Of a thyng I am bethowth:
    ȝondyr is a blynd knyth I xal go to,
    And sone a whyle here xal be wrowth.   1130

Here þe knyth goth to blynde Longeys and seyth:

    Heyl, sere Longeys, þu gentyl knyth,
    Þe I prey now ryth hertyly
    Þat þu wylt wend with me ful wyth;
    It xal be for þi prow veryly.

1115 *sn Aramathia] lost at edge of leaf*   1118 request] *MS.* resquest; *rest first written,*
-q- *added over* t *but* s *uncorrected*   1122 *sd* two] *MS.* ij

Longeus
    Sere, at ʒour comawndement with ʒow wyl I wende 1135
    In what place ʒe wyl me haue,
    For I trost ʒe be my frend.
    Lede me forth, sere, oure sabath ʒou save!

Primus miles
    Lo, sere Longeys, here is a spere,
    Bothe long and brood and sharp anow;   1140
    Heve it up fast þat it wore þere,
    For here is game. Show, man, show!

Here Longeys showyth þe spere warly and þe blood comyth ren-
nyng to his hand, and he auantorysly xal wype his eyn.

Longeys
f. 188   O, good lord, how may þis be
    Þat I may se so bryth now?
    Þis thretty wyntyr I myth not se,   1145
    And now I may se, I wote nevyr how.
    But ho is þis þat hangyth here now?
    I trowe it be þe maydonys sone –
    And þat he is now. I knowe wel how
    Þe Jewys to hym þis velany han don.   1150

Here he fallyth down on his knes.

    Now, good lord, forgyf me that
    Þat I to þe now don have,
    For I dede I wyst not what.
    Þe Jewys of myn ignorans dede me rave;

    Mercy, mercy, mercy, I crye!   1155

Þan Joseph doth set up þe lederys, and Nychodemus comyth to help
hym.

Nicodemus
    Joseph ab Aramathy, blyssyd þu be!
    For þu dost a fol good dede.
    I prey the lete me help þe,
    Þat I may be partenere of þi mede.

1148 maydonys] *MS.* mayndonys   1155 *Line in right margin*

Joseph
> Nychodemus, welcome indede!   1160
> I pray ʒow ʒe wole help þerto;
> He wole aqwyte us ryth weyl oure mede,
> And I haue lysens for to do.

Here Joseph and Nychodemus takyn Cryst of þe cros, on on o ledyr and þe tother on another leddyr. And qwan [he] is had down, Joseph leyth hym in Oure Ladys lappe, seyng þe knytys turnyng hem; and Joseph seyth:

Joseph
> Lo, Mary, modyr good and trewe,
> Here is þi son, blody and bloo;   1165
> For hym myn hert ful sore doth rewe.
> Kysse hym now onys eer he go.

Maria Virgo
f. 188v   A, mercy, mercy, myn owyn son so dere!
> Þi blody face now I must kysse.
> Þi face is pale withowtyn chere,   1170
> Of meche joy now xal I mysse.
> Þer was nevyr modyr þat sey this,
> So here sone dyspoyled with so gret wo;
> And my dere chylde nevyr dede amys.
> A, mercy, Fadyr of hefne, it xulde be so!   1175

Joseph
> Mary, ʒour sone ʒe take to me,
> Into his grave it xal be browth.
Maria
> Joseph, blyssyd evyr mot þu be,
> For þe good dede þat ʒe han wrowth.

Here þei xal leyn Cryst in his grave.

Joseph
> I gyf þe þis syndony þat I have bowth,   1180
> To wynde þe in whyl it is new.

1163 *sd* he] *omitted in MS.*

Nichodemus
  Here is an onyment þat I haue browth,
  To anoynt withall myn lord Jhesu.

Joseph
  Now Jhesu is withinne his grave,
  Wheche I ordeyn somtyme for me.   1185
  On þe, lord, I vowche it save,
  I knowe my mede ful gret xal be.

Nichodemus
  Now lete us leyn on þis ston ageyn,
  And Jhesu in þis tombe stylle xal be;
  And we wyl walke hom ful pleyn.   1190
  Þe day passyth fast I se.
  Farewel, Joseph, and wel ȝe be,
  No lengere teryeng here we make.
Joseph
  Sere, almythy God be with þe,
  Into his blysse he mote ȝou take!   1195

Maria
f. 189   Farewel, ȝe jentyl princys kende,
  In joye evyr mote ȝe be!
  Þe blysse of hefne withowtyn ende,
  I knowe veryly þat ȝe xal se.

*Here þe princys xal do reuerens to Oure Lady and gon here way and
leve þe Maryes at þe sepulchre. Cayphas goth to Pylat seyng þus:*

Cayphas
  Herk, sere Pylat, lyst to me,   1200
  I xal þe telle tydyngys new;
  Of o thyng we must ware be
  Er ellys hereafter we myth it rewe.

  Þu wotyst weyl þat Jhesu,
  He seyd to us with wordys pleyn,   1205
  He seyd we xuld fynd it trew
  Þe thryd day he wold ryse ageyn.

1188 sn Nichodemus] *suspension mark covered by paper guard*   1196 princys] *MS.
unusual abbreviation mark for* ri   1199 sd] Here . . . way *and in right margin*   1200]
nota *in left margin above line*;   Incipit hic *in right margin (scribe B)*   1207 ageyn] *MS.*
agey

Yf þat hese dyscyplys come, serteyn,
And out of his graue stele hym away,
Þei wyl go preche and pleyn seyn   1210
Þat he is reson þe thryd day.

Þis is þe cowncel þat I gyf here:
Take men and gyf hem charge þerto,
To weche þe grave with gret power
Tyl þe thryd day be go.   1215

Pylat
Sere Cayphas, it xal be do!
For as ȝe say þer is peryl in;
And it happened þat it were so,
It myth make our lawys for to blyn.

ȝe xal se, ser, er þat ȝe go   1220
How I xal þis mater saue,
And what I xal sey þerto,
And what charge þei xal haue.

Come forth ȝe, ser Amorawnt
And ser Arphaxat; com ner also,   1225
Ser Cosdram and ser Affraunt,
And here þe charge þat ȝe must do.
Serys, to Jhesu-is grave ȝe xal go
Tyl þat þe thryd day be gon,
And lete nother frend nor fo   1230
In no wey to towche þe ston.

Yf ony of hese dyscipelys com þer
To fech þe body fro ȝou away,
Bete hym down, have ȝe no fere,
With shamful deth do hym day.   1235

In payn of ȝour godys and ȝour lyvys
Þat ȝe lete hem nowth shape ȝou fro,
And of ȝour chyldere and ȝour wyfys,
For al ȝe lese and ȝe do so.

1224] hic *written twice in left margin the first preceded by* nota *(scribe B)*

Primus Miles

f. 189v   Sere Pylat, we xal not ses;   1240
            We xal kepe it strong anow.
Secundus Miles
            3a, and an hunderyd put hem in pres
            Þei xal dey, I make avow!

Tertius Miles
            And han honderyd? Fy on an honderyd! And an
                                    honderyd þerto!
            Þer is non of hem xal us withstonde.   1245
Quartus Miles
            3a, and þer com an hunderyd thowsand and mo,
            I xal hem kylle with myn honde!

Pylat
            Wel, serys, þan 3our part 3e do
            And to 3our charge loke 3e take hede;
            Withowtyn wordys ony mo,   1250
            Wysly now þat 3e procede.

Here þe knytys gon out of þe place.

            Lo, ser Cayphas, how thynkyth 3ow?
            Is not þis wel browth abowth?
Cayphas
            In feyth, ser, it is sure anow,
            Hardely haue 3e no dowth.   1255

Arfaxat (secundus)
            Let se, ser Amaraunt, where wele 3e be?
            Wole 3e kepe þe feet or þe hed?
Ameraunt
            At þe hed, so mote I the!
            And hoso come here he is but ded.

1244 honderyd! And an honderyd] *in MS.* honderyd *written* C *in both cases*   1251 *sd*]
in right margin;   gon] *letter deleted after* gon   1256, 1258, 1260, 1262, 1264 *sn*]
speaker's names renumbered j^us, ij^us, j^us, iij^us, iiij^us *on left of name; suspension marks of
numbers on right largely lost at edge of leaf*   1257–8] So mote I the I wole be at þe hed
deleted between the two lines

Arfaxat (secundus)
    And I wole kepe þe feet þis tyde,   1260
    Þow þer come both Jakke and Gylle.
Cosdram (tertius)
    And I xal kepe þe ryth syde,
    And hoso come I xal hym kylle.

Affraunt (quartus)
    And I wole on þe lefte hand ben,
    And hoso come here he xal nevyr then;   1265
    Ful sekyrly his bane xal I ben
        With dyntys of dowte.
f. 190   Syr Pylat, haue good day!
    We xul kepyn þe body in clay
    And we xul wakyn wele þe way   1270
        And wayten all abowte.

Pylatus
    Now, jentyl serys, wole ȝe vowchsaffe
    To go with me and sele þe graffe?
    Þat he ne ryse out of þe grave
        Þat is now ded.   1275
Cayphas
    We graunte wel, lete us now go.
    Whan it is selyd and kepte also,
    Than be we sekyr withowtyn wo,
        And haue of hym no dred.

Tunc ibunt ad sepulcrum Pilatus, Cayphas, Annas et omnes mi-
lites, et dicit

Annas
    Loo, here is wax ful redy dyght,   1280
    Sett on ȝour sele anon ful ryght;
    Þan be ȝe sekyr, I ȝow plyght,
        He xal not rysyn agayn.

1264 *sn quartus*] MS. *Arabic* 4   below 1267] syr pilat *catch words for quire V*   1268]
nota *in left margin*   1273 þe] *letter deleted after* þe

Pilatus

On þis corner my seal xal sytt
And with þis wax I sele þis pytt.   1285
Now dare I ley he xal nevyr flytt
    Out of þis grave, serteayn.

Annas

Here is more wax ful redy, loo.
All þe cornerys ȝe sele also,
And with a lokke loke it too,   1290
    Than lete us gon oure way.
And lete þese knytys abydyn þerby;
And yf hese dysciplys com preuyly
To stele awey þis ded body,
    To vs they hem brynge without delay.   1295

Pilatus

On every corner now is sett my seale,
Now is myn herte in welthe and wele.
f. 190v   This may no brybour awey now stele,
    Þis body from vndyr ston.
Now, syr buschopp, I pray to the,   1300
And Annas also, com on with me,
Evyn togedyr, all we thre
    Homward þe wey we gon.

As wynde wrothe,
Knyghtys, now goht   1305
Clappyd in cloth,
    And kepyth hym well.
Loke ȝe be bolde
With me for to holde;
ȝe xul haue gold   1310
    And helme of stele.

*Pylat, Annas and Cayphas go to þer skaffaldys and þe knyghtys
seyn:*

1296 *sn Pilatus*] MS. Pilatas *possibly corrected to* Pilatus

Affraunt (4)
  Now in þis growunde
  He lyth bounde,
  Þat tholyd wounde
    For he was fals.   1315
  Þis lefft cornere
  I wyl kepe here,
  Armyd clere,
    Both hed and hals.

Cosdran (3)
  I wyl haue þis syde   1320
  Whatso betyde;
  If any man ryde
    To stele þe cors
  I xal hym chyde
  With woundys wyde,   1325
  Amonge hem glyde
    With fyne fors.

Ameraunt (primus)
  The hed I take,
  Hereby to wake,
  A stele stake   1330
    I holde in honde.
  Maystryes to make,
  Crownys I crake,
  Schafftys to-shake
    And schapyn schonde.   1335

Arfaxat (secundus)
  I xal not lete
  To kepe þe fete,
  They ar ful wete,
    Walterid in blood.

1312 þis] tyde *deleted after* þis   1316 lefft] *second* f *written over a* t   1328 sn] jᵘˢ
altered to ijᵘˢ *by addition of minim*   1335] sle fre & bonde *added* + *caret above line (scribe*
B)   1336 sn] 2ᵘˢ *altered to* jᵘˢ   1338 wete] *considerable erasure and later alteration in*
the middle of word

He þat wyll stalke   1340
Be brook or balke,
Hedyr to walke,
   Þo wrecchis be wood.

Primus Miles

f. 191   Myn heed dullyth,
Myn herte fullyth   1345
   Of slepp.
Seynt Mahownd,
Þis beryenge grownd
   Þu kepp!

Secundus Miles

I sey þe same   1350
For any blame
   I falle.
Mahownd whelpe,
Aftyr þin helpe
   I calle!   1355

Tertius Miles

I am hevy as leed,
For any dred,
   I slepe.
Mahownd of myght,
Þis ston tonyght,   1360
   Þu kepe!

Quartus Miles

I haue no foot
To stonde on root
   By brynke.
Here I aske   1365
To go to taske
   A wynke.

Tunc dormyent milites et ueniet Anima Christi de inferno cum Adam et Eua, Abraham, John Baptist et alijs.

1356 sn, 1362 sn] MS. *Arabic 3 and 4 with suspension mark*

Anima Christi
    Come forthe, Adam, and Eue with the,
    And all my fryndys þat herein be;
    To paradys come forthe with me   1370
        In blysse for to dwelle.
    Þe fende of helle þat is ȝour foo,
    He xal be wrappyd and woundyn in woo.
    Fro wo to welthe now xul ȝe go,
        With myrthe evyrmore to melle.   1375

Adam
    I thanke þe, Lord, of þi grett grace
    That now is forȝovyn my grett trespace;
    Now xal we dwellyn in blysful place,
        In joye and endeles myrthe.
    Thorwe my synne man was forlorn,   1380
    And man to saue þu wore all torn,
    And of a mayd in Bedlem born,
        Þat evyr blyssyd be þi byrthe!

Eua
f. 191v   Blyssyd be þu, lord of lyff!
    I am Eue, Adam-is wyff;   1385
    Þu hast soferyd strok and stryff
        For werkys þat we wrought.
    Þi mylde mercy hath all forȝovyn,
    Dethis dentys on þe were drevyn,
    Now with þe, lord, we xul levyn,   1390
        Þi bryght blood hath us bowth.

Johannes Baptista
    I am þi cosyn, my name is John.
    Þi woundys hath betyn þe to þe bon.
    I baptyzid þe in flom Jordon
        And ȝaff þi body baptyze.   1395
    With þi grace now xul we gon
    From our enmyes everychon,
    And fyndyn myrthis many on
        In pley of paradyse.

1368–75 *unusually large red numeral* 35 *in right margin*   1388 hath] *MS.* hahth *third* -h
deleted   1398 fyndyn] *MS.* fyndȳs *with* -s *dotted for deletion*

Abraham
    I am Abraham, fadyr trowe,   1400
    Þat reyned after Noes flowe;
    A sory synne Adam gan sowe
        Þat clad us all in care.
    A sone þat maydenys mylk hath sokyn,
    And with his blood oure bonde hath brokyn;   1405
    Helle logge lyth vnlokyn,
        Fro fylth with frende we fare.

Anima Christi
    Fayre frendys, now be ʒe wunne,
    On ʒow shyneth þe sothfast sunne;
    Þe gost þat all grevaunce hath gunne   1410
f. 192   Ful harde I xal hym bynde.
    As wyckyd werme þu gunne apere
    To tray my chylderyn þat were so dere,
    Þerfore, traytour, heuermore here
        Newe paynes þu xalt evyr fynde.   1415

    Thorwe blood I took of mannys kynde,
    Fals devyl, I here þe bynde,
    In endles sorwe I þe wynde,
        Þerin evyrmore to dwelle.
    Now þu art bownde, þu mayst not fle;   1420
    For þin envyous cruelté
    In endeles dampnacyon xalt þu be
        And nevyr comyn out of helle.

Beliall
    Alas, herrow! Now am I bownde
    In helle gonge to ly on grounde;   1425
    In hendles sorwe now am I wounde
        In care evyrmore to dwelle.
    In helle logge I lyʒ alone;
    Now is my joye awey al gone,
    For all fendys xul be my fone –   1430
        I xal nevyr com from helle.

1407–10] *for marginal additions to left and right, see Appendix 5*   1425 ly on] *erasure after*
ly; on *added above line*   1431–39 sd] *for marginal additions to left and right see Appendix 5*

Anima Christi
Now is ʒour foo boundyn in helle
Þat evyr was besy ʒow for to qwelle.
Now wele I rysyn, flesch and felle,
   Þat rent was for ʒour sake,   1435
Myn owyn body þat hynge on rode;
And be þe Jewys nevyr so wode
It xal aryse both flesch and blode –
   My body now wyl I take.

Tunc transiet Anima Christi ad resuscitandum corpus; quo resusci-
tato, dicat Jhesus:

f. 192v *Jhesus*
Harde gatys haue I gon   1440
And peynes sofryd many on,
Stomblyd at stake and at ston
   Nyʒ thre and thretty ʒere.
I lyght out of my Faderys trone
For to amende mannys mone,   1445
My flesch was betyn to þe bon,
   My blood I bledde clere.

For mannys loue I tholyd dede,
And for mannys loue I am rysyn up rede;
For man I haue mad my body in brede,   1450
   His sowle for to fede.
Man, and þu lete me þus gone,
And wylt not folwyn me anone,
Such a frende fyndyst þu nevyr none
   To help þe at þi nede.   1455

Salue sancta parens, my modyr dere,
All heyl, modyr, with glad chere!
For now is aresyn with body clere
   Þi sone þat was dolve depe.
Þis is þe thrydde day þat I ʒow tolde   1460
I xuld arysyn out of þe cley so colde.
Now am I here with brest ful bolde,
   Þerfore no more ʒe wepe.

1439 *sd* Jhesus] *most of final -s lost at edge of leaf*   1449 up rede] *letter erased, -r- added*
above line

Maria
>Welcom, my lord, welcom, my grace!
>Welcome, my sone and my solace!   1465
>I xal þe wurchep in every place,
>>Welcom, lord God of myght!
>Mekel sorwe in hert I leed
>Whan þu were leyd in dethis beed,
>But now my blysse is newly breed,   1470
>>All men may joye þis syght.

Jhesus

f. 193
>All þis werlde þat was forlorn
>Shal wurchepe ȝou bothe evyn and morn;
>For had I not of ȝow be born
>>Man had be lost in helle.   1475
>I was deed and lyff I haue,
>And thorwe my deth man do I saue;
>For now I am resyn out of my graue
>>In hevyn man xal now dwelle.

Maria
>A, dere sone, þese wurdys ben goode,   1480
>Þu hast wel comfortyd my mornyng moode.
>Blyssyd be þi precyous bloode
>>Þat mankende þus doth saue.

Jhesus
>Now, dere modyr, my leve I take,
>Joye in hert and myrth ȝe make,   1485
>For deth is deed and lyff doth wake
>>Now I am resyn fro my graue.

Maria
>Farewel, my sone, farewel, my childe!
>Farewel, my lorde, my God so mylde!
>Myn hert is wele þat fyrst was whylde,   1490
>>Farewel, myn owyn dere love!

1473 wurchepe ȝou] ȝou *added above line after* wurchepe   1478 I am resyn MS. I
āresyn *with curved mark below* a-   1480 ben] *letter or letters obliterated before* ben
1490 hert is] is *added above line* + *caret*

Now all mankynde beth glad with gle,
For deth is deed, as ȝe may se,
And lyff is reysed endles to be
    In hevyn dwellynge above.   1495

Whan my sone was naylyd on tre
All women myght rewe with me,
For grettere sorwe myght nevyr non be
    Than I dede suffyr, iwys.
f. 193v   But þis joy now passyth all sorwe   1500
Þat my childe suffryd in þat hard morwe,
For now he is oure alderers borwe
    To brynge us all to blys.

Tunc evigilabunt milites sepulcri et dicit Primus Miles:

Primus Miles
    Awake, awake!
    Hillis gyn quake   1505
    And tres ben shake
        Ful nere atoo.
    Stonys clevyd,
    Wyttys ben revid,
    Erys ben devid –   1510
        I am servid soo.

Secundus Miles
    He is aresyn, þis is no nay,
    Þat was deed and colde in clay;
    Now is he resyn belyve þis day,
        Grett woundyr it is to me.   1515
    He is resyn by his owyn myght
    And forth he goth his wey ful ryght;
    How xul we now us qwytte
        Whan Pylat doth us se?

Tertius Miles
    Lete us now go   1520
    Pilat ontoo;
    And ryght evyn so
        As we han sayn,

1509 revid] rewi *deleted before* revid   1512, 1520, 1528 *sn*] MS. *Arabic* 2, 3,
4   1514 Now is he] he *omitted Block*

Þe trewth we say:
Þat out of clay   1525
He is resyn þis day
        Þat Jewys han slayn.

Quartus Miles
    I holde it best.
    Lete us nevyr rest
    But go we prest   1530
        Þat it were done.
    All heyl, Pilatt,
    In þin astat!
    He is resyn vp latt
        Þat þu gast dome.   1535

Pilat
    What, what, what, what!
    Out upon the! Why seyst þu þat?
    Fy vpon the, harlat!
        How darst þu so say?

f. 194   Þu dost myn herte ryght grett greff,   1540
    Þu lyest vpon hym, fals theff;
    How xulde he rysyn ageyn to lyff
        Þat lay deed in clay?

Primus Miles
    ȝa, þow þu be nevyr so wroth
    And of these tydandys nevyr so loth,   1545
    ȝitt goodly on ground on lyve he goth,
        Qwycke and levynge man.
    Iff þu haddyst a ben þer we ware,
    In hert þu xuldyst han had gret care,
    And of blysse a ben ryght bare,   1550
        Of colore bothe pale and whan.

Pilatus
    Or ȝe come there
    ȝe dede all swere
    To fyght in fere
        And bete and bynde.   1555

1544 sn] *numeral(?) deleted after* j^us

All þis was trayn,
ȝour wurdys wore vayn;
Þis is sertayn,
   ȝow fals I fynde.

Secundus Miles
Be þe deth þe devyl deyd,   1560
We were of hym so sore atreyd,
Þat for fer we us down leyd,
   Ryght evyn vpon oure syde.
Whan we were leyd upon þe grounde,
Stylle we lay as we had be bounde,   1565
We durst not ryse for a thowsand pounde,
   Ne not for all þis worlde so wyde.

Pilatus
Now fy upon ȝour grett bost!
All ȝour wurchep is now lost;
In felde, in town and in every cost   1570
   Men may ȝou dyspravyn.
f. 194v Now all ȝour wurchep it is lorn,
And every man may ȝow wel scorn,
And bydde ȝow go syttyn in þe corn
   And chare awey þe ravyn.   1575

Tertius Miles
ȝa, it was hyȝ tyme to leyn oure bost;
For whan þe body toke aȝen þe gost,
He wold a frayd many an ost,
   Kynge, knyght and knave.
ȝa, whan he dede ryse out of his lake,   1580
Þan was þer suche an erthequake,
Þat all þe worlde it gan to shake;
   Þat made us for to rave.

Quartus Miles
ȝa, ȝa! Herke, felawys, what I xal say:
Late us not ses be nyght nor day,   1585
But telle þe trewth ryght as it lay,
   In countré where we goo.

1560, 1576, 1586, 1596 *sn*] *MS. Arabic* 2, 3, 4, 2   1573 wel] *MS.* we   1580 whan]
d *deleted after* whan;   lake] k *deleted before* lake

And than I dare ley myn heed,
Þat þei þat Crystys lawys leed,
They wyl nevyr ses tyl they be deed   1590
    His deth þat brought hym too.

Primus Miles
Be Belyall, þis was now wele ment!
To þis cowncell lete us consent,
Lett us go tellyn with on assent
    He is resyn up þis day.   1595
Secundus Miles
I grawnt þerto and þat forthryght,
Þat he is resyn by his owyn myght;
For þer cam non be day nor nyght
    To helpe hym owte of clay.

Pilatus
f. 195   Now, jentyl serys, I pray 30w all,   1600
Abyde stylle a lytyl thrall,
Whyll þat I my cowncel call
    And here of þer councell.
Primus Miles
Syr, att 30ur prayour we wyl abyde
Here in þis place a lytel tyde.   1605
But tary not to longe, for we must ryde,
    We may not longe dwelle.

Pilatus
Now, jentyl serys, I pray 30w here,
Sum good cowncel me to lere;
For sertys, serys, without dwere,   1610
    We stounde in ryght grett dowte.
Cayphas
Now trewly, sere, I 30w telle,
þis matere is both fers and felle,
Combros it is þerwith to melle
    And evyl to be browth abowte.   1615

1602 my] *possible suspension mark above -y*

Annas

    Syr Pylat, þu grett justyse,
    Þow þu be of wittys wyse,
    3it herke ful sadly with good devyse
        What þat þu xalt do.
    I counsel þe, be my reed,   1620
    Þis wundyrful tale pray hem to hede,
    And upon þis 3eve hem good mede,
        Bothe golde and sylver also.

    And, sere, I xall telle 3ow why
    In 3oure erys prevyly,   1625
    Betweyn us thre, serteynly.
        Now herk, serys, in 3our erys.

Hic faciant Pilatus, Cayphas et Annas priuatim inter se consilium.
Quo finito dicat

Annas

f. 195v   For mede doth most in every qwest,
    And mede is mayster bothe est and west.
    Now trewly, serys, I hold þis best,   1630
        With mede men may bynde berys.

Cayphas

    Sekyr, sere, þis counsell is good.
    Pray þese knyhtys to chaunge þer mood;
    3eve them golde, feste and food,
        And þat may chaunge þer wytt.   1635

Pylatt

    Serys, 3oure good councel I xall fulfylle.
    Now, jentyl knyhtys, come hedyr me tylle;
    I pray 3ow, serys, of 3our good wylle
        No ferther þat 3e flytt.

    Jentyl knyhtys, I 3ow pray   1640
    A better sawe þat 3e say:
    Sey þer he was cawth away
        With his dyscyplis be nyght;
    Sey he was with his dyscyplis fett.
    I wolde 3e worn in 3oure sadelys sett,   1645
    And haue here golde in a purs knett
        And to Rome rydyth ryght.

Quartus Miles
    Now, syr Pylatt,
    We gon oure gatt.
    We wyll not prate   1650
       No lengere now.
    Now we haue golde
    No talys xul be tolde
    To whithtys on wolde,
       We make þe avow.   1655

Pilatus
    Now, 3e men of myth,
    As 3e han hyght,
    Euyn so forthryght,
       3oure wurdys not falle.
    And 3e xul gon   1660
    With me anon,
    All everychon,
       Into myn halle.

Primus Miles
f. 196   Now hens we go
    As lyth as ro,   1665
    And ryght evyn so
       As we han seyd,
    We xul kepe counsel.
    Wheresoevyr we dwell
    We xul no talys tell,   1670
       Be not dysmayd.

Hic uenient ad sepulcrum Maria Magdalene, Maria Jacobi et Maria Salome, et dicit Maria Magdalene:

Magdalen
    Swete systeryn, I 3ow besech,
    Heryght now my specyal speche;
    Go we with salvys for to leche
       Cryst þat tholyd wounde.   1675

1648 *sn*] *MS. Arabic* 4   1656 men of] men of *written twice, second deleted*   *1671 sd*]
in left margin is added finem prima die nota *(scribe B)*; Jacobi] *MS.* iacobi   1672–5]
large red numeral 36 in right margin

He hath us wonnyn owt of wreche,
The ryght wey God wyl us teche
For to seke my lorde, my leche;
   His blood hath me vnbownde.

Sefne develys in me were pyght,   1680
My loue, my lord, my God almyght,
Awey he weryd þo fyndys wight
   With his wyse wurde.
He droff fro me þe fendes lees,
In my swete sowle his chawmere i–ches;   1685
In me belevyth þe lorde of pes;
   I go to his burryenge boorde.

Maria Jacobi
   My systerys sone I woot he was;
   He lyth in here as sunne in glas,
   Þe childe was born by oxe and asse   1690
      Vp in a bestys stall.
   Thow his body be gravyd vndyr gres,
f. 196v   Þe grete godhede is nevyr þe lasse;
   Þe lord xal rysyn and gon his pas
      And comfortyn his frendys all.   1695

Maria Salome
   My name is Mary Salomé,
   His modyr and I, systerys we be,
   Annys dowterys we be all thre;
      Jhesu, we be þin awntys.
   The naylis gun his lemys feyn,   1700
   And þe spere gan punche and peyn;
   On þo woundys we wold haue eyn,
      Þat grace now God graunt vs.

Maria Magdalene
   Now go we stylle
   With good wyll   1705
      Þer he is leyd.

1680 Sefne] *MS.* vij   1685 In] *in left margin*   1696–7] systerys dowterys bothe *deleted between the two lines*

He deyd on crowch,
We wolde hym towch
   As we han seyd.

Tunc respicit Maria Magdalene in sepulcro dicens:

Where is my lord þat was here,   1710
Þat for me bledde, bowndyn in brere?
His body was beryed ryght by þis mere
   Þat for me gan deye.
Þe Jewys, fekyll and fals fownde,
Where haue þei do þe body with wounde?   1715
He lyth not upon þis grownde,
   Þe body is don aweye.

Maria Jacobi
To my lorde, my love, my frende,
Fayn wolde I salve aspende,
And I myght aught amende   1720
   His woundys depe and wyde.
To my lorde I owe lowlyté,
Bothe homage and fewté,
I wolde with my dewté
   A softyd hand and syde.   1725

Maria Salome
f. 197   To myghtfful God omnypotent
I bere a boyst of oynement;
I wold han softyd his sore dent,
   His sydys al abowte.
Lombe of love, withowt loth,   1730
I fynde þe not, myn hert is wroth;
In þe sepulcre þer lyth a cloth
   And jentyl Jhesu is owte.

Angelus
Wendyth forth, ʒe women thre,
Into þe strete of Galylé;   1735
ʒour savyour þer xul ʒe se
   Walkynge in þe waye.

1712 ryght] *MS.* rygh   1735 strete] g *deleted after* strete

3our fleschly lorde now hath lyff,
Þat deyd on tre with strook and stryff;
Wende forth, þu wepynge wyff,   1740
    And seke hym, I þe saye.

Now goth forth fast, all thre,
To his dyscyplys fayr and fre,
And to Petyr þe trewth telle 3e,
    Þerof haue 3e no dreed.   1745
Spare 3e not þe soth to say,
He þat was deed and closyd in clay,
He is resyn þis same day
    And levyth with woundys reed.

Maria Magdalene
    A, myrthe and joye in herte we haue,   1750
    For now [he] is resyn out of his graue,
    He levyth now oure lyf to saue,
        Þat dede lay in þe clay.
Maria Jacoby
f. 197v   In hert I was ryght sore dysmayd,
    The aungel to us whan þat he sayd   1755
    Þat Cryst is resyn. I was affrayd
        Þe aungel whan I say.

Maria Salome
    Now lete us all thre fulfylle
    Þe angelys wurde and Goddys wylle.
    Lett us sey with voys wul shrylle,   1760
        "Cryst þat Jewys dede sle,
    Oure lord þat naylyd was on þe rode
    And betyn out was his bodyes blode,
    He is aresyn, þough they ben wode" –
        A, lorde, 3itt wele þu be!   1765

Maria Magdalene dicit Petro et ceteris apostolis:

1750 sn *Maria Magdalene*] *end of word lost at edge of leaf*   1751 he] *omitted in MS.*

[*Maria Magdalene*]
    Bretheryn, all in herte be glad;
    Bothe blythe and joyful, in herte ful fayn!
    For ryght good tydandys haue we had
    Þat oure lord is resyn agayn.
    An aungel us bad ryght þus sertayn   1770
    To þe, Petyr, þat we xulde telle
    How Cryst is resyn þe which was slayn,
    A levynge man evyrmore to dwelle.

Maria Jacobi
    To lyve is resyn ageyn þat lorde
    The qwych Judas to Jewys solde;   1775
    Of þis I bere ryght trewe recorde
    By wurdys þat þe aungel tolde.
    Now myrth and joye to man on molde!
    Euery man now myrth may haue,
    He þat was closyd in cley ful colde   1780
f. 198   This day is resyn owt of his grave.

Petrus
    Sey me, systeryn, with wurdys blythe,
    May I troste to þat ʒe say?
    Is Cryst resyn ageyn to lyve
    Þat was ded and colde in clay?   1785
Maria Salome
    Ʒa, trostyth us truly, it is no nay;
    He is aresyn, it is no les.
    And so an aungel us tolde þis day
    With opyn voys and speche expres.

Johannes
    Ʒa, þese be tydyngys of ryght gret blys,   1790
    Þat oure mayster resyn xulde be.
    I wyl go renne in hast, iwys,
    And loke my lord yf I may se.

1766 sn Maria Magdalene] *omitted in MS.*   1769–81] *for marginal and textual additions and alterations see Appendix 5*   1776 trewe] *letter deleted before* trewe   1788–97] *for addition in left margin See Appendix 5*   1790 ʒa] be ʒ *deleted after* ʒa

Petrus
    For joye also I renne with the,
    My brothyr John, as I þe say.   1795
    In hast anon evyn forth go we,
    To his grave we renne oure way.

Hic currunt Johannes et Petrus simul ad sepulcrum, et Johannes
prius venit ad monumentum sed non intrat.

Johannes
    The same shete here I se
    Þat Crystys body was in wounde,
    But he is gon. Wheresoever he be   1800
    He lyth not here upon þis grownde.

Petrus intrat monumentum et dicit Petrus:

Petrus
    In þis cornere þe shete is fownde,
    And here we fynde þe sudary
f. 198v   In þe whiche his hed was wounde
    Whan he was take from Calvary.   1805

Hic intrat Johannes monumentum dicens:

Johannes
    The same sudary and þe same shete
    Here with my syth I se both tweyn.
    Now may I wele knowe and wete
    Þat he is rysyn to lyve ageyn.
    Onto oure bretheryn lete us go seyn   1810
    Þe trewth, ryght hevyn as it is:
    Oure mayster lyvyth þe whech was slayn,
    Allmyghty lorde and kynge of blys.

Petrus
    No lengere here wyll we dwelle,
    To oure bretheryn þe wey we take.   1815
    The trewth to them whan þat we telle
    Grett joye in hert þan wul þei make.
1805 Calvary] *another letter, ?u , altered to* –v–

Hic Petrus loquitur omnibus apostolis simul collectis.

Beth mery, bretheryn, for Crystys sake!
Þat man þat is oure mayster so good
From deth to lyve he is awake,   1820
Þat sore was rent upon þe rood.

Johannes
As women seyd so haue we fownde;
Remevyd awey we saw þe ston.
He lyth no lengere vndyr þe grownde,
Out of his graue oure mayster is gon.   1825
Omnes congregati Thomas
We haue grett woundyr everychon
Of þese wurdys þat ȝe do speke;
A ston ful hevy lay hym vpon,
From vndyr þat ston how xulde he breke?

Petrus
f. 199   The trewth to tellyn it passyth oure witt;   1830
Wethyr he be resyn thorwe his own myght
Or ellys stolyn out of his pitt
Be sum man prevély be nyght.
That he is gon we saw with syght,
For in his graue he is nowth;   1835
We cannot tellyn in what plyght
Out of his graue þat he is browth.

Maria Magdalene goth to þe graue and wepyth and seyth:

Maria Magdalene
For hertyly sorwe myn herte doth breke,
With wepynge terys I wasch my face.
Alas, for sorwe I may not speke!   1840
My lorde is gon þat hereinne wase,
Myn owyn dere lorde and kynge of gras
Þat sefne deuelys fro me dyd take.
I kannat se hym, alas, alas!
He is stolyn awey owt of þis lake.   1845

1838 sorwe] *letter blotted, -o- written above line*   1839–44] *large red numeral* 37 *in right margin*   1843 sefne] *MS.* vij   1844 kannat] se *deleted after* kannat

Aungelus
    Woman þat stondyst here alone,
    Why dost þu wepe and morne so sore?
    What cawse hast þu to make such mone?
    Why makyst þu such sorwe and wherefore?
Maria Magdalene
    I haue gret cawse to wepe evyrmore,   1850
    My lord is take out of his grave,
    Stolyn awey and fro me lore;
    I kannot wete where hym to haue.

Hic parum deambulet e sepulcro dicens:

    Alas, alas, what xal I do?
    My lord awey is fro me take.   1855
f. 199v   A, woful wrecche, whedyr xal I go?
    My joye is gon owth of þis lake.
Jhesus
    Woman, suche mornynge why dost þu make?
    Why is þi chere so hevy and badde?
    Why dost þu sythe so sore and qwake?   1860
    Why dost þu wepe so sore and sadde?

Maria Magdalene
    A grettyr cawse had nevyr woman
    For to wepe bothe nyth and day
    Than I myself haue, in serteyn,
    For to sorwyn evyr and ay.   1865

    Alas, for sorwe myn hert doth blede,
    My lorde is take fro me away.
    I muste nedys sore wepe and grede,
    Where he is put I kannot say.

    But, jentyl gardener, I pray to the,   1870
    If þu hym took out of his graue,
    Telle me qwere I may hym se,
    Þat I may go my lorde to haue.

1847 wepe and morne] and wepe *repeated after* morne   1865 For] & *deleted before*
For

Jhesus
    Maria!   *spectans*

Maria Magdalene
    A, mayster and lorde, to þe I crave   1875
    As þu art lord and kynge of blys,
    Graunt me, lord, and þu vowchesave,
    Thyn holy fete þat I may kys.

Jhesus
    Towche me not as ȝett, Mary!
    For to my Fadyr I haue not ascende;   1880
    But to my bretheryn in hast þe hyȝ,
    With these gode wurdys here care amende.
f. 200 Sey to my bretheryn þat I intende
    To stey to my Fadyr and to ȝowre;
    To oure Lord, both God and frende,   1885
    I wyl ascende to hevyn towre.

    In hevyn to ordeyn ȝow a place
    To my Fadyr now wyl I go;
    To merth and joye and grett solace,
    And endeles blys to brynge ȝow to.   1890
    For man I sufferyd both schame and wo,
    More spyteful deth nevyr man dyd take;
    Ȝit wyl I ordeyn for al this, lo,
    In hevyn an halle for mannys sake.

Maria Magdalyn
    Gracyous lord, at ȝour byddyng   1895
    To all my bretheryn I xal go telle
    How þat ȝe be man levynge,
    Quyk and qwethynge, of flesch and felle.
    Now all hevynes I may expelle,
    And myrth and joy now take to me;   1900
    My lord þat I haue louyd so wele,
    With opyn syght I dede hym se.

    Whan I sowght my lord in grave,
    I was ful sory and ryght sad,
    For syght of hym I myght non haue;   1905
    For mornynge sore I was nere mad.

1895 sn Maria Magdalyn] *very end of name lost at edge of leaf*   1906 For] *letter deleted after* For

Grettere sorwe ȝit nevyr whith had
Whan my lord awey was gon.

But now in herte I am so glad,
So grett a joy nevyr wyf had non.   1910

How myght I more gretter joye haue
Than se þat lorde with opyn syght,
The whiche, my sowle from synne to saue,
From develys sefne he mad me qwyght.

There kan no tounge my joye expres   1915
Now I haue seyn my lorde on lyve.
To my bretheryn I wyl me dresse
And telle to hem anon ryght belyve;
With opyn speche I xal me shryve
And telle to hem with wurdys pleyn,   1920
How þat Cryst from deth to lyve,
To endles blys is resyn ageyn.

Bretheryn, all blyth ȝe be!
For joyful tydyngys tellyn I kan.
I saw oure lord Cryst – lyste wel to me –   1925
Of flesch and bon, quyk levynge man.
Beth glad and joyful as for than
For trost me trewly it is ryght thus;
Mowth to mowth, þis [is] sertayn,
I spak ryght now with Cryst Jhesus.   1930

Petrus
A woundyrful tale, forsothe, is this!
Ever onowryd oure lord mote be!
We pray þe, lord and kynge of blys,
Onys þi presence þat we may se
Ere thu ascende to thi magesté.   1935
Gracyous God, if þat ȝe plese,
Late us haue sum syght of the
Oure careful hertys to sett in ease.
                                   Amen.

Explicit apparicio Marie Magdalene.

1923 blyth] *MS.* bllyth   1929 is] *omitted in MS.*   Final explicit] *very end of last*
word lost at edge of leaf

NOTES

The notes to the plays are intended to function in a number of ways. The first is to explain those passages where it seems to me that for some reason the text is obscure. The second is to provide a context of thought. This is a far less extensive element than in the *Mary Play* because of the greater narrative emphasis in the *Passion*. The third purpose is to demonstrate actual dependencies, where the playwright is basing his text closely on another work. The fourth purpose is to indicate the stage action of the play where this is not clear in the text; and the fifth briefly to indicate any liturgical associations. I have also occasionally drawn attention to the blending of pageant and play material, but the main discussion of this is contained in the Introduction and the Appendices.

For the short titles used in the notes, full bibliographical references will be found in the Bibliography.

The following abbreviations are used throughout:

EETS OS/ES	Early English Text Society Ordinary Series/ Extra Series
MED	*Middle English Dictionary*
OED	*Oxford English Dictionary*
PL	*Patrologia Latina*

PASSION PLAY I

1–164   The first part of the Passion opens with two prologues: one by Demon, who immediately identifies himself as Lucifer/Satan, and one by John the Baptist. The function of the first part of Lucifer's prologue is similar to that of many opening speeches in the cycle pageants, to give a narrative context to what follows. But it is presented from Lucifer's own viewpoint, where the history of the world is seen as his own struggle for power through the spreading of sin. Thus the story moves straight from his first failure in heaven to the signs of his coming failure, which he does not recognise as such, on earth. This also sets the scene for the conspiracy against Christ which follows, which is seen as part of Lucifer's machinations. He then turns his attention to demonstrating his power by wooing man, the audience, to sin.

John the Baptist picks up Lucifer's temptation of the audience (I. 129–32) but does not answer it directly. Instead he takes one of the main themes of the play, the coming of mercy, and shows the relation between sin and mercy: man cannot sin in the expectation of mercy, but on the other hand having sinned he must not despair of mercy. Lucifer's confident picture of sin leading to inevitable damnation is thus modified into a subtler and more hopeful view of man's sinfulness, looking forward to the new law of Christ. *Quia in inferno nulla est redempcio* (I. 48) will not in future be the only law.

1–3   The names Lucifer and Satan, though sometimes used for different devils, are here one and the same, as in *Cursor Mundi*, ll. 479–80, and Chaucer *Canterbury Tales* Monk's Tale ll. 2004–5.

Demon is '3*our* lord' (i.e. the audience's) because he is 'prince of þis werd' ('Princeps huius mundi', John xii, 31; xiv, 30).

6   As 'tower' is appropriate to the height of heaven, so 'dungeon' is to the depth of hell, and also to its function as the prison of mankind. For a depiction of the threefold division, heaven, earth and hell, see for example *Piers Plowman* B Prologue ll. 13–19.

7–8   The interweaving of attractive words ('reward') and terrifying prospects is characteristic of the wooing of man by personified sins and devils. The aim is didactic presentation of temptation, not naturalistic, though the two blend and interweave.

13–20   The fall of Lucifer and the rebel angels forms an almost inevitable part of the medieval re-telling of the story of mankind; providing an explanation for the creation of man, the existence of the serpent, and the temptation of Adam and Eve.

The nature of the angels and their fall is discussed by Augustine in *De Civitate Dei*, Bk. XI, 33; XII, 1–2, 6 and 9. Biblical sources for the war in heaven and the fall of Lucifer are Job iv, 18; Isaiah xiv, 12–15; Ezechiel xxviii, 1–2, 15, 17; Luke x, 18; II Peter ii, 4; Jude i, 6; Apocalypse xii, 7–9; *et al.*

16   Lucifer is always shown as the highest of the angels. *Berere of lyth* translates the name; cf. 'Lighteborne', Lucifer's companion in *Chester* I.

17   *in my tayle* 'after me' or 'in my retinue'. Perhaps there are overtones of 'arse'; cf. *Canterbury Tales* Summoner's Prologue ll. 1685–1706.

The whole phrase is curiously like that in the Book of John the Evangelist (James, pp. 187–93) found in use amongst the Albigensians but in existence elsewhere: 'and he drew with his tail the third part of the angels of God' (p.

189). I owe the reference to Miss Jane Dignum. The similarity is noted by Miriam J. Benkovitz in 'Some notes on the "Prologue of Demon" of *Ludus Coventriae*', *Modern Language Notes* 60 (1945) p. 81.

19 *tweyn aȝens on* 'two in exchange for one' or 'two set against one' (i.e. a third of the angels fell with him, or so he claims. He is after all the father of lies, John viii, 44).

20 It was commonly held that one order of angels out of the ten fell with Lucifer, that order being replaced by man; see *Towneley* I ll. 254–65. *Cursor Mundi* provides a somewhat different version, ll. 411–32, though the traditional one is referred to later (ll. 511–16).

22 *I gan þer do play* 'I performed there' or 'I caused to be performed there'. Though the precise meaning is not certain, it does not seem necessary to emend *do* to 'to' (as Bevington). *do* seems to be a loose usage of the auxiliary 'do'; perhaps confused with uses like *han . . . do sowth* (II. 123).

24 *þe fyrst day*. Presumably the first day *after* the creation was finished; see Genesis ii and iii.

27–32 See Matthew iv, 1–11; Mark i, 13; Luke iv, 1–13.

30 This is what the devil said at the time to tempt Christ: 'That he hath given his angels charge over thee, and in their hands shall they bear thee up, lest perhaps thou dash thy foot against a stone' (Matthew iv, 6, quoting Psalm xc, 11–12). Christ did not put it to the test, though according to Matthew angels ministered to him after the third temptation.

32 The temptations were usually linked with particular sins: gluttony (*York* XXII, l. 47, *Chester* XII, l. 173, *N. town* 23 [22], l. 106); vainglory (*York*, l. 93, *Chester*, l. 173, *N. town*, l. 144); and covetousness (*York*, l. 131, *Chester*, l. 174, *N. town*, l. 147). *Chester* makes use of the common link with the temptation of Adam: Adam fell, Christ withstood (*Chester*, ll. 169–216). See also Comestor, col. 1556; *Vita Christi* pp. 111–14; *Ministry and Passion* ll. 69–88; Mirk, pp. 83–4; *Stanzaic Life* pp. 177–9.

34–5 Cf. Luke x, 1 (though there said of the seventy-two disciples) and, less close, Mark vi, 7.

36–8 Lucifer very briefly runs through Christ's healing miracles which are mainly contained in Matthew xv, xvii and xx, Mark iii, v and vii–x, Luke i, v–viii and xviii, and John v and ix. Ll. 36–7 seem to reflect Matthew xv, 31. The raising of Lazarus, the culmination of the ministry, appears only in John (xi, 1–44).

40 Mary Magdalene is named in the gospels as the woman out of whom seven devils were cast (Mark xvi, 9; Luke viii, 2). She was also identified in the Middle Ages with the woman with the box of ointment (Matthew xxvi,

6–13; Mark xiv, 3–9; Luke vii, 37–50 and John xii, 1–8), who is furthermore said by John to be the sister of Lazarus (xi, 2). All are brought together in *Mary Magdalen* ll. 631–924. See also Appendix 2 and II. 1680–86.

The inconsistency of Mary's forgiveness being mentioned here before it has happened does not exist once the interpolated passage is removed (see Appendix 2, ll. 1–64).

41 'He claims to be God's son and born of a virgin'. Though in the gospels and in the plays, Christ frequently refers to his Father in heaven and could be said to claim to be God's son (e.g. Matthew xvi, 15–17 and especially John v, 17–47, and see below I. 421), the only reference to 'born of a virgin' is that in Matthew i, 23, quoting Isaiah vii, 14: 'Ecce virgo concipiet et pariet filium'.

45 Those in hell, i.e. all mankind except Enoch and Elijah. See for example *Middle English Sermons*, p. 171, and for Enoch and Elijah, *Chester* XXII, ll. 221–60.

48 'Because in hell there is no redemption'. *Þis tyxt of holde* is based on Job vii, 9, but derived immediately from Matins of the Office of the Dead (*Breviary* II, 278; *Horae* p. 107). It almost always appears in support of the Old Law, Justice or the devil; see for example *Piers Plowman* B XVIII l. 149; *Deuelis Perlament* (Hymns p. 50) l. 280. Satan in *York* XXXVII, attributing the text to Solomon as well as Job, uses two versions of it against Christ (ll. 281–8), and the Evil Angel in the *Castle of Perseverance* threatens Mankind's soul with it (*Castle* ll. 3095–6).

51–2 Lucifer presumably refers to the false witness brought against Christ; see below I. 536–42.

54 Computations of the wounds of Christ were often made in the Middle Ages; see for example Brown *Lyrics XV*, pp. 153 and notes on pp. 322–3; and also *Reynes, Commonplace Book* notes on pp. 369–72.

55 *countyrfe*. In view of the scribe's occasional tendency to omit final letters (e.g. at I. 182, 187, 190, 251 below) it is possible that Bevington is right to emend to *countyrfet*. This is not the scribe's normal spelling of the word, however, and a spelling of 'contrive' is equally possible. The reference is to Judas.

56 Revenge is a common motive for Lucifer's actions (see below I. 59). *gyf* is probably a *3 sg. pr.* without ending; see note to I. 197.

58 The proverb is a common one. Mercy uses it in *Mankind* (l. 750) in the form nearest to this one. Richard Hill, the London grocer, gives a Latin version in his commonplace book among 'Diwers good prowerbis': 'In whom I trust most, sonnest me deseyvith. In quo confido, leniter me decipit ipse' (p. 130). For further examples see Whiting T492.

61–2 Lucifer's cruelty in revenge is ironically juxtaposed with his wooing of mankind. His words are reminiscent of Christ's often repeated appeal to man: 'I loue þe, þenne loue me' (the form it takes in the poem *Wofully araide* (*Lyrics XV*, p. 157) l. 11), though the sentiments are reversed.

65–87   At l. 65 begins Lucifer's description of the extremes of contemporary fashion. The elements of costume which are satirised are very similar to those attacked in the late fourteenth century and right through the fifteenth; see Owst, pp. 404–11 and for general discussion Davenport 'Lusty fresche galaunts' in *Aspects of Early English Drama* ed. Paula Neuss. Many of the 'abuses' mentioned parallel items in the Statutes relating to Apparel (especially those of 1463/4, effective 1465), e.g. wearing of 'Sateyn' and 'Furre of Ermyn' by those below the rank of knight; the stuffing of the doublet with 'Wolle, Coton or Cadas'; wearing short gown, jacket or cloak which reveals 'his pryve Membres and Buttokkes'; restricting the length of 'pykes' on shoes to two inches; restricting the wearing of 'close Hoses' (*Statutes of the Realm*, II, pp. 399–402).

It has been suggested that Lucifer is himself dressed in the costume he describes. Lucifer in *Wisdom* appears first in 'dewyllys aray' and then as a 'prowde galonte' because, as he himself says,

> . . . for to tempte man in my lyknes,
> Yt wolde brynge hym to grett feerfullnes,
> I wyll change me into bryghtnes,
>   And so hym to-begyle,
> Sen I xall schew hym perfyghtnes,
> And wertu prove yt wykkydnes;
> Thus wndyr colors all thynge perverse;
> I xall neuer rest tyll þe Soule I defyle.   (ll. 373–80)

Despite the similarity of aim, however, Lucifer in the *Passion Play* is making no attempt to conceal his devilish nature from the audience (the Lucifer in *Wisdom* is tempting characters in the play) and it is likely that he appears as devil throughout.

my dysgysyd varyauns may well mean costume characteristic of the servants of the devil and that he is describing an 'ideal'; i.e. 'Observe the variety of my fashionably-dressed, diverse (adherents)' (I. 65). Certainly the brief description of female dress at l. 101–6 is of this kind. Lucifer may have made use of members of the audience for examples. The description of Pryde in Medwall's *Nature* (I, ll. 739–78) forms quite a close parallel to this passage.

66–7   'Everything arranged naturally and appropriately, and each part matching its counterpart'. Lucifer pretends to see the extremities of fashion that follow as clothing appropriate and natural to the form and shape of man (cf. *of proporcyon*, I. 78 below).

69   The proud priests in Piers Plowman wear 'pyked' shoes (B XX l. 218) and they are mentioned as articles of pride in the confession section of

Myrc's *Instructions for Parish Priests* (l. 1033). The satire is an old one, but still alive in the late fifteenth century; see note to I. 65–87 above.

70–2   Broadly speaking there are two kinds of hose in the late fifteenth century, those made as two separate stockings and those joined at the crutch and covering the buttocks. *hosyn enclosyd* would be the latter (see 'close Hoses' in note to I. 65–87 above); the more expensive, more showy and better-class style. Hose of both kinds were held up at the waist by attaching to a short, tough jacket (*dobbelet*) by a number of laces (*poyntys*) with tags (*aglottys*) for threading the laces through the holes in the doublet. Twenty-four silver-tagged laces would make a considerable show; see Cunnington, pp. 108–9, and, for late-fifteenth century men's fashions in general, pp. 134–52, and Kelly and Schwabe, I, pp. 39–42.

73   The shirt was an undergarment, parts of which were allowed to show at neck and sleeves. *holond* is linen-cloth originally from the Netherlands province of Holland, frequently used for shirts.

74   *stomachere* is a decorative piece of material worn across the chest over the shirt (Cunnington, pp. 135 and 139); *reynes* is a fine linen-cloth from Rennes in northern France.

75   'Though you are poor, let pride have its way'.

77–8   The doublet was frequently padded out to produce a quite disproportionate upper half to the body, as described in I. 79–80 (see note to I. 65–87 above).

80   *to an* . . . 'so that you are in [lit. 'have'] . . .'

81   The gown, the outermost garment, was usually open down the front and often long, though the three yards of material could be used in a costly fashion to make a short gown as Pride's is:

> Than have I suche a short gown
> Wyth wyde sleves that hang adown –
> They wold make some lad in thys town
> A doublet and a cote.   (*Nature* I, ll. 767–70)

Three yards of material is clearly intended to sound excessive, but Cornelius' gown in *Fulgens and Lucres* is made from seven (I, ll. 740–2).

81–2   'Make sure you always set out to emulate those who are above you in rank'. The Statutes of Apparel tried to restrict certain types of dress to certain ranks as well as attempting to curb excessive fashions; see note to I, 65–87 above.

83   The dagger was also a fashionable accoutrement, though I. 91 shows that it was not purely for decoration; cf. Medwall's Pryde (*Nature* I, ll. 773–8).

85–6 Long hair became fashionable again in the later fifteenth century. Medwall's Pryde has 'syde here' hanging six inches below his ears (*Nature* I, ll. 755–8). Both versions of I. 85 make the same point. The first reference for 'side locks' in the *OED* is 1848 (*Vanity Fair*), for 'side hair' 1861 (*Great Expectations*); s.v. **Side** *sb.¹* V 23b. The latest *OED* Supplement gives an earlier quotation for **side-locks** in a somewhat different sense (Randle Holme, 1688); s.v. **side** *sb.¹* V 27. It is likely, however, that it is **Side** *a.* (see sense 3b 'long') that is being used here and in Medwall, and perhaps also in Randle Holme.

None of the explanations of MS. *j schrewe* seems to me very satisfactory (Bevington 'I swear'; Happé 'I curse'; Davies 'I curse (?)'), but I can only offer further suggestions: *i-schrewe* (imperative) (a) in the sense of 'disfigure' (s.v. *OED* **Shrew** *v.* 2), or (less likely) (b) 'adorn' a form of **shroud** (s.v. *OED* **Shroud** *v¹.* 1b). For comments on the *i-* prefix see the note to *Mary Play* l. 1430.

87 'A tall narrow hat for covering the top of your head'.

89 'Take your pleasure in the great oaths and in lechery'.

91–2 Taking the law into their own hands by getting together a gang of thugs was a not uncommon feature of fifteenth-century life among some of the gentry; see H. S. Bennett, *The Pastons and their England* (C.U.P., 1922) pp. 180–92. Here again the follower of Lucifer is being encouraged to imitate the upper classes. See also the advice given by the devil in *A Dispute between a Good Man and the Devil* (*Minor Poems*, I, pp. 338–9) ll. 382–91.

94 *sevyle and canoun.* Probably adjectives used as nouns, 'secular and ecclesiastical law', but possibly adjectives governing *precept* and *comawndement* in the previous line.

95 The idea that oaths by parts of Christ's body renewed his passion was a common one; see for example Owst pp. 420–1; *Canterbury Tales* Pardoner's Tale ll. 472–5 and 708–9; *Chester* XXIV ll. 417–20; and also Woolf *Lyrics* Appendix G, pp. 395–400. It appears in pictorial form in the wall painting at Broughton, Buckinghamshire (reproduced in Woodforde *The Norwich School of Glass-painting in the Fifteenth Century* (London 1950) plate XLI, and see ch. 7).

101–8 Having described the over-dressed man, Lucifer now turns to the woman, often in similar terms – imitation of the gentry, overspending – but developing a connection with lechery.

101–4 'A beggar's daughter, making a great effort to imitate a gentlewoman, dressed as well as she can manage; and if she hasn't enough money, this is the new trick, through her secret pleasures to get it from some man.'

105 The v-shaped collar edged with fur, derived from Burgundy, was

common in England from early to late fifteenth century; for details of female
costume see Cunnington, pp. 153–68 and Kelly and Schwabe I, pp. 42–5.

106   'A sign under which to sell lechery . . .'

107–8   'And those that won't pay, will still have enough; and [she'll] tell
them it's for love – she can't refuse it.'

109   Concealing the vices under new, viirtuous, names is a common
enough device. It occurs, for example, in *Speculum Christiani* (p. 232):

> Dissolucion in felyschipe is trowede myrth. Curyosite of clothynge and
> of othere temperal thynges is taken for honeste. Couetyse is called true
> puruyance of purchacynge. Wast ouerspens is called largys and fredam of
> hert, and so of other vices, *et cetera*.

Of the theatrical uses of the device Medwall's *Nature* comes nearest to this
one though only Wrath/Manhood have the same names (I, ll. 1200–31).
Veronica O'Mara, University of Leeds, has drawn my attention to a sermon
in Sidney Sussex College, Cambridge, MS. 74, containing a series of
equivalences similar in some ways to those in the play (f. 205v): 'pride of
aray or cloþing'/'honeste', 'lecherie'/'doyng of kynde', 'coveitise'/'wysdam
a man to helpen hymself'.

114   'At all assizes and [judicial] sessions, let perjury be in charge'.

115   Either 'Let Gluttony remain and abstinence be absent', or, less likely,
'Gluttony [called] relaxation; let Abstinence be absent'. It depends whether
Lucifer's list of sins concludes with Envy or breaks and picks up again with
Gluttony. 'Rest' is not an obvious new name for 'Gluttony'.

116   'And mock him who tries to make you virtuous'.

118   *eneryth þe dyvicyon eternal* 'be for ever set apart from God'.

119   'Though Christ cleverly try many ruses'.

121   'Remember [all this, you], our servants, whose souls are mortal'. For
alternative explanations see Davies (p. 239) and Bevington (p. 485). Another
problem is the word *mortall*. No soul is mortal (i.e. subject to death) so
presumably the idea is 'souls which are affected/threatened by the death of
the body'; or it is an error for 'immortall' (cf. *fynyte* for *infynyte*, *Mary Play* l.
705).

123   Perhaps reminiscent of Christ's words, 'For where there are two or
three gathered together in my name, there am I in the midst of them'
(Matthew xviii, 20).

125   The opening of John the Baptist's prologue is made up of translated
excerpts from John's words from the gospels expanded with traditional
teaching.

126–8   Cf. Mark i, 7, 'There cometh after me one mightier than I, the latchet of whose shoes I am not worthy to stoop down and loose', and Luke iii, 16 'but there shall come one mightier than I, the latchet of whose shoes I am not worthy to loose'.

129   The MS. reading *I councel þe ȝe reforme all wronge* may be correct in view of *Mary Play* l. 1396, but there the change is from formal to informal addressing a single person, not from singular to plural in addressing a crowd. See, however, the change at l. 149–56 below.

131–2   Cf. Matthew iii, 2, 'Do penance: for the kingdom of heaven is at hand'.

133–7   Based on the quotation from Isaiah xl, 3, 'Prepare ye the way of the Lord, make straight in the wilderness the paths of our God' (which in an adapted form is connected with John the Baptist in Matthew, Mark and Luke and quoted by him in John) and on Isaiah xxx, 21, 'And thy ears shall hear the word of one admonishing thee behind thy back: This is the way, walk ye in it: and go not aside neither to the right hand, nor to the left'.

136   'Keeping straight on;'.

142–3   The danger of over-confidence in God's mercy on the one hand and of despair of it on the other was a frequent topic of teaching; see *Religious Pieces* pp. 10–11 and *Lay Folk's Catechism* pp. 78–81 (especially the Latin on p. 78); *Canterbury Tales* Parson's Tale ll. 693–705; *Speculum Christiani* pairs 'ouerhope' and 'wanhope' p. 80, and see also pp. 100 and 112–15. *Jacob's Well* uses Isaiah xxx, 21 for a moralisation about keeping to the middle way, but not in relation to presumption and despair (pp. 258–9).

149–56   The change between singular and plural pronouns here is more explicable and less abrupt than in l. 129. The first line of the stanza continues the general statement from the previous stanza, the rest of the stanza elaborates and develops it in a preciser (? a more intimate) way. These are presumably the *Grete cawsys* of l. 147.

158   'joined in unity'.

164sd   This is the only use of the word 'stage' as opposed to 'scaffold' in the plays.

of/after þe hoold lawe seems to mean dressed in the manner described in the Old Testament (Exodus xxviii, 4–42; xxxix, 1–30; see also Exodus xxix, 5–9, and Leviticus viii, 7–9 and 13) which is clearly open to a wide variety of interpretation. There is an almost archaeologically reconstructed version in the *Nuremburg Chronicle* f. 33 (see Elisabeth Rucker, *Die Schedelsche Weltchronik* (Munich, 1973) and Meg Twycross 'Apparell comlye' in *Aspects* pp. 44–5) and a somewhat differently imagined representation in a Flemish narrative painting of Joachim and Anne in the Musée St. Sauveur, Bruges (reproduced in Adey Horton, *The Child Jesus* (New York, 1975) pl. 92). Cf. also the description of Aaron in the Lucerne Easter play *Staging of Religious Drama*, p. 135.

The costume described here suggests something fairly loosely envisaged as a red robe with a blue furred tabard over it and one of the variety of 'non-contemporary' mitres – e.g. one worn sideways on, a 'beehive-shaped' one, a soft squarish one, one with side lappets. For some illustrations of the variety, see: Mayo (1984) pl. 13; Rushforth (1936) figs. 39, 138, 140, 160, 164; *Biblia Pauperum* pp. 97 and 116 (Aaron); Cave pl. 191; *Child Jesus* pll. 17, 20, 26, 31, 32; *Golden Age* pl. 34B; Meiss pll. 342, 573, 777, 863.

skarlet can refer to the richness of the cloth, but at this date and in view of the emphasis on colour elsewhere in the description it seems more likely that it means 'bright red' (see *MED* **scarlet** *n.* and *adj.*).

There are on the scaffold Annas, two doctors of the law, the messenger and an unnamed official (? Gamaliel) carrying his own or Annas' staff of office. The messenger is dressed as a Saracen (see Twycross, *Aspects* p. 46). The *gret knop* on the furred caps was characteristic of representations of Jewish costume; see for a variety of Jewish hats with 'knops' the *Offering of the Jews* in Albert Châtelet, *Early Dutch Painting* (Oxford, 1981) pl. 76, especially the figure to the right of the altar.

165–6 'As a bishop I am appointed specifically to ensure peace, and [as] judge of the Jews to maintain the law'.

167–8 Probably a construction with omitted relative: 'I . . . shall command [that] no men . . .'

169 'Immediately make known to me any who . . .'

172 'And especially I must maintain our laws'. The emphasis in Annas' speech on the law prepares the way for the complaints against Christ and also makes use of the traditional opposition of the Old Law of justice and the New Law of mercy symbolised by Christ. Cf. the use of this opposition in the N. town *Woman Taken in Adultery* (Block, pp. 200–9).

178–80 Despite the fact that Christ emphasised that he came to fulfil the law of the Old Testament (Matthew v, 17) and that the Ten Commandments were one of the bases of his teaching, the Old Law, the Laws of Moses and the Synagogue together, are frequently used in the Middle Ages to symbolise the rigour of justice without mercy, and therefore of harshness, cruelty and even injustice.

184 The Jews, at the time being under Roman rule, frequently make use of an imagined danger to Caesar's law as well as their own, especially in order to provoke Pilate to action. Cf. John xix, 12 and below ll. 310–13.

194–5 Rewfyn and Leyon though referred to as Pharisees (l. 223 and 288sd) are primarily presented as the secular counterparts of Annas and

Caiaphas – the laws civil and canon. The development from those who closely observe the Jewish law, the Pharisees, to legal officials is an easy one. In *Cursor Mundi* the Pharisees are called 'maisters o þat lau' (l. 13577–8).

The names are not biblical. Ruffyn is one of the devils mentioned in *Chester* I, l. 260, and it is commonly used elsewhere in the same way (*OED* sv. **Ruffin**).

195–6 '. . . who, with Caiaphas your cousin, know the way to put this matter right'.

196 Annas was Caiaphas' father-in-law (John xviii, 13) and so *cosyn* is loosely appropriate (*MED* s.v. **cosin(e)**).

197 *revyfe*. An example of a 3rd present singular verb without ending. Davis (*Non-Cycle Plays* p. xxxix) notes a number of these in the B text of the Norwich Grocers' pageant. See also *perverte* 218, *present* 295, *werke* 322 and 325, *ete* 518sd, *ete*, *drynke* 821, and probably *gyf* 56, *come* II sd I.

199 Arfexe is the Saracen messenger. The name may derive from *Arphaxat* (one of Pilate's knights; see II. 1225) which appears in the Ashmole poem on the Resurrection as 'Arfax' (see note to II. 1224–6). The English plays name minor characters far less often than the continental plays do. See, for example, the lists at the end of Mons *Le Livre de Conduite* (pp. 619–31) or Lucerne (*Staging of Religious Drama* pp. 300–1).

208sd Caiaphas is dressed identically with Annas except that over his scarlet gown he wears a red tabard rather than a blue one. *aftyr þe old gyse* could mean the same as *after þe hoold lawe* (I. 164sd), but it is difficult to be sure what a doctor's robe or gown of the Old Law would look like. It could on the other hand simply mean 'not contemporary'. The *furryd cappys* are presumably similar in style to those of Annas' doctors (see I. 164sd and note).

209–10 '. . . I represent here in person bishops of the law with all due ceremony', taking *sensyble* (as Bevington does) to mean 'apparent to your eyes'.

211–12 'I, Caiaphas, am a judge [endowed] with powers capable of removing all errors that create discord in our laws'.

214 'And all possible subjects [of importance] are evident to me'.

216 'My decision on what is right or wrong is final'.

217 A preposition appears to be missing, but which is not clear. 'Of, from, in' would all give good sense. In view of the somewhat parallel I. 212, I have used 'in' with the meaning 'who is inconstant in [following] our laws' or perhaps 'creates discord in our laws'. 'Of' or 'from' would give a meaning 'divergent' for *varyable*.

219   'We must seek a way to bring him into disrepute'.

223   *jewgys of Pharasy*, perhaps 'judges of the Pharisaic sect' but more probably a reference simply to their legal status.

224   *procede be prossesse* 'continue in the same way'.

229   *ageyns all kende* 'against the course of nature'.

230 and 240   *hem*. The first example could be plural referring to the *meraclis* or singular referring to Christ. The second example must refer to Christ; cf. II. 1237.

244   'He shall not escape from my grasp'.

244sd   *in þe mene tyme*. This is the first indication in the stage directions of the overlapping actions which are an important part of the stagecraft of the Passion Play; see Introduction pp. 26, 29–30 and Eleanor Prosser, *Drama and Religion in the English Mystery Plays* (Stanford, 1961) pp. 119ff. It is also the first mention of the 'place' or *platea*.

   tabardys in the case of Annas and Caiaphas may refer to one of the Old Testament liturgical garments; for Rewfyn and Leyon they are presumably simple tabards, unless they represent a garment associated with doctors of the law. *ray* is a striped material, according to Stella Mary Newton associated with Jews and orientals (*Renaissance Theatre Costume* (London, 1975) p. 139). That it also had a connection with the dress of officials of the law courts is clear from the contemporary illustrations of the courts (published in *Archaeologia* 39, pp. 358–60 and 362) now in the library of the Inner Temple and dating probably from the reign of Edward IV. The Courts of Chancery, King's Bench, Common Pleas and the Exchequer are all shown and each contains officials in garments of 'ray', ranging from ushers and sergeants to the King's coroner and the Masters of the Court. No judges wear 'ray' garments. It is this legal association that clearly lies behind the use of *ray tabardys* and *hodys* for Rewfyn and Leyon. I am most grateful to Theodore de Welles, formerly of Records of Early English Drama, Toronto, for drawing my attention to these illustrations. Ray garments in association with civic officials can be seen in the illustration of the 'mayor-making ceremony' in Ricart's Calendar (1479) in the Bristol Record Office (*The Maire of Bristowe is Kalendar by Robert Ricart*, ed. Lucy Toulmin Smith, Camden Society, ns 5, 1872, frontispiece).

256sd   On Rewfyn and Leyon as 'judges' see note to I. 194–5.

267   *delacyon*. Block has *declaracion*; Bevington reads (correctly) *delacion*. Is Leyon deliberately mocking the messenger's rather pompous word?

275   *se ȝour presens* 'attend you', see also I. 260 and 265.

288sd   *here clerkys* i.e. the doctors of Annas and Caiaphas; *Pharaseus* i.e. Rewfyn and Leyon.

The position of the *oratory/cownsel hous* is not clear. A necessary preposition has been mistakenly written with the abbreviation for 'and'. This could most easily be a mistake for an abbreviated 'in', but it is also possible that 'at', 'by', or 'near' were intended. Even if *in* is right there is no certainty that the oratory into which they then go is in the middle of the *platea*. It could refer to the *myd place* in a row of scaffolds, or to the meeting point alone and not to the position of the *oratory*.

The oratory itself is set out with stools and cushions as a council house would have been for a meeting. Is the writer thinking of the use of chapels like St Stephen's at Westminster or St William's chapel at York?

294 '... that some call God's son'.

295 Either 'He performs miracles and then claims ...', with *present* as a third person singular verb without ending (see note to I. 197 above); or 'He performs miracles and says in this place/now ...', with *sythe* as a misreading by the scribe of 'seythe' (as Block suggests s.v. *sythe* in Glossary p. 399), but *seyth* is not elsewhere spelt with final -*e*. The meaning is little affected.

298 The *prevy menys* are presumably the (implied) underhand methods by which Christ wins people over. Though it could mean that people go over secretly or that the Jews find out by secret methods, these seem less likely in a context where the Jews suggest no secrecy about the conversions.

301 *þis*. Block reads 'þus' and comments 'perhaps corrected to *þis*' (p. 235).

304 'I cannot consider him [to be] without guilt', or 'I cannot sentence him without [proof of] wrongdoing'. If the latter, what follows is a very sudden but theatrically not impossible conviction on Caiaphas' part.

309 *eretyk* and *tretour* – in the fifteenth century in England both capital offences, one religious and one secular. The statute of Heresy (*De heretico comburendo*), by which heresy could be punished by death, was passed in 1401 (*Statutes of the Realm*, II, pp. 125–8).

313–14 'The reason why we are here [is] to maintain the law and to speak the truth'.

328 *Pan* '[If you do,] then'. Cf. I. 525 below.

333–40 Caiaphas, Rewfyn, Leyon and all the doctors condemn Christ out of hand, only Annas maintains a semblance of justice in advising the seeking of evidence.

334 It is possible that Annas suggests *nine* days because of the fading of a nine days' wonder (cf. Chaucer *Troilus and Criseyde* IV, 588 and Whiting W555); but nine is a common mystical and arbitrary number.

342sn The speaker cannot logically (or grammatically, *we all*) be Annas, as it is he who has just propounded the scheme. It seems most likely to belong to all the others.

342 After the departure of the Jews the curtains of the oratory are apparently drawn to (see I. 518sd).

342sd This section (to I. 348) is deleted in the manuscript and recopied on f. 143v with slight variations. The text here gives the reading of f. 142v with corrections from f. 143v. For the passage omitted here see Appendix 1.
  enteryth, presumably into the 'place'.

343–6 Peter's words take up the promise of Christ's coming contained in John the Baptist's prologue, though the emphasis is now more strongly on mercy.

352 See I. 141–62 if the reference is within the play. John discussed 'walking' in terms of balancing hope in God's mercy with fear of his judgment. Peter shifts the emphasis to the love of God and neighbour (I. 359–66). Both are paths that lead to salvation.

353 The idea of Christ as a healer or physician is a common one, drawn ultimately from the healing miracles of the gospels; see also *Vita Christi* pp. 140 (quoting Chrysostom) and 680.

352–7 *prophecyed/applyed/deny it/aspyed*. The rhymes clearly depend upon the pronunciation of the final unstressed syllable of *prophecyed* and *aspyed* as '-it'. The alterations in I. 355 (see Textual notes) are a result of the scribe removing a similar form there. *3e* has been overwritten *it*; *be* added above the line, and *deny it* altered to *deny=id*. The lines now read:

> Wherefore what he comawndyth loke 3e applyed
> Þat som of 3ow be blynd, it may not be deny=id

The scribe appears to have disliked or found suspect this kind of rhyme; see 'Reconsideration' pp. 42–6 for similar changes made in the *Assumption of the Virgin* later in the manuscript. A similar rhyme 'leyt/seyt' ('laid/say it') appears in the Reynes Nine Worthies piece (ll. 3/4, p. 236).

356 Cf. John i, 10. The blind, the deaf and the dumb are given a moral interpretation in *Middle English Sermons*, pp. 146–8; the dumb alone in Mirc p. 96. See also *Vita Christi* pp. 243–4.

358 'I ought to call you deaf as regards spiritual hearing'.

361–6 The image of the single foot of love occurs in Augustine's commentary on Psalm 9, v. 16 (I. p. 83), in *Middle English Sermons* p. 77, and briefly in *Jacob's Well* p. 126. In his commentary on Psalm 33 (v. 6), however, Augustine says: 'Thy feet are thy charity. Have two feet, be not lame. What are thy two feet? The two commandments of love, of thy God, and of thy Neighbour. With these feet run thou unto thy God . . .' (I. p. 361). The two loves are a commonplace deriving from Matthew xxii, 37–40; see *Mary Play* ll. 453–68 and note. Bede relates the feet of the Passover to the two loves (see below note to I. 735).

362   'Which should bear up the spiritual and most important side of man'.

367–70   Cf. Mirc p. 96 for the linking of dumbness and lack of confession. The emphasis on 'oral' confession, *be mowthe*, may be a reaction against Lollard suspicion of it (Hudson, pp. 19 and 146).

373   The commonplace image of the physician is nicely sharpened into reality through the reference to payment.

374   As Christ says in the N. town *Woman Taken in Adultery* (ll. 19–20):

> Man, I cam down all for þi loue,
> Loue me ageyn, I aske no more.   (Block, p. 201)

383–4   Zacharias ix, 9. All the evangelists describe the Entry into Jerusalem; Matthew (xxi, 5) and John (xii, 15) quote the prophecy. The moral interpretation which follows is a common one; see, for example, *Meditationes* p. 594, *Vita Christi* p. 490. The idea of meekness is specifically introduced by Matthew ('mansuetus'). It is not in Zacharias which has 'poor' ('pauper'). For further comment, see Appendix 1.

398   Christ entered traditionally by the Golden Gate (see Fabri I, 458–9). Only the direction from which he came appears in the gospels.

386–90   John's words pick up Demon's opening speech which is largely concerned with Pride.

395–8   Peter and John are apparently pictured inside the city and therefore act as a spatial link between the conspiracy scenes and the entry of Christ. They also prepare for Christ's appearance by announcing his message of mercy in advance. Without the episode of the ass (see Appendix 1) the action is considerably tightened and swifter moving and Christ's first appearance, by being delayed, is made that much more exciting.

398sd   *here entrith þe fyrst prophete* is added in the margin to the left of the stage direction. The addition indicates an adaptation of this section which instead of leaning towards naturalism, as the play does, introduces the ritual element of a Palm Sunday procession or a typical civic entry. The citizens do already see the entry of Christ in terms of a royal entry into the city (see I. 401–2) but the penitential costume deliberately contrasts with the pomp of such a worldly affair (see I. 406sd). For the Palm Sunday procession see Young I, 90–8, and for the preparations for a civic entry see REED *York* pp. 137–43, 145–52 (1486) and REED *Coventry* pp. 89–91 (1498).

406sd   The citizens spread their clothes for Christ to step down onto, not for the procession to walk over as is usually shown. Pilate's messenger in the *Gospel of Nicodemus* does the same (ch. 1) relating it to the Entry.

407–14   The first two lines are a near-translation of *Benedictus qui venit in nomine Domini* used as part of an antiphon of the Palm Sunday service (*Missal*

258; from Mark xi, 9; cf. Matthew xxi, 9 and Luke xix, 38). The adaptation thereafter is not close to the gospels but is turned towards the dominant idea of mercy, to lead into Christ's first words.

410sd. None of the gospels mentions flowers but they are a part of the Palm Sunday service (*Missal* 253, 255 and 257). The processional movement around the place to meet different groups is made possible by the place and scaffold staging.

    Gloria laus is a processional hymn for Palm Sunday. In the Sarum Processional (f. 46) the first verse is sung at the second station by seven boys in some high place; the choir repeating it after each subsequent verse. This is the 'gerlis' and '*Gloria laus*' of *Piers Plowman* B XVIII l.7.

411sn The absent speaker's name could be one of the children or one of the citizens. If *beforn on seyth* means 'one in front' then it is a child, if it means 'before these actions take place', then probably one of the citizens.

414–15 If the speech at l. 411 follows the singing of *Gloria laus*, the cry for mercy directly introduces Christ's opening words. It may however have been divided from them by the hymn (see previous note).

    Immediately below l. 414, at the foot of f. 145, is the addition *here entreth þe parte off the ij^{de} prophete*. For the significance of this see the note to 398sd above. The phrase *entreth þe parte* seems odd; *entreth* implies a human actor, *parte* a role. *MED* gives no evidence for a specific meaning like 'character' though 'role, office, duty' in general terms appear. In the Sarum Palm Sunday procession there are two prophecies (Young, I p. 93).

415 Christ's first words emphasise the new law of mercy; cf. 2 Corinthians vi, 2. This line and the three following were borrowed to introduce the added section on f. 143 (see Appendix 1).

418 Cf. John xii, 31.

420 *shewyd experyence* 'demonstrated'; Bevington emends to 'shewyd [by] experience'.

423–4 'The greatest of truths shall now be tested and a perfect harmony between God and man'. Christ presumably refers to the final testing of the bond between God and man which will be created by his own death; cf. Lucifer's words at l. 43–4.

427–34 Cf. Matthew xx, 30–1 and Luke xviii, 35–43. The belief of both blind men in Christ is made apparent as it is in Matthew ix, 27–30 and Luke xviii, 42.

428 The context does not demand the meaning 'most' for *must*, but it seems more appropriate.

435 Cf. Luke xviii, 42.

436   *mortal* ?'physical', ?'of this world'. Or is *mortal peyn* 'damnation'?

437–8   John xx, 29 – an ingenious application of Christ's words to Thomas.

442sd   Again the movement of characters in the place is emphasised by the stage directions.

443–58   Only Luke (xix, 41–4) records Christ's weeping over Jerusalem, though his words here bear little relation to the gospel or to other works which record this episode. *York* XXV (ll. 470–81) derives mainly from Luke with the added explanation that the destruction of Jerusalem is a result of the crucifixion; *Chester* XIV (ll. 209–24), like *York*, depends on Luke but attributes the destruction to the Jews not receiving Christ (derived from Luke xix, 44). See also *Vita Christi* pp. 494–6 and *Blickling Homilies* pp. 76–9. The prophecy was always related to the destruction of Jerusalem by Vespasian and Titus (as was that in Matthew xxiii, 34–9) and details in Christ's speech here – the vengeance of God, the failure of food supplies – relate to that. The ultimate source is the siege and destruction of Jerusalem in Josephus, *Wars of the Jews*.

447–8   The transition from MS. *3e* (l. 447) to *þei* (l. 448) is very awkward but it may be intentional and I have allowed it to stand. Cf. I. 539–40 where the transition is natural.

458   Rounds off the speech by repeating the first line with variation.

459–74   Cf. Mark xiv, 12–16; Luke xxii, 8–13; and, less close, Matthew xxvi, 17–19. I. 473–4, which are not in the gospel accounts, are reminiscent of the assurance Christ gives at the fetching of the ass (Matthew xxi, 3 and Mark xi, 3). Only Luke names the two disciples as Peter and John.

459   The word *maundé* is here used for the Passover feast. It derives from 'Mandatum (novum)' the first word of the first antiphon sung at the washing of feet on the Thursday before Easter (Maundy Thursday; 'In Coena Domini', *Missal* 311). It was used for that ceremony and then generalised to the whole service and hence to the Last Supper.

459–66   The disciples' eagerness to serve Christ is underlined by the running-together of their speeches (cf. I. 475–8).

478sd   The meal at the house of Simon the Leper (Matthew xxvi, 6–13 and Mark xiv, 3–9) is blended with the Last Supper to the extent that Simon becomes the servant bearing the pitcher of water (Mark xiv, 13 and Luke xxii, 10). The account in the *Metrical Life* also blends the two episodes, including the box of ointment incident (ll. 1938–69). In the additions to the *Passion Play* the two episodes are more fully blended (see Appendix 2).

494sd   The scaffold of Simon's house may remain 'closed' (i.e. the curtain drawn to) until I. 662sd.

495   *cald Syon* MS. *calsydon*. The house of the Last Supper was traditionally placed on Mount Sion (see Fabri I, pp. 289–91, 308–9). As Christ and his disciples were therefore on the way to Sion, and since nothing has so far been found to relate the path to the stone 'chalcedony', it seems reasonable to emend, as Bevington has done, to *cald Syon*. There is no other instance of a form of the word 'call' with single 'l' in the *Mary Play* or *Passion Plays*, but the form exists elsewhere in the manuscript (see, for example, Block p. 169, l. 21). Halliwell and Happé divide it as *cal Sydon* but there seems no obvious reason for a mention of 'Sydon' here. For further discussion see 'Reconsideration' pp. 40–2.

  be goostly ordenawns 'by spiritual design'. The playwright is perhaps here making use of some of the meanings of Sion to add further to the significance of Christ's speech – Sion (the church) shall convey us to Sion (heaven), see 'Reconsideration' pp. 41–2.

499   *Contewnyng in pees* 'continuing in harmony'. Bevington emends to *contenwing* but *contunen* is an occasional variant of *continuen* (*MED*, s.v.).

502   Cf. *Mary Play* l. 1212. This is the first (oblique) reference to Christ's coming death.

515   'There the greatest of all joys is ensured for you', perhaps the blessing brought upon the house by the taking of the Last Supper there. Possibly an echo of Christ's words on entering Zaccheus' house (Luke xix, 9). Bevington places l. 515 after l. 518 but there seems no need. Cf. Christ's more extended greeting to Simon in *Mary Magdalen* ll. 619–25.

518sd. *ete*. Christ 'enters' and 'eats' the Paschal lamb. The form *ete* is either a form of 'eateth' (see note to l. 197), or an infinitive with the scribe once again writing a Tironian nota for a preposition (here 'to').

  This is one of the most striking uses of juxtaposition of two actions: the joy and peace of the Last Supper set against the anger and confusion of the conspiracy. The use of curtaining is shown in *sodeynly onclose*. Annas is reporting on the failure of their previous plan, see l. 333–40. He is also responding to the scene of Christ's entry which has just concluded. The various agents of the conspiracy must have been returning to the closed scaffold towards the end of the previous episode.

525   In *Than* is implied 'if we do that then'. Cf. l. 328 above.

526–7   Cf. John xi, 48. The implication here differs slightly from that in John, in that the conversion of all to Christ is seen here as a result of the Romans taking over rather than a cause.

528   *here* i.e. 'the people's'.

532–4   John xi, 50 and xviii, 14. *Cursor Mundi* draws attention to the irony of the remark, Christ's death is indeed necessary to save all people (ll.

14526–31), and the dramatic Palm Sunday 'sermon' draws attention to Caiaphas' unwitting prophesying, see Carleton Brown, 'Caiaphas as a Palm-Sunday Prophet', in *Anniversary Papers by Colleagues and Pupils of George Lyman Kittredge* (Boston, Mass., 1913) pp. 105–17.

536   This is the first mention of the false witness which is to be brought against Christ since the Demon's prologue, I. 51–2.

543sn   *Gamalyel* is named here for the first time (see note to I. 164sd). A Gamaliel is one of the list of leaders of the Jews in *Gospel of Nicodemus* (ch. 1); and one is named as a Pharisee in Acts v, 34, and as Paul's teacher in Acts xxii, 3.

556   According to the gospels Jesus had not claimed to be king. As recorded by John he fled when the people wished to make him king (vi, 15). See, however, Matthew ii, 2, xxi, 5; Luke xix, 38–40; John i, 49–50, xii, 13 and 15.

561–2   See Matthew xxvi, 61, and cf. John ii, 19–21 where it is explained as referring to his own body.

563   MS. *conseyve* removes the rhyme and Block (p. 246) suggests *constreyn* which gives good sense.

565–6   This is certainly implied in many of Christ's sayings, e.g. Matthew xix, 28. Cf. Symon's words to Christ at I. 512.

571–4   The suggested punishments are in the main realistic with only an occasional move towards the extremities of saints' legends (I. 553–4). Here what is stressed is the deterrent effect of the criminal left hanging on the gallows.

582sd   For the text omitted here see Appendix 2.

597   'For covetousness, I will stay awake with them and...'

612   'The silver is ready provided we can come to an agreement'.

617   The last character to quote *termys* was Lucifer (I. 58). The language of the market which follows characterises the degradation of Judas and his actions. He is called *mercator pessimus* in the *Breviary* (I, dcclxxviii) and in *Meditationes* (p. 602).

618   Whiting M629; meaning 'ready money ensures that a bargain is made'.

620   Money in a glove sounds more like a gift than an ordinary business deal.

625   *Smyth up* 'Strike hands [and seal the bargain]'.

626   Judas re-states his obsession with monetary payment (cf. I. 595) but now as a public statement.

631–8 These are the two commonest reasons given for the necessity of Judas' picking Christ out: that many of those sent to take him had never seen him, and that Christ and his disciples dressed all alike. The latter is interesting from the point of view of costuming in the play in that it confirms the use of the style of robe and cloak normal for his disciples and often for Christ in the visual arts, which has little to do with contemporary styles of dress.

o dyscypil. It was sometimes said that St James the Less was so like Christ that 'he was taken of mony peple for Criste. Wherefore Iudas ȝafe a token of kyssenge to the Iewes, leste that thei scholde have been disseyvede in the takenge of oure Saviour Criste' (Higden's *Polychronicon* in Trevisa's translation, IV, p. 349); cf. *Legenda* 295, and see the altar-piece in St. Peters, Leuven, where the disciple sitting next but one to Christ's left at the Last Supper is remarkably like Christ (Schiller II, pl. 99).

662sd The secrecy of the Jews' plotting is emphasised by their taking leave of each other by signs or gestures (*be contenawns*). Their stealthy departure contrasts with the suddenness of the drawing back of the curtain around the Last Supper scaffold. The action on the scaffold of the Last Supper is now played against the silent threat of the surrounding Jews. When the curtain is drawn back, the Paschal meal has already been eaten. Christ's expounding of it, emphasises the fulfilling of the Old Law.

ech in ere degré perhaps implies an expected seating arrangement for the disciples. In Michel's *Passion* there is a seating plan; see p. 266.

665–6 Exodus xii, 1–11.

667–70 *swete bredys* and *bytter sokelyng* represent the biblical 'azymos panes' ('unleavened bread') and 'lactucis agrestis' ('wild lettuce') of Exodus xii, 8. For the latter Lucerne used 'wilden lattich', Revello 'latuce' and Mons 'laitues' (see *Staging of Religious Drama*, pp. 125–6 and the references in the 'Reference Titles and Detailed Bibliography' under Lucerne, Revello and Mons).

'Suckling' in English usually means 'honeysuckle' or 'clover', and 'honysokles' are named in *Stanzaic Life* as the bitter herbs used by the Jews before the Passover (l. 4714). It is possible that *sokelyng* was felt to be an appropriate word but, since the meal had already been eaten, it is not clear what, if anything, appeared on stage. In Michel's *Passion* it is directed that all signs of the Passover feast should be removed before the Last Supper commenced (p. 266): 'Here it is to be understood that the apostles will remove everything which is on the table and leave only the cloth there, then they will put a chalice in the middle of it and some sacramental wafers'.

669 No mention is made here or later of the intestines (Exodus xii, 9).

take. The tense of this verb is inconsistent with the others in the section and should perhaps be emended to 'toke' or 'haue take', though the present tense is not impossible.

671–4 They are not specifically said to have stood, otherwise the passage is remarkably close to that in Exodus: 'And thus you shall eat it: you shall gird your reins, and you shall have shoes on your feet, holding staves in your hands, and you shall eat in haste: for it is the Phase (that is the Passage) of the Lord' (xii, 11). The costuming of the Last Supper at Mons is described in some detail: 'Note that all the apostles ought here to have white shoes on their feet and to be girt with leather girdles or napkins over their clothes, their cloaks removed, and they have a white staff in their hands, like a pilgrim's staff' (*Le Livre de Conduite*, p. 279). The Exodus passage describing the Passover feast was read at the Mass on Good Friday (*Missal* 317–18).

675 The Paschal meal, the *fygure* or foreshadowing, is to be replaced by the Eucharistic sacrifice of the mass. The Paschal lamb of the Old Law is balanced against the *newe lomb* (I. 685), Christ, the Agnus Dei, of the New Law.
  Perby 'from it'.

676 A deliberate play on *hed* meaning 'master'.

677–8 The *fygure* will be made apparent to them through the sacramental act (*mystery*) of the transubstantiation of the bread, or wafer, at the mass into Christ's body and blood.

678 *in forme of bred* is a commonly recurring phrase to describe transubstantiation; see *Minor Poems*, I, pp. 24–5; *Meditations on the Supper* l. 215; *Metrical Life* l. 2045; carols 317–19 in Greene and note on p. 422.

679–82 Cf. Luke xxii, 15–16. The repetition *desyre/desyryd* is almost certainly a result of the repetition 'desiderio/desideraui' in the gospel.

682 'For from this time on . . .'. Bevington suggests 'of this (food)', but the source (Luke xxii, 16) clearly indicates the former; 'Dico enim uobis quia ex hoc non manducabo illud . . .'.

683–4 An omitted relative, 'which' or 'that', links the two lines.

684–6 Not only does the repetition of *sacryfyce* interweave Old and New Laws, but the two are rhetorically linked by the use of *sacryd* (I. 685).

686sd More than any of the other vernacular English plays this one emphasises the institution of the sacrament of the eucharist, not only by using the sacramental wafer (*oblé*), but also by keeping close to the actions and in some cases words of the mass. The rubrics of the *Missal* (615–17) perhaps indicate to some extent Christ's gestures.

687 *þe* can be either 'thee' or 'the'. The former produces a slightly awkward repetition with l. 688; the latter an abrupt change from third to second person. The presence of *art* makes the former the more likely.

689–90 The point is presumably made to justify the need for the Father's power to turn the bread into Christ's flesh and blood since Christ is here acting as man (the priest) and not God, and the crucifixion has not yet taken place.

695   The idea that the words of consecration effected the change of bread and wine into body and blood is referred to by Comestor: 'ex virtute horum verborum fit transsubstantiatio' (col. 1618) and see *Legenda* (pp. 930–1). See also *Towneley*, p. 316, ll. 328–9 and *Twenty-Six Political Poems*, p. 105, ll. 65–8. In *apparens* and *þe very flesche and blod* the difference between 'accident' (outward appearance) and 'substance' (inner essence), and hence the nature of transubstantiation, is brought out.

696   *þis* here and at l. 701 and 703 is the *oblé*, the consecrated wafer.

699–700   The celebration of the Passover was decreed at the moment of the Israelites' departure from Egypt. As it was the means to save them from the final plague of the killing of the first-born (Exodus xii, 3, 7 and 12–14), it could be said that eating of the lamb contributed to the destruction of Pharaoh, but the relationship is not obvious. Pharaoh is, however, commonly equated with the devil, e.g. 'Israel populum Christianum, Pharao diabolum significat', *Glossa Ordinaria*, I, col. 186.

706   John i, 29 and 36.

708   Ludolph of Saxony has a similar point by point *gostly interpretacyon* of the Paschal meal, *Vita Christi* p. 577. It occasionally coincides in detail with that given here. See also Bede (PL 91, coll. 306–7), *Legenda* pp. 929–30, *Speculum Christiani* p. 182 and the sermon in British Library MS. Arundel 279, ff. 2–5. (I am grateful to Dr Veronica O'Mara for this last reference.) It is used in the play to confirm the continuity of Old and New Laws.

710   The line seems to mean 'Therefore ensure that your minds are responsive to what I shall say'. This is not an easy reading and the commonness of the collocation 'apply (your) wit' (*MED* s.v. **ap(p)lien**) makes it possible that it originally read *3our wyttys loke 3e applye.*

711   The repetition of *bred* is awkward and is almost certainly an error for 'lamb', because though Christ is talking about the *oblé* ('bread') he is referring to it as though it were the Paschal lamb.

711–50   The eight precepts taught are clearly shaped so as to be applicable both to members of the audience and to the disciples. The positioning of the fourth, 'if you cannot understand, simply believe', gives additional emphasis to the third, 'the sacrament is Christ as God and man', which is already stressed by having two stanzas instead of the usual one. The only other precept with two stanzas is the final one; rhetorically appropriate as a conclusion but also stressing the importance of constant vigilance against evil. It is clear from l. 817–20 that the playwright is here concerned with eucharistic belief and not simply with belief in Christ as God and man. In view of this it seems not unreasonable to see in I. 719–26 a combating of doubts about transubstantiation which were current at the time in Lollardy. The following stanza underlines this by its emphasis upon the necessity of belief regardless of understanding.

713   *Vita Christi*, 'tertio, sine fermento peccati, cum panibus azymis, per conscientiae sinceritatem' ('thirdly, without the yeast of sin, with un-leavened bread, through sincerity of conscience'); see also Bede col. 306.

718   *Vita Christi*, 'secundo, cum lactucis agrestibus, per amaram de peccatis omnibus cordis contritionem' ('secondly, with wild lettuce, through bitter contrition of heart for all sins'); *Legenda*, 'cum amaritudine dolendo de peccatis omnibus' ('with bitterness of weeping for all sins'); and Bede.

719–26   *Vita Christi* and *Legenda* both take the head and feet to refer to Christ's divinity and humanity in which all must believe. See also Bede, and for a casual and different explanation, Lydgate *Virtues of the Mass* ll. 41–8 (*Lydgate* p. 89).

727   For the unusual form of the past participle cf. II. 273 and note.

727–30   Bede has a similar explanation in discussing the 'intestinis' and this passage (col. 306). *Vita Christi* does not comment on this section.

731–2   *Vita Christi* 'quarto, renibus accinctis, per castitatem' ('fourthly, with reins girt up, through chastity'); and Bede 'In hoc significat correc-tionem humanae concupiscentiae' ('By this is signified the correction of sensual yearning').

735   *Vita Christi*, 'quinto, pedibus calceatis, per affectionum a terrenis elongationem' ('fifthly, with feet shod, through desire of being far from earthly things').
    Bede is nearer to the play with prophets and apostles as examples. He also sees this as related to the two loves, of God and of our neighbour.

739–52   Neither *Vita Christi* ('careful control of oneself') nor Bede ('the two testaments to defend us') comes near to this.

740   *þe exawmplys* to be taught are presumably those of virtuous men referred to in I. 736.

743–6   Again, neither *Vita Christi* ('with spiritual eagerness and accom-panying delight') nor Bede, who has several explanations (col. 307), is near.

753   *awngellys mete* or 'angels food' is a common expression for the sac-ramental wafer; see Lydgate *Virtues of the Mass* ll. 361–84 (*Lydgate* pp. 103–4), Greene, carol 318, st. 3, and *Minor Poems*, I, p. 179, l. 248 ('Angeles Brede').

754   The staging of this episode is important. It appears that the disciples come up one by one to Christ (*come forth seryattly*) to receive the sacrament; but where is he standing? He is usually shown at the table with his disciples sitting around it. Does he here come in front of the table (as a priest before the altar) and minister the sacrament from there, thus emphasising still further the liturgical associations? For a pictorial representation of this, see Schiller II pl. 109.

755–8   Great stress was laid on the importance of receiving the sacrament in a proper state of mind and body (deriving from 1 Corinthians xi 29); see *Minor Poems* I, p. 180, ll. 269–71; *Towneley* XXVI ll. 330–3; *26 Political Poems*, pp. 105–6, ll. 73–80; *Lay Folk's Catechism*, p. 66, ll. 326–7; and *Lay-Folk's Mass Book*, pp. 122–7, especially p. 122, ll. 21–9.
   'Lord, [how] to receive this spiritual food properly exceeds my understanding, because no man can, of his own nature, possess the quality necessary to receive it with too much honour'.

761–2   Peter properly prepares himself by a form of confession and contrition; cf. *Religious Pieces* p. 45, and note also I. 718 above.

763   The words of the mass are 'Hoc est enim corpus meum' – the 'wordys fyfe' of Christ's speech in the *Towneley* Resurrection (XXVI l. 329). It is perhaps an oversight that the playwright has used the tag *flesch and blode*, but *Vita Christi* points out that the one, bread or wine, contains the other (p. 587); see also *26 Political Poems*, p. 105, ll. 57–60.

765–70   Again the taking of the sacrament in the proper state of mind and body is stressed. *Meditationes* records the doubt of whether Judas was there or not (p. 598), but leaves no doubt that he was (p. 602). Comestor stresses that he was not there (col. 1618). The doubt arises because John, the only evangelist to mention his departure, does not describe the institution of the sacrament.

770sd   Judas like the others returns to his own seat.

771–4   The account of Christ's foretelling of the betrayal is close to Matthew (xxvi, 21–4) and Mark (xiv, 18–21), but in the play there is no dipping of the hand into the dish.

775   As with the individual taking of the sacrament so also here each disciple, one after the other, denies betraying Christ. Only Judas is given the question.
   Lines 775–8 are marked by the scribe as a four-line stanza; I have divided it into two couplets. In view of the repetition of *Lord, it is not I* it would probably be more satisfactory to make that a separate, extra-metrical line and begin the couplet with Judas's question.

776   Matthew xxvi, 25, 'Ait illi: Tu dixisti'.

778   Cf. John xiii, 27, 'Quod facis, fac citius', quoted in *York* XXVII l. 90.

In *York* (though the institution of the sacrament section is on a missing leaf) and in *Chester* XV it is clear that Judas leaves after the washing of feet and the institution of the sacrament. It is often explained in the commentaries that the other disciples did not know why Judas was leaving.

778sd The sentence does not make sense without a subject for *xal mete*. Since the devil meets Judas immediately after it is clear that he is the subject. Bevington emends somewhat differently but with the same result.

If Lucifer does not return here, he acts, as John the Baptist does, simply as a prologue. The choice offered by the stage direction is a clear sign of theatrical and not literary intention.

782 Judas is one of those (with Cain) who remain in hell after the Harrowing; see for example *York* XXXVII ll. 303–12.

783 Again the stress is not only on the betrayal but also on Judas's taking the sacrament in a state of sin.

785 These are Lucifer's first expressed doubts about the wisdom of killing Christ and bringing him to hell. They do not quite square with his reaction to the devil in hell at II. 528–31 – but a year separates them in performance.

787 Cf. Christ's words 'Quod facis, fac citius' (see note to I. 778 above).

791–2 John xiii, 31 and cf. xii, 23 and 28. The Latin is 'Nunc clarificatus est Filius hominis: et Deus clarificatus est in eo', and there is no doubt that it affected the choice of words in the play.

793–4 Christ's sorrow for Judas is not in the gospels, nor in any of the cycle plays, but Comestor explains 'Turbatus est' (John xiii, 21) as meaning 'misericorditer compatiens Judae, quem notabat' ('mercifully feeling for Judas, whom he was indicating'), col. 1617.

795 The delaying of the taking of the second part of the eucharist until after the prophecy of the betrayal and after Judas' departure is only found in N. town. In *Chester*, the only other play with a pageant containing the institution of the sacrament, it follows immediately. There is no gospel warrant for it.

In theatrical terms it means that the slow receiving of the bread is separated by Judas' accusation and departure from the slow receiving of the wine, which is apparently staged in exactly the same way. The major difference between the two is in the change of emotional tone after the departure of Judas from doubt and suspicion to unalloyed brotherhood and affection, even though there is an awareness of the certain progression to Christ's passion and death.

799–804 Adapted from and expanding the gospel accounts; cf. Matthew xxvi, 27–8; Mark xiv, 23–4 and Luke xxii, 20. It is possible that Luke xxii, 19 'Do this for a commemoration of me' is reflected in I. 800.

807–8   Cf. John xv, 13.

810   These words are taken from one of the post-Resurrection speeches of Christ to Peter (John xxi, 15–17). The words are repeated in a nearly similar way three times and are usually understood as meaning 'Teach my people'. That meaning is included here but by transferring them to this occasion they can also be used to give emphasis once again to the eucharist.

814   That is, by the words that Christ has spoken at the Supper (see note to I. 695 above).

818   Cf. the emphasis already laid on this, I. 719–26, and see the note to I. 711–50.

824sd   The episode of the washing of feet occurs only in John (xiii, 4–16). This stage direction (as the next shows) is misplaced. It does not seem from John as though Christ begins with Peter though he does so in all the cycles; no doubt because he is the only one to protest.

825ff   The playwright seems to be combining here the solution to the argument about precedence with Christ's direction to his disciples to love one another. It is a neat merging of a number of themes from the gospels.

828sd   This is the only indication that I know of a particular term being used for 'stage direction' in medieval English drama. The directions in the manuscript are not written in red, so are not strictly 'rubrics'; but they stand in the same relation to the text as the rubrics in service books do.

829–40   An expansion of John xiii, 6–9.

838   *his* seems a little strange, but as Peter changes from *I* to *we*, it could be that he is offering and asking for the agreement of his fellow disciples.

840sd   It appears that the slow stylised process of the receiving of the eucharist is repeated here with the washing of feet.

841–8   Cf. John xiii, 12–14.

849–53   There is nothing exactly like this in John's gospel but compare xiii, 34–5 and xv, 9–13. Perhaps it is partly a reminiscence of Psalm cxxxii which is one of the psalms sung during the washing of the feet on Maundy Thursday (*Missal* 311). Through the Last Supper section there is, however, a recurrent emphasis on the need for love and brotherhood between men in order to ensure their salvation (see I. 679, 713, 826), a counterpart of Christ's love that made that salvation possible.

854–8   Cf. Luke xviii, 31–4.

861–75   Cf. Matthew xxvi, 31–5; Mark xiv, 27–31. Only Mark has 'before the cock crow twice'.

873–4   'Peter, with regard to that, do not make promises [which go] beyond what you know'. Davies accepts the manuscript reading *Petyr þu ferthere* but adds 'sayst' after *þu*. This is one solution. Block and Bevington read *þu* as *yn*. I am reluctant to do this because it is the only example of this spelling for **in** in *Mary* or *Passion Plays*, and as far as a scan of the rest of the manuscript reveals the only example in the whole manuscript. It seems to me an easy error for the scribe to write *Petyr, þu* expecting a verb which did not exist and failing to correct his error, but Davies may be right that a verb is missing. If so it makes for a cumbersome line.

880   *Betany*. Gethsemane and the Mount of Olives are in the general direction of Bethany, as any pilgrim to the Holy Land would know.

884sd   None of the gospels mentions Bethany. Matthew and Mark name Gethsemane; Luke, the Mount of Olives; and John says that they went over the brook Cedron. The commentators follow one or other or combine them.

The stage direction is accurate in saying *Betanyward* since from Sion to Gethsemane is in the direction of Bethany, and it was in Bethany that Christ and the disciples were staying before coming to Jerusalem for the Passover. It is, however, almost certainly a narrative rather than a staging direction since no location 'Bethany' is required in the play, and it may simply have been derived from I. 880.

889   See note to I. 854–8 above.

893   The oil of mercy is salvation; cf. *Towneley* III, l. 46; X, l. 9; *Mary Magdalen* l. 759; and *Deuelis Perlament* l. 348 (*Hymns* p. 52). The image is a common one, most fully developed in the Legend of the Cross (see *Legends of the Holy Rood*, p. 64 ll. 87–90 and *passim*).

Many images and themes connected with salvation are drawn together here: the overthrowing of the devil's power (890), man's soul as bride of Christ (892), the oil of mercy (893), the reconciliation of God and man (896), Christ's brotherhood with man (897), the power of love and the satisfying of justice in the balance of man for man (900). The iteration of the idea of 'the time has come' (I. 881, 887) appears also in *Cursor Mundi*, ll. 14908, 14959, 14989 *et al*.

900   Cf. I. 502.

900sd   For a possible staging of the park see the garden of paradise or Magdalene's garden on the first day, or Gethsemane on the second day in the Lucerne plans; *Staging of Religious Drama*, endpiece. The nature of the *Mount of Olyvet* as part of the stage setting is not made clear. It is required only here.

901   As in Luke (xxii, 39–41) the disciples remain together when Christ goes aside to pray.

904   Christ's physical agony is stressed in Luke in the sweating of blood (xxii, 43–4). The physical trembling was perhaps suggested by the phrase

'The spirit is indeed willing but the flesh weak', actually applied to the disciples by Christ (Matthew xxvi, 41; Mark xiv, 38).

909–16　The sudden change from prayer for the removal of the obligation to suffer, to acceptance of it, parallels the gospel accounts (Matthew xxvi, 39; Mark xiv, 36; Luke xxii, 42). There, however, the change is marked by 'nevertheless/but' ('Uerum tamen/sed'), and the play seems to need 'but' rather than 'and' at I. 913, though a pause in the action could well be used to the same effect. The two-stanza lyric of 'Christ's Prayer in Gethsemane' (*Lyrics XIV*, p. 82), however, is almost exactly parallel in marking the change by 'And'. In all three gospels Christ asks for 'this chalice' to be taken away.

arn (I. 911) seems inconsistent with the singular subject, though the combination of singular subject and plural verb is not an uncommon one in the fifteenth and sixteenth centuries.

917–20　The emphasis on the disciples' lack of concern for Christ's suffering is only obliquely referred to in the gospels. It is, however, a commonplace in later realisations of the scene.

920sd　Only Matthew and Mark have Christ's three prayers; Luke has one and John does not report the incident (see Matthew xxvi, 37–46; Mark xiv, 33–42 and Luke xxii, 41–6).

925–6　Luke xxii, 44. At Lucerne and Revello a painter concealed below the staging spattered Christ's face with paint to represent the bloody sweat (*Staging of Religious Drama*, p. 108).

933–6　Christ's words strike an unfortunate note of self-righteousness through the playwright's desire to re-emphasise his blamelessness and self-sacrifice. It is one of the inevitable dangers (which he usually manages to avoid) of presenting ideas through characters.

936sd　Only in Luke does an angel appear 'confortans eum' ('strengthening him'). The chalice frequently appears, often with a host, in art; see Schiller II, pll. 151 and 152. It is derived from the metaphorical *calix* of the gospels. It presents a complex message in as much as the chalice and host mean nothing without the death of Christ. They therefore symbolise the necessity of that death as well as recalling the Last Supper.

938　Probably 'sent you this now/here', though 'sent you this gift' is not grammatically impossible.

941　This refers to the decision to save mankind taken by the Trinity. It is dealt with fully in the *Mary Play* (see especially ll. 1199–1246) and at the very least suggests an audience familiar with the idea, if not a reference to that play (l. 590).

944　*dede*. Bevington translates 'death', which is possible though there is only one other use of the form in the two parts of the *Passion Play* (II. 1448). It seems more likely to mean 'deed', since an action (the redemption) has been mentioned but only by implication a death.

945–8   A further emphasis on the eucharist, bringing it into contemporary time (*all presthood*). The image is not merely visual (I. 936sd) but is also explained verbally.

948sd   The sudden ascent of the angel may imply raising machinery, but there is no other evidence for it in the play nor is there any need for a heaven scaffold, and it is more likely that he quickly leaves the place. It may be a problem of narrative or staging direction.

953–6   There is some similarity between these lines and the responsory on Maundy Thursday 'Una hora . . .' (*Missal* 310).

954   'You make no attempt to stay awake.' This rather cumbersome expression seems nevertheless preferable to the broken sentence suggested by Bevington which is almost unsayable.

960–4   There are a number of echoes of the *Northern Passion* in these lines. I. 960 is close to one in the same episode in the poem (l. 502); I. 961–2 contain parts of two lines (ll. 325–6) which occur in an earlier part of the poem, and I. 963–4 have a very general similarity with l. 510 and the identical l. 327.

964sd   It is implied here by *goth into þe place* that the *park* was a separate location.
Just as the Jews parted *be contenawns* so Judas now leads them to Christ in the same way. Lanterns, torches, weapons, swords, staves, and clubs are all mentioned in the gospels. *white arneys and breganderys* is an accurate description of the kind of mixed armour often worn in the fifteenth century; a combination of flexible body armour (*breganderys*) and pieces of rigid shell armour (*white arneys*). See Kelly and Schwabe, I, p. 70 and pl. XXVIII i. Many fifteenth-century paintings of the taking of Christ illustrate this kind of armour – often of a somewhat fantastic nature (see for example *Early Dutch Painting* pl. 66).

965–92   The incidents from the various gospels are here woven together: the falling of the Jews from John; the kiss from Matthew, Mark and Luke; the cutting off of the ear in all, though Christ's words are taken from Matthew.

968   John xviii, 4 'Quem quaeritis?'.

973   Christ's willing submission (contrasting with his prayers in the garden) is emphasised by the repetition of *þat wyl not fle* from I. 966.

976sd   This was seen as a revelation of Christ's hidden power, his ability to resist and therefore of his willingness to undergo the passion; see for example *Vita Christi* p. 611.

977–84   Another cluster of borrowings and reminiscences of the *Northern Passion* appears here; borrowings in I. 977 and 981 (ll. 537 and 539) and reminiscences and verbal similarities in I. 983–4 (ll. 539–41).

992   Matthew xxvi, 52. The playwright makes the rhetorical relationship closer by using *smyth/smete* for Matthew's 'acceperint/peribunt', as the parallel passage in the Apocalypse does using 'occiderit/occidi' (xiii, 10).

1001–4   The taunt is adapted from later in the passion; see Matthew xxvii, 40 and 42, Mark xv, 30–2, Luke xxiii, 37 and 39.

1017–26   See Matthew xxvi, 55; Mark xiv, 48–9; Luke xxii, 52–3; and the *Northern Passion*, ll. 591–3.

1028   Perhaps a forward echo to 'Father forgive them for they know not what they do', one of the seven words from the cross (see II. 800–2).

1032sd   Once again the actions overlap in movement. As Christ is driven and dragged from the place, Mary Magdalene observes him and crosses to Mary. Normally John is the one to report the taking of Christ to Mary, but there is evidence of another tradition where Mary Magdalene is the bearer of the news; see *Lamentacion of oure Lady*, *Archiv* (1887) p. 455. I am grateful to Dr C. W. Marx for drawing my attention to this reference.

1033   The verse changes to a long line and a more formal and measured language.

1045–76   Mary's lament combines a number of traditional elements paralleled in earlier and contemporary works (lyrics, prose and verse laments) and in the liturgy. Some of the elements occur in laments of Mary at the cross or after Christ's death, and one at least (the pallor of Christ's face, l. 1064) is not particularly appropriate here. See Gray, *Themes and Images* pp. 135–9, Woolf *Lyrics* pp. 239–73 for a general discussion of Compassion lyrics, and Young I, pp. 492–513 for the development of the *planctus*. There are laments on this occasion in *Lamentacion of oure Lady*, p. 455 and *Meditationes* p. 603.

1057   Bevington and Davies add 'not' after *I*. It is possible that this is the intended reading since the question is awkward.

1060   *prongys* is not a common word. It is perhaps suggested by the use of 'wommanes prongys' for the pains of childbirth, since it was generally believed that the sufferings of Mary at the Passion balanced her lack of suffering at the birth of Christ. The *swerd* (I. 1058) that Simeon prophesied should pierce Mary's soul (Luke ii, 35) was usually interpreted as referring to the Passion, and perhaps there is a figurative reference to that.

1063   *betwyx tweyn bestys*; the ox and ass of the Nativity. A commonplace in most descriptions and illustrations but drawn from *Pseudo-Matthew* (ch. 14) which in turn draws it from an interpretation of Isaiah i, 3 and of Habacuc iii, 2 (Septuagint reading: 'thou shalt be known between the two living creatures').

1068   *now* perhaps repeated in error.

1071–2   It is somewhat unusual to find Mary able to comfort herself with the knowledge that Christ's suffering will have a triumphant end; cf. the confidence of Mary Jacobi at the sepulchre, II. 1692–5.

1075–6   The play comes to a sad though very low-key ending in Mary's final prayer for pity for mankind and herself. No stage direction exists to show how the play ended visually, but it should not be forgotten that the procession leading Christ away may have remained visible (and perhaps distantly audible) during the last scene.

PASSION PLAY II

1sd   Opening a play with a procession of the characters is a feature of some continental plays (e.g. Lucerne, Seurre; see M. Blakemore Evans, *The Passion Play of Lucerne* (New York, 1943) pp. 215–20, and *Staging of Religious Drama*, p. 261). Here it seems to be no more than a ceremonial way of getting the actors into their positions. Scaffolds are specified for Herod, Pilate, and (probably, but not certainly, together) Annas and Caiaphas.

This is the only place in the *Passion Play* where an expositor is mentioned. He functions as a prologue, putting the following action into the context of the preceding part of the Passion, and acting as a temporal link. The *doctorys wede* is presumably here contemporary dress (unlike Annas' and Caiaphas' doctors' costumes in *Passion* I). The name *Contemplacio* has possibly been borrowed from the *Mary Play*. It is certainly more integral to that play (see Notes to *Mary Play* 1sn).

1   *gret with gode*, perhaps 'greeted/filled with goodness/charitable feelings', perhaps simply 'welcomed/honoured'. The rhyme with *rode* and the spelling *gode* make the meaning 'greeted/great with God' unlikely (but cf. II. 5/7 below). Davies suggests, 'greeted with good things' (p. 279).

6   This is the only information there is about the pattern of performance of the two parts of the *Passion Play*. Only the short *Killing of the Children* has similar references to a yearly progression in the story, and there it covers three years (ll. 25–6 and 561–2) and is tied to St Anne's day.

10   See I. 415ff.

11–12   See I. 753ff.

12   *evyr with us to abydyn for mannys sake*. A gloss on the significance of the Last Supper, placing it in a liturgical as well as a historical context.

13–14   See I. 599ff.

15–16   See I. 965ff.

16   *about mydnyth*. No time is stated in the gospels but this is one tradition, perhaps derived from the association of the canonical hours with the seven works of the Passion. The same phrase is used in an English version of the Latin hymn *Patris sapiencia* often found in Primers (Maskell, II, p. 40, n. 14; and cf. p. x). Frequently however the phrase 'hora matutina' is simply translated by such phrases as 'at morne tyde' or 'in þe nyȝt'. See Woolf *Lyrics* for a brief discussion of the relation of lyrics to the canonical hours and the Latin hymn (pp. 235–7), and *Lay Folk's Mass Book*, pp. 82–7 for a parallel English and Latin text of *Patris Sapiencia*.

20sd   The early introduction of Herod is striking for its unexpectedness. It prepares for his appearance later (at II. 377sd), and builds up the sense of threat against Christ. His opening speech is a typically blustering tyrant's one. This is Herod Antipas, son of Herod the Great, though the distinction is not always observed in the Middle Ages (see S. S. Hussey, 'How many Herods in the Middle English Drama?' *Neophilologus* 48 (1964) pp. 252–9).

26   *Mahownde* – literally 'Mahomet' but doing duty for all devils and pagan gods. *þe lawys of Mahownde* are presumably the same as the laws that Annas and Caiaphas are defending, but Herod is said in *Vita Christi* to have been a pagan who became a Jew for love of his wife (p. 632). He is perhaps being seen here as an exotic eastern potentate rather than a Jew. No-one in *Passion* I refers to *Mahownde*, and in *Passion* II it is only Herod and the knights at the tomb who do so.

29   *Crystyn* is apparently anachronistic, but is not really so since Christ already has many followers.

31–2   Two of the punishments already suggested for Christ (see I. 571 and 553). The latter is the punishment meted out to the murderers of the child in Chaucer's Prioress' Tale (l. 633).

35   'To force them into dungeons to be gnawed by dragons'. Satan too uses dragons in dungeons as tortures (see II. 492 below), and Herod in *York* XXXI claims that dragons are terrified by his anger, ll. 12–13.

37–40   This Herod is correctly linked with the death of John the Baptist (Matthew xiv and Mark vi).

51   'You are the final arbiter'. Cf. Caiaphas' use of the term: 'To seuere ryth and wrong in me is termynable' (I. 216).

63   Herod is presumably not intended to connect Jesus with Christ whom he has already casually mentioned, or even perhaps with Christians. It is apparently the *wondrys* that raise Herod's interest rather than overthrowing

the laws; see II. 65 and 68 and notes to II. 398–413 and 406, and cf. Luke xxiii, 8.

66   Lucifer's charge against Christ in I. 41 (see note).

67   One of the charges of the Jews against Christ; see note to I. 566.

71   'under our jurisdiction' – *with* may be an error for 'within'. Herod governed in Galilee, see below II. 347–53.

85   Cf. II. 347 below.

88–9   Herod, like Caiaphas, Herod and Pilate in *York* (XXIX, ll. 64–86; XXXI, ll. 33–54 and XXX, ll. 126–48) and Pilate in *Towneley* (XXIV, ll. 65–72), retires to his bed. It is practically a way of removing a character from the action for a while (and a reason for drawing a curtain), but it also suggests a certain self-indulgence and the comfort and luxury of their lives in contrast with Christ's.

89sd   As Herod's scaffold closes (it opens again at II. 377), the action swings first to the 'place' as the messenger runs in and then to the bustle of Annas' and Caiaphas' scaffold. Circling round the 'place' becomes more frenzied in *Passion* II. As with the appearance of Herod, the playwright manages another surprise (yet contrasting) opening.

96ff   Contemplacio left the detailed story of the Passion at the point where Christ was taken (II. 16); the messenger takes it on from there with an eye-witness account (*I was hem among*). He not only conveys the excitement but also the doubts about what is happening – if that is how II. 113 is to be understood.

97   *ner-to kachyd*. The meaning is clear (the messenger was 'almost struck'), the forms however are not. Under **ner** *adv. 2. MED* gives '*ben* [*ner*] *to cacched*' as 'to almost receive (a blow)' with this as the only quotation, but does not record under **cacchen** a form of the verb *ben cacched*. Nor is it clear whether *to* belongs with *ner* or with *cacched*. Neither *ner-to* nor *to-cacched* is recorded in *MED* or *OED*. I have assumed a form *ner-to* on an analogy with later 'near-upon' and taken *was kachyd* to mean 'was given' (cf. *OED* s.v. **Catch** *v*. I, 11 (where, however, the earliest example (1583) is not a very certain one), and **Near** *adv.²* II, 15, for a similar kind of construction but using the infinitive).

98–101   Cf. I. 989–92.

104–11   See I. 965–84. The incidents are reversed in the messenger's re-telling.

112   There is no mention of the part played by Judas.

120   Once again it is Annas who initiates the action, though in the gospels it is Caiaphas who is said to be high priest for that year.

123 'We have often had you searched for diligently'.

125 The mercenary nature of the purchase is stressed in I. 617–25; see also note to I. 617.

128–9 'You have often thwarted us and others as well, so now it is absolutely necessary to kill you'. *bryng þe a dawe*, literally 'bring you out of day'.

130–1 In John it is Annas who asks about Christ's disciples and doctrine (xviii, 19), though the speaker's identity is not immediately obvious.

132–3 Either Caiaphas is attempting at first to conceal his antagonism for Christ by rather blatant support of him or he is mocking him.

134–7 Christ replies as in John xviii, 20–1, the playwright keeping very close to the bible text. This is true of much of this section, allowing for movement from one gospel account to another.

138–41sd As John xviii, 22; transforming description into direct speech.

142–5 As John xviii, 23. In John, Christ is then sent to Caiaphas.

150–3 Both Matthew (xxvi, 61) and Mark (xiv, 58) report this as an accusation; John gives it as Christ's own words of prophecy much earlier on (ii, 18–22). According to *Ministry and Passion* the Jews made four accusations against Christ: claiming that he was God's son; contradicting the law; claiming to be able to destroy the temple and rebuild it in three days; and forbidding tribute to Caesar (ll. 2281–5). *Vita Christi* gives three of these, omitting that relating to God's son, and shows how they were false (p. 630).

154–5 All the gospels contain this as a question or an accusation; see Matthew xxvi, 63, Mark xiv, 61, Luke xxii, 70 and John xix, 7.

162–8 Drawn from Matthew xxvi, 62–3 (Mark xiv, 60–1). The playwright successfully manages to reveal Caiaphas' growing anger. In Matthew he adjures Christ by the living God ('per Deum uiuum'). The *sonne and þe mone* was no doubt felt to be less Christian-sounding. In the *Metrical Life* Caiaphas calls on the Trinity (l. 2359).

169–72 The playwright follows Mark's direct answer, 'I am' ('Ego sum', xiv, 62). The rest is reported in Matthew, Mark and Luke, but the playwright makes the reference to the Day of Judgment specific, rather than implicit as it is in the gospels.

173–7 At this, Caiaphas rent his garments in Matthew (xxvi, 65–6) and Mark (xiv, 63–4). For Caiaphas's words, the playwright remains close to the gospels.

178–9 The crowd, which plays an important role in *Passion* II, speaks for the first time. The formal threefold repetitions of the *Mary Play* now reflect the threatening mob. In these days of large numbers of extras it is easy to overestimate its size. Judging by the speaking parts and references the number is around ten or eleven, or if the doctors and messenger are included, fourteen or fifteen. There seems no reason to put it higher. Cf. *a ten personys* and Judas, who come to take Christ in *Passion* I (964sd).

181sd   Matthew and Mark have two mockings, one at the high priest's and one at Pilate's house. Luke has only the high priest's (except for Herod and the white robe) and John only Pilate's. As the gospel harmonies do, but with considerably more freedom, the plays blend and put events in their own order. The details of this, the first mocking, are much as they are in Matthew, Mark and Luke; though the sitting on a stool is traditional and not biblical, appearing in *Chester* XVI (a '*cathedra*', 69sd); *Towneley* XXI ('a light buffit', l. 351) and *York* XXIX ('a stole', l. 356).

183–5   Developed from the account in Matthew (xxvi, 67–8), Mark (xiv, 65) and Luke (xxii, 64).

185sd   'And he shall strike [him] on the head'. This is the first of the Latin marginal stage directions of which there are a number in the second part though none in the first part of the Passion.

189–93   The fourth Jew's *now wole I a newe game begynne* transforms the simple taunting of the 'blindfold' Christ to say who has hit him into a specific game with a chanted refrain (cf. *Towneley* XXI, l. 344 'a new play of yoyll').

If, as seems likely, part of the chant describes the movements of the game, it involved 'circling' (by the players) or 'spinning' (of the guesser) – *whele*; 'plucking' – *pylle*; and 'identifying the plucker' – *ho was þat*? It therefore seems to be a version of the guessing game 'Hot Cockles' (Opies, under 'Stroke the Baby', pp. 292–4) and related to the chasing game 'Blind Man's Buff' and 'Frog in the Middle' (Opies, pp. 117–20 and 122). One version of 'Blind Man's Buff' has a ring of players circling a blindfold 'chaser' and involves the identifying of the 'striker'; 'Frog in the Middle' has a seated 'chaser' and in the oldest version 'plucking' or 'pinching' by the other players. The 'guesser' in the play, Christ, makes no attempt to identify the 'plucker' and thereby end the game; a perhaps just perceptible underlining of his willing acceptance of his role.

Owst provides two sermon references (pp. 510–11) to the mocking of Christ seen as a game, one of which includes a chanted refrain:

> A bobbid, a bobbid, a biliried;
> Smyte not her, bot thu smyte a gode!

But the idea of a game is present in the gospel accounts and the Opies comment on the possibility of the tormentors of Christ themselves knowing one such as 'Hot Cockles'.

194ff   The first remark is not addressed to Peter but neatly draws attention away from Christ to him. *York* (XXIX ll. 87–106) uses the same device at greater length. The two women derive from Matthew's and Mark's accounts of the incident, the cousin of Malchus (*'cognatus'*) from John's – providing the three denials. In the gospels, the 'cousin' does not directly associate Peter with the cutting off of Malchus' ear (see I. 789–990sd, II. 98–101). The whole is a skilful blending and developing of the four accounts. *York* develops the potential of the scene more fully (XXIX ll. 87–169).

199sd   'And the cock shall crow'.

210–11   The oath is particularly mentioned in Matthew xxvi, 72, but for the second denial. The third, as in Mark xiv, 71, is accompanied by cursing and swearing.

212sd   'And the cock shall crow'.

213sd   The look and the weeping are recorded in Luke xxii, 61–2. Peter and Magdalene are the archetypal repentant sinners. For a discussion of Peter's weeping, see *Legenda* pp. 369–70 and *Vita Christi* p. 625, and for his grief and penitence Bodley *Resurrection* ll. 267–398.

217   Peter immediately thinks of Christ's mercy, Judas only of his own sin (see below II. 250–3).

219   See I. 869–76.

222–3   Christ's look is generally seen as one of pity which provokes penitence, see *Vita Christi*, pp. 624–5.

230   There seems no reason to suppose that the *mothalle* of *Passion* II is the same structure as the *lytil oratory* of *Passion* I, given the year's gap between the two parts of the play. The action which takes place at each is very different (see Introduction pp. 24 and 28–9).

237   Pilate was in direct control over Judaea, Samaria and Idumaea. The fifteenth-century Harley translation of Higden's *Polychronicon* translates 'Iudea' as 'Iewery' (I, p. 103).

238/9   *comawndyd/prayd.* Though by no means impossible, the past tense is a little unexpected. Could this be another confusion between final – *yth* and -*yd*? Cf. *levyth* I. 727, *Shewyth* II. 273 and *Mary Play* 'Dauyd, Davyd/ Dauyth, Davyth' ll. 431, 736; 1256, etc./1003; 429.

239   There are few reminders before this that the action up to II. 258 takes place during the night.

242   The *oure of prime* was traditionally that at which Christ was brought before Pilate:

Hora prima, dominus
be-fore pylate was browthe   (*Lyrics* XV, p. 137)

See also *Horae*, p. 49 and *Metrical Life*, l. 2413, and note to II. 16 above.

243sd   *comith . . . bryngith*. The suspensions should perhaps be expanded *comyt, bryngyt*; cf. *byddyt* I. 900sd. See also notes to II. 646sd and 856.

249sd   The brevity of the treatment of this incident is in a way illusory, since the hanging Judas presumably remains in full view of the audience for some time. There is no suggestion here of the spectacular effect of the bursting belly; see REED *York* p. 48 (the Saucemakers' pageant) or Michel's *Passion* 'Here Judas' belly splits and the guts fall out and the soul departs', p. 347.
　　Judas' remorse was acknowledged but his damnation was seen to be a result of his despair in the mercy of God (in contrast with Peter, see above II. 217); see *Vita Christi* p. 628. The point is not brought out here clearly but his recognition of his sin results in raving (*I am wax wood*) rather than the tears which characterise the repentant sinner (see above II. 213sd). The incident follows Matthew xxvii, 3–5.

256   Cf. Annas' earlier remark, II. 125.

270   Annas' reversal of the order of Luke xxiii, 5 is perhaps the reason why Pilate does not pick up the implication that Christ is from Galilee.

273   *Shewyth* is an unusual spelling of *shewyd*, 'shown to the people by trickery'. The phrase is parallel to *wrowth be nygramancye* (II. 272). Cf. note to II. 238/9 and I. 727.

275   Cf. John xix, 12. With this the Jews begin to play on Pilate's loyalty to and fear of Caesar.

282–5   Cf. Matthew xxvii, 13 and Mark xv, 4. Christ is silent in the gospels and here, hence Pilate's question, preceded presumably by a pause. The phrase *lawys newe* (II. 284) is not in the gospels and was perhaps intended to hint at Christ's New Law.
　　II. 284–5 are close to *Northern Passion* ll. 1143–4.

286–9   'I care nothing for their accusation, provided that they do not injure their own, or others', souls'.
　　By his remarks at II. 288–9 Christ may mean that he seeks death, which is his Father's will, and therefore only cares for the instruments of his death in that their souls are at risk.

290–2   Pilate plants the claim to kingship in Christ's mouth since he has made no such claim, only been accused of it (II. 276). *sone of Gode* has not even been suggested to Pilate nor in the gospels is he concerned at all with the claim. Cf., however, *Metrical Life* ll. 2440–3, and *Northern Passion* l. 919, where in only one manuscript is the idea suggested to him in advance, and Herod's automatic association of Christ's claims to be king and son of God (II. 66–7 below).

II. 295 and 297 are paralleled by ll. 1161 and 1162 in the *Northern Passion*.

298–301   Perhaps an expansion of John iii, 15 and 16, but Christ further discusses his role of saviour in John v, 17–47 and vi, 35–41 and 44–59.

306   This is the only example of the word *obecyon* recorded in *MED*.

306–7   Cf. Luke xxiii, 4 and 14–15, and John xviii, 38.

308–9   'The law decrees that without guilt he cannot be sentenced to death'.

310–13   The First Doctor speciously takes up Pilate's words: the law can only condemn the guilty. He, Pilate, is the law; they, the Jews, know Christ's guilt. It is, however, the mention of reporting to the Emperor that brings Pilate back to the attack.

314–23   John xviii, 29–31. The insertion of *ʒe seyn* (ll. 322) implies that it is Pilate or the Romans who have made this rule, and therefore it is up to Pilate to do something about Christ.

325   *Pat* '[is] so that' (as Bevington).

326–7   John xix, 15.

328–35   In all the gospels Pilate asks this question (Matthew xxvii, 11; Mark xv, 2; Luke xxiii, 3; John xviii, 33); Christ's reply appears in Matthew (xxvii, 12) and Luke (xxii, 4). Pilate's further question does not appear but seems to be implied in Christ's reply in John xviii, 36, 'My kingdom is not of this world.'

336–7   Pilate returns to his position at II. 306–7.

338–45sd   Annas' almost incoherent speech conveys well his growing irritation at Pilate's refusal to condemn Christ. The crowd is once again mustered in support, only to see the impetus dissipated by the question of Christ's origins.
    'And they shall cry:'

346–9   Pilate, as he seems to do also in Luke (xxiii, 6), picks up the reference to Galilee as a way out of an impossible situation.

347   *outborn.* I find Kokeritz's explanation that 'out' means 'ought, at all' unsatisfactory (H. Kokeritz, '"Out born" in *Ludus Coventriae*', *Modern Language Notes* 64 (1949) pp. 88–90). Christ was surely born or he wasn't. The only way it seems to me in which it could make sense would be if *born* were taken to mean 'carried' – i.e. was Mary 'carrying' Christ at all while living in Nazareth? If not impossible, this seems over-ingenious. It is pretty

clear from ll. 352 that Pilate is concerned with birth not pregnancy and certainly that is the way that Caiaphas takes it. It seems better either to take *outborn* as a momentary creation of Pilate's excitement meaning simply 'born', or to assume, as Bevington does, that *out* is an adverb preceding the verb *born* and means 'out of this district, abroad'. The latter gives reasonable sense but the word order is rather awkward, and the former seems marginally more likely.

The question of exactly how the playwright was treating the idea of Christ being born in Galilee is a problematic one. The matter does not arise in the *Northern Passion* (see pp. 96–7), and in the other plays of the period from England there is some variety. In *Chester* Pilate assumes that Christ was born in Galilee (XVII. 151), in *York* Annas states that he was born there (XXX l. 514) but nothing more is made of it, in the *Ordinalia* (*Passio* ll. 1605–7) Pilate asks if Christ is from Galilee and Annas replies that he was born in 'bethlem iudi'. He does not go so far as to say that Bethlehem is in Galilee. Did the Passion playwright know that Bethlehem was in Judaea and not Galilee? In the notes which follow I have assumed that he did.

354–61 Caiaphas' long-winded reply merely emphasises the fact that Christ is from Galilee. He goes far beyond the bounds of truth, however, to substantiate his statement. Christ was not born in Galilee. Bethlehem, Christ's birthplace, is as Caiaphas himself says in Judaea, *Bedlem Judé*. By this blatant, stated and re-stated falsehood the playwright seems to be re-emphasising Caiaphas's total disregard of the truth, allowing him a joke at the expense of the foreigner, Pilate, and giving his supporters time by his long-windedness to adjust to the extremity of the lie that they are being asked to subscribe to. It is presumably an indication of the success of his tactic that after ll. 361 no-one actually denies the truth of what he says. See further, note to ll. 385.

362–74 The length of this speech and its rattling pace reflect Pilate's relief and a release of tension. For a somewhat similar reason the reply of the First Doctor is a return to commonplace civilities.

363 Pilate seems to mean: 'since I know that he *was* born in Galilee, I must [now] necessarily consider the facts of the situation (i.e. ?the implications, ?what is the correct next move)'.

377sd The *gret hast* is partly to provide an increase in Christ's suffering, partly because there is no overlap in the action at this point. The *etc.* at the end of the stage direction probably results from the lack of space left for the normal 'and . . . xal say'. It is just possible, however, that it signifies something else; perhaps the existence at one time of another copy with fuller directions.

in astat – seated in his chair of estate with his knights around him. The 'chair of estate' is the canopied seat, sometimes raised on a step or two in which rulers are usually shown sitting in contemporary illustrations.

all þe Jewys knelyng . . . The wording of the description of the Jews seems
to suggest that they are on the scaffold. It is more likely that they are in the
'place' and that the scribe, short of space, has amalgamated the two descriptions rather ambiguously.

378ff. The episode of Christ before Herod appears only in Luke (xxiii,
7–12).

381–2 The dividing of a speech in mid-sentence between two characters
only occurs here, though the situation at I. 459–66 and 475–8 is similar. It
perhaps reflects the formal nature of their office, or possibly the identity of
their purpose as with the disciples in *Passion* I.

385 In Luke and in most of the English vernacular treatments of the
episode it is clear that Herod is in Jerusalem. Here, however, the Second
Doctor talks as though Herod is in Galilee. That this is the playwright's
intention seems clear from II. 70–1 where Herod talks of Galilee (*oure
jurresdyccyon*) as *þis cowntré*. Christ is therefore taken from Jerusalem to
Galilee and back again. It is impossible to know how familiar the playwright
was with the topography of the Holy Land but one should remember again
the familiarity of pilgrimages and of pilgrim accounts in the late fifteenth
century. The 'place' could well allow the sense of real journeying that the
playwright appears to want.

392 See Luke xxiii, 12.

395 See above II. 62–73 and Luke xxiii, 8. The trial before Herod can be an
awkward repetition. By introducing him early, the playwright creates him
as a character, making his attitudes known and sufficiently interesting to the
audience to alter the focus of the scene from confrontation between Christ
and an antagonist to character study. The fact that Christ does not speak
enhances this effect.

398–413 The same accusations are repeated: destroying the law, witchcraft, claiming to be king of the Jews and the son of God. The accusation of
witchcraft does not occur in the gospels but is a natural way for his enemies
to describe his miracles. In the *Gospel of Nicodemus* he is described as *maleficus*
'a magician' (p. 316), and later *magum/maleficium* (p. 394). Herod was said to
have thought Christ a sorcerer ('incantator', *Vita Christi* p. 632). The greater
emphasis here on *soserye* (l. 402), *nygramancye* (l. 404) and *meraclys* (l. 409)
serves to reveal Herod's bias and to explain his impatience with other
matters.

406 Caiaphas's *ȝe must take hede* perhaps gives an indication of Herod's lack
of interest in the accusations (see Herod's words at II. 414–17).

408 *ten monthis* – an arbitrarily chosen number apparently; cf. *nyn days* I.
334.

414–17 Herod's dismissive attitude to the accusations is clearly shown.

421–7 Herod's interest in Christ's miracles derives from Luke xxiii, 8; see note to I. 63 above.

429 *o meracle* 'signum aliquod' (Luke xxiii, 8).

433sd Christ's silence contrasts here with his earlier readiness to speak. In the other plays, contrary to the gospels, he remains silent almost throughout the trials, perhaps through the influence of Isaiah liii, 7. 'He was offered because it was his own will, and he opened not his mouth: he shall be led as a sheep to the slaughter, and shall be dumb as a lamb before the shearer, and he shall not open his mouth'. The whole of this chapter was applied to the Passion, and read, with the Passion according to Luke, at mass on the Wednesday in Holy Week (*Missal* 287–8). See Woolf *Mystery Plays* pp. 256–7, who a little overstates Christ's silence.

438–41 Herod's words are very similar to Pilate's at II. 613–16 below.

450–1 '. . . but [silent] as a deceitful trick so that we should not accuse him.'

461sd There is no biblical warrant for this scourging. Luke xxiii, 11 reads: 'And Herod with his army set him at nought, and mocked him . . .' The idea is perhaps derived from Pilate's words after also finding him guiltless: 'I will chastise him therefore, and release him' (xxiii, 16). In *Northern Passion* Herod has Christ beaten, the only other example I know of (l. 996). In *York* XXXI, Herod is so annoyed that he goes to fight Christ and has to be forcibly restrained (ll. 291–6) but he eventually refuses to punish him because he is guiltless (ll. 398–403).

470–4 This is the first of the separate five-line stanzas rhyming *abbba*; the second is at II. 612. They resemble the final lines of the thirteener (see Appendix 2, ll. 13–17) or part of the romance stanza, though the *a* lines are here more variable in length and number of syllables. There is one occurrence of a five-line stanza of this sort rhyme-linked with a quatrain (at II. 41ff.) and one 'double' one also producing a nine-line stanza (at II. 519ff.). The other two are consecutive (at II. 580 and 585).

479–80 Cf. Luke xxiii, 12.

486sd Herod does not command the *whyte clothe* nor is its meaning explained in the play. *Vita Christi* gives the traditional explanation that it was a fool's garment, and says that it was shaped like a scapular, hanging from the neck at front and back (p. 632). It also indicates other meanings: a sign of Christ's purity and of his priesthood (p. 633). *York* explains the white gown, XXXI ll. 335–52, as does *Chester*, XVI ll. 195–202, and *Ordinalia: Passio*, ll. 1779–86, in the traditional way.

The timing of the movement around the place becomes important for the first time, so that the arrival back at the moothall shall coincide with the end

of Pilate's wife's scene (II. 563), seventy-six lines and some business later.
The episode of Pilate's wife's dream is elaborated from Matthew xxvii,
19. The dream was normally associated with Satan's belated realisation that
Christ's death would be disastrous to his power; see for example *Vita Christi*
p. 636; *Ministry and Passion* ll. 2243–52; *York* XXX, ll. 149–306; *Ordinalia:
Passio* ll. 1907–34.

487   *rochand*, perhaps 'regent' with 'o' for 'e' as is not uncommon in this
text.

487–98   It is possible that the twelve-line stanza beginning at II. 487 is
intended to be a quatrain and an octave. Having followed the scribe in seeing
dynt/flynt as intended to rhyme with *sent/brent* (cf. II. 1728), I have departed
from him in not dividing off II. 495–8 as a separate quatrain where the
rhyming link is so much more marked; cf. II. 362–73 marked by the scribe as
a twelve-line stanza.

496 and 500   A rather glaring example of inconsistency in as much as Satan
refers casually to Jesus at II. 496 and then introduces him as a new topic at II.
500.

503–6   See note to I. 32.

507–10   Satan's irritation at Christ's behaviour is much in the manner of his
earlier remarks (as Lucifer), I. 25–60.

511–14   The thoroughness of his preparations is ironic in view of his
discovery that he needs to save Christ.

521   The *oure of none* was the hour of Christ's death:

Ora nona, dominus
Hys spryt he dyd vp-yelde   (*Lyrics* XV, p. 138)

See also *Horae*, p. 56, and note to II. 16 above.

524–7   It is not explained how the *devyl in helle* knows of the danger, but
Comestor (col. 1628) explains that Satan knew through the rejoicing of
those in hell, which *Vita Christi* explains was a result of the raising of Lazarus
from the dead (p. 636). Similar ideas occur in the conversation between
Satan and Hades in the Gospel of Nicodemus (ch. 4) on which this is loosely
based.

529   'Unless some trick helps, I am in a predicament'.

541   He does not explain very clearly what Pilate is to be made to believe—
presumably, the necessity of saving Christ (II. 533). To some extent the lines
(II. 532–41) give the impression of Satan's rapid re-planning.

543sd   Presumably Satan enters the closed scaffold (Pilate's) from which
Pilate's wife bursts.

Since the shirt was an undergarment, it seems likely that MS. *and here shert* should read *in here shert*. The similarity between abbreviated *in* and the nota for 'and' is close (cf. I. 244sd and note). The *kyrtyl* is the garment next up. 'Shirt' at this date can apply to a female garment, the smock, and it is only later that the 'shirt' becomes specifically male (cf. *Romeo and Juliet* II iv 109).

564–71   The demands of the Doctors become briefer and more insistent as Pilate's attempts to avoid the condemnation of Christ fail.

572–5   Cf. *Northern Passion* ll. 1015–18.

575–7   Luke xxiii, 14–15.

581–5   Cf. Matthew xxvii, 15; Mark xv, 6; Luke xxiii, 17.

582   Cf. *Northern Passion* l. 1022 (Additional MS.)

591ff.   With the return of the crowd, the playwright uses again the direct-ness of couplet speeches, cf. II. 314–37.

592–3   Cf. Matthew xxvii, 21 and Luke xxiii, 18–19. In the play Pilate offers to free Christ three times as in Luke.

594–5   Matthew xxvii, 22; Mark xv, 12.

596–7   Matthew xxvii, 22; Mark xv, 13; Luke xxiii, 21. *Crucifigatur* is from Matthew, here and at l. 599.

598–9   Matthew xxvii, 23; Mark xv, 14; Luke xxiii, 22–3.

603sd   Pilate's private words with Christ are reported only in John (xix, 9–11). The action suggests a scaffold with an inner area visible to the audience and from which they can also hear the dialogue.

606–7   Cf. *Northern Passion* ll. 1121–2 (Cambridge MSS.)

613–22   John xix, 10–11. The play follows the gospel account closely. Only ll. 619–20 are additional.

626sd   *in to* presumably means no more than 'to'. Cf. the note to 603sd.

627–8   Cf. *Northern Passion* ll. 1174–6 (Additional MS.)

638   Perhaps derived from 'thou art not Caesar's friend' of John xix, 12.

641   Only recorded in Matthew xxvii, 24. I have found no other use of the name *Artyse* except as a variant of 'Artus' in French romance; *s.v.* **Artis le Bloi** in Flutre, *Tables des noms propres*.

642sd   'Here one shall bring water'.

645–6   'Sanguis eius super nos et super filios nostros' (Matthew xxvii, 25).

646sd   'And they shall cry:'

bryngith. The suspension should perhaps be expanded *bryngyt* (see notes to II. 243sd and 856).

648   No gospel has the repetition of 'no cause' as late as this. It could reflect John xix, 12, but see *Gospel of Nicodemus* (ch. 9). The repetition serves to whip up the anger of the onlookers.

652   'We have no king but Caesar', John xix, 15.

655–656sd   The sentencing of Christ is carried out partly as in a contemporary court. Annas and Caiaphas apparently flank Pilate as he sits in judgment. In *Ordinalia: Passio* (ll. 2215–30) also seats are formally arranged (*cathedra* and *scabella*) and a bar is set up.

661ff   The First and Second Doctors' speeches are in marked contrast in their formality to the previous howling for Christ's blood. There is perhaps a momentary return to their previous tone at II. 671.

664sd   'And he shall run'.

665   The names of the two thieves in the *Gospel of Nicodemus* (ch. 10) are Dismas ('Dimas' in some MSS.) and Gestas. They are unnamed in the bible. Gestas frequently appears, as here, as Gesmas or Jesmas. *Legenda* has Dismas, who was converted, and Gesmas, who was damned (p. 223); *Metrical Life* Dismas and Jesmas (ll. 2764–5). They are unnamed in *York* and *Chester*. The speaker's name at II. 815 below is *Jestes*.

671   Pilate to the end asks for evidence against Christ. Eventually he gives way; according to Matthew (xxvii, 24) because he saw he was getting nowhere and to avoid a riot; in Mark (xv, 15) to satisfy the people; and in Luke (xxiii, 23) because the clamour of the Jews prevailed.

672sd   'And they shall all cry with a loud voice saying: . . .'

677–8   As it must have been obvious to the audience that those who were waiting to seize Christ were neither knights nor gentlemen born, these words do much to turn Pilate finally into a mere puppet. They could be seen as a final gesture of support for Christ by Pilate in the knowledge that they were in vain. It is a rather pathetic indication that Pilate is still far from understanding the nature of Christ's kingship.

679–90   The sentence of Pilate appears very briefly in *Gospel of Nicodemus* (ch. 9). The enumerating of each action is like a verbal Instruments of the Passion series. For a poem on this subject see *Legends of the Holy Rood*, pp. 170–93.

681   The pillar was still shown to pilgrims to Jerusalem in the fifteenth century. It was of stone and a part was in Rome (*Vita Christi* p. 638).

690   That is, long enough to go through both feet.

693–5   Cf. *Legenda* p. 223, 'Sed postea unus conversus, scilicet Dismas, qui erat a dextris, sicut dicitur in evangelio Nicodemi, et alius damnatus, scilicet Gesmas, qui erat a sinistris.' ('But one [was] later converted, namely Dismas, who was on the right, as it says in the Gospel of Nicodemus, and the other damned, namely Gesmas, who was on the left').

696sd and 698sd   Unlike the situation in *York*, *Chester* and *Towneley*, the scourging, crowning and mocking are here carried out with no dialogue, except the words of the First Jew preceding the scourging (II. 697–8); cf. *York* XXXIII ll. 336–419; *Chester* XVI ll. 307–54; *Towneley* XXII ll. 125–51.

   with forkys. A frequent way of showing the crowning with thorns in the later Middle Ages was with the crown being forced down over Christ's head with sticks. See for example Schiller II pll. 251–4, and the description in Mirk p. 121.

   to berynt 'to carry it'; cf. II. 733.

707–18   Close to Luke xxiii, 28–30 but considerably expanded. The expansions occur in II. 709–10, 713–14, and 716–18. The first (709–10) fairly certainly refers to the destruction of Jerusalem under Titus and Vespasian (cf. I. 443–58). The second (713–14) is simply a natural extension of the previous lines, with again perhaps a suggestion of the destruction in *wher xal be oure dwellyng*, in as much as this was the beginning of the dispersal of the Jews. The last (716–18) is a vision of the Last Judgment (cf. Isaiah ii, 21). *Vita Christi* (p. 648) gives a similar explanation of Christ's words. See also *Ministry and Passion* ll. 2424–6.

718sd   As with the movements of Christ before his betrayal, there is a pattern of moving and pausing, giving the impression of the fifteenth-century 'stations' paintings of Jerusalem (see for example *Early Dutch Painting* pl. 117) or a pilgrim tour of the sacred sites. It is interesting that in *Mary Magdalen*, the Maries going towards the sepulchre momentarily talk in terms of the pilgrim tour (ll. 995–1005).

   The incident of Simon of Cyrene appears in Matthew (xxvii, 32), Mark (xv, 21) and Luke (xxiii, 26).

719–26   The excessive politeness of the First Jew conceals a threat which is soon revealed when Simon refuses to carry the cross. The usual explanation for getting Simon to carry the cross was the need to hurry a weary Christ to his Crucifixion lest Pilate should change his mind (see *Vita Christi* pp. 649–50 and *Meditationes* p. 605).

727   Fabri records Simon's unwillingness to carry Christ's cross (I, p. 445). The same unwillingness appears in all the cycles but only in *Chester* is it because he disapproves of Christ's death (XIVA ll. 21–8). It no doubt stems from the word 'angariauerunt' ('forced') in Matthew and Mark.

739sn   For an account of the story of Veronica, see *Oxford Dictionary of Saints* s.v. The later part of the story, interweaving with that of Pilate and the miraculous healing of the emperor Tiberius, is told in *Legenda* pp. 232–3, drawn from *Gospel of Nicodemus*. It is dramatised in *Ordinalia: Resurrexio*, ll. 1587–2360. Fabri outlines the story as it relates to Christ (I, p. 443). There is no mention of the incident in the gospels. In the earliest version of the story it is at a previous time that the image of Christ's face is acquired on the handkerchief (for an example of this see *Legenda* p. 233). Note that the significance of the *kerchy* is not explained or commented on in the play beyond Christ's words at ll. 745–6. Possibly it was displayed to the audience, possibly (but less likely) Veronica merely reacted to the miraculous image. Veronica's part in the *Ordinalia* at this point is missing from the manuscript (see I, p. 428).

739   The addition of *3e* seems to give a more natural syntax and rhythm, but it is not a certain emendation.

746sd   In all the gospels the nailing of Christ to the cross is dealt with in a single verse. Under the influence of centuries of meditation on the sufferings of Christ all the plays extend this, usually with the element of the badly spaced holes bored for the nails. Only the Cornish *Ordinalia* in England have the legend of the forging of the nails (ll. 2669–739).

The cross is flat on the ground. In *Ministry and Passion* it is already in position (ll. 2431–6) before Christ is nailed to it. *Meditationes* offers both possibilities (pp. 605–6).

751–70   There is a practical problem with the nailing of the hands. Nails are only mentioned twice (767 and 770) which should mark the moments of nailing. It is not necessary for a medieval playwright to describe every move made by an actor, but they frequently do, especially if, as in this case, it is important to draw attention to Christ's sufferings. The following is one possibility: 2 takes one arm; 3 takes the other and is joined by 4. Since the holes are bored too far apart, 2 suggests stretching Christ out (763–4). As Christ's hand reaches the holes, 3 tells 4 to drive in the nail (767) as he holds the rope. 4 and 1 drive in the nails, though only 4 responds verbally, as 3 and 2 hold the ropes (770). The only slight awkwardness is that 4's '*þat I graunt*' etc., looks like a reply to 3's '*Dryve in þe nayl*' etc.

763   The stretching of Christ's body with ropes was an early addition to the sufferings of Christ on the cross. *Vita Christi* discusses this (p. 652). All the plays, including the *Ordinalia*, have the incident. See also *Northern Passion*, pp. 187–92.

763–4   'Fasten on a rope and stretch him out, and I'll pull against you'.

768   'And see if the flesh and sinews hold firm'.

773   The *nayl perto mad ful mete* of Pilate's sentence (II. 690).

774sd   The dancing around the cross as it lies on the ground is unique to this play. It functions in the same way as the earlier mocking games; see II. 182–93.

775   *takkyd* is ironic as it implies 'temporarily fixed'.

783–6   Adapted from Matthew xxvii, 40 and 42, Mark xv, 32 and the earlier saluting of Christ as king of the Jews at the mocking.

786sd   The crowd, now passively observing, is used to set up the crosses of the thieves.

790   The Second Jew echoes Pilate's words at II. 692.

790sd   Once again significant incidents are enacted in dumb show or at least action without set dialogue. The dicing and fighting and the setting up of the thieves' crosses is a background to the lament of Mary. The three Maries are Mary Magdalene, Mary Salome and Mary Jacobi. The swooning of the Virgin Mary is referred to in meditations and by pilgrim guides, particularly in relation to two moments. The first time is when she sees Christ led to Crucifixion (Fabri I, pp. 446–7) and the second as Christ dies on the cross (*Meditationes* p. 607). But these were frequently multiplied; see *Margery Kempe* pp. 187–93 and Bodley *Burial* pp. 155 and 157.
    Leysere is unrecorded elsewhere as an adverb and perhaps should be emended to *at leysere* 'at length'.

791–8   Mary's words to some extent echo her earlier and longer lament in I. 1045–76.

799–802   The first of the Seven Words from the Cross (see *Meditationes*, p. 607 and *Vita Christi* pp. 661–71). This one is reported only in Luke (xxiii, 34).

803ff   The words of mockery from the separate gospels are drawn together in the Jews' cries (cf. Matthew xxvii, 40 and 42, Mark xv, 29 and 32). II. 813–14 are an expansion, ironically drawing on the theme of mercy (especially ironic in view of the first of Christ's words from the cross).

815   As in Luke (the incident only occurs there; xxiii, 39–42) the thief, Jestes (Jesmas), picks up the words of the Jews, but the repetition is here made closer. Jestes is the alternative name for the damned thief (see above note to II. 665). He is said to blaspheme Christ but his explicit denial of his godhead (II. 817–18) does not appear in the gospel. Here however it is made to contrast with the saved thief's explicit expression of faith (II. 820).

817   'But I do not find it at all credible'.

819–25   The latter part of Dysmas' speech is taken from Luke (xxiii, 41). The word 'mercy' does not appear there however. In *Vita Christi* the thief's words are seen as a sign of confession, contrition and satisfaction (p. 659).

827–30   Luke xxiii, 43; the second of the Words from the Cross.

831–8   Through Mary's very human words the playwright is able to draw attention to Christ's mercy in his first and second words from the cross and lead into (II. 839–40) his third word, which is addressed to her. Mary's complaint of Christ's neglect appears in Fabri I, p. 388 and elsewhere.

843–4   Christ's third Word (John xix, 26–7). Comestor's heading for his chapter 174 which deals with this is 'Quod virgo virgini commissa est' ('How a virgin is entrusted to a virgin') col. 1631.

846–54   Mary's apparent lack of understanding because of her grief is frequently used as a way of allowing Christ again to explain the reason for his Crucifixion.

847   *Vita Christi* (p. 663) and *Meditationes* (p. 607) both comment on Christ's using the neutral, seemingly harsh, word 'woman', so as not to increase Mary's sufferings.

848   It is common to think of the redemption as a 'buying back' (its literal meaning) and by extension the paying of a ransom; cf. II. 954.

849   'For this is the will and intention of my Father'.

854sd   It is usually Mary Magdalene who is pictured embracing the foot of the cross.

855–8   As in the Bodley *Burial*, Magdalene attempts to control Mary's outbursts (e.g. ll. 508–10), though frequently she is shown as overcome with grief herself. The idea that Mary's grief increased Christ's suffering was a common one (see e.g. *Meditationes* p. 606).

856   *cheuith*   The suspension should perhaps be expanded *cheuyt* (see notes to II. 243sd and 646sd).

859–62   Cf. Gray *Lyrics*, no. 22, l. 4 (and note on pp. 110–11). Mary frequently asks to die with or instead of Christ; see for example *Meditationes*, p. 606.

866sd   Pilate, Caiaphas and Annas have been at Pilate's scaffold since immediately after the sentencing of Christ (696sd).

867–74   With Caiaphas' words the play returns to the gospel accounts (Matthew xxvii, 42–3; Mark xv, 31–2; Luke xxiii, 35 and 37).

874sd   Pilate mimes the writing on the board which is to be affixed above Christ's head and himself fixes the board to the cross. This follows John (xix, 19–22) which alone of the gospels has Pilate inscribing the board. *Vita Christi* records that it was the custom of the Romans to place the reason for the death of those crucified on the cross (p. 654).

879   'Quod scripsi, scripsi' John xix, 22; quoted in *York* XXXVI, l. 114 and slightly adapted in *Towneley* XXIII, l. 555.

881–4   The fourth Word from the cross: 'Heloi, Heloi lama sabacthani'. The form of the word *Heloy* is as it is in Mark (xv, 34; cf. Matthew xxvii, 46). With this speech the stanza form changes. Up to this it has been mainly quatrains and couplets; from here onwards the romance stanza predominates (see Introduction pp. 8–9 and Appendix 4).

885–6   As *Vita Christi* says, these are the words of Christ's manhood, which was suffering, not of his godhead (p. 665).

886   *peynde* is perhaps a by-formation from **peinen** 'to punish' or **pinen** 'to torment', giving a meaning 'suffer' (*MED* **peinen** 3. (a)) or 'languish' (*MED* **pinen** 6). *MED* relates it to **pinden** 'to enclose' and suggests a series of meanings 'to pinch, press; thrust, stab (sb.), pierce' none of which seems to fit here. Moreover, the evidence given for these meanings is slight, consisting solely of the *Catholicon Anglicum* (s.v. **Pynde**, p. 280) equating **pinden** with Latin *trudere* 'to press, thrust' besides the usual *includere* 'to enclose'.

889–92   Matthew xxvii, 47–9 and Mark xv, 35–6. *Hely* is Elias (or Elijah) the prophet who was taken alive into heaven (4 Kings ii, 11) and with Enoch was expected to come to challenge Antichrist in the last days.

893–6   Christ's fifth Word (John xix, 28), 'sitio' ('I thirst'). *Meditationes* gives both the spiritual and the physical explanations: the thirst for the salvation of man (cf. *Piers Plowman* B XVIII ll. 366–8), and thirst from dryness; and stresses the latter (p. 607). The play hints at the spiritual meaning (II. 894).

897   *hoberd* is only recorded from the N. town plays in *MED*. *MED* tentatively suggests a derivation from 'Robert', but it is perhaps rather connected with 'hob' ('a rustic') and ?'hobgoblin'. It is one of the many words of abuse that are used in the plays.

898   In Matthew (xxvii, 34) a drink of wine and gall is offered to Christ before the Crucifixion; in John, vinegar is offered after his cry of 'sitio' (xix, 29). The two have been blended as a result of the association with Psalm lxviii, 22, 'And they gave me gall for my food, and in my thirst they gave me vinegar to drink'. For the association of the texts, see, for example, *Vita Christi* p. 667.

907   *on þe newe gett* 'in the new fashion' i.e. by pulling a face (II. 908).

911–12   The figure on the cross is finally seen as a scarecrow.

913   Luke xxiii, 46; normally the seventh Word though it is not uncommon for the order of the last two to be reversed. It is given here partly in Latin (II. 913) 'Into thy hands, O Lord', and partly in English (II. 915). *domine* does not occur in Luke, but it does in the liturgical use of the phrase (see *Breviary* I, dccxiv and II. 230).

917   Uniquely here Christ indicates his intention of harrowing hell.

920   John xix, 30; normally the sixth Word, 'Now it is finished'. The final
two words have been reversed in order, perhaps because of the apparent
conclusiveness of the latter. *Vita Christi* says, 'All that was foretold of me in
the law and prophets, and whatever was written of me, and the work of
human redemption and all my work which I had to do in the world "is
finished" and perfected' (p. 669). In *Piers Plowman* (B XVIII ll. 57–9)
Christ's life also ends with these words, and they follow Christ's final lines
in *Chester* XVIa, ll. 356–9.

916   The word *fest* could mean either 'fast' or 'feast/festival'.

921–92   The whole of this passage seems to have been included as an
afterthought in the course of the new blending of pageant and play material
(see Introduction pp. 8–9). It is not possible, however, as it was in *Passion* I,
to identify and remove all interpolated material. Despite its awkwardness,
therefore, I have retained the passage in the main text.

931–2   John's emphasis on Christ's willing sacrifice for man is an appropriate repetition of a commonplace idea.

933   See above II. 844–6.

937–44   Mary's words serve as a meditation on the sufferings of Christ for
man; John's as a commentary on the meaning of those sufferings; cf. the
similar method used in the thirteenth century 'Stonde wel, moder, vnder
rode' Brown *Lyrics XIII* pp. 89–91.

949–51   John briefly presents the mystery of the redemption. All men by
Adam's sin must go to hell after death; Christ by dying as a man, yet sinless,
provides the 'grace' necessary for sinful man to have the opportunity of
heaven.

954   *bye*. Though commonplace the word brings alive the idea contained in
the Latin-based word 'redeem' (L. *redemere* 'to buy back'); cf. II. 848 and
note.

968sd   See above note to II. 790sd. The word *semi-mortua* occurs in *Meditationes* pp. 607 and 608 in relation to Mary's swooning.

974   In *Meditationes* and *Vita Christi*, Mary, John and the other Maries all
remain with Christ after his death. In view of II. 1163sd it seems likely that
that was the original situation in the *Passion Play*. After the burial they return
to a house on Mount Sion (*Meditationes*, p. 611), John's house (*Vita Christi*,
p. 674), Magdalene's house (*Meditations on the Supper*, l. 1061).

985   The temple introduces another scaffold unused except for this stanza.
For the probable pageant source of this whole passage, see Proclamation ll.
395–8 (Appendix 4, ll. 10–13). See above note to II. 921–92.

993ff   It is impossible to know how the original Harrowing of Hell was managed in the *Passion Play*. The readjustment and interpolation of material here has however resulted in a very striking juxtaposition of the dead and the 'living' Christ (the *Anima Christi*).

In *Chester*, *York* and *Towneley*, the Deposition intervenes between Crucifixion and Harrowing, but in many non-dramatic treatments of the story Christ's descent into hell is shown as following immediately on his death; see for example, *Meditationes*, p. 612; *Vita Christi*, p. 692; *Northern Passion*, ll. 1807–9. In the N. town pageants (according to the Proclamation) the thirtieth showed the death of Christ and the departure of Mary and John; the next showed Longeus and the first part of the Harrowing; the thirty-second, Deposition, Burial, Setting the Watch and possibly Resurrection, and the thirty-third, the second part of the Harrowing, the Resurrection and Christ's visit to his mother. There was, therefore, a somewhat unusual order existing there as well (see Appendix 4). The episode is not biblical but is an article in the Creed (Apostles' and Athanasian) and appears as a narrative in the *Gospel of Nicodemus* (Part II: *Descensus Christi ad Inferos*).

Pictorially Anima Christi usually appears simply as the risen Christ with cross-banner, but there are signs of more elaborate theatrical treatments e.g. Mons 'la Divinité, qui est comme une ame en ung pavillon de vollete, doit la apparoir' ('the Godhead [the Anima Christi], who is like a soul in a tent of gauze, must appear there'), *Livre de Conduite* p. 383.

1003–5 Anima Christi should appear from the cross to make the point clear, but there is no evidence of how it was done. At this point attention is drawn to the contrasting Christs.

1006–8 A simple but effective joining of the promise of the institution of the sacrament at the Last Supper and the establishment of it through Christ's death.

1010–12 The *Stanzaic Life* comments that it was the same body that Christ raised to life (ll. 7293–6).

1016sd 'nota anima latronis' is the first of the marginal annotations which indicate later use of the *Passion Play* section of the manuscript (see below App. 5).

1017–18 Psalm xxiii, 7. This verse is commonly used both for Christ breaking down the gates of hell and for his triumphal entry into heaven at the Ascension. In the services in the *Missal* it is related to Advent (30 and 48) and the Annunciation (727 and 763*). For its use in church drama see Young I, pp. 149–77.

1019 *Sorwatorie*: an otherwise unrecorded word. Perhaps a combination of 'sorwe' and 'purgatorie'.

1029 Belial at last voices the realisation of what Satan had feared (II. 516), and the words of the Demon in hell are now confirmed (II. 524–7). Satan's place, as *the* devil, is now taken by Belial.

1042   As Anima Christi enters hell so the action moves back to his dead body on the cross.

1046   'That this was indeed the son of God', Matthew xxvii, 54; cf. Mark xv, 39, Luke xxiii, 47. The *Quod* is an adaptation, interestingly in Latin, which fits the quotation into the stanza (cf. *Gospel of Nicodemus* p. 342). As before his death there are a series of denials of Christ's divinity, so his death is followed by a series of affirmations, of which this is the most explicit.

1047ff   The Second Knight translates the same Latin to produce his own affirmation. The marvels that accompanied Christ's death are described by the soldiers as actually taking place. Various means were used to create such effects, but for those here there is no evidence; cf. Coventry Drapers' accounts, 1565, 'Item [paid] to porter for keveryng [covering] the Earth quake ijs' (elsewhere money is spent on a barrel for the earthquake), REED *Coventry* p. 230; and for other effects see *Staging of Religious Drama*, p. 167.
       The earthquake is mentioned in Matthew xxvii, 51. The darkness is usually envisaged as an eclipse (as the Jews explain it in *Gospel of Nicodemus* ch. 11) and was staged like that at Lucerne with a reversible sun and moon (*Staging of Religious Drama*, p. 148); but smoke was also used there (ibid. pp. 149 and 197).

1055–8   The playwright is expanding, as the commentators do, on the conversion of the Gentile (Roman) Centurion.

1059   Nichodemus is mentioned only in John's gospel (xix, 39 and earlier), but his role is considerably developed in *Gospel of Nicodemus* ch. 11.

1067–78   One of the signs of the confusion of the manuscript text here is the repetition of the words of the Centurion. His speech is developed here, as in ll. 1055–8, as an expression of faith, though less as internal monologue and more as evangelising address.

1078   Joseph of Arimathea's request for Christ's body and his burial of it appear in all the gospels. He is said to be a wealthy man (Matthew xxvii, 57) and a secret follower of Christ (John xix, 38).

1091–8   Joseph's reasons for wanting to take down Christ's body stem ultimately from John xix, 31.

1099   *Baramathie*. The *B* has been added from the Latin preposition *ab*, 'Joseph ab Aramathia'. The *Ordinalia: Passio* (l. 3099) also has this form, 'iosep baramathia'.

1099–1122   Note that Pilate is still presented in a sympathetic light.

1101–2   In John (the only source) it is the Jews who ask Pilate for permission to break the legs of the crucified to make sure all are dead before the sabbath (John xix, 31). This and the Longeus episode precede the mention of Joseph, as they do in *Chester* XVIA, *York* XXXVI and *Towneley* XXIII. The

Northern Passion has a very similar order to that in the play, and there is verbal reminiscence at ll. 1099 and 1101 (cf. *NP* ll. 1853–4).

1103   The soldiers here and later are invariably called *milites* 'knights'. I have therefore used the word 'knight' throughout, both to describe the characters and to translate Latin *miles, milites*. What the word implies about their appearance is suggested in a comment by Bonnivard who acted in a play of St Blaise as a child: 'because the Latin story said *milites*, the soldiers, who only acted there as executioners, were dressed as knights (*chevalliez*), which therefore made me think that emperors only used knights as executioners' (1563) (original in *Les Mystères* II, p. 88). I am grateful to my colleague Dr L. R. Muir for drawing my attention to this reference.

1122sd   *heldyn hym in þe face*. Foster (*Northern Passion* II, p. 95) links this with *Northern Passion*, but it is as likely to derive from John xix, 36–7: 'For these things were done, that the scripture might be fulfilled: *You shall not break a bone of him*. And again another scripture saith: *They shall look on him whom they pierced*' (quoting Zacharias xii, 10); though it is true that in John the piercing of Christ's side is interposed between the action of the soldiers (33) and the comments on it.

1123–6   Cf. John xix, 33.

1129–55   The Longeus episode derives ultimately from John xix, 34, but is much developed. No name appears there. It is usually given in the Latin sources as Longinus but all the English plays (including the Cornish *Ordinalia*) have 'Longeus'. *Vita Christi* gives two versions of the story (pp. 674–5), in one of which Longinus is blind. It is also told in *Legenda* pp. 202–3, and he is briefly mentioned in *Gospel of Nicodemus* ch. 16.

1134   The knight's joke turns out to be true. Longeus's sight is restored.

1138   Shylock (*Merchant of Venice* IV i 36) swears by 'our holy Sabbath' but I know of no other use of 'Sabbath' in oath or asseveration. Longeus's use of *oure* aligns him with the Jews though later he seems to dissociate himself from them (l. 1150). The problem no doubt arises from the uncertain shifting in the Middle Ages between 'Jews' as a term for the persecutors of Christ – as in the names of the tormentors in this play – and a more sympathetic awareness of Jews as the people from whom Christ himself sprang and which numbered among them the prophets and patriarchs and characters like Joseph of Arimathea and Nichodemus.

1142   'Shove, man, shove!'

1142sd   An indication of how this effect was managed in the Rome *Passion* is contained in the hollow-shafted lance (*Staging of Religious Drama* p. 124).

1148–9   The speech seems to show Longeus's gradual realisation of his action; hence the break in l. 1149 emphasises his final understanding. The line is otherwise difficult to make sense of.

1155   For the repetition cf. I. 414 and *Mary Play* l. 1099.

1155sd   Nichodemus clearly stays in the background during the earlier episode (II. 1059 onwards). He is normally present, and is certainly necessary for the taking down of Christ from the cross; see II. 1163sd. Cf. Mons, 'Note to get ready here four new ladders for taking Christ down, for the carpenter and others can well help with it without speaking' (*Livre de Conduite*, p. 389). *Ordinalia: Passio* (ll. 3151–9) almost describes how it was done with apparently only two people and taken with the description here suggests Joseph on a short ladder in front of Christ ready to receive his body, and Nichodemus on a longer ladder withdrawing the nails from hands and then feet.

1163sd   The sudden reappearance of Mary suggests a conflation of material. Though it would be easy to bring her back from the temple in time for the Deposition, the sources and the unnecessary addition of a further scaffold make it far more likely that she was originally intended to remain nearby throughout.

Joseph sees the knights turning away and lays the body of Christ in Mary's lap. The scene is reminiscent of a *pietà*. See *Meditationes* pp. 608–10 and Bodley *Burial* ll. 392–832 for an elaborate description of both incidents.

1168–75   Mary's brief lament again makes use of traditional elements; see II. 791–8 and I. 1045–76 above.

1179sd   No indication is given of the kind of tomb but the usual one pictorially was still the 'table-top' kind. It has corners which are sealed later (II. 1280ff), a stone top (II. 1188), and a *lefft cornere* (II. 1316), a *syde* (II. 1320), and places where Christ's head and feet are located (II. 1328 and 1337). See however Fabri I, pp. 399ff; and Comestor (col. 1634) and *Meditationes* (p. 610), both quoting from Bede.

1180   *syndony*. The word could simply mean 'linen-cloth'. It is derived from Matthew xxvii, 59 and Luke xxiii, 53, 'sindone' meaning 'in fine linen'. It is sometimes used as if it meant 'shroud'. The grave clothes are usually described as a 'sudarium' for the head and bandages or shroud for the body; see for example *Vita Christi* p. 681.

1182–3   Cf. John xix, 39.

1185   Cf. Matthew xxvii, 60.

1199   The Maries are said to remain by the sepulchre (as Mary Magdalene and another do in Matthew xxvii, 61); but there is no indication of when they leave. When Christ appears to his mother she is alone (II. 1456) and the Maries reappear at 1671sd going *to* the sepulchre. Once again the text is too uncertain here to know what the original intention was.

1200   In the right margin *Incipit hic* has been added by a later hand. There are a number of alterations and additions in this hand, almost all apparently relating to the extracting of a Resurrection play from the latter part of the *Passion Play*. For these alterations and additions see the textual notes to ll. 1016sd, 1200, 1224, 1256sn–64sn, 1268, 1328 and 1336sn, 1407–10, 1431–9sd, 1671, 1769–81 and 1788. For a discussion of these alterations see Appendix 5.

1200ff   This episode appears only in Matthew xxvii, 62–6. Caiaphas' speech (ll. 1200–15) is a paraphrased and padded out version of the words of the chief priests and Pharisees.

1216–51   Pilate's response is quite different in Matthew: 'You have a guard: go, guard it as you know' (v. 65). In the play he talks as one of the Jews (e.g. *our lawys* ll. 1219) and wholeheartedly embraces Caiaphas's suggestion. In the vernacular versions in England it is usually Pilate who orders the watch; see for example *Chester* XVIII, *York* XXXVIII (and *Towneley* XXVI, the *York* text); *Ordinalia: Resurrexio* ll. 361–6; *Ministry and Passion* ll. 2643–4. In *Metrical Life* ll. 3054–63 it is Pilate's idea but he does not himself order the watch.

1224–6   These knights, except for Affraunt, are the same as those listed in the *Reynes Commonplace Book* (article 78, p. 257) as 'The iiij knyghtis þat wechyd sepulc[re]' and in Bodleian Library MS. Laud misc. 23, f. 114v. *Affraunt* is there 'Iheraunt/gerrant'. Similar names occur in the poem on the Resurrection in Ashmole 61, ff. 138v–44v:

> Syr Cosdram & ser Emorant,
> Syr Arfax & ser Gemorant.

The only name which has a biblical origin is *Arphaxat*, son of Sem (Genesis x, 22). It appears in the biblical genealogy on f. 21v of the N. town manuscript. It is also the name of one of the magicians overcome by SS. Simon and Jude in Persia ('Arfaxat'; James, pp. 464–5). *Cosdram* may be derived from a form of Chosroes, king of Persia; cf. 'Cosdras' in Lydgate's *Assembly of the Gods*, l. 473, and 'Cosdre' in Capgrave's *Abbreuiacion of Chronicles* p. 75 ('Arphaxat' also appears there, pp. 18 and 19). However he appears also as the Amiral Cosdram, nephew of the Sultan of Coyne, in *Guy of Warwick* (ll. 2905, 3109 and 3945) and since Amoraunt is the Sultan of Egypt's giant champion killed by Guy (st. 95ff.) it seems more likely that the names are derived from romance. Affraunt is a cousin of Tideus in the Thebes romances, Gemorant (the variant in the Ashmole poem) may well be related to Guymerraunt, the giant in *Octovian Imperator*, l. 921. I am grateful to JoAnna Dutka, University of Toronto, for putting me on the track of romance giants.
  Except for *Amoraunt* (repeated at ll. 1256) they appear in the text only here. As with those in the French plays, they are clearly intended to sound exotic. *Chester* has a different but similarly exotic group (XVIII, ll. 78–9). The order here is: 1. Amoraunt, 2. Arphaxat, 3. Cosdram, 4. Affraunt.

1240–47   The boasting is characteristic of all the knights of the watch in the plays. As with Herod's boasts at Christ's birth, it emphasises the powerlessness of humans against the power of God.

1251sd   Unless *out of* should be *into* this can hardly be the *platea*, since the knights remain near enough to address Pilate again at II. 1268–71 in terms which suggest they have not left but are just about to. At 1279sd, however, they are said to go with Pilate, Annas and Caiaphas to the sepulchre (Annas having appeared from nowhere), implying that they have not yet left.

1256–67   From the dialogue it sounds as though the knights are already at the sepulchre (*here* at II. 1259 and 1265; and cf. 1251sd) and it may be that the repetition at II. 1316–39 is a result of the blending of material from different sources both describing the knights actually at the sepulchre. Affraunt's speech which makes clear that they are still with Pilate is in the romance stanza whereas the others are in quatrains. Theatrically, however, there is no difficulty in seeing this section as looking forward to the positions that they intend to take up – childish but typical of the knights. The positions they describe here are apparently the ones they take up at II. 1316–39.

1273   The sealing is mentioned only in Matthew (xxvii, 66) and in relation to the Jews (but see also the apocryphal *Gospel of Peter*, vv. 31–3, in James p. 92). In *Gospel of Nicodemus* the Jews imprison Joseph of Arimathea and seal the gate. In the morning Joseph has gone and the seals are intact (ch. 12). This incident may have affected the treatment of the sepulchre here. In *Vita Christi* the sealing of the sepulchre is briefly discussed (p. 686). This unusual episode is depicted on one of the Norwich cathedral cloister roof bosses (photograph in Anderson, *Drama and Imagery* plate 13d).

1279sd   'Then Pilate, Caiaphas, Annas and all the knights shall go to the sepulchre'. From this point on, Latin stage directions become normal, possibly as a result of greater dependence upon non-Passion play material.

1286–7   Pilate shows by his trust in the seals that his fear is only of others coming to steal Christ's body. In *Vita Christi* it is suggested that, without intending it, the Jews bore witness to the Resurrection through their sealing of the tomb (p. 686).

1290   There is an element of the conjuror's locked cabinet in the treatment of the tomb. *Meditationes* says that Christ rose with the tomb still shut, 'ipso monumento clauso' (p. 616); see below, note to 1439sd.

1304–11   Pilate, before he leaves, changes to the short-line romance stanzas associated particularly with the knights. Because of the shortness of the line, rhyme and rhythm become far more pronounced. Pilate, Annas and Caiaphas go to *per* scaffolds; probably two, Pilate's and Annas and Caiaphas's, if the original arrangement is still being followed.

1312–39   The knights appear to take up the positions they have previously chosen. The positions they described at II. 1256–67 are the natural ones around a table-top tomb – right and left sides, head and foot. Two of the positions they name here, however, *lefft cornere* and *þis syde* are somewhat ambiguous. It is just possible that the sepulchre was seen by the audience from one side only, that the four knights are all more or less visible grouped around this side, and that the change from precise locations to ambiguous references reflects this. For the alteration to the numbering of the knights see note to II. 1200 above.

1313   *lyth bounde* i.e. in grave clothes.

1332–5   'To perform great deeds, I break heads, shatter lances and work destruction'. *schapyn* is probably an infinitive, the construction having broken down.

1340/1343   *He/þo wrecchis*; the delay of the noun subject has allowed the number to change.

1347   See note to II. 26.

1351   'However much I'm blamed [for it].'

1353   'child of Mahomet' or 'puppy of Mahomet'. Probably just another way of calling on 'Mahomet' himself. See above note to II. 26.

1362–7   The general meaning is clear, 'I can't stand any longer; I must go to sleep'. More literally it seems to mean, 'I cannot stand upright on the ground. I ask now that I may go and engage in/try out sleeping' (*OED* **Task** *v*. 3) or '. . . may take on sleeping as my job' (*OED* **Task** *sb*. II. 5). For *haue no foot* cf. *Ayenbite of Inwit* I, p. 56, l. 30.

1367sd   'Then the knights shall sleep and Anima Christi shall come from hell with Adam and Eve, Abraham, John the Baptist and others.' The sleeping of the knights heralds not as usual the resurrection of Christ but a triumphal procession of the souls rescued from hell. The situation in the Proclamation is somewhat puzzling. In the thirty-second pageant the watch is set and, it is said, the body rises from the tomb and terrifies the knights. In the following pageant, however, Anima Christi is said to raise the body to life again, and no knights are mentioned at all. For Proclamation, see Appendix 4.

1372–3   The power of Satan was said to be limited after Christ's death because no longer would all the dead go to hell. In all the Harrowing of Hell pageants Satan is bound as well as losing almost all his prisoners, see below II. 1416–23. The idea of the binding comes from Apocalypse xx, 2: 'And he laid hold on the dragon the old serpent, which is the devil and Satan, and bound him for a thousand years'.

1380–1   Adam briefly draws attention to the balancing of his and Christ's acts.

1391 *bowth*. See note to II. 954.

1404–7 The syntax of Abraham's speech is not clear. The simplest solution is to take *A sone* as an exclamation 'Ah, son!'; but it seems odd for Abraham to address Anima Christi thus, even though Jesus is a descendant of his, besides which it seems unnecessary for him to point out to Anima Christi that hell is broken open. I have taken the rather more awkward explanation, that it is disjointed syntactically, and that II. 1404–5 are a kind of musing contemplation on the manner of man's salvation, linked to II. 1406 by the parallel variation of *Helle logge lyth vnlokyn* with *oure bonde hath brokyn*. The omission of 'And' in II. 1405 will, of course, remove the difficulty.

1406 Hell is always referred to as a *logge* in this section. It is not another word for 'limbo' however, since Belial at II. 1428 also refers to it as the place of his perpetual punishment. It is also used elsewhere in the *N. town* text, e.g. p. 26, l. 315; p. 176, l. 239.

1407–10 For the later marginal additions, see Appendix 5.

1412–15 At the temptation of Adam and Eve in the Garden of Eden, the devil betrayed man, therefore he will be punished as a traitor.

1421 *envyous* initially of the blessed state of Adam and Eve in paradise.

1430–3 The devil is given bound into the power of Hades in *Gospel of Nicodemus* ch. 24 (Second Latin version).

1431–39sd For the later marginal additions, see Appendix 5.

1434–6 Cf. *Meditationes*, 'Tempus est ut excitem corpus meum; vadam, et reassumam illud' ('It is time for me to arouse my body; I shall go and re-assume it') p. 613. Cf. II. 1009–12 above.

1439sd 'Then Anima Christi shall go to revive his body; and when it is revived, Jesus shall say:'

Anima Christi goes to the tomb and Christ rises from it. The normal pictorial representation of the Resurrection is of Christ stepping from an open tomb, but the commentators stress that it was closed. Given the emphasis upon the seals, it is perhaps intended that Christ should rise here without disturbing the top of the tomb. There is unfortunately no indication of how it was to be done.

1440–3 The first two lines are from the fourteenth-century English *Harrowing of Hell* (pp. 4–5). They are nearest to the Auchinleck version:

> Hard gates haue y gon
> & suffred pines mani on; (ll. 43–4).

The fourth line seems to be an adaptation of *Harrowing* l. 45. There is no further connection. Nearly the same phrase, 'Harde gates I have go', appears in John of Grimestone's preaching book (quoted in Gray, *Themes and Images*,

p. 139) as the opening of a brief complaint of Christ. It seems as though at least one of the lines had a life of its own apart from the poem.

1443   Thirty-three is Christ's traditional age at the Crucifixion; cf. *Mary Play* l. 1070.

1448–51   The essential meaning of Christ's life and death is expressed succinctly and simply (cf. *Towneley* pp. 313–16, *Chester* pp. 345–6). This stanza is in the manner of the complaints of Christ. The other Resurrection speeches take this form and both mention the eucharist; see *Towneley* p. 316, ll. 322–33; *Chester* p. 345, ll. 170–85.

1449   *rede.* The *r* is a superscript correction but it is not clear what the original letter was. Since signs of both ascender and descender remain it may have been a *d* repeated from the previous line, *dede*, and corrected to a long *r*. *rede*, a form of **rade** *adv.*, seems the most likely word (cf. *MED* **rad(e** *adj.* and **rad(e** *adv.*). Davies reads 'red' and explains 'i.e. stained with blood' (p. 330).

1456   *Meditationes* contains the episode of Christ's resurrection appearance to his mother (pp. 616–17); as does the *Legenda*, pp. 241–2, and *Vita Christi*, pp. 699–700. *Stanzaic Life* says that though it is not recorded in the gospels it is unthinkable that Christ did not visit her (ll. 7765–88). For an opposing point of view see *Lyf of Oure Lady* p. 90. The episode does not appear in the other civic plays but is included in the *Ordinalia* with the almost inevitable 'Salve sancta parens!', *Resurrexio*, pp. 37–41.
   Salve sancta parens is the incipit of one of the sequences for the mass of the Blessed Virgin Mary from Christmas to Purification (*Missal* 772*). The rest of the text has no relevance, but the incipit was traditionally associated with Christ's greeting to his mother. For the place where the incident took place see Fabri I, pp. 347–8; *Margery Kempe* p. 75. In *Meditationes* she is still in the house of the Last Supper (p. 612); according to the Proclamation (*A4* 45) she is in the Temple.

1464–7   The rhetorical repetition of *Welcom* is paralleled by the farewells of ll. 1488–9. Cf. the similar thanks and farewells in the Annunciation episode of the *Mary Play* (ll. 1352–5, 1376–9).

1472ff   Christ's and Mary's words form a kind of counterpoint to their speeches at the Crucifixion. Then, salvation was promised in sorrow, now it is accomplished in joy.

1486   An adaptation of 'O mors ero mors tua' (antiphon for Holy Saturday (*Breviary*, I, dccci) and a prophecy of the Crucifixion (Osee xiii, 14)), and perhaps the antiphon before mass on Easter Day, 'Christus resurgens ex mortuis jam non moritur, mors illi ultra non dominabitur: quod enim vivit, vivit Deo, alleluya, alleluya' (*Missal* 357–8). Mary briefly elaborates the idea at ll. 1493–5.

1502   *oure alderers borwe* 'the surety of us all'.

1503sd   'Then the knights of the sepulchre shall wake and the First Knight says:'
As with the setting of the watch (II. 1200ff.) this episode appears only in Matthew (xxviii, 4 and 11–15). It is made quite clear from what they say that they are aware of Christ's Resurrection.

1505–10   The great earthquake is recorded only in Matthew xxviii, 2 and *Gospel of Nicodemus* ch. 13. At Mons, the coming of the angels to open the tomb is accompanied by a great noise from hell and the ground is to tremble (*Livre de Conduite*, p. 412).

1522–4   Matthew says that they told 'all things that had been done' (xxviii, 11).

1534–5   The Fourth Knight, besides being truthful, is also abrupt, and no doubt partly provokes Pilate's spluttering response.

1536–43   The violence of Pilate's reaction is no doubt also due to the unexpectedness of the news, since his concern had merely been with the body being stolen away.

1560–7   There seems little doubt that though the knights fall asleep they are also aware of what is going on around them. The Second Knight's words seem to echo Matthew xxviii, 4, 'And for fear of him [the angel], the guards were struck with terror, and became as dead men'. The guards are often pictured with their eyes open; see for example *Early Dutch Painting* pl. 67.

1574–5   Cf. one of the jibes at Christ on the cross, above II. 911–12.

1584   The Fourth Knight skilfully turns the truth into a weapon. It is difficult to decide whether the words of the Fourth Knight express a serious intention or are merely a counter-attack on Pilate, threatening him with spreading the news of Christ's Resurrection. Judging by their readiness to take a bribe, the latter is the more likely. The words of the knights in any case serve to reinforce the facts of Christ's resurrection; that body and soul came together (II. 1577), that he rose by his own strength (II. 1597), that he is alive (II. 1546–7).

1589–91   'That those who teach Christ's laws, will never rest until those who brought him [Christ] to his death, are dead'.

1600   Pilate's tone changes immediately he is challenged. There is no longer the sense of a man caught in an impossible moral position, as there is in the earlier trial scenes. Much may well be due to the change from Play to pageant material.

1608   It is perhaps worth noting that Pilate and Annas and Caiaphas retired to separate scaffolds at II. 1311sd yet are here together again.

1615   'Difficult to resolve'.

1620–3   Cf. Matthew xxviii, 12, in which the chief priests give a large sum of money to the guards to keep them quiet.

1621   *hede* 'hide'.

1627sd   'Here Pilate, Caiaphas and Annas take counsel privately between themselves. When they have finished, he [Annas] shall say:'

1628–31   By emphasising the secrecy, the playwright skilfully draws attention to what is otherwise a piece of commonplace cynicism, put forward by an expert. Also as Rosemary Woolf says, the playwright gives a 'fresh twist to the theme, since here the denunciatory generalisation of the satirist becomes the satisfied observation of the villain.' (*Mystery Plays*, p. 277).
   The seeming proverbs are not recorded from elsewhere by Whiting (M490), but for the general idea compare his entries for **Gift** G66 and 88, **Gold** G296 and 302, **Law** L110, **Man** M322, **Money** M627, 630–1, **Penny** P124 and **Penny-man** P129.

1630   *þis*, i.e. using bribery.

1642–4   Cf. Matthew xxviii, 13.

1647   The reason for sending the knights to Rome, apart from getting rid of them, is not apparent. It may have been suggested by the fact that according to the play they are Roman soldiers.

1650–5   In all the plays the knights are bribed and agree to keep silence, as in Matthew xxviii, 15.

1657–9   'As you have agreed, exactly, from now, do not fail your promises'. *falle* (rhyming with *halle*) seems an unlikely variant of 'fail'; but 'fall' seems to require a preposition. Whichever is followed, the meaning is little changed.

1671   The marginal addition *finem prima die nota* ('end to the first day, note') is connected with an apparent later extracting of sections of the text for separate performance. See note to II. 1200 above, and Appendix 5.

1671sd   'Here Mary Magdalene, Mary Jacobi, and Mary Salome shall come to the sepulchre. And Mary Magdalene says:'
   The post-Resurrection period is very varied in the four gospels. Traditionally, however, it is the three Maries who come to the sepulchre, even though only Mark records it. The whole episode was one of the major developments of church drama (see *Visitatio Sepulcri* in Young, I, pp. 401ff.) but the centrepoint of that development, the *Quem queritis*, is completely absent here.

1673 'Listen carefully now to what I have to say'. *Specyal* seems to have been transferred from the 'hearing' to the 'speaking'.

1674 Mark (xvi, 1) records that the Maries bought spices to anoint Christ, and Luke (xxiv, 1) that they prepared them.

1676/1679 Mary's words seem more appropriate *after* her knowledge of the Resurrection than *before*. But see Mary Jacobi's words (ll. 1688–95) where far more stress is laid on the certainty of Christ's rising than on the misery of his death. There is unusually almost no sense of mourning in Mary's words.

1680ff For earlier episodes in Mary Magdalene's life, see *Passion* I, note to l. 40, and Appendix 2.

1685 'Chose his dwelling-place in my sweet soul'; 'sweet' presumably because purified by Christ's forgiveness (see ll. 1680–4). The alternative reading *I ches* ('I chose his dwelling-place in my sweet soul') gives a slightly odd meaning but is by no means impossible. For *i-ches* cf. *i-cast, Mary Play* l. 1430, and *i-schrewe*, l. 85 (and notes). It may be part of the old verb **ichesen** or a new formation.

1687 *his burryenge boorde* 'his burial feast' or 'his funeral table'. A slab of marble was shown in Jerusalem as that on which Christ was laid out after his death; see Fabri I, p. 373. Perhaps the same idea, though of a wooden board, is contained here.

1688 According to tradition the Virgin Mary, Mary Jacobi and Mary Salome were all daughters of Anne, each by a different husband. The relationship is laid out in the N. town manuscript (f. 37) in a genealogical table, in the *Reynes Commonplace Book* (pp. 191–5), and in *Legenda* (p. 586). The extended family of Mary was also a favourite subject for artists and sculptors in the later Middle Ages, see for example Rushforth, pp. 198–202 and fig. 97; *Norwich School*, pp. 21–2; *Glass at All Souls*, pp. 26–9 and figs. XIII–XIV; *Child Jesus* pll. 12 and 98, and front cover (the Holy Kindred altarpiece by Derick Baegert from Dortmund).

1689 'He alighted in her in the same way as the sun in glass'. This looks like the common image of the conception of Christ, but the emphasis is usually upon the conception taking place without breaking Mary's virginity, and therefore upon the passing of the sun's rays through the glass without doing it any damage. Here the image is a more striking one of the sun illuminating the glass itself; cf. Joseph's words to Mary in *Mary Play*, ll. 1406–7.

1692 A conventional alliterative phrase not very appropriate here.

1694–5 Mary Jacobi's great confidence in Christ's Resurrection is most unusual at this point, where emphasis is usually upon the sadness of Christ's terrible death.

1696–9 The repeated mention of relationships trivialises a potentially moving episode, and makes the abrupt change to the tortures of the Passion (ll. 1700) very awkward.

1700 *feyn* may be: (i) 'join, attach' i.e. to the cross, from **feien** *v.1.*, but the usual sense of the verb is 'unite'; (ii) 'mortally wound' an otherwise unrecorded verb from **feie** *adj.*, 'doomed'; or (iii) 'enfeeble' ('?make faint', Block's suggestion, p. 388) from **feinten** *v.* with the loss of final *t*. A use of **fain** 'glad' seems impossible. It could be that the verb is delayed until the next line and that *lemys feyn* means 'beautiful limbs', or that emendation to *freyn* (from **fraien** *v.2* 'to bruise, injure') is necessary, as Davies suggests (p. 339). Block's suggestion still seems to me most satisfactory.

1701 'And the spear pierced and tormented [him]'.

1709sd 'Then Mary Magdalene looks into the sepulchre, saying:'
There is no mention of the laying aside of the stone, nor does the playwright make use of what seem like the inevitable words of the angel 'Quem queritis?' ('Whom do you seek?) from the Easter trope, as *Chester* (l. 345) and *York/Towneley* (ll. 235–6/382–3) do. Instead the playwright seems to have expanded the words given to Mary Magdalene in John (xx, 2) when reporting to the disciples (ll. 1710–18). In the *Ordinalia: Resurrexio* (l. 781) the angel greets the Maries with a statement 'I know whom ye seek' adapted from the trope.

1711 *brere* i.e. the crown of thorns.

1712 *mere*. The primary meaning is 'boundary'; then it comes to mean 'boundary marker', then 'marked place', and here probably not much more than 'particular place'.

1732 *a cloth* i.e. the *sindony* of l. 1180.

1734–49 Expanded from Matthew xxviii, 7 and Mark xvi, 7 (who mentions Peter).

1756–7 The fear of the Maries is either stated or implied in the angel's words in all the gospels.

1764 *they*, i.e. the Jews.

1765sd 'Mary Magdalene says to Peter and the other apostles:'
Chester also includes the report to the disciples and the running to the sepulchre of Peter and John (an important part of many church plays; see Young I. pp. 307–68). In John it is only Magdalene who reports to the disciples, and only John records the Peter and John incident (xx, 2–8).

1766–81 These two speeches very much more successfully convey the joy of the Resurrection.

1769–88 For the later alterations to the text, see Appendix 5.

1797sd 'Here John and Peter run together to the sepulchre, and John arrives first at the monument but does not enter'.

There are occasional similarities between the stage direction and John xx, 4, especially 'et venit primus ad monumentum'. The word 'Monumentum' has not previously been used. Because the writer is writing in biblical words it does not necessarily mean that he is not thinking in theatrical terms, but they no longer apply to the staging of the *Passion Play*.

1798 John looking in sees only the sheet, as in John xx, 5.

1801sd 'Peter enters the monument and Peter says:'

1802–5 Peter, going in, sees the *shete* and *sudary* (John xx, 6–7). The gospel account is no doubt the reason for the division of the linen cloth for the first time into shroud and head-cloth.

1805sd 'Here John enters the monument saying:'

The whole incident of Peter and John was elaborately explained by many commentators (see for example *Vita Christi* pp. 704–5), but there is no hint of that here.

1806–9 In the gospel the sight of the inside of the monument is sufficient to convince John of Christ's Resurrection. Here the playwright switches the emphasis to the grave clothes, but makes the same point. Elsewhere (for example *Vita Christi*) Peter and John are said to believe that Christ has gone, but not that he has risen from the dead.

1817sd 'Here Peter speaks to all the apostles gathered together:'

1826sh The speech heading is difficult to interpret. The first word is certainly *omnes*, the second could be expanded as *congregati* or *congregatis* but only the first would agree with *omnes*. Davies, following Block's suggestion (p. 333), emends to *omnibus congregatis* (p. 343). Though the forms are awkward the meaning seems quite clear, namely that Thomas voices the doubts of all the other disciples. In the *Ordinalia: Resurrexio* (ll. 893–1138) Thomas carries on a long defence of his doubts against Mary Magdalene and all the apostles one after the other.

'All gathered, Thomas'.

1830 Peter's reaction to the feelings of the other disciples expressed by Thomas is clear from the change from enthusiastic announcement of the Resurrection to doubt. Many versions of the episode suggest that neither Peter nor John was sure of the meaning of the empty tomb (*Ministry and Passion*, l. 2704; *Metrical Life* ll. 3226–9). The difficulty of interpretation goes back to the gospel where in v. 8 it is said of John that 'he saw, and believed'; but this is followed by 'For as yet they knew not the scripture, that he must rise again from the dead' (v. 9).

1838 *Meditationes* explains this strange switch from belief in Christ's Resurrection, to doubt and sorrow, by saying that she was so overwhelmed with grief that she did not remember the words of the angel (p. 618).

1843   The repetition of the seven devils reference (see above ll. 1680–3 and below ll. 1914) suggests separate pageants rather than continuous play.

1846–53   Cf. John xx, 13.

1853sd   'Here let her walk away from the sepulchre a little, saying:'

1858–61   Cf. John xx, 15. It is apparent from ll. 1870 that Christ is dressed as a gardener.

1862–73   Magdalene's reply is simply an extended repetition of her reply to the angel, until ll. 1870 when the playwright makes use of the second half of John xx, 15.

1874   *Maria* is written in large letters, each one rubricated, spaced out across the text space of the page.

1874sd   *spectans* 'looking carefully' could refer to Mary, for the first time looking at Christ; but it could be the other way round; his looking at her making her realise who he was.

1874–5   Cf. John xx, 16. Mary's reply uses a translation of the biblical 'Rabboni'.

1879–94   The first stanza is quite a close paraphrase (with expansions) of John xx, 17. The second stanza is an expansion and explanation of the preceding one, to some extent using Christ's earlier words to his disciples from John xiv, 2–3.

1929   The emendation is supported by the contemporary copy of this stanza on f. 201.

1936–8   These lines merely refer to the later appearance of Christ and are not a true ending to the *Passion Play*.

1938sd   'Here ends the appearance to Mary Magdalene.' This is the first practical indication that what precedes was once a separate pageant.

f. 143 The leaf interpolated into *Passion I*, showing blots and corrections. Photograph reproduced by permission of the British Library (BL MS Cotton Vespasian D VIII).

APPENDICES

The following section of text is an interpolation into *Passion* I, probably originating in pageant material. Apart from the opening quatrain (borrowed from I. 415–18 of the main text) and the re-copied final lines (1*A*44–9; cf. I. 343–8), the passage is written entirely in thirteeners. The incident is not mentioned in the Proclamation but unlike other episodes, which take a whole stanza, there is only part of a stanza to describe the main action of both the Last Supper and Judas's betrayal of Christ.

The passage is contained on a single leaf, f. 143, which was written later than the rest of this part of the manuscript and then inserted between leaves 7 and 8 of quire N. The leaf, judging by the ink blots already on it when it was written on, was a piece of scrap paper. Lines 44–9 are repeated from f. 142v where they have been deleted.

The passage contains the incident of the fetching of the ass and its foal which the main scribe or someone directing him decided was necessary to the story. It introduces Christ early in the play and spoils the effect of the Entry into Jerusalem heralded by Peter's sermon and John's excited words of preparation (I. 395–8). The vagueness of the stage direction at l. 43 suggests a practical uncertainty about the addition.

The source of the incident is Matthew xxi, 1–7, Mark xi, 1–7 and Luke xix, 29–35. John has only the riding into Jerusalem on a young ass ('asellum' xii, 14). Matthew and John both refer to the prophecy in Zacharias ix, 9, but in Matthew it is quoted relatively precisely and refers to 'an ass, and a colt the foal of her', while in John it is loosely quoted as 'an ass's colt'. Confusion about what Christ was riding on therefore exists from the beginning (see below, notes to ll. 8 and 17sd). *York* (XXV) and *Chester* (XIV) both contain the incident and though they are equally confused about the ass and/or foal in the text it is clear what happened practically. In *Towneley* there is no Entry

into Jerusalem. The *Ordinalia: Passio* has stage directions all referring
to ass and foal ('asinum et pullum/asino et pullo' 172sd, 190sd and
216sd) and Matthew twice refers to both (ll. 192–3 and 218–19).
Finally a stage direction at 264sd records that Jesus shall mount 'upon
the ass and foal' ('super asinam et pullum') almost exactly as in
Zacharias. What actually did happen is not clear.

f. 143 r & v

f. 143 *Jhesus*

    Frendys, beholde þe tyme of mercy,
    The whiche is come now withowt dowth;
    Mannys sowle in blys now xal edyfy,
    And þe prynce of þe werd is cast owth.

    Go to ȝon castel þat standyth ȝow ageyn,   5
    Sum of myn dyscyplis, go forth ȝe to.
    Þere xul ȝe fyndyn bestys tweyn,
    An asse tyed and here fole also.
    Vnlosne þat asse and brynge it to me pleyn.
    Iff any man aske why þat ȝe do so,   10
    Sey þat I haue nede to þis best, certeyn,
    And he xal not lett ȝow ȝour weys for to go.
      Þat best brynge ȝe to me.

Primus apostolus

    Holy prophete, we gon our way,
    We wyl not ȝoure wourd delay;   15
    Al so sone as þat we may
      We xal it brynge to the.

Here þei fecch þe asse with þe fole; and þe burgeys seyth:

Burgensis

    Herke, ȝe men, who ȝaff ȝow leve
    Thus þis best for to take away?
    But only for pore men to releve   20
    This asse is ordayned, as I ȝow say.

10 man] MS. mas   18 ȝow] e *written above -o-, and -o- itself written over an* e   19
þis] ff *deleted after* þis;   away] *second a written over another letter*   20 pore] *a large blot*
before pore *which was there before the leaf was written on.*   21 asse] MS. assa, *the -a is*
dotted for deletion, an e *is written above*;   ordayned] -a- *written over* ? r

Philippus
 Good sere, take this at no greff,
 Oure mayster us sent hedyr þis day;
 He hath grett need withowt repreff,
 Þerfore not lett us I þe pray   25
   Þis best for to lede.
  Burgensis
f. 143v Sethyn þat it is so, þat he hath ȝow sent,
 Werkyth his wyll and his intent.
 Take þe beste as ȝe be bent,
   And evyr wel mote ȝe spede.   30

Jacobus minor
 This best is brought ryght now here, lo,
 Holy prophete, at þin owyn wylle.
 And with þis cloth anon also
 Þis bestys bak we xal sone hylle.
Philippus
 Now mayst þu ryde whedyr þu wylt go,   35
 Thyn holy purpos to fulfylle.
 Thy best ful redy is dyth þe to,
 Both meke and tame þe best is stylle.
   And we be redy also,
 Iff it be plesynge to þi syght,   40
 The to helpe anon forthryght
 Vpon þis best þat þu were dyght,
   Þi jurney for to do.

Here Cryst rydyth out of þe place, and he wyl; and Petyr and John
abydyn stylle. And at þe last whan þei haue don þer prechyng, þei
mete with Jhesu.

Petrus
 O, ȝe pepyl dyspeyryng, be glad!
 A grett cawse ȝe haue and ȝe kan se.   45
 Þe lord þat all thynge of nought mad
 Is comynge ȝour comfort to be.

22 this] *a large blot above*   22–3] *A large blot has moved the beginning of the line to the*
right; the line reads Thus this best to take, *a mistaken repetition of part of 19 and*
deleted   25 I] y *deleted before* I   44 dyspeyryng] *third* -y- *written over an* e

All ʒour langoris salvyn xal he,
ʒour helthe is more than ʒe kan wete.

Notes to Appendix 1

1–4   These lines are borrowed from Christ's triumphal entry into Jerusalem (I. 415–18).

5   The word used in the gospels is '*castellum*', 'a village'.

6   Either 'go forth to [it]' or 'go forth, you two'. In view of the earlier part of the line, the former is more likely.

8   Only Matthew has both ass and foal (v. 7) and the disciples are asked to bring both (cf. stage direction at l. 17).

10–12   Matthew xxi, 3, Mark xi, 3; cf. Luke xix, 31.

14sn   James the Less and Philip (unnamed here as in the gospels) are seen later to be the two disciples told to fetch the ass (see below ll. 22sn and 31sn). In York and Chester the disciples are Peter and Philip; in the *Ordinalia: Passio* they are Matthew and James the Greater.

17sd   The stage direction contradicts Christ's request (l. 9), and the words of the *burgeys* (ll. 19ff); unless 'with þe fole' merely defines which *asse* it is. No further mention is made of the foal, even though in Mark and Luke there is no doubt that it is on the foal that Christ rides. In *Meditationes* he rides one after the other (p. 594).

18–19   Mark xi, 5, Luke xix, 33.

20–1   Comestor (col. 1598) and *Meditationes* (p. 594) have this explanation.

33–4   Matthew xxi, 7, Mark xi, 7, Luke xix, 35.

43sd   This stage direction seems like a rather casual cobbling-up of loose ends.

44–9   These lines are repeated from f. 142v. In two cases they supply words missing in the earlier copy (see textual notes to ll. 345 and 348). This suggests either that the scribe was correcting the second version himself (they are obvious enough corrections) or that he had access to another copy of the play and was not simply taking the text from f. 142v.

f. 148v which contains the series of cancelled catchwords showing the scribe's changes of plan for additions to the Last Supper section. Photograph reproduced by permission of the British Library (BL MS Cotton Vespasian D VIII).

The following section of text is the second interpolation into *Passion* I. It consists of two sections, continuous in the manuscript: the repentance of Mary Magdalene (f. 149) and the foretelling of the betrayal (ff. 150–1). These three leaves, now designated quire O, are interpolated between quires N and P. At the foot of f. 148v (the last leaf of quire N), there are a series of three catchwords and three speakers' names. Only one of each is left undeleted. The deleted catchword (1) at the foot of the page in a red scroll: *now cownterfetyd*, shows that the text originally ran straight from f. 148v, 'here Judas Caryoth comyth into þe place', to f. 152 where Judas enters with the speech: *Now cowntyrfetyd I haue a prevy treson* – as in the main text of this edition. The scribe, probably when including *Passion* I in his new manuscript, decided to insert the section on ff. 150–1 beginning with Jesus's words: *Myn hert is ryth [sory]* (catchword 2). Having written that section he then changed his mind and decided to include before it the section beginning with Mawdelyn's speech: *As a cursyd [creature]* (catchword 3). In order to enter this economically between the two parts of the text already written, he had to fit it onto a single leaf. The writing especially on the recto of f. 149 is therefore very cramped; the number of lines rising from twenty-five on f. 148v to thirty-three on f. 149r. This was his last change and the catchwords that lead into this therefore remain undeleted at the foot of f. 148v.

The episode of the anointing of Christ by a woman at a meal is reported in Matthew, Mark, Luke and John. Matthew and Mark place it two days before the Passover at the house of Simon the Leper, John six days before apparently at the house of Lazarus, Martha and Mary. In Luke the incident of anointing occurs much earlier in Christ's ministry at the house of Simon the Pharisee. The woman is named Mary only in John. The proximity in three of the gospels of the Last Supper and the anointing (together with the fact that the anointing takes place at a meal) was no doubt the main reason for the occasional combination of the two incidents, as in *Metrical Life*, ll. 1936–2109. The introduction of the forgiveness of Magdalene here in *Passion* I directly contradicts the prologue of the Demon (I. 40) where Magdalene's forgiveness is described as already obtained. The time lapse between the two would no doubt have made the contradiction less noticeable to an audience, however.

At the end of the Magdalene section the stage direction has been

altered by the deletion of 'gohth here outh' after 'Mary Mawdelyn'.
This deletion has been taken to indicate that Magdalene was intended
to be present throughout the Last Supper and the Betrayal. It is
almost certainly the work of the main scribe, since the deletion was
made before the stage direction was underlined in red, but as a part of
a series of piecemeal alterations it cannot by itself carry the authority
given to it. It was perhaps suggested by the unusual fact that it is
Mary Magdalene that carries the news of Christ's capture to the
Virgin Mary later in the play.

The effect of the second addition, the foretelling of the betrayal, is
to produce a doubling-up with the episode at I. 771–6. The repetition is not obvious, however, because the later version is verbally so
brief. The episode mainly consists of a lengthy development of the
disciples' replies. As with the prior appearance of Christ in the
interpolation on f. 143 (see Appendix 1), this prior view of the Last
Supper alters the tone and dilutes the impact of the episode. The
audience knows of the betrayal because Judas slips out of the closed
scaffold of the Last Supper to perform it (I. 583ff.), and the addition
therefore adds nothing necessary to the narrative.

The first section is almost entirely in thirteeners, and the second
entirely in octaves (ababbcbc). Neither incident is specifically described in the Proclamation.

f. 149 r & v

f. 149 *Maria Magdalene*
    As a cursyd creature closyd all in care,
    And as a wyckyd wrecche all wrappyd in wo,
    Of blysse was nevyr no berde so bare
    As I mysylf þat here now go.
    Alas, alas! I xal forfare   5
    For þo grete synnys þat I haue do,
    Lesse than my lord God sumdel spare
    And his grett mercy receyve me to.
      Mary Mavdelyn is my name.
    Now wyl I go to Cryst Jhesu,   10
    For he is lord of all vertu,
    And for sum grace I thynke to sew,
      For of myself I haue grett shame.

4 As] *letter deleted after* As

A, mercy, lord, and salve my synne!
Maydenys floure, þu wasch me fre!   15
Þer was nevyr woman of mannys kynne
So ful of synne in no countré.
I haue be fowlyd be fryth and fenne,
And sowght synne in many a ceté;
But þu me borwe, lord, I xal brenne,   20
With blake fendys ay bowne to be.
   Wherefore, kynge of grace,
With þis oynement þat is so sote
Lete me anoynte þin holy fote,
And for my balys þus wyn sum bote,   25
   And mercy, lord, for my trespace.

Jhesus
   Woman, for þi wepynge wylle
Sum socowre God xal þe sende.
Þe to saue I haue grett skylle,
For sorwefful hert may synne amende.   30
All þi prayour I xal fulfylle,
To þi good hert I wul attende
And saue þe fro þi synne so hylle
And fro sefne develys I xal þe fende.
   Fendys, fleth ȝour weye!   35
Wyckyd spyrityS, I ȝow conjowre,
Fleth out of hire bodyly bowre!
In my grace she xal evyr flowre
   Tyl deth doth here to deye.

Maria Magdalene
f. 149v   I thanke þe, lorde, of this grett grace.   40
   Now þese sefne fendys be fro me flytt,
I xal nevyr forfett nor do trespace,
In wurd nor dede, ne wyl nor wytt.
Now I am brought from þe fendys brace,
In þi grett mercy closyd and shytt,   45
I xal nevyr returne to synful trace
Þat xulde me dampne to helle pytt.

24 anoynte] noyy *deleted after* a–   31 I xal] *the stroke of an* ?x *deleted before* I   33 so]
hende *deleted after* so   34 sefne] *MS.* vij; xal] x *written over an* a   38 she xal] x
deleted before she   41 sefne] *MS.* vij

    I wurchep the on knes bare;
Blyssyd be þe tyme þat I hedyr sowth,
And þis oynement þat I hedyr brought,   50
For now myn hert is clensyd from thought
    Þat fyrst was combryd with care.

Judas
    Lord, methynkyth þu dost ryght ylle
To lete þis oynement so spylle;
To selle it yt were more skylle   55
    And bye mete to poer men.
The box was worth of good moné
Thre hunderyd pens, fayr and fre;
Þis myght a bowht mete plenté
    To fede oure power ken.   60

Jhesus
    Pore men xul abyde.
Ageyn þe woman þu spekyst wronge,
And I passe forth in a tyde;
Off mercy is here mornyng songe.

*Here Cryst restyth and etyth a lytyl and seyth syttyng to his disciplis
and Mary Mawdelyn:*

ff. 150–51

f. 150   *Jhesus*
    Myn herte is ryght sory and no wondyr is,   65
Too deth I xal go and nevyr dyd trespas.
But ȝitt most grevyth myn hert evyr of this:
On of my bretheryn xal werke þis manas.
On of ȝow here syttynge my treson xal tras,
On of ȝow is besy my deth here to dyth;   70
And ȝitt was I nevyr in no synful plas
Wherefore my deth xuld so shamfully be pyght.

---

53 ylle] y *apparently altered from* i   58 Thre hunderyd] MS. iij. C.   64 *sd* Mary
Mawdelyn] *after* Mawdelyn, gohth here outh, *not underlined, deleted in red ink*   66
Too] MS. Thoo, h *dotted for deletion*   67 grevyth] g *much altered or written over another*
letter   71 no] syn *deleted after* no

Petrus
My dere lord, I pray the þe trewth for to telle,
Whiche of vs ys he þat treson xal do?
Whatt traytour is he þat his lord wold selle? 75
Expresse his name, lord, þat xal werke þis woo.
Johannes
If þat þer be on þat wolde selle so
Good mayster, telle us now opynly his name.
What traytour is hym þat from þe wolde go,
And with fals treson fulfylle his grett shame? 80

Andreas
It is ryght dredfull such tresson to thynke,
And wel more dredfful to werk þat bad dede.
For þat fals treson to helle he xal synke,
In endles peynes grett myscheff to lede.
Jacobus maior
It is not I, lord, for dowte I haue drede, 85
Þis synne to fulfylle cam nevyr in my mende.
Iff þat I solde þe, thy blood for to blede,
In doyng þat treson my sowle xulde I shende.

Matheus
f. 150v   Alas, my dere lord, what man is so wood
For gold or for sylvyr hymself so to spylle? 90
He þat þe doth selle for gold or for other good,
With his grett covetyse hymself he doth kylle.
Bartholomeus
What man soevyr he be of so wyckyd wylle,
Dere lord, among vs, tell vs his name all owt;
He þat to hym tendyth þis dede to fulffille, 95
For his grett treson his sowle stondyth in dowt.

75 lord wold] þat *repeated after* lord *and not deleted*   79 þe wolde] þat *repeated after* þe
and not deleted

Philippus
   Golde, sylver and tresoour sone doth passe away,
   But withowtyn ende evyr doth laste þi grace.
   A, lord, who is that wyll chaffare þe for monay?
   For he þat sellyth his lord to grett is þe trespace.   100
Jacobus minor
   That traytour þat doth þis orryble manace,
   Bothe body and sowle I holde he be lorn;
   Dampnyd to helle pytt, fer from þi face,
   Amonge all fowle fyndys to be rent and torn.

Symon
   To bad a marchawnt þat traytour he is,   105
   And for þat monye he may mornyng make.
   Alas, what cawsyth hym to selle þe kyng of blys?
   For his fals wynnynge þe devyl hym xal take.
Thomas
   For his fals treson, þe fendys so blake
   Xal bere his sowle depe down into helle pytt.   110
   Resste xal he non haue, but evyrmore wake
   Brennyng in hoot fyre, in preson evyr shytt.

Thadeus
   I woundyr ryght sore who þat he xuld be
   Amongys vs all, bretheryn, þat xuld do þis synne.
f. 151   Alas, he is lorn, þer may no grace be,   115
   In depe helle donjeon his sowle he doth pynne.
Jhesus
   In my dysche he etyht, þis treson xal begynne;
   Wo xal betydyn hym for his werke of dred.
   He may be ryght sory swych ryches to wynne,
   And whysshe hymself vnborn for þat synful ded.   120

---

100 is þe] *a letter obliterated after* þe   106 monye] may *deleted before* monye   107
hym] y *deleted after* hym   120 And] *MS.* Ad

Judas
> The trewth wolde I knowe as leff as ȝe,
> And þerfore, good sere, þe trewth þu me telle,
> Whiche of vs all here þat traytour may be;
> Am I þat person þat þe now xal selle?

Jhesus
> So seyst þiselff, take hed att þi spelle.   125
> Þu askyst me now here if þu xalt do þat treson;
> Remembyr þiself, avyse þe ryght welle,
> Þu art of grett age and wotysst what is reson.

Here Judas rysyth prevély and goth in þe place and seyt: Now cowntyrfetyd.

128 *sd* cowntyrfetyd] fetyd *trimmed away at edge of leaf*

Notes to Appendix 2

1   The incident which follows is recorded in Matthew (xxvi, 6–13), Mark (xiv, 3–9) at the house of Simon the Leper, and in Luke (vii, 37–50) at the house of Simon the Pharisee. In John it is referred to (xi, 2) and narrated (the host is not named but Martha, Mary's sister, is said to have served) in xii, 1–8. *Metrical Life* places the Last Supper in the house of Simon the Leper (as in the *Passion Play*, I. 478sd–486) and precedes it by the incident of Magdalene's anointing of Christ's feet (ll. 1936–57). Magdalene is forgotten, as is the house of Simon the Leper, once the incident is over, which causes no problem in a narrative poem but cannot happen in a play.

5–6   Mary and Peter were types of the penitent sinner. Only in Luke is this incident concerned with the forgiveness of sins.

19   In Luke she is 'a woman that was in the city, a sinner' (vii, 37).

24   In John it is Christ's feet which are anointed, in Luke his head and feet, and in Matthew and Mark his head.

27–30   An emphasis on her penitence; in Luke it is her love and her faith that win her forgiveness (vv. 47 and 50).

34   Mark xvi, 9 and Luke viii, 2 name Mary Magdalene as the woman from whom seven devils were cast; see I. 40 and II. 1608–14.

44   *brace*. The most likely meaning is 'embrace, hold', but *MED* (**brace** *n.*) does not give this and *OED* (s.v. Brace *sb²*.) has only one example, in 1589. The only other possiblity, and it seems to me a remote one, is 'strap' or 'fastening' (*MED* **brace** *4(a)*); but this is in restricted use, refers to small fastenings and is not related to restriction of freedom, as it would need to be to make sense here. The meaning exists in the verb (s.v. **bracen** *v.1*). Under **Brace** *v¹*, *OED* notes: 'some of the senses are taken directly from those of **Brace** *sb².*' In this case the opposite seems to have happened.

53ff   It is Judas who voices the complaint in John (xii, 4–6). In Matthew and Mark it is the disciples.

58   The sum is mentioned in Mark (xiv, 5) and John (xii, 5). It was traditionally connected with Judas's acceptance of the thirty pence as the price of Christ's betrayal, replacing the lost 10 per cent cut of the profit from the selling of the ointment, which as treasurer of the disciples he considered himself entitled to (see for example *Ministry and Passion* ll. 1921, 1927–32 and 2047–50 and note to ll. 1917–32).

61–3   Matthew xxvi, 10–11, Mark xiv, 6–7; cf. John xii, 7–8.
   'Poor men will remain. You speak wrongly against the woman considering that I in a while shall depart'.

63sd   Christ's actions here have not the solemnity of those in the later Last Supper scene.
   It is possible that Mary Magdalene was to remain on the scaffold until the curtains closed again but equally possible that she was to remain throughout and then go on to report to Mary. It is impossible to be quite sure what was intended or indeed whether the scribe himself had thought it through.

65   This is the beginning of the foretelling of the betrayal; cf. the later version II. 771–6.

65–72   Christ expresses his grief at his approaching death and that he will be betrayed by one of his own disciples though he is innocent. His own declaration of his innocence (ll. 66 and 71–2) brings expression of character and exemplary demonstration somewhat into conflict (cf. I. 933–6 and note). His grief (John xiii, 21) is explained by Comestor (col. 1617) as grief for Judas's damnation.

69–70   The repetitions successfully build up the tension of the scene (see Woolf, *Mystery Plays*, p. 234, for a sympathetic examination of this treatment of the episode).

73ff   The speeches that follow form an accumulating denunciation of the traitor.

85–6   James varies the denunciations with doubt of himself. He is the only one to use the words of the gospels, though he uses them in denial not as a question (Matthew xxvi, 22; Mark xiv, 19).

93–100   Bartholomew and Philip return to asking for the name of the traitor.

95   The meaning seems to be 'He who goes to him (i.e. Christ) to carry out this act', but it may be that *to hym tendyth* means 'intends in himself' – a more satisfactory meaning but a rather unusual use of 'to' (?cf. 'thinks to himself').

105   The '*mercator pessimus*' of the liturgy (see note to I. 617).

113–16   Thadeus's speech draws the denials and questions to a close by turning the questioning to the other disciples.

117–20   'He that dippeth his hand with me in the dish, he shall betray me. The Son of man indeed goeth, as it is written of him: but woe to that man, by whom the Son of man shall be betrayed: It were better for him, if that man had not been born.' Matthew xxvi, 23–4; Mark xiv, 20–1 is very similar.

124   Judas is the first to ask the question of himself. In Matthew and Mark (and at I. 771–6) all the disciples ask.

124–5   Matthew xxvi, 25. Christ's words, '*Tu dixisti*', were taken to mean 'You ask, but you in fact know' (see Comestor col. 1617).

128   That is: 'You are old enough to know the meaning of what you are doing'.

APPENDIX 3

Now between the two parts of the Passion Play are a series of stanzas describing a procession. They have nothing to do with the play, but were written here when the manuscript of *Passion* I was separate (see Introduction pp. 2–8), on one of the leaves left blank after the play at the end of the manuscript. Though they have nothing to do with the play, they are an important witness to associated dramatic activity and to the nature of the earlier manuscript as a playbook.

Speaking apparently to a mixed lay and clerical audience (ll. 9 and 11), two doctors explain and comment on a procession of apostles and (presumably) others. The language is at times aureate and at others plain. The stanza form is a quatrain.

f. 163 r & v

f. 163   *Primus doctor*
                O, thou altitude of al gostly ryches,
                O, þu incomperhensibele of grete excyllence,
                O, þu luminarye of pure lyghtnes,
                Shete oute þi bemys ontyl þis audyens!

          Secundus doctor
                O, *Fily altissimi* clepyd by eternalyté,   5
                Hele þis congregacyon with þe salve of þi passyon;
                And we pray þe, *Spiritus Paraclyté*,
                With þe fyre of þi love to slake all detraccyon.

          Primus doctor
                To þe pepyl not lernyd, I stonde as a techer,
                Of þis processyon to ʒeve informacyon;   10
                And to them þat be lernyd, as a gostly precher,
                That in my rehersayl they may haue delectacyon.

          Secundus [doctor]
                Welcome, of þe apostelys þe gloryous qwere:
                Fyrst Petyr, ʒour prynce and eke ʒour presydent,
                And Andrewe, ʒour half-brother, togedyr in fere,   15
                That fyrst folwyd Cryst be on assent.

1, etc. *sn*] *Arabic numerals with no suspension mark*   13 *sn doctor*] *omitted in MS.*

Primus [doctor]

    O, ʒe tweyn luminaryes, Jamys and Jhon,
    Contynualy brennyng as bryght as þe sonn-bem;
    With þe chene of charyté bothe knyt in on,
    And offeryd of ʒour modyr to Cryst in Jherusalem.   20

Secundus [doctor]

f. 163v   Welcome, Phelypp, þat conuertyd Samaryan,
    And conuertyd þe tresorere of þe qwene Candas;
    With Jamys þe Lesser, that *apud Jherosolyman*
    Was mad fyrst patryarke by þe ordenauns of Cephas.

Primus [doctor]

    Heyl, Mathew, the apostel and also evangelyst,   25
    That was clepyd to þe flok of gostly conuersacyon
    From thyrknes of concyens þat ʒe were in fest;
    With Bertylmew, þat fled all carnall temptacyon.

Secundus [doctor]

    Heyl, Symeon Zelotes, þus be ʒour name,
    And Judas, þat bothe wel lovyd Oure Lord;   30
    Thereffore ʒe haue bothe joye and game
    Wher nevyr is stryff but good acorde.

Primus [doctor]

    Heyl, Poul, grett doctour of þe feyth
    And vessel chosyn be trewe eleccyon;
    Heyl, Thomas, of whom þe gospel seyth   35
    In Crystys wounde was ʒour refeccyon.

Secundus [doctor]

    Heyl, John Baptyst, most sovereyn creature
    That evyr was born be naturall conseyvyng,
    And hyest of prophetys, as wytnessyth scrypture;
    Heyl, [voys] þat in desert was allwey cryeng.   40

Primus [doctor]

---

19 chene] ?l *deleted before* chene   17, etc. *sn* doctor] *omitted in MS.*   22 Candas]
MS. Cavdas   24 Cephas] id est Petyr *added above* Cephas   25 etc. *sn*] *Arabic
numerals with suspension mark*   40 voys] *MS.* joys

Notes to Appendix 3

1–8   The opening is apparently an invocation to the Trinity: ll. 1–4 to the Father, ll. 5–6 to the Son, and ll. 7–8 to the Holy Spirit.

5   'Son of the highest'; cf. Mark v, 7 and Luke viii, 28, both times spoken by evil spirits.
    by eternalyté. Possibly 'everlastingly' or possibly 'by virtue of your everlasting nature'.

7   'Holy Spirit' – the words are not usually used together and perhaps should be considered as two names here: 'Spirit, Paraclete'. The name *Paraclete* is only used in John's gospel (ch. xiv, xv and xvi).

8   Love is the attribute of the Holy Spirit; see *Mary Play* l. 464.

9–12   For the unlearned factual information is given, for the learned spiritual interpretation.

13   The choir of the apostles comes first. The order of the first five and Matthew is the same as that in Luke vi, 14–16 (cf. Matthew x, 2–4). The sharing of feast-days is perhaps the reason for upsetting that order (see Philip and James, May 1st; Simon and Jude, October 28th). This does not affect Peter, however, who shares June 29th with Paul.

14–16   Peter is always seen as the leader of the disciples. Andrew is Peter's brother; so *3our half-brother* must, like *3our prynce and eke 3our presydent*, be in relation to the rest of the apostles and mean something like 'spiritual brother'. Peter and Andrew are usually reckoned the first disciples to be called; see Comestor (col. 1557) and *Metrical Life* l. 830–5.

16   *be on assent* 'wholeheartedly'.

17–20   These are James the Great and John the Evangelist, sons of Zebedee. *With þe chene of charyte bothe knyt in on* perhaps derives from *Legenda* where they are said to be 'of one love and of one study and of one will' (*Golden Legend* V, p. 97). Their mother was said to be Mary Salome, half-sister of the Virgin Mary (*Legenda* p. 586).

20   See Matthew xx, 20–3.

21–2   For Philip's conversion of Samaria, see Acts viii, 5–13; for his conversion of the treasurer of Queen Candace of Ethiopia, see Acts viii, 27–39. The manuscript reading *Cavdas* presupposes that the *n* of *Candas* has at some stage been mis-read as a *u* and then written *v*.

23–4   James the Less was bishop of Jerusalem (*Legenda* p. 296; Eusebius, Bk. 2, I, p. 72). *Cephas* is one of Peter's names (Gk. 'a rock'), as the gloss *'id est Petyr'* makes clear (John i, 42). Philip and James share the same feast-day (May 1st).

26–7   '[You] who were called from the darkness of conscience that you were set firmly in, to the company of [those living the] spiritual life' (cf. *Legenda* p. 622).

28   There seems no special reason why this attribute rather than another should be attached to Bartholomew (unless *carnall* is to be understood as 'of the world', see *Golden Legend* V, p. 34), nor for putting Matthew and Bartholomew together; unless the Gospel of Matthew found in India and said to have belonged to Bartholomew is a connection (Eusebius Bk 5, x, pp. 213–14 and *Golden Legend* V, p. 37).

29–30   Simon (Zelotes) and Jude share the same feast-day (October 28th). They were said to be brothers, traditionally sons of Mary Jacobi as was James the Less. They preached together in Persia (*Golden Legend* VI, pp. 75–80).

33–4   The name Paul is interpreted by Isidore as *electus* 'elected' (VII, ix, 9). He also quotes Acts xii, 2, where Paul is 'elected' by the Holy Spirit.

35–6   'Your [spiritual] refreshment / Your relief [from doubt] was through Christ's wounds'. The reference is to John xx, 25–8. The idea of Christ's wounds as refreshment occurs frequently elsewhere; for example, *Missal* 755*, Brown *Lyrics XV*, p. 1.

37–40   John the Baptist seems to be the first of the next group, perhaps the prophets and patriarchs (cf. carol 309, st. 4, Greene p. 188). *Vita Christi* describes John's conception slightly differently '. . . the conception of the Precursor appears miraculous because it was not only by nature but through nature helped by divine grace' (p. 16).

40   Isaiah xl, 3: 'The voice of one crying in the desert. Prepare ye the way of the Lord, make straight in the wilderness the paths of our God'. See also the note to I. 133 and 135. The manuscript reading 'joys', though it makes sense grammatically, makes no sense in relation to John's ministry, and the line is so nearly a quotation from Isaiah that the emendation seems certain.

APPENDIX 4

As explained in the Introduction (pp. 8–9) there is an intrusion of text written in romance stanzas into the couplets and quatrains of the play after l. 880, and, after l. 1765, of text written regularly in octaves. The romance stanzas appear in two blocks, II. 881–1042 and II. 1264–1765. These two sections contain (i) the end of the Crucifixion, the taking of Mary to the Temple and the first part of the Harrowing of Hell, and (ii) the setting of the watch and sealing of the tomb, the second part of the Harrowing, and the Resurrection, including the visit to the Virgin Mary, the waking of the watch, report to Pilate and the bribing, and the visit of the Maries to the sepulchre. II. 1765 to the end is in octaves and contains the visit of the Maries to the disciples, the visit of Peter and John to the Sepulchre, and the appearance of Christ to Mary Magdalene and her report to the disciples. The romance stanzas are continuous, the octaves almost so (except for three quatrains). The only section of mixed stanzas in the second part of *Passion* II occurs between the two romance blocks, II. 1043–1263, and contains the reaction of Centurio (twice), Joseph of Arimathea's request to Pilate for Christ's body, the Longeus episode, the burial of Christ and the beginning of the setting of the watch. It consists of 31 quatrains, 11 octaves, 1 single line and a single romance stanza.

It is impossible to be certain about the origin of this material, but it is interesting to note that if the episodes contained in the mixed section are removed from the Proclamation description, the order becomes the same as that of the play as it appears in the manuscript.

In other words if the scribe or the organiser of the present compilation, working with the pageants represented by the Proclamation,
decided to use the (?) *Passion Play* sections for Longeus, Joseph of
Arimathea, the Burial and the beginning of the setting of the watch,
and inserted it as a block of text into the compilation (as it appears in
II. 1043–1263), he would have had to have removed the pageant
versions of those episodes from the positions indicated by the Proclamation and would have ended up with the order in the play as it
now stands.

It is also worth noting in relation to this that in the romance and
octave sections Latin stage directions predominate (2:1, 7:1, and 6:1),
whereas in the mixed section there are no Latin stage directions at all
but ten English ones similar in fullness, practicality and continuity to
those contained in the first part of *Passion* II. In that part there are 44
English directions, many of them very full, and only 9 Latin ones, all
brief and all but one in the margin.

The obvious conclusion is that the mixed section is drawn from
copy of a kind similar to that of the first part of *Passion* II (i.e. a
continuous play) if not from the *Passion Play* itself, and that the
romance and octave sections are drawn from a different kind of
copy, in all likelihood the pageant material reflected in the Proclamation.

The subject matter of the romance and octave sections often
corresponds quite closely with the descriptions in the Proclamation.
This is noticeable in the description of Mary and John at the cross,
the Harrowing of Hell, Christ's visit to his mother, and the visit of
the Maries to the sepulchre and the subsequent events. In the Mary
and John episode, Mary's mourning and swooning, John's comforting and leaving Mary in the Temple, all appear in both. Two
incidents, the divided Harrowing and Christ's visit to his mother are
especially important as occurring only here amongst all the English
plays. The visit to the sepulchre and the subsequent events are
commonplace items and the similarity between Proclamation and
play is therefore less significant. Nevertheless in order and incidents
the Proclamation and play are close.

Furthermore, the incident of John taking Mary to the Temple,
contained in the Proclamation and in the romance section of the play,
conflicts with the later situation in the mixed section where Mary
appears to remain at the foot of the cross.

There seems incidentally little doubt that there was already similarity between the contents of the play and those of the pageants. The

seven words of Christ from the cross, specifically mentioned in the Proclamation, already appear in the first part of *Passion* II (i.e. before l. 880) and continue into the romance section. It remains a possibility that *Passion* II was still incomplete and that as time ran out the writer fell back on making a simple and rather haphazard patching together of newly written play material and old pageant material, though this seems less likely to me than that we are here dealing with the scribe who deliberately suppressed the ending of the play in order perhaps to extend its range (comprehensiveness again) and to make the transition to the later pageants more straightforward.

The text of the Proclamation for the six pageants which overlap with the latter part of *Passion* II is given here for comparison. The relationship between Proclamation and play is set out in the notes.

The text of this appendix is not covered in the Glossary.

f. 7   *Primus vexillator*
       In þe [thirtieth] pagent, þei bete out Crystys blood,
       And nayle hym al nakyd upon a rode tre;
       Betwen two thevys – iwys they were to wood! –
       They hyng Cryst Jhesu; gret shame it is to se.
f. 7v   Seven wurdys Cryst spekyth, hangyng upon þe rode,   5
       Þe weche ʒe xal here, all þo þat wyl þer be.
       Þan doth he dye for oure allther good.
       His modyr doth se þat syth; gret mornyng makyth she,
           For sorwe she gynnyth to swowne.
       Seynt John, evyn þer as I ʒow plyth,   10
       Doth chere Oure Lady with al his myth;
       And to þe temple anon forthryth
           He ledyth here in þat stownde.

       Secundus vexillator
       We purpose to shewe in oure pleyn place
       In þe [thirty-first] pagent, þorwe Godys myth,   15
       How to Crystys herte a spere gan pace
       And rent Oure Lordys bryst in ruly plyth.
       For Longeus, þat olde knyth, blynd as he was,
       A ryth sharpe spere to Crystys herte xal pyth.
       Þe blod of his wounde to his eyn xal tras,   20
       And, þorwe gret meracle, þer hath he syth.

1 thirtieth] *MS.* xxx^{ti}   3 two] *MS.* ij   4 is] *MS.* was *deleted; is written above*   5
seven] *MS.* vij   15 thirty-first] *MS.* xxxj^{ti}

Than in þat morn
Crystys soule goth down to helle,
And þer ovyrcomyth þe fende so felle;
Comfortyth þe soulys þat þerin dwelle, 25
And savyth þat was forlorn.

Tertius vexillator
Joseph and Nycodemus, to Cryst trew servaunt,
In þe [thirty-second] pagent, þe body þei aske to haue.
Pylat ful redyly þe body doth hem graunt;
Þan þei with reverens do put it in grave. 30
Þe Jewys more wyckyd þan ony geawnt,
For Crystys ded body, kepers do þei craue.
Pylat sendyth four knytys þat be ryth hardaunt
To kepe þe blody body in his dede conclaue.

f. 8 And ȝit be his owyn myth, 35
The body þat was hevy as led,
Be þe Jewys nevyr so qwed,
Aryseth from grave þat þer lay ded,
And frayth than every knyth.

Primus vexillator
In þe [thirty-third] pagent, þe soule of Cryst Jhesu 40
Xal brynge all his frendys from helle to paradyse.
Þe soule goth than to þe grave, and, be ryth gret vertu,
Þat body þat longe ded hath loyn, to lyf aȝen doth ryse.
Than doth Cryst Jhesu onto his modyr sew,
And comfortyth all here care in temple þer she lyse. 45
With suche cher and comforth his modyr he doth
                                          indew
Þat joy it is to here þer spech for to devyse.
And than
Oure Lady of hefne so cler,
In herte sche hath ryth glad chere; 50
Whan here sone þus doth apere
Here care awey is tan.

---

28 thirty-second pagent] *MS.* xxxij page   33 four] *MS.* iiij   40 thirty-third]
MS. xxiij   42 be ryth] ryth *added above* + *caret*   48 And than] *written in right
margin*

Secundus vexillator
> In þe [thirty-fourth] pagent, xal Maryes thre
> Seke Cryst Jhesu in his grave so coolde.
> An aungel hem tellyth þat aresyn is he.   55
> And whan þat þis tale to them is tolde,
> To Crystys dyscyplis with wurdys ful fre
> They telle these tydyngys with brest ful bolde.
> Than Petyr and John, as ȝe xal se,
> Down rennyn in hast ouer lond and wolde   60
>> The trewth of þis to haue.
> Whan þei þer comyn, as I ȝow say,
> He is gon from vndyr clay;
> Þan þei wytnesse anoon þat day
>> He lyth not in his grave.   65

f. 8v   *Tertius vexillator*
> Onto Mary Mawdelyn, as we haue bent,
> Cryst Jhesu xal than apere,
> In þe [thirty-fifth] pagent,
> And she wenyth he be a gardenere.
> Mary, be name, verament,   70
> Whan Cryst here callyth with spech ful clere,
> She fallyth to ground with good entent
> To kys his fete with gladsom chere.
>> But Cryst byddyth here do way;
> He byddyth his feet þat sche not kys   75
> Tyl he haue styed to hefne blys.
> To Crystys dyscyplys Mary, iwys,
>> Than goth þe trewth to say.

53 thirty-fourth] MS. xxxiiij^{ti}   68 thirty-fifth] MS. xxxv^{ti}   74 Cryst] d *deleted*
after Cryst

Notes to Appendix 4

1   There are two scourgings in the play, at II. 462sd–469sd (ordered by Herod) and at
II. 696sd (ordered by Pilate). The road to Calvary interposes between the latter and the
nailing which begins at II. 746sd. The Proclamation obviously cannot cover every
incident and in a number of cases dramatic effect no doubt rather than complete
coverage was the aim in choosing which incidents to describe. Differences in order
between play and Proclamation are therefore often more significant than absence of
incident or episode.

5   The seven words from the cross occur at II. 800–2 (Father forgive them), 829–30 (This day . . . in paradise), 843–4 (Woman, behold thy son), 881–4 (Eloi, eloi), 893–6 (I thirst), 913–15 (Into thy hands), and 920 (It is finished). The romance stanzas begin at II. 881 at the fourth word.

7–13   Christ dies at II. 920. Mary laments between II. 921 and 968, and swoons at 968sd. John almost immediately takes her to the Temple II. 984sd. This is a continuous section in the play as it is in the Proclamation.

16–21   The Longeus episode does not follow here in the play but is placed much later (II. 1130sd–55) after the first part of the Harrowing of Hell, the reactions of the Centurion, etc., and Joseph of Arimathea's visit to Pilate. Everything after the Harrowing of Hell is in the mixed section of text.

22–6   In the play the Harrowing follows immediately after Mary has been installed in the Temple but only to the point where Christ enters hell having overcome Belial. The comforting of the souls (what there is of it) does not occur separately from the leading-out of the souls after II. 1367sd.

27–30   Nicodemus appears alone at II. 1059–66 (an isolated romance stanza), then Joseph alone. It is only Joseph who asks for Christ's body from Pilate (II. 1084ff.). Joseph and Nicodemus take down Christ's body at II. 1155sd–63sd after the Longeus episode. There follows a brief pietà scene.

31–4   The setting of the watch begins at II. 1200 with a request for guards from Caiaphas alone. In the play the sealing of the tomb (II. 1280–1311) is interposed between this and the knights taking up their positions (II. 1312–67).

35–9   There is some confusion here since the Resurrection is described again at 4A 42–3 after the second part of the Harrowing.

40–52   The latter part of the Harrowing is at II. 1367sd–1439sd, leading straight into the Resurrection and the Visit to Mary as here.

53   The Visit to the Sepulchre is preceded by a long episode of the waking and reporting of the knights to Pilate (II. 1503–1671) not mentioned in the Proclamation.

53–65   The episodes are described here in the order and form which they have in the play. Regular octaves take over from the romance stanzas at II. 1776, the beginning of the Maries' report to the disciples.

66–78   Apart from the conversation with the angel (II. 1838–57) the episode of Mary and Christ as gardener is as it is in the play.

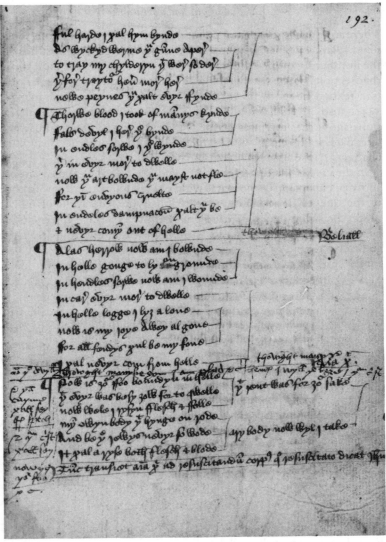

f. 192 which towards the foot of the page contains some of the additions and alterations to the Resurrection section made by scribe B. Photograph reproduced by permission of the British Library (BL MS Cotton Vespasian D VIII).

Later additions and alterations

There are a small number of alterations and marginal additions to the
text of *Passion* II. These are related to other changes, such as those in
the numbering of the knights at the sepulchre, and to the indications
that sections of the text were being extracted for playing separately
(see textual notes to II. 1016sd, 1200, 1224, 1256sn ff., 1407–10,
1431–39sd, 1671sd, 1769–81 and 1788). In as much as these alterations show that the manuscript was being put to practical use at a
later date, it is perhaps worthwhile to try and reconstruct the textual
changes, trivial as in many cases they are.

In the case of the first group (A(i) and (ii), ff. 191v–2) they simply
show an expansion of the Harrowing of Hell to include a part for one
of the thieves (II. 1016sd), presumably when the spirit of Christ
meets the saved one as in Chester XVII (ll. 255–72) – not included
here – and for Cain (II. 1407–10). Unfortunately almost all the
additional text must have been written out elsewhere. The only part
given here is an incipit and an explicit of a speech by the devil
gloating over those left to him in hell – notably, it seems, Cain.

The second group of alterations (B, ff. 197v–8) interestingly
shows a very tentative attempt to change the source of the Maries'
information about Christ's Resurrection from the angel to Christ
himself. This presumably reflects a change, or an intended change,
elsewhere in the play perhaps to include the appearance of Christ to
the Maries; but there is no sign of this in the manuscript.

Two attempts seem to have been made, since besides the marginal
alterations there is another simpler (and more successful) way suggested of removing the references to the angel. This is indicated in
the text at II. 1770–2: changing *aungel* to *bade*, deleting *bad* and
changing *Cryst* to *he*, thus:

> An bade us ryght þus sertayn
> To þe, Petyr, þat we xulde telle
> How he is resyn þe which was slayn.

The more elaborate set of alterations of II. 1778–81 itself has alterna-
tives, but these have been deleted (see Block pp. 330–1, facsimile ff.
197v–8 and textual notes to the following appendices). As with the
Harrowing of Hell additions it is likely that the full corrected text

was written out elsewhere, though in this case the main manuscript seems to have been used for drafting the changes.

All these additions and alterations are the work of a single scribe (Scribe B), who was also at work elsewhere in the manuscript copying out missing text, correcting and updating (see 'Reviser B', facsimile p. xxiv).

A (i)

f. 191v *Abraham*
        . . .
        Helle loge lyth vnlokyn,   1406
            Fro fylth with frende we fare.

        Anima Cayn
            [Speech to be added]

        Anima Christi
            Fayre frendys, now be ʒe wunne;
            On ʒow shyneth þe sothfast sunne.   1409

                                    . . .

A (ii)

f. 192   *Beliall*
            I xal nevyr com from helle.   1431

        nota ye devyll
            Thowght many be gon, I am glad *etc.*   1431a
            . . .
            Hens I wyll ye bere.   1431b

        and yan Cayme xall sey his spech
        And yan Crist xall sey
            Now ys your foo *etc.*   1432

1407] nota anima cayn *in left margin*   1408–10] *some deleted words ending* as folow
fayere frendys *in left margin*   1431] *in right margin* thowght many & c   1431a *sd*]
in left margin   1431a] *interlined between 1431 and 1432*   1431b] *in right
margin*   1431b *sd*] *in left margin*   1432 *and sd*] *in left margin*

B.

f. 197v–198

Maria Magdalene dicit Petro et ceteris apostolis:

Bretheryn all, in herte be glad!   1766
Bothe blythe and joyful, in herte ful fayn!
For ryght good tydandys haue we had
Þat oure lord is resyn and aperyd to us serteyne;   (1769)

Lyk as he dyede, nakyd as he was borne.   (1770)
And commande us to go to Peter and John and his
                                        dyscipulis all, (1771)
And tell to yow he wolde apere in lyknes as he was
                                        beforn (1772)

Maria Jacobi
To lyve is resyn ageyn þat lorde,   1774
The qwych Judas to Jewys solde,
Of þis I bere ryght trewe recorde
By wurdys þat þe aungel tolde.
Allso he aperyd to us with body bolde,   (1778)
And he schewyd us his woundis fyve,   (1779)
He þat was closyd in cley ful colde,   (1780)
And þerfor beleve us þat he is man alyve.   (1781)

Petrus
Sey me, systeryn, with wurdys blythe,   1782
May I troste to þat 3e say?
Is Cryst resyn ageyn to lyve
Þat was ded and colde in clay?
Maria Salome
3a, trostyth us truly, it is no nay,
He is aresyn, it is no les;   1787
And so he badd us tell yow þis daye   (1788)
With opyn voys and speche expres.

(1771) to go] *added above* + *caret*   (1772) beforn] *end of word lost at edge of leaf*   (1778)] *heavily corrected from* for . . aperyd to us with handis fytte and hert borde   (1779) And he] ?for ?*deleted after* And   (1779)–(1780)] *between these is deleted* both handis and fytte and þe wound in his syde

GLOSSARY

The *Linguistic Atlas of Late Middle English* has re-affirmed for me the value of complete word listings and the Glossary that follows is, like that of the *Mary Play*, intended to contain examples of every English word and spelling used in the main text and in Appendices 1–3. If there are more than four examples of a word or spelling, two line references are given, followed by 'etc.'. Where there are four or fewer examples, one to four references are given without an 'etc.'. Where it seemed to me important, and where it was possible, I have listed all examples. No line references are given for very common words unless there is a less common variant in the text. References to the two parts of the *Passion Play* consist of 'I.' or 'II.' followed by line number or numbers; references to the Appendices consist of *1A*, *2A* or *3A* followed likewise by line number or numbers. References to different forms of an individual word are separated by a semi-colon; e.g.: '**gret(e), grett, greet** . . . I.2, 79 etc.; I.89, II.1693, *2A6*, *3A2*; I.45, II. 893 etc.; II.773 . . .' means that there are examples of the form **gret** in lines 2 and 79 of *Passion* I and a number of others (at least five in all); of **grete** in lines 89 of *Passion* I, 1693 of *Passion* II, 6 of Appendix 2, and 2 of Appendix 3; of **grett** in lines 45 of *Passion* I and 893 of *Passion* II, as well as a number of others; and of **greet** in line 773 of *Passion* II.

Verbs are listed under their infinitives where such a form exists in the text.

In the alphabetical sequence, initial *i* and *j*, *g* and *ȝ* are treated as separate letters, but initial *þ* is combined with *th*, and *u* with *v*. Medial *þ* and *th*, *u* and *v* are also combined. The very few words with initial *y* are listed in their normal alphabetical position and cross-referenced, but medial and final *y* have been treated throughout as *i*.

For the purposes of alphabetical order, words with bracketed letters are treated as though the bracketed letters did not exist. They are, however, placed after forms with no brackets; e.g. **hast** precedes **hast(e)**.

The series of meanings given towards the beginning of each entry is intended to cover all the varieties found in the main text and Appendices 1–3. Occasionally glosses are given for individual words or phrases. No glossary can give enough information about any one word, and to enable a reader to gain easy access to further information, every entry is followed by the relevant headword in the *Middle English Dictionary* (*MED*), as far as that

has been published (up to **sheden** at the time of writing). Thereafter, there
are occasional references to the *Oxford English Dictionary* (*OED*), if a connection between the fifteenth-century and the modern form is not obvious.

a, ha *interj.* ah!, oh! (expressing horror, surprise, pleasure etc., or used in
  invocation) I. 779, 993 etc.; II.887 (**a, ha** *interj.*)
a *prep.* (reduced form of various prepositions in unstressed position) **brynge
  þe a dawe** kill you (lit. 'take you out of day'; see **dai** *n.*5(b)) II.129 (cf.
  II.149)
a *see also* **haue**
a(n), han *indef.art.* a, an I.4, 9 etc.; I.23, 87 etc.; II.1244; **a ten personys** ten
  people I.964sd (**a** *indef.art.*)
abed *adv.* in bed II.537 (**abedde** *adv.*)
abey *v.* obey I.838; *3?sg.pr.* **obeyth** is subject II.1032 (**obeien** *v.*)
abhomynable *adj.* odious, hateful I.386 (**abhominable** *adj.*)
abyde, abydyn *v.* dwell, remain, stay, await, wait I.19, 334 etc.; I.879,
  II.12,1292; *3sg.pr.* **abydyth** II.260; *3pl.pr.* **abydyn** 1*A*43sd; *imp.pl.* **abyde**
  II.1601; *pr.p.* **abydyng** I.1034 (**abiden** *v.*)
about, abouth, abowt(e), abowth, abowtyn *prep.* about, around, on
  II.16, 181sd; I.244sd, 337, 406sd; II.265sd; II.774sd, 1729; I.641, 988sd,
  II.89sd, 486sd; I.824sd (**aboute(n** *prep.*)
aboute, abowte, abowth, abowtyn *adv.* about II.130; II.517, 1271, 1615;
  I.419, II.1253; I.662sd (**aboute(n** *adv.*)
above *adv.* above I.363, II.1495; (as adj.) I.796 (**above(n** *adv.*)
abovyn *prep.* above II.874sd (**above(n** *prep.*)
absent *adj.* absent I.115 (**absent** *adj.*)
abstynawnce *n.* self-denial, abstemiousness I.115 (**abstinence** *n.*)
abundauns, habundawns *n.* abundance, wealth, quantity, intensity I.64;
  I.360 (**aboundaunce** *n.*)
acorde, of–corde *n.* agreement, harmony I.162, 3*A*32; I.424 (**accord** *n.*)
acordyth *v.* *3sg.pr.* agree, be in agreement, match I.341; *1pl.pr.subj.* **acorde**
  I.612; *pr.p.* **acordynge** I.67; *p.p.* **acordyd** I.580 (**accorden** *v.*)
acuse *v.* accuse II.439, 451; *3pl.pr.* **acuse** II.166; *p.p.* **acusyd** II.283
  (**ac(c)usen** *v.*)
acusyng *vbl.n.* accusing II.286, 315 (**ac(c)using(e** *ger.*)
advercyté *n.* misfortune, harm I.449, 1050 (**adversité** *n.*)
aferd(e) *p.p.* frightened, afraid II.449, 516; II.450 (**afered** *ppl.*)
affeccyon *n.* love, friendship, desire I.61, 679, 1040 (**affecioun** *n.*)
affrayd *p.p.* afraid, frightened II.1756 (**affraien** *v.1.*)
afore *adv.* previously II.874sd (**afore** *adv.*)
afore *prep.* in front of II.790sd (**afor(e** *prep.*)
after, aftyr *conj.* after II.246, 543sd; I.28, 770sd (**after** *conj.*)
after(e), affter(e), aftyr *prep.* after, for, according to I.92, 164sd etc.;
  I.176, 293; II.782sd; I.63; I.126, 208sd etc. (**after** *prep.*)
af(f)tyr *adv.* afterwards I.549, II.709; I.554 (**after** *adv.*)

agayn, ageyn, aȝen *adv.* again II.997, 1011, 1283, 1769; I.502sd, 562 etc.;
   I.804sd, 928sd etc. (**ayen** *adv.*)
agast *p.p.* afraid I.919, 967, II.551 (**agasten** *v.*)
age *n.* **of grett age** old enough, adult 2A128 (**age** *n.*, cf.2.a)
ageyn *prep.* against, towards, opposite I.184, 278 etc. (**ayen** *prep.*)
ageyn, aȝen *adv. see* **agayn**
ageyns, aȝens *prep.* against, contrary to, in preparation for I.28, 229, II.30,
   387; I.19, 164 etc. (**ayen(e)s** *prep.*)
aglottys *n.pl.* metal ends (of a lace or 'point') I.72 (**aglet** *n.*)
agresyth *v. 3sg.pr.* terrifies, frightens II.1049 (**agrisen** *v.*)
ay *adv.* ever, for ever II.1016, 1865, 2A21 (**ei** *adv.*)
al, all(e) *n.* all I.519, 964sd, II.1239; I.775sd, II.161 etc.; II.274, 298 (**al**
   lim.adj & n.)
al, all(e), hall *adj.* all I.59, 206 etc.; I.14, 76 etc.; I.289, 296 etc.; I.883, II.370
   (**al** *lim adj. & n.*)
al, all *adv.* all, at all, altogether II.817, 938, 1729, 1A16; II.469sd, 943 etc. (**al**
   adv. & conj.)
alas, allas *interj.* alas (exclamation of grief, pity etc.) I.452, 1059 etc.; II.173,
   699 etc. (**alas** *int.*)
alderers *n.poss.pl.* **oure alderers** of us all II.1502 (**al** *lim adj. & n.* and OED
   All *a., sb.* and *adv.*, D)
algatys *adv.* anyway, in any case II.600, 653 (**al-gate(s** *adv.*)
alyawns *n.* alliance, close agreement or association I.62 (**allia(u)nce** *n.*)
alythe *v. imp. sg.* come down, descend II.775 (**alighten** *v.1.*)
allmyghty, al(l)mythty, almythy *adj.* almighty II.1813; I.947; II.5;
   II.799, 1194 (**al-mighti** *adj.*)
allwey *adv.* always, all the time 3A40 (**al-wei, -wei(e)s** *adv.*)
almyght *adj.* almighty II.1681 (**al-might** *adj.*)
almost *adv.* almost II.401, 866 (**al-most** *adv.*)
alofte *adv.* raised, held up I.1032sd (**aloft(e** *adv.*)
alon(e) *adv., adj.* alone II.327, 652; I.724, 962 etc. (**al-on(e** *adv. & adj.*)
along *adv.* out, extended II.746sd (**along, alonges(t** *adv. & prep.*)
alow *v.* recognise, reward I.646 (**allouen** *v.*)
also *adv.* also I.40, 46 etc. (**also** *adv.*)
altitude *n.* highest point, summit 3A1 (**altitude** *n.*)
am *see* **be(n)**
amat *adj.* **make . . . amat** confound, get the better of II.115 (**amat** *adj.*)
amen *interj.* amen II.827, 1939 (**amen** *interj.*)
amende *v.* make amends for, relieve, remedy I.196, II.992 etc.; *imp.sg.*
   amende II.1882 (**amenden** *v.*)
amendys *n.* reparation, amends I.860 (**amende(s** *n.*)
amys *adv.* wrong, improperly II.142, 145 etc. (**amis** *adv.*)
among(e), amongys *prep.* among, with I.4, 14 etc.; I.962, II.1326, 2A104;
   II.16, 947, 2A114 (**among(es** *prep.*)
amonge *adv.* together II.1076 (**among(es** *adv.*)

an *see* **a(n); haue**

and *conj.* and, if I.2, 11 etc.; considering that, since 2A63 (**and** *conj.*)

angel(l)ys *see* **aungel**

any, ony *adj.* any I.170, 191 etc.; I.1036, II.29, 60; (as *pron.*) II.778; II.1232; (as *adv.*) **ony mo** II.1108, 1250 (**ani** *lim adj.*)

anythyng, onythynge *n.* anything II.1117; **for onythynge** at all events, in particular I.635 (**ani-thing** *phrase & n.*)

anoynt(e) *v.* anoint II.1183; 2A24 (**enointen** *v.*)

anon(e), anoon *adv.* at once, immediately I.39, 169 etc.; II.1453; I.988sd, II.99, 230 (**an-on** *adv. & conj.*)

another, anothyr *pron.* another II.274, 756, 846; I.675, II.688 (**other** *pron.*)

another *adj.* another I.825, II.351, 1163sd (**other** *adj.*)

anow, inow *n.* enough, plenty I.557, II.1096; I.107 (**inough** *n.*)

anow, inow *adv.* enough, sufficiently II.265, 772 etc.; I.644 (**inough** *adv.*)

anow *adj.* abundant, enough I.12, II.220 (**inough** *adj.*)

ansuere *n.* answer II.243sd; *n.pl.* **answerys** I.31 (**answere** *n.*)

answere *v.* answer II.358, 637; *2sg.pr.* **answeryst** II.162; *3sg.pa.* **answerd** II.452 (**answeren** *v.*)

ap(p)ere *v.* appear I.1021, II.47, 1412; I.510; *3sg.pr.* **ap(p)eryth** I.4; II.41; *3sg.pa.* **aperyd** II.548 (**ap(p)eren** *v.*)

apostel, apostyl *n.* apostle, disciple 3A25; I.342sd; *n.pl.* **apostelys** II.12, 16. 3A13 (**apostle** *n.*)

apparens *n.* sight, perception I.696 (**ap(p)araunce, -ence** *n.*)

appendyth *v.* *3sg.pr.* belongs, is appropriate to I.944 (**ap(p)enden** *v.*)

appetyde *n.* natural inclination II.88 (**ap(p)etit** *n.*)

applyed *v.* *2pl.pr.subj.* (+ *pron.* 'it') perform it I.354; *pr.p.* **applyande** striving I.134 (**ap(p)lien** *v.*)

aprevyn *v.* *3pl.pr.* demonstrate, confirm II.1045 (**ap(p)reven** *v.*)

aproche *v.* come near I.64 (**ap(p)rochen** *v.*)

aqwyte *v.* **aqwyte us . . . our mede** reward us II.1162; *p.p.* **aqwhyte** repaid, satisfied I.374 (**acquiten** *v.*)

ar(e) *see* **be(n)**

aray *n.* clothing I.468; **in good aray** in proper form, in good condition II.806 (**arrai** *n.*)

aray *v.* prepare I.133, 163; *p.p.* **arayd** dressed, costumed I.208sd (**arraien** *v.*)

arere *v.* raise up I.50 (**areren** *v.*)

aryse, arysyn *v.* arise II.1438; II.1461; *imp.pl.* **aryse** I.977; *p.p.* **aresyn** II.1458, 1512, 1764, 1787 (**arisen** *v.*)

arm *n.* arm II.752, 755, 760; *n.pl.* **armys** II.790sd (**arm** *n.*)

armyd *p.p.* in armour II.1318 (**armen** *v.*)

arn *see* **be(n)**

arneys *n.* body armour (see note) I.964sd (**harneis** *n.*)

arryn *v.* torment, drag (about) II.696sd; *1sg.pr.* **harry** II.498 (**herien** *v.2.*)

art *see* **be(n)**

as *adv.*, *conj.* as, like I.10, 34 etc.; as if I.648, 848; **as who seyth** like one who says, as if he said II.223 (**also** *adv.*; **as** *conj.*)

asay *v.* try, test, have a taste, try out I.585, 588 etc.; *imp.pl.* **asay** II.457; *1sg.pa.* **hasayd** II.505; *p.p.* **asayd** II.184 (**assaien** *v.*)

asayl *v.* attack I.192; *3sg.pr.* **asalys** I.39 (**assail(l)en** *v.*)

ascende *v.* ascend II.1886; *3sg.pr.* **ascendyth** I.948sd; *2sg.pr.subj.* **ascende** II.1935; *p.p.* **ascende** II.1880 (**ascenden** *v.*)

asclepe, aslepe *adv.* asleep I.928sd; II.537 (**aslepe** *adv.1.*)

asencyon *n.* **hyest asencyon** topmost point I.68 (**ascensioun** *n.*)

asyde *adv.* to one side, apart II.790sd (**aside** *adv.*)

askape *v.* escape II.77 (**escapen** *v.*)

aske, askyn *v.* ask II.1084; II.874sd; *1sg.pr.* **aske** II.1365; **haske** I.762; *2sg.pr.* **askyst** *2A*126; *3sg.pr.subj.* **aske** *1A*10; *pr.p.* **haskyng** II.838; *imp.pl.* **aske** II.136, 137; *3sg.pa.* **haskyd** II.104; *p.p.* **askyd** II.828 (**asken** *v.*)

asondyr, asondre, asundyr *adv.* apart I.1060; I.928; II.895 (**asonder, -re** *adv.* & *pred. adj.*)

aspey, aspy(e) *v.* see, discover, spy out I.173; II.890; I.575, 982, II.1114; *1pl.pr.* **aspye** I.298; *2pl.pr. subj.* **aspye** II.71; *p.p.* **aspyed** I.357 (**aspien** *v.*)

aspende *v.* give, devote II.1719 (**aspenden** *v.*)

asse *n.* ass I.384, II.1690 etc. (**asse** *n.*)

assent *n.* **with/be on assent** unanimously, all/both together II.1594, *3A*16 (**assent** *n.*)

assystent *adj.* **to hym assystent** helping/assisting him, attendant on him I.30 (**assistent, -ant** *adj.*)

ast *see* **haue**

astat(e) *n.* rank, social position, authority, office, splendour I.82, 164sd etc.; I.90; (see also note to II.377sd) (**estat** *n.*)

asundyr *see* **asondyr**

at(t) *prep.* at, according to, to, in I.32, 76 etc.; II.1604, *2A*125 (**at** *prep.*)

atende, attend(e) *v.* take heed, attend, muster I.464; I.393; *2A*32; *imp.pl.* **attende** I.531 (**attenden** *v.*)

atoo *see* **two, to**

atreyd *p.p.* afraid, frightened II.1561 (**atreien** *v.*)

attendauns *n.* **to his attendauns** to follow/wait on him I.33 (**attenda(u)nce** *n.*)

auantorysly *adv.* by chance, accidentally II.1142sd (**auntrousli** *adv.*)

audyence, audyens *n.* hearing, audience; **gevyth lordly audyence** listen politely II.21; *3A*4 (**audience** *n.*)

aught, owth, howth *adv.* at all, in any way, possibly II.1720; I.775; I.978 (**ought** *adv.*)

avyse *v.* *imp.sg./pl.* (reflexive) consider, take thought II.114, 254, 336, *2A*127; *p.p.* **avysyd, art þu avysyd?** have you considered? I.765 (**avisen** *v.*)

avyse *n.* advice, opinion I.185, II.589 (**avis** *n.*)

avysement *n.* **have avysement** take counsel I.579 (**avisement** *n.*)
aungel *n.* angel I.936sd, 948sd, II.1755; *n.poss.* **angelys** II.1759; *n.pl.* **angel-(l)ys** I.17, 30; I.14; *n.pl.poss.* **awngellys** I.753 (**aungel** *n.*)
avow *n.* **make avow** promise, assure (you), swear II.140, 774, 1243, 1655 (**avou(e** *n.*)
away, awey(e) *adv.* away II.584, 662 etc.; II.912, 1294 etc.; II.1717 (**awei** *adv.*)
awake *v.imp.sg./pl.* wake up I.918, 953, II.1504; *p.p.* **is awake,** has awakened II.1820 (**awaken, -ien** *v.*)
awngellys *see* **aungel**
awntys *n.pl.* aunts II.1699 (**aunte** *n.*)

bad *v. see* **byd(de)**
bad(de) *adj.* wicked, miserable 2A82, 105; II.1859 (**badde** *adj.*)
baylé *n.* jurisdiction II.83 (**bailli(e** *n.1.*)
bak *n.* back II.939, 1A34; *n.pl.* **bakkys** II.108 (**bak** *n.*)
bakward *adv.* backwards I.1032sd, II.107 (**bak-ward(es** *adv.*)
balys *n.pl.* sins, miseries 2A25 (**bale** *n.1.*)
balke *n.* ridge; **be brook or balke** anywhere II.1341 (**balk(e** *n.*)
bane *n.* death II.1266 (**bane** *n.*)
baptyze *n.* baptism II.1395 (**baptis(t** *n.2.*)
baptyzid *v. 1sg.pa.* baptised II.1394 (**baptisen, -izen** *v.*)
bar(e) *v. see* **bere**
bare *adj.* bare, destitute II.456, 1550, 2A3, 48 (**bar** *adj.*)
bareyn *adj.* barren, childless II.711 (**barain(e** *adj.*)
barelegged, -leggyd *adv.* and *adj.* barelegged I.406sd; II.656sd (**bar-leg, -legged** *adj. & adv.*)
barfot *adv.* barefoot I.406sd (**bar-fot, -foted** *adj. & adv.*)
barfot-goyng *vbl.n.* going barefoot II.509 (*see* **bar-fot, -foted** *adj. & adv.*)
bargany *n.* deal, transaction I.624, 627 (**bargain(e** *n.*)
barre *n.* bar (of a court of law) II.655, 656sd (**barre** *n*).
basyn *n.* basin, bowl I.824sd, 828sd (**bacin** *n.*)
batte *n.* blow II.184 (**bat** *n.*)
be, by(e) *prep.* by, with I.27, 47 etc.; I.119, 610 etc.; I.577 (**bi** *prep.*)
be(n), bene, beyn *v.* be I.20, 41 etc.; I.156, 319 etc.; I.152; I.115; *1sg.pr.* **am** I.1, 5 etc.; *2sg.pr.* **art** I.687, 765 etc.; *3sg.pr.* **is** I.3, 10 etc., **ys** I.945, 2A74; *pl.pr.* **ar(e)** II.1338; I.261, 265 etc., **arn** I.195, 366 etc., **be** I.45, 351 etc., **ben** I.121, 214 etc., **been** I.313; *sg.pr.subj.* **be** I.75, 204 etc.; *pl.pr.subj.* **be** I.134, 255 etc.; *imp.sg./pl.* **be** I.136, 151 etc.; *imp.pl.* **beth** I.741, II.115 etc.; *1/3sg.pa.* **was(e)** I.15, 16 etc.; II.1841; *2sg.pa.* **wace** I.988, **wore** I.943, II.1381, **were** II.1469; *pl.pa.* **were** I.30, 31 etc.; *1pl.pa.* **ware** II.1548, **where** I.396; *2pl.pa.* **worn** II.1645, *3pl.pa.* **weryn** I.14, 666, II.300, **wore** I.804sd, II.1557; *sg.pa.subj.* **were** I.361, 537 etc.; *1/3sg.pa.subj.* **wore** II.842, 1035, 1141; *2pl.pa.subj.* **ware** II.980; *3pl.pa.subj.* **were** I.988sd; *p.p.* **be** I.264, 773 etc., **ben** I.995, II.1548, 1550 (**ben** *v.*)

because, becawse *conj.* because I.305, II.284; I.406, II.385, 448, so that II.451 (**bicause** *conj.*)

bed(de), beed *n.* bed II.549; II.543sd; II.1469 (**bed** *n.1.*)

bedellys *n.pl.* spokesmen, messengers I.34 (**bidel** *n.*)

befalle *v. 3sg.pr.subj.* happen, befall I.485, II.1090; *3pl.pr.* **befallyth** II.68; *p.p.* **befalle** I.291 (**bifallen** *v.*)

before, beforn *adv.* before, in front, first II.223; I.164sd, 410sd etc. (**bifore(n** *adv.*)

before, beforn *prep.* before, in front of I.175, II.126, 782sd; I.164sd, 287 etc. (**bifore(n** *prep.*)

befornseyd *ppl.adj.* already-mentioned, aforesaid I.518sd (**bifore-** *pref.*)

began *see* **begynne**

begat *v.2sg.pa.subj.* begot II.713 (**biyeten** *v.*)

beggerys *n.pl.* beggars I.88; *n.poss.* **beggerys** I.101 (**begger(e** *n.*)

begyle *v.* trick, deceive I.243, II.558 (**bigilen** *v.*)

begynne *v.* begin I.705, II.74, 189, 2A117; *3sg.pr.* **begynnyth** II.918; *1sg.pa.* **began** I.13; *3sg.pa.* **began** II.199, 341; *p.p.* **begonne** II.508 (**biginnen** *v.*)

begynnyng *vbl.n.* beginning I.491, II.675, 698 (**biginning(e** *ger.*)

beheldyth *v. 3sg.pr.* look at, behold, see II.195; *2pl.pr.subj.* **beholde** I.311; *imp.sg.* **beheld** II.843; *imp.pl.* **beheld** I.150, **beheldyth** II.867, **behold(e)** I.519; I.415, 1A1, **byholde** I.65 (**biholden** *v.*)

behyndyn *adv.* behind II.939 (**bihinde(n** *adv. & pred. adj.*)

behove *v. 3sg.pr.subj.* is necessary/proper I.913 (**bihoven** *v.*)

bey *n.* a low-born person, servant I.71 (**boie** *n.1.*)

bey *see also* **by(e)** *v.*

beyn *see* **be(n)**

beleve, belef *n.* faith I.435; **to bryng . . . in belef** to convince II.541 (**bileve** *n.*)

beleve, belevyn *v.* believe, have confidence I.529, 725, II.211; I.428, 442, II.809; *1sg.pr.* **beleve** II.820; *3sg.pr.* **belevyth** II.1686; *1pl.pr.* **beleve** I.409; *3pl.pr.* **beleve** I.437; **belevyn** II.298 (**bileven** *v.2.*)

belyve *adv.* suddenly, at once II.1514, 1918 (**blive** *adv.*)

bemys *n.pl.* rays of light (fig.) 3A4 (**bem** *n.1.*)

benyng *adj.* gracious, kind I.1067 (**benigne** *adj.*)

bent *p.p.* **be bent** intend, are resolved 1A29 (**benden** *v.1.*)

berde *n.* woman 2A3 (**birde** *n.1.*)

bere *v.* bear, carry, give birth to I.362, II.143 etc.; *1sg.pr.* **bere** II.1727, 1776; *3sg.pr.* **beryth** II.721, 738sd; *pr.p.* **beryng** I.469, 478sd; *1sg.pa.* **bare** I.1063; *3sg.pa.* **bar** II.98; *p.p.* **bore** I.780, **born** I.41, 448 etc.; *inf.* + 'it' **to berynt** II.698sd, 733 (**beren** *v.1.*)

berere *n.* **berere of lyth** light-bearer (translation of 'Lucifer') I.16 (**berer(e** *n.*)

bery *v.* bury II.1085, 1091, 1094; *2pl.pr.* **bery** II.1121; *p.p.* **beryed** II.1712 (**birien** *v.*)

beryenge, burryenge *adj.* **beryenge grownd** grave, cemetery II. 1348;
  burryenge boorde (see note) II.1687 (**biriing(e** *ger.*)
berynt *see* **bere**
berys *n.pl.* bears II.1631 (**ber(e** *n.1.*)
beseche *v.* entreat, pray II.813; *1sg.pr.* **besech(e)** II.1672; I.921; *1pl.pr.*
  beseche II.7; *pr.p.* **besekyng** II.20 (**bisechen** *v.*)
beseen, beseyn *p.p.* dressed, costumed, equipped, furnished, laid out
  I.964sd; I.164sd, 288sd (**bisen** *v.*)
besekyng *see* **beseche**
besy *adj.* busy, diligent, eager, constant I.402, 749, II.1433, 2A70 (**bisi** *adj.*)
besyde *prep.* next to, beside I.903 (**biside(s** *prep.*)
besyly *adv.* eagerly, diligently II.123, 845 (**bisili** *adv.*)
best *n., adj., adv.* best I.74, 182 etc. (**best** *adj. & adv.*)
best(e) *n.* animal, creature *1A*11, 13 etc.; *1A*29; *n.poss.* **bestys** II.1691, *1A*34;
  n.pl. **bestys** I.86, 1063, *1A*7 (**best(e** *n.*)
bestad *p.p.* placed, situated II.995 (**bistad** *ppl.*)
Betanyward *adv.* **to Betanyward** towards Bethany I.884sd (*OED* **-ward**
  suffix)
bete *v.* beat, scourge II.181sd, 573, 1555; *3pl.pr.* **bete** II.554, **bety** I.1044,
  betyn II.461sd; *imp.pl.* **bete** II.456, 468, 1234, **betyth** II.180; *p.p.* **betyn**
  II.469sd, 473, 683sd (**beten** *v.1.*)
beth *see* **be(n)**
bethynke *v.* **bethynke þe** consider II.223; *p.p.* **am bethowth** am mindful
  II.1128 (**bithinken** *v.*)
bety(n) *see* **bete**
betydyn *v.* come to, befall *2A*118; *3sg.pr.subj.* **betyde** happens, occurs
  II.1321 (**bitiden** *v.*)
betyth *see* **bete**
betray *v.* betray I.956; *p.p.* **betrayed** I.771, II.13, 251, 621 (**bitraien** *v.*)
bettyr *adj.* better, preferable I.773, 995, II.1641 (**bettre** *adj.*)
betweyn, betwyn *prep.* between II.1626; I.144 (**bitwene** *prep.*)
betwyx *prep.* between I.159, 424 etc. (**bitwix(e** *prep.*)
by(e), bey *v.* buy, redeem, I.107; I.623, II.954, 2A56; I.106; *3pl.pa.* **bowth**
  II.125; *p.p.* **bowth** I.74, 99, II.1180, 1391, **bowht** *2A*59 (**bien** *v.*)
by(e) *see also* **be**
by and by *adv. phrase* one by one I.840sd (**bi and bi** *phrase*)
byd(de) *v.* request, order II.538; II.1574; *3sg.pr.* **byddyth** I.976sd, II.567,
  byddyt I.900sd; *3sg.pa.* **bad** I.939, II.100 etc. (**bidden** *v.*)
byddyng(e) *vbl.n.* command II.1895; II.1028 (**biddinge** *ger.*)
byholde *see* **beheldyth**
bynd(e), byndyn *v.* bind, tie I.1018, II.518; I.231, II.573 etc.; II.696sd;
  1sg.pr. **bynde** II.1417; *imp.pl.* **bynde** II.681; *3pl.pa.* **bownd** II.554; *p.p.*
  bounde II.1565, **boundyn** II.1432, **bownd(e)** II.264; I.1000, 1043,
  II.1420, 1424, **bowndyn** II.1711, **bowne** forced *2A*21 (**binden** *v.*)
byrthe *n.* birth II.1383 (**birth(e** *n.*)

byttyr *adj.* bitter I.668, 715, 718, 762; **byttyr bred** leavened bread I.711
   (**bit(t)er** *adj.*, and cf. *OED* **Sour-dough** *sb.*)
byttyrnesse *n.* malice, ill–will I.712 (**bit(t)ernesse** *n.*)
blak(e) *adj.* filthy, black II.744; 2A21, 109 (**blak** *adj.*)
blame *n.* blame, guilt, fault I.226, 288, II.278, 1351 (**blame** *n.*)
blame *v.* blame I.324; **am/be to blame** am/are at fault/to blame II.221, 572
   (**blamen** *v.*)
blasfemyng *vbl.n.* blasphemy II.181 (**blasfeminge** *ger.*)
blasfemyth *v.* *3sg.pr.* blasphemes II.174 (**blasfemen** *v.*)
blede *v.* bleed II.1866, 2A87; *1/3sg.pa.* **bledde** II.1447, 1711 (**bleden** *v.*)
blew *adj.* blue I.164sd (**bleu** *adj.*)
blyn *v.* cease, come to an end II.1219 (**blinnen** *v.*)
blynd(e) *adj.* blind I.355, 430 etc.; II.1130sd (as *n.*) **blynd(e)** I.37; I.349
   (**blind** *n. & adj.*)
blynde *v.* deceive, delude I.228 (**blinden** *v.*)
blyndnesse *n.* delusion, stupidity II.710 (**blindnes(se** *n.*)
blys(se) *n.* blessedness, joy, bliss II.854, 954 etc.; I.417, 517 etc. (**blis(se** *n.*)
blysful *adj.* blessed, happy II.1378 (**blisful** *adj.*)
blyssyd *adj.* blessed, holy, precious I.157, 1063 etc. (**blessed** *ppl.*)
blyssyd *see also* **blyssyth**
blyssyng *vbl.n.* consecration, blessing I.693 (**blessinge** *ger.*)
blyssyth *v.* *3sg.pr.* blesses, makes the sign of the cross I.438sd, 990sd; *p.p.*
   blyssyd blest, fortunate I.407, 437 etc. (**blessen** *v.* and **blessed** *ppl.*)
blyth(e) *adj.* happy, joyful II.1923; II.1767, 1782 (**blithe** *adj.*)
blod(e) *see* **blood(e)**
blody *adj.* bloody II.469sd, 1005, 1165, 1169 (**blodi** *adj.*)
bloo *adj.* livid, bruised II.1165 (**blo** *adj.*)
blood(e), blod(e) *n.* blood I.678, 797 etc.; II.1482; I.697, 802sd, II.645;
   I.763, 936 etc. (**blod** *n.*)
bobbyd *p.p.* beaten II.1065 (**bobben** *v.*)
body *n.* body I.44, 79 etc.; *n.poss.* **bodyes** II.1008, 1763 (**bodi** *n.*)
bodyly *adj.* physical, of the body I.432, 438, 2A37 (**bodili(ch** *adj.*)
boyst *n.* jar, box II.1727 (**boist(e** *n.*)
bold(e) *adj.* fearless, confident, brazen, presumptuous, shameless II.659;
   I.151, 309 etc. (**bold** *adj.*)
boldnes *n.* confidence, assurance I.99 (**boldnesse** *n.*)
bon *n.* bone II.1393, 1446, 1926; *n.pl.* **bonys** II.36, 462, 784, 1124 (**bon** *n.1.*)
bonde *n.* bonds, confinement II.583, 1405 (**bond** *n.*)
bone *n.* favour, request II.1090 (**bon** *n.2.*)
bonet *n.* hat I.87 (**bonet** *n.*)
borde, boorde *n.* table, meal I.772; II.1687 (see note) (**bord** *n.*)
bore *see* **bere**
borys *n.pl.* holes (bored in the cross to receive the nails) II.758 (**bore** *n.1.*)
born *see* **bere**
borwe *n.* **oure alderers borwe** the ransom for us all II.1502 (**borgh** *n.*)

borwe *v. 2sg.pr.subj.* save, redeem *2A*20 (**borwen** *v.*)
bost *n.* bragging, boasting II.1568, 1576 (**bost** *n.*)
bote *n.* remedy, relief *2A*25 (**bote** *n.1.*)
both(e) *num.* both; (as *corr.conj.*) I.94, 450 etc.; I.311, 457 etc.; (as *adj.*)
II.1807; II.689; (as *n.*) II.668; *3A*19, 30; **bothyn** I.144 (**bothe** *num.*)
bounde, boundyn *see* **bynd(e)**
bountevous *adj.* generous, beneficient I.9 (**bountevous** *adj.*)
bow *v.* bow, be obedient II.1028 (**bouen** *v.1.*)
bowht *see* **by(e)** *v.*
bownd(e), bowndyn, bowne *see* **bynde** *v.*
bowre *n.* **bodyly bowre** body *2A*37 (**bour** *n.*)
bowth *see* **by(e)** *v.*
box *n.* jar, box *2A*57 (**box** *n.2.*)
brace *n.* embrace, hold *2A*44 (*OED* **Brace** *sb.²* 3)
bras *n.* brass II.493 (**bras** *n.*)
brawnchis *n.pl.* branches, sprays I.405 (**braunch** *n.*)
bred *n.* bread, loaf I.29, 678 etc.; *n.pl.* **bredys** I.667 (**bred** *n.*)
brede *n.* breadth II.367, 1450 (**brede** *n.2.*)
brederyn *see* **brother**
breed *p.p.* begotten, born II.1470 (**breden** *v.3.*)
breff *adj.* brief I.117 (**bref** *adj.*)
breganderys *n.pl.* flexible body armour (see note) I.964sd (**briganders, -ine(s** *n.*)
breke *v.* break II.448, 462 etc.; *imp.pl.* **brekyth** II.151; *p.p.* **brokyn** II.1405 (**breken** *v.*)
brenge *see* **bryng(e)**
brenne *v.* burn *2A*20; *pr.p.* **brennyng** I.1032sd, II.490, *2A*112, *3A*18; *p.p.* **brent** I.320, 537 etc. (**brennen** *v.*)
brere *n.* thorn (the crown of thorns) II.1711 (**brer** *n.*)
brest *n.* breast II.939, 1462; *n.pl.* **brestys** II.92 (**brest** *n.1.*)
brest *v.* burst, break I.1048, II.214, 527; *2sg.pr.* **brest** II.795; *1pl.pr.* **brest** II.766 (**bresten** *v.*)
brethellys *n.pl.* wretches II.493 (**brethel** *n.*)
bretheryn *see* **brother**
brybory *n.* swindling, stealing I.90 (**briberie** *n.*)
brybour *n.* trickster, thief II.1298 (**bribour** *n.*)
bryght *see* **bryth** *adj.*
bryng(e), bryngyn *v.* bring I.6, 598 etc.; II.38, 656sd etc.; I.784, II.510; *1sg.pr.* **bryng(e)** II.647; II.92; *2sg.pr.* **bryngyst** II.284; *3sg.pr.* **bryngyth** I.936sd, II.410, **bryngith** II.243sd, 646sd (see notes); *1pl.pr.* **bryng** II.324; *3pl.pr.* **bryng(e)** II.117sd, 563sd; II.1295; *imp.sg.* **brenge** I.778, **bryng(e)** II.132, 641; I.1004, II. 974, *imp.pl.* **bryng(e)** I.1005, II.48; II.148, 655, *1A*9, 13; *pr.p.* **bryngyng** II.634; *1sg.pa.* **brought** *2A*50; *1pl.pa.* **browth** II.317; *3pl.pa.* **brought** II.1591; *p.p.* **brought** *1A*31, *2A*44, **brouth** II.72, **browt** II.149, **browth** I.96, 109 etc. (**bringen** *v.*)

brynke *n.* ?ground (lit. 'bank, edge, brink'; perhaps 'edge of the grave'?) II.1364 (see note) (**brinke** *n.*)

bryth, bryght *adj.* bright, resplendent, clear, fair I.14, 17 etc.; II.1391, 3A18 (**bright** *adj.*)

bryth *adv.* clearly II.1144 (**brighte** *adv.*)

brokyn *see* **breke**

bronston *n.* brimstone, sulphur II.493 (**brim-ston** *n.*)

brood *adj.* broad II.1140 (**brod** *adj.*)

brook *n.* brook, stream II.1341 (**brok** *n.3.*)

brother, brothyr *n.* brother, fellow-man I.848, 897; I.391, II.1795; *n.poss.* **brotherys** I.375; *n.pl.* **brederyn** I.663, **bretheryn** I.333, 695 etc. (**brother** *n.*)

brought, brouth, browt, browth *see* **bryng(e)**

burgeys *n.* burgess, citizen 1A17sd (**burgeis** *n.*)

burryenge *see* **beryenge**

buschop(p), busshop *n.* bishop, high priest II.139; II.1300; I.164sd, II.238; *n.pl.* **buschopys** I.210, 288sd, 518sd, 662sd, **buschoppys** II.244, **bus-shoppys** II.608, 696sd (**bishop** *n.*)

but *conj.* but, only, except, unless I.19, 20 etc.; **but yf** unless II.678 (**but** *conj.*)

cace *see* **cas(e)**

cadace *n.* stuffing, padding I.77 (**cadace** *n.*)

calabere *n.* a kind of fur (from Calabria in southern Italy) I.105 (**Calabre** *n.*)

calle, kalle *v.* call, cry out, summon I.294, 558 etc.; I.111, II.638; *1sg.pr.* **call** I.863, II.1602, **calle** II.1355; *2sg.pr.* **kallyst** I.1001; *3sg.pr.* **callyth** II.66; *2pl.pr.* **call** I.123; *3pl.pr.* **calle** II.500; *p.p.* **callyd** I.113, (emend.) **cald** I.495 (**callen** *v.*)

cam *see* **com(e)**

can, kan *v.* *1/3sg.pr.* can, know how to, be able I.102, 198etc.; I.7, 206etc.; *2sg.pr.* **canst** II.441, **kanst** I.963, II.616, **kone** II.845; *1pl.pr.* **can** II.375, **kan** I.464, II.342, **cone** II.120; *2pl.pr.* **can** II.148, **kan** I.348, 540, 974, II.336, **kone** II.671; *3pl.pr.* **con** II.137, **kan** I.222, II.344; *2/3sg.pr.subj.* **kan** II.807, 808, 870; *2pl.pr.subj.* **kan** I.344; could *1sg.pa.* **cowde** II.505; *2sg.pa.* **kowdyst** I.784; *3sg.pa.* **cowde(n)** II.577; II.1071; (also neg.) *1sg.pr.* **cannot** I.304, **kannat** II.1844, **kannot** II.1853, 1869; *3sg.pr.* **kan-not** II.453; *1pl.pr.* **cannot** II.1836, **kannot** II.278 (**connen** *v.*)

canoun *n.* or *adj.* ecclesiastical (law) I.94 (**canoun** *n.1.*)

cappe *n.* hat, cap I.164sd (see note); *n.pl.* **cappys** I.208sd (**cappe** *n.*)

care *n.* sorrow, distress, suffering II.926, 960 etc. (**care** *n.1.*)

care *v.* *imp.pl.* worry about, consider I.73 (**caren** *v.*)

careful *adj.* sorrowful, sad II.742, 1938 (**careful** *adj.*)

carnall *adj.* fleshly, physical 3A28 (**carnal** *adj.*)

cas(e), cace *n.* state of affairs, situation, state, matter, accusation, case I.302; I.182, 221 etc.; I.997 (**cas** *n.*)

cast, castyn *v.* throw, cast, devise II.790sd; II.181sd; *3sg.pr.* **castyth**
 II.257sd; *3pl.pr.* **cast** I.410sd; *imp.pl.* **cast** II.749; *3sg.pa.* **kest** II.222; *p.p.*
 cast I.15, 406sd, 418, 546, 728, *1A4*, **kast** II.532; **cast 3ou** set yourselves,
 contrive I.133, 734 (**casten** *v.*)
castel *n.* village, town *1A5* (**castel** *n.*)
cause, cawse *n.* reason, cause I.334, 388; II.324, 435 *1A45*; *n.pl.* **cawsys**
 I.147 (**cause** *n.*)
cause, cawse *v.* cause I.100, 351; I.349, II.982; *3sg.pr.* **cawsyth** *2A*107
 (**cause** *v.1.*)
cawth *see* **kachyd**
celestyal *adj.* heavenly, celestial I.366 (**celestial** *adj.*)
certayn, sertayn, serteyn *adj.* and *n.* certain, indubitable II.1010; II.1558,
 1929; I.251, **in serteyn** truly II.1864; (as *n.*) **a serteyn of** a certain number
 of I.410sd (**certain** *adj.* and *n.*)
certefye *v.* *2pl.pr.* report (officially) I.169 (**certifien** *v.*)
certeyn, sertayn, serteayn, serteyn *adv.* truly, indeed *1A*11; I.310, 895,
 II.1770; II.1287; I.560, 645, II.479, 1208 (**certain** *adv.*)
ces *see* **ses(e)**
ceteseynys *n.pl.* citizens I.398sd, 406sd (**citisein** *n.*)
cetéward, cetyward *adv.phrase* **onto/to þe cety-/cetéward** towards the
 city I.397; I.380 (*OED* **-ward** *suffix*)
cety(e), ceté, cyté *n.* city II.10; II.270; I.392, 447, 458, *2A*19; I.400, 442sd
 (**cité** *n.*)
chaffare *v.* trade, sell *2A*99 (**chaffaren** *v.*)
chalys *n.* chalice, cup I.799, 936sd, 945 (**chalice** *n.*)
chapmen *see* **schapman**
chare *v.* **chare awey** drive off II.1575; *imp.pl.* II.912 (**charen** *v.1.*)
charge *n.* instructions, duty, obligation, task I.189, II.1213 etc. (**charge**
 n.)
charge *v.* order, request I.208; *1sg.pr.* **charge** I.1029, II.22 etc.; *3sg.pr.*
 chargyth II.381, 384; *1pl.pr.* **charge** II.280, 571; *3sg.pa.* **chargyd** II.933
 (**chargen** *v.*)
charyté *n.* spiritual love, loving-kindness I.713, 826 etc. (**charité** *n.*)
chastément *n.* due admonition, corrective punishment I.113 (**chastiement**
 n.)
chastyté *n.* purity I.732 (**chastité** *n.*)
chaunge *v.* change, alter II.981, 1633, 1635; *imp.pl.* **chaunge** II.929
 (**chaungen** *v.*)
chawmer(e) *n.* room, dwelling II.562; II.1685 (**chaumbre** *n.*)
chef *adj.* most important, pre-eminent I.215; (or *n.*) leader, sovereign power
 I.57, 75, 114 (**chef** *n.* or *adj.*)
cheke *n.* cheek II.140, 141sd (**cheke** *n.*)
cheke *v.* choke, strangle II.455 (**choken** *v.*)
chene *n.* chain *3A*19; *n.pl.* **cheynes** II.31, **chenys** II.518 (**chaine** *n.*)
cher(e) *n.* spirits, mood, joy, appearance, behaviour I.963, II.856; I.508,

II.935 etc.; **make . . . chere** comfort, keep in good spirits I.883 (**chere** *n.1.*)

chese *v.* select, choose II.567; *p.p.* **chosyn** 3A34 (**chesen** *v.*)

cheverelle *n.* kid leather I.72 (**cheverel(le** *n.*)

chevesauns *n.* method, device, expedient I.103 (**chevisaunce** *n.*)

cheuith *v.* 3sg.pr. **cheuith us sore** grieves us greatly II.856 (see note) (**cheven** *v.*)

chyde *v.* abuse II.1324 (**chiden** *v.*)

chyld(e), childe *n.* child II.925; I.1072, II.1174; II.796, 990 etc.; *n.poss.* **childys** II.983; *n.pl.* **chyldere** II.1238, **chyldyr** II.646, 708, **chylderyn** I.410sd, 451, 666, II.1413 (**child** *n.*)

chosyn *see* **chese**

cyrcumstawns *n.* **with al þe cyrcumstawns** with all due formality I.210 (**circumsta(u)nce** *n.*)

cyté *see* **cety(e)**

clad *v.* 3sg.pa. (fig.) clothed, enveloped II.1403 (**clothen** *v.*)

clay, cley *n.* ground, grave II.1269, 1513 etc.; II.1461, 1780 (**clei** *n.*)

clappyd *p.p.* wrapped II.1306 (**clappen** *v.*)

claryfyed *p.p.* glorified (see note) I.791, 792 (**clarifien** *v.*)

clene *adj.* clean, pure, chaste II.643, 744, 846 (**clene** *adj.*)

clene, cleen *adv.* completely, fully I.155; I.457 (**clene** *adv.*)

clenly *adv.* neatly, splendidly, suitably I.288sd (**clenli** *adv.*)

clennes *n.* purity, continence I.732 (**clennesse** *n.*)

clensyd *p.p.* freed 2A51 (**clensen** *v.*)

clepe *v.* call, name, summon I.358; *p.p.* **clepyd** I.3, 26 etc. (**clepen** *v.*)

clere *adj.* bright, magnificent, pure, clear, fine I.74, 728, II.1052, 1458 (**cler** *adj.*)

clere *adv.* fully, wholly, openly II.557, 1318, 1447 (**cler** *adv.*)

clerk(e) *n.* scholar, learned man II.1073; II.497; *n.pl.* **clerkys** officials, legal advisers I.288sd (**clerk** *n.*)

cleve *v.* stick together II.896 (**cleven** *v.1.*)

cleve *v.* break I.1056; 3pl.pa. **clevyd** II.1508 (**cleven** *v.2.*)

closyd *p.p.* enclosed, enveloped 2A1, 45; **closyd in clay/cley** buried II.1747, 1780 (**closen** *v.*)

cloth(e) *n.* cloth, garment I.70, II.181sd etc.; II.486sd; *n.pl.* **clothis** I.406sd, II.461sd etc. (**cloth** *n.*)

clothyng *n.* dress, clothes I.637 (**clothing** *ger.*)

clowdys *n.pl.* clouds II.1053 (**cloud** *n.*)

clowte *n.* blow II.97 (**clout** *n.3.*)

cok *n.* cock I.875, II.222 (**cok** *n.1.*)

colde *adj.* cold, chilled with grief I.1045, II.1461 etc. (**cold** *adj.*)

colere *n.* collar I.85, 105 (**coler** *n.*)

colour, colore *n.* colour I.1064, II.1551 (**colour** *n.*)

com(e), comyn *v.* come I.802sd, 836, II.89sd, 1431; I.126, 132 etc.; II.242, 1423; 1sg.pr. **come** I.377, 600, 902, 929; 2sg.pr. **comyst** I.907, II.826;

3sg.pr. **comyth** I.244sd, 272sd etc., **comith** II.243sd (see note), ?**come**
II.1sd; *pl.pr.* **com** I.502sd, II.135, 377, 1293, **come** I.287, 988sd etc.,
comyn I.775sd, **cvm** I.641; *sg./pl.pr.subj.* **com** II.1232, 1246, **come**
II.70, 516 etc.; *imp.sg.* **com** II.785, 1301, **come** I.1009, II.459 etc.; *imp.pl.*
com II.969, 1225, **come** I.754, II.787 etc., ?**comyth** II.192; *pr.p.* **com-
yng(e)** I.346, 372 etc.; *1A*47; came *1/3sg.pa.* **cam** I.1, 650sd etc., **kam**
I.353; *1pl.pa.* **cam** II.103; *p.p.* **come** I.392, 416 etc. (**comen** *v.*)
comawnde *v.* order, present (one's) compliments I.167, II.738; *1sg.pr.*
   comawnd(e) II.1103; II.372, 470; *3sg.pr.* **comawndyth** I.354, II.245,
   666, *pl.pr.* **comawnde** II.229, 486; *imp.sg.* **comawnde** II.240; *3sg.pa.?*
   comawndyd II.238; *p.p.* **comawndyd** I.665, 699, 731, II.379 (**com-
   maunden** *v.*)
comawndement, cowmawndement *n.* rule, commandment, order, request I.93, 169 etc.; I.746; *n.pl.* **comaundementys** precepts, (Ten) Commandments I.357 (**commaundement** *n.*)
combryd *p.p.* overwhelmed *2A*52 (**combren** *v.*)
combros *adj.* troublesome, difficult II.1614 (**combrous** *adj.*)
comendable *adj.* praiseworthy, admirable II.54 (**com(m)endable** *adj.*)
comende *v.* *1sg.pr.* entrust, commend II.915 (**commenden** *v.*)
comfort(e) *n.* support, consolation, relief I.346, *1A*47; I.410, II.988 (**comfort** *n.*)
comforte, comfortyn *v.* comfort, cheer, console, relieve I.1071; II.1695;
   imp.sg. **comforte** II.991; *imp.pl.* **comfort** II.865; *p.p.* **comfortyd** II.1481
   (**comforten** *v.*)
comonys, comownys *n.* the ordinary people, the commons II.786sd; I.324
   (**communes** *n.*)
comoun *adj.* **þe comoun peple** the commons, the ordinary people II.610
   (**commune** *adj.*)
compayné *n.* body of people, gathering II.212 (**compaignie** *n.*)
comparycyon, comparison *n.* **make c.** (**to/vnto**) claim equality (with)
   I.71; I.81 (**comparisoun** *n.*; cf. **comparacioun** *n.*)
compleyn *v.* *2pl.pr.* make a complaint, appeal I.170 (**compleinen** *v.*)
compleyntys *n.pl.* charges, accusations II.282 (**compleint(e** *n.*)
con(e) see **can**
concyens *n.* mind, heart, conscience I.130, *3A*27 (**conscience** *n.*)
concludyd *p.p.* refuted, frustrated II.128 (**concluden** *v.*)
conclusyon *n.* end, principle, judgment I.525, II.308; **had conclusyon** was
   defeated/confuted I.29 (**conclusioun** *n.*)
conferme *v.* endorse, strengthen I.378 (**confermen** *v.*)
confermyng *vbl.n.* affirmation I.908 (**conferminge** *ger.*)
confesse *v.* *2pl.pr.* confess I.369; *imp.sg.* **confesse** I.155 (**confessen** *v.*)
confydens *n.* trust, firm belief I.376 (**confidence** *n.*)
confusyon *n.* destruction, ruin I.5, 51 etc. (**confusioun** *n.*)
congregacyon *n.* gathering, audience *3A*6 (**congregacioun** *n.*)
conyng *adj.* learned, clever II.497 (**conning** *ppl.*)

coniunccyon *n.* (natural) unity I.158 (**conjunccioun** *n.*)

coniure, conjowre *v.* *1sg.pr.* solemnly charge/order II.167; 2A36; *1pl.pr.* **coniure** II.524 (**conjuren** *v.*)

conqweryd *p.p.* overcome, taken possession of I.387 (**conqueren** *v.*)

conseyvyng *vbl.n.* conception (of a child) 3A38 (**conceivinge** *ger.*)

consent *v.* agree II.1593 (**consenten** *v.*)

consolacyon *n.* comfort I.1038 (**consolacioun** *n.*)

conspiracy *n.* conspiracy, plotting I.50 (**conspiracie** *n.*)

constreyn *v.* compel, oblige I.905, (emend.) I.563 (**constreinen** *v.*)

contenawns *n.* signs, gestures, bearing, looks I.662sd, 884sd, 964sd (**contenaunce** *n.*)

contenue *v.* continue I.227; *pr.p.* **contewnyng** I.499 (see note) (**continuen** *v.*)

contynent *adj.* chaste I.733 (**continent** *adj.*)

contynualy *adv.* continuously, forever 3A18 (**continuel(l)i** *adv.*)

contrary *n.* opposite, anyone in opposition I.173 (**contrarie** *n.*)

contré *see* **countré**

contrycyon *n.* remorse, contrition I.369, 718, 762 (**contricioun** *n.*)

contryve *v.* plan, devise I.567 (**contreven** *v.*)

conuey, convey *v.* control, lead, guide I.496; I.528; *1sg.pr.* **convey** I.213; *pr.p.* **conveyng** I.964sd (**conveien** *v.*)

conuersacyon *n.* way of life (see note) 3A26 (**conversacioun** *n.*)

conuertyd *v.* *3sg.pa.* converted 3A21, 22 (**converten** *v.*)

convocacyon *n.* synod, assembly, convocation I.518sd (**convocacioun** *n.*)

copelyd *p.p.* joined I.158 (**couplen** *v.*)

cordewan *n.* Cordovan leather I.69 (**cordewan(e** *n.*)

cordys *n.pl.* ropes I.1000, 1018, 1043 (**corde** *n.*)

corn *n.* corn II.911, 1574 (**corn** *n.*)

corner(e) *n.* corner II.1284, 1296; II.1316, 1802; *n.pl.* **cornerys** II.1289 (**corner** *n.1.*)

correcte *v.* punish I.242; *imp.pl.* **correcte** II.82 (**correcten** *v.*)

correxion *n.* punishment I.236 (**correccioun** *n.*)

cors *n.* body II.1323 (**cors** *n.*)

corteyn *n.* curtain II.543sd (**curtin(e** *n.*)

cosyn *n.* (near) relation, cousin (see note to I.196) commonly used as a term of address I.196, 200 etc.; *n.poss.* **cosynys** II.205 (**cosin(e** *n.*)

cost *n.* **every cost** everywhere II.1570 (**coste** *n.*)

costyous *adj.* expensive, costly I.70 (**costious** *adj.*)

covetyse *n.* greed, covetousness I.112, 597, II.504, 2A92 (**coveitise** *n.*)

counawnt *n.* agreement II.255 (**covenaunt** *n.*)

councel(l), counsel(l), cowncel(l), cowncelle, cownsayl *n.* advice, counsel, plan, body of advisers, council I.123, II.1636; II.1603; II.1668; II.1632; I.181, 186 etc.; I.302, 341, II.1593; II.417; I.193; **kepe counsel** keep quiet (about it) II.1668; **take/takyth cowncel(le** consult, consider I.221, II.114; II.417 (*see also* **cowncel(l)/cownsel hous**) (**counseil** *n.*)

councel, counsel *v. 1sg.pr.* advise I.129; II.1620 (**counseilen** *v.*)

countyrfe *v.* manage, conspire I.55 (see note) (cf. **contreven** *v.*)

countré, cowntré, contré *n.* region, country I.337, 573 etc.; II.70; II.349 (**contré(e** *n.*)

course *v.* curse I.448 (**cursen** *v.*)

cowardly *adv.* disgracefully, in a cowardly way II.215 (**couardli** *adv.*)

cowde(n) *see* **can**

cowmawndement *see* **comawndement**

cowncel(l)/cownsel hous *n.* meeting-house II.603sd; II.656sd; I.288sd, 518sd (**counseil** *n.*)

cowncel(l), cowncelle, cownsayl *see* **councel(l)**

cownterfete *v.* imitate, make up, contrive I.102; *imp.sg.* **cowntyrfete** I.540; *p.p.* **cowntyrfetyd** I.583, 993, 2A128sd (**countrefeten** *v.*)

cowntré *see* **countré**

craft(e) *n.* cleverness, trickery, trick, skill, art II.543; II.402; *n.pl.* **craftys** II.272 (**craft** *n.*)

crafty *adj.* clever, skilful II.497 (**crafti** *adj.*)

crake *v.* crack, break II.895; *1sg.pr.* **crake** II.1333 (**craken** *v.*)

crave *v. 1sg.pr.* pray II.1875 (**craven** *v.*)

creature *n.* creature, created being, person I.742, 1067 etc. (**creature** *n.*)

credens *n.* trust, credence I.564, 698 (**credence** *n.*)

crenseyn *n.* crimson colour I.70 (**cremesin** *n. & adj.*)

cresset(t)ys *n.pl.* cresset (oil) lamps I.656; I.964sd (**cresset** *n.*)

cry *n.* shout, shouting I.988sd, 1032sd (**cri(e** *n.*)

cry(e), cryen *v.* cry, shout, call out I.856; I.786, II.696sd, 715; II.590sd, 880sd; *1sg.pr.* **crye** II.1155; *3sg.pr.* **cryeth** I.990sd; *1pl.pr.* **crye** II.597; *pr.p.* **criyng** II.89sd, **creyng** I.414, II.553, 3A40; **crye out on me** cry out against me I.786 (**crien** *v.*)

crystenyd *v. 3sg.pa.* baptised II.37 (**cristnen** *v.*)

Crystyn *n.* and *adj.* Christian II.29, 41, 47, 52; *n.pl.* **Crystyn** II.33 (**Cristen** *adj. & n.*)

crokyd *adj.* crippled, lame I.351, 359; (as *n.*) I.37, II.423 (**croked** *ppl.*)

cros(se) *n.* cross II.511, 596 etc.; II.650, 672 etc.; *n.pl.* **crosses/-ys** II.787; II.790sd (**cros** *n.*)

crowch *n.* cross II.1707 (**crouche** *n.*)

crowe *n.* crow II.912 (**croue** *n.*)

crowyn *v.* crow II.222; *p.p.* **crowe** I.875 (**crouen** *v.*)

crowne, kroune *n.* crown of the head/of a cap, head, crown (of thorns) I.87, 164sd; II.698sd; *n.pl.* **crownys** II.1333 (**coroune** *n.*)

crowne *v. imp.pl.* crown II.683; *p.p.* **crownyd** I.781 (**corounen** *v.*)

cruelly *adv.* cruelly, harshly II.965 (**cruelli** *adv.*)

cruelté *n.* cruelty II.1421 (**cruelté** *n.*)

cvm *see* **com(e)**

cure *n.* cure, care, duty I.371, 749) **do ʒoure besy cure** work diligently I.749 (**cure** *n.1.*)

curyng *vbl.n.* protection I.87 (**curing** *ger.*)
cursyd *p.p.* sinful 2A1 (**cursed** *ppl.*)
cusshonys *n.pl.* cushions I.288sd (**quishin** *n.*)
custom *n.* custom, tradition II.581 (**custum(e** *n.*)

daggare *n.* dagger, knife I.83 (**daggere** *n.*)
day, dawe *n.* day I.24, 204 etc.; **o/a/of dawe** (lit. 'out of day') to death II.38, 129, 149; *n.pl.* **days** I.28, 38 etc. (**dai** *n.*)
day *see also* **dey(e)**
dayly *adj.* constant I.1038 (**daili** *adj.*)
dayly *adv.* daily, every day I.11, 82, 180, II.411 (**daili** *adv.*)
dame *n.* lady II.563 (**dame** *n.*)
dampnacyon *n.* damnation I.390, 769, II.1422 (**dampnacioun** *n.*)
dampne *v.* condemn, damn II.482, 2A47; *p.p.* **dampnyd** II.547, 555, 2A103 (**dampnen** *v.*)
dare, dur(st) *v.* *1sg.pr.* dare II.116, 1075, 1286, 1588; I.863; II.157; *2sg.pr.* **darst** II.1539; *1pl.pr.* **durst** II.1566; *3pl.pr.* **dare** I.654 (**durren** *v.*)
daungere, dawngere *n.* control, danger II.1057; I.244, 1004 (**daunger** *n.*)
dawe *v.* *3sg.pr.subj.* dawns, breaks II.239, 246 (**dauen** *v.*)
dawe *see also* **day**
dawncyn *v.* dance II.774sd (**dauncyn** *v.*)
debat *n.* **make debat** quarrel, disagree I.84 (**debat** *n.*)
declaracyon *n.* **made declaracyon** explained I.163 (**declaracioun** *n.*)
declinande, declynyng *pr.p.* tending, inclining, turning aside I.136; I.146 (**declinen** *v.*)
ded(e) *n.* action, deed 2A120; I.180, 536 etc.; *n.pl.* **dedys** I.130, 368, II.82, 257 (**dede** *n.*)
ded(e), deed *adj.* dead I.38, 808 etc.; II.300, 424, 546, 1753; II.1006, 1476 etc. (**ded** *adj.*)
dede *n.* death II.1448 (**deth** *n.*)
dede *see also* **do(n)**
dedly *adv.* **synnyst dedly** commit mortal sin I.154 (**dedli** *adv.*)
deed *see* **ded(e)** *adj.*
def *adj.* deaf I.358; (as *n.*) I.350 (**def** *adj.* (& *n.*))
defawte, defawth *n.* flaw, sin, crime, guilt II.577; I.191, II.309 etc. *n.pl.* **defawtys** II.474 (**defaut(e** *n.*)
defende *v.* protect I.802, 819; *3sg.pr.subj.* **defende** II.4; *p.p.* **defendyd** denied, refused II.832 (**defenden** *v.*)
defye *v.* defy II.506 (**defien** *v.*)
degré(e) *n.* rank, (proper) position, order I.253, 662sd; I.690; *n.pl.* **degrees** I.82; **in every/eche degré** in every way II.306, 915, II.444, **in no (maner) degré** (+ *neg.v.*) in any way, at all I.1052, II.376, 727 (**degré** *n.*)
dey(e), dye, day *v.* die I.42, 312 etc.; I.533, II.640 etc.; I.412, II.511, 704, 1058; I.316; *2sg.pr.* **deyst** II.1079; *3sg.pa.* **deyd** II.3, 1560, 1707, 1739; *p.p.* **deyd** II.946 (**dien** *v.*)

deyté *n.* deity, Godhead I.691 (**deité** *n.*)

delacyon *n.* delay I.260, 267, 543 (**dilacioun** *n.*)

delay *n.* delay I.271, 590 etc. (**delai(e** *n.*)

delayd *p.p.* delayed I.43 (**delaien** *v.1.*)

dele *n.* **nevyr a dele** not at all I.822 (**del** *n.2.*)

delectacyon *n.* pleasure, enjoyment *3A*12 (**delectacioun** *n.*)

delycyous *adj.* spiritually rich/enjoyable I.759 (**delicious** *adj.*)

delyte *n.* pleasure I.89 (see note), II.62 (**delit(e** *n.1.*)

delyveré *n.* release, freeing II.658 (cf. **deliveri** *n.*)

delyuere, delyver(e), delyvyr *v.* free, give (up), hand over, rescue II.850, 873; II.485; II.1025; II.14; *imp.sg.* **delyuere** I.931, **delyvere** II.592, 649; **dylyuere** II.649; *p.p.* **delyveryd** I.436, II.335 (**deliveren** *v.*)

dem(e) *v.* judge, condemn, think I.304; II.172, 436; *1sg.pr.* **deme** II.693; *imp.sg.* **deme** II.545; *imp.pl.* **demyth** II.321; *p.p.* **dempt** II.655 (**demen** *v.*)

demawnde *n.* request II.484 (**demaunde** *n.*)

dene *n.* sound II.543sd (**dine** *n.1.*)

deny(e), deney *v.* deny, refuse, renounce, fail to acknowledge, foil, prevent I.301; I.53, 168 etc.; I.108, 891 (**denien** *v.*)

dent, dynt *n.* blow, wound II.1728; II.488; *n.pl.* **dentys** II.1389, **dyntys** II.1267 (**dint** *n.*)

departyng *vbl.n.* death (lit. 'departure') II.865 (**departing(e** *ger.*)

departyth *v. 3sg.pr.* goes away, departs II.968 (**departen** *v.*)

depe *adj.* deep II.1721, *2A*116 (**dep** *adj.*)

depe *adv.* deep II.1459, *2A*110 (**dep(e** *adv.*)

dere *v.* harm, injure II.145 (**deren** *v.*)

dere *adj.* dear, beloved I.877, 885 etc. (**dere** *adj.*)

derk(e), dyrk *n.* dark, gloomy II.510; II.492, 1039, 1052; II.1050 (**derk** *adj.*)

derlyng *n.* beloved I.779, II.831, 973 (**dereling** *n.*)

descendyth *v. 3sg.pr.* comes down, descends I.936sd (**descenden** *v.*)

desert *n.* desert, wilderness *3A*40 (**desert** *n.2.*)

desyre *n.* longing, desire I.679, II.977; *n.pl.* **desyrys** I.63 (**desir** *n.*)

desyre *v. 1sg.pr.* wish, long II.64; *3sg.pr.* **desyryth** II.69; *2sg.pr.subj.* **desyre** I.80; *1sg.pa.* **desyred** II.395; *p.p.* **desyryd** I.680, II.420 (**desiren** *v.*)

deth *n.* death I.55, 323 etc.; *n.poss.* **dethis** II.1389, 1469 (**deth** *n.*)

deth *see also* **do(n)**

detraccyon *n.* slander, reproach *3A*8 (**detraccioun** *n.*)

devid *p.p.* deafened II.1510 (**deven** *v.1.*)

devyl, deuyl *n.* devil I.778sd, II.455 etc.; I.819, II.761; *n.poss.* **develys** II.850; *n.pl.* **develys** II.489, 492 etc., **deuelys** II.1843 (**devel** *n.*)

devyse *n.* intent II.1618 (**devis** *n.*)

devocyon, devoscyon *n.* reverence, devotion, piety I.797; I.83 (**devocioun** *n.*)

devoyde *v. 1sg.pr.* drive out, remove I.124; *pr.p.* **devoydyng** I.386 (**devoiden** *v.*)

devowtest *adj.* (as *n.*) most devout/pious I.1034 (**devout** *adj.*)
dew(e) *adj.* proper, appropriate I.381, II.75; I.66, 756 (**du(e** *adj.*)
dewté *n.* service, tribute II.1724 (**dueté** *n.*)
dyce *n.pl.* dice II.790sd (**de** *n.*)
dyd *see* **do(n)**
dye *see* **dey(e)**
dyght(e) *see* **dyth**
dyligens, dilygens, dylygens *n.* duty, industry, diligence I.277, 381, II.52;
 II.75; II.382, 1111; **do þi dylygens** make an effort II.430 (**diligence** *n.*)
dylyuere *see* **delyuere**
dymysse *v. 1sg.pr.* release, free II.663 (**dismissen** *v.*)
dynt(ys) *see* **dent**
dyrk *see* **derk(e)**
dysceyvyth *v. 3sg.pr.* tricks, misleads II.444 (**deceiven** *v.*)
dysche *n.* dish, plate 2A117 (**dish** *n.*)
dyscypil, dyscypyl, dyscyple *n.* disciple (of Christ) I.636; I.774sd; II.100,
 124; *n.pl.* **dyscipelys** II.1232, **disciplis** I.518sd, 928sd, 2A64sd, **dysciplis**
 I.916sd, 948, **dysciplys** I.502sd, 694sd etc., **dyscyplis** II.1643, 1644,
 1A6, **dyscyplys** II.1208, **discipulis** I.53, **discipulys** I.900sd, **dyscipulis**
 I.964sd, **dyscipulys** I.442sd, 483 etc., **dyscypulys** I.57, 494sd, 662sd,
 762sd, **dysypulys** I.33 (**disciple** *n.*)
dyscrecyon *n.* discretion, moderation I.60 (**discrecioun** *n.*)
dysgeysyd, dysgysyd, -sed *p.p.* dressed strangely/elaborately/
 fashionably I.102; I.65 (as *adj.*); I.964sd (**disgisen** *v.*)
dysmayd *p.p.* alarmed, frightened II.1671, 1754 (**dismaien** *v.*)
dyspeyre *v.* despair I.154; *pr.p.* (as *adj.*) **dyspeyryng** I.343, 1A44 (**de-
speiren** *v.*)
dysperacyon *n.* despair (of God's mercy) I.143, 161 (**desperacioun** *n.*)
dyspyte, dyspyth *n.* contempt, shame, insult I.1031, II.588, 706, 965; I.550
 (**despit** *n.*)
displesauns *n.* annoyance, harm I.56 (**displesaunce** *n.*)
dysplese *v.* displease II.852; *imp.pl.* **dysplese** II.735 (**displesen** *v.*)
dyspoyle *v.* strip II.573; *p.p.* **dyspoyled, -yd** II.1173; II.700 (**despoilen** *v.*)
dysposycyon *n.* order, inclination, temperament I.66, 716 (see note to
 I.66–7) (**disposicioun** *n.*)
dysprave, dyspravyn *v.* condemn, speak against, find fault with I.1025;
 II.1571 (**depraven** *v.*)
dysprevyd *p.p.* refuted, denied II.673 (**dispreven** *v.*)
dysseuerawns *n.* separation I.159 (**disseveraunce** *n.*)
dystyllyth *v. 3pl.pr.* runs, trickles I.926 (**distillen** *v.*)
dystrye, dysstroye, distroye, dystroy(e) *v.* destroy, kill, ruin I.300;
 II.55; I.212; I.701; II.407, 804; *3sg.pr.* **dystroyt** I.180; *3sg.pr.subj.* **dystroye** II.147; *p.p.* **dystroy** I.445, **dystroyd** I.188, II.40, 401, 625 (**des-
troien** *v.*)
dystruccyon *n.* destruction, death I.542, 700 (**destruccioun** *n.*)

dyth *v.* prepare, set, arrange, condemn, betake oneself, treat II.61, 2A70; *3sg.pr.subj.* **dyth** I.660; *p.p.* **dyght(e)** II.1280, *1A*42; II.966, **dyth** *1A*37 (**dighten** *v.*)

dyverce *adj.* various I.35 (**divers(e** *adj.*)

dyvercyté *n.* variety I.65 (see note to I.65–87) (**diversité** *n.*)

dyvicyon *n.* **dyvicyon eternal** endless separation (from God) I.118 (**divisioun** *n.*)

dyvide *p.p.* split, destroyed I.425 (**dividen** *v.*)

do(n) *v.* do, perform, carry out, act, put, take, cause to be, make, (and as *aux.*) I.131, 151 etc.; I.236, 402 etc.; *1sg.pr.* **do** I.828, II.1477; *2sg.pr.* **dost** I.409, II.131 etc., **doyst** I.873; *3sg.pr.* **doth** I.178, 566 etc.; *1pl.pr.* **do** I.184, 519, II.1029; *2pl.pr.* **do** I.801, 842 etc.; *3pl.pr.* **do** I.1060, II.52 etc., **doth** II.47; *3sg.pr.subj.* **do** I.245; *2pl.pr.subj.* **do** II.1239; *imp.sg.* **do** I.155, II.430, 1100; *imp.pl.* **do** I.239, 749 etc., **doth** II.697; *pr.p.* **doyng** 2A88; *1sg.pa.* **dede** I.924, 934 etc., **dyd** 2A66; *2sg.pa.* **dedyst** II.255, 811, 815; *3sg.pa.* **dede** I.704, 705 etc., **dyd** I.331, 510 etc.; *pl.pa.* **dede** I.670, 671 etc.; *p.p.* **do** I.805, II.82 etc., **don(e)** I.332, 475 etc.; II.1070, 1531; **do wey** stop II.819 (**don** *v.*)

dobbelet *n.* doublet I.78 (**doublet** *n.*)

doctour *n.* learned man, cleric *3A*33; *n.poss.* **doctorys** II.1sd; *n.pl.* **doctorys** I.164sd, 208sd (**doctour** *n.*)

doctryne *n.* teaching, doctrine II.131 (**doctrine** *n.*)

doggys *n.pl.* wretches (lit. 'dogs') II.47, 52 (**dogge** *n.*)

doyng, doyst *see* **do(n)**

dolfol, dolful *adj.* sorrowful, sad II.856; II.958 (**dolful** *adj.*)

dolour *n.* suffering, sorrow II.958 (**dolour** *n.*)

dolve *p.p.* buried II.1459 (**delven** *v.*)

dome *n.* **gast dome** sentenced, condemned II.1535 (**dom** *n.*)

dome, dowm *adj.* dumb I.350 (as *n.*), 367; I.37 (as *n.*) (**domb** *adj.*)

domynacyon *n.* lordship, control I.45 (**dominacioun** *n.*)

domysday *n.* the Day of Judgment II.170 (**domes–dai** *n.*)

don(e) *see* **do(n)**

dongeon, donjeon *n.* prison I.6, II.510; 2A116; *n.pl.* **doongenys**, II.35, **doungenys** II.492 (**dongoun** *n.*)

dore *n.* door, gate II.1039 (**dor(e** *n.*)

doseyn *num.* dozen I.72 (**dosein(e** *num.*)

dost, doth *see* **do(n)**

doute, dowt(e), dowth *n.* doubt, uncertainty, fear, danger II.132; 2A96; II.1030, 1611, 2A85; I.416, 639, II.1255, *1A*2 (**dout(e** *n.*)

dowm *see* **dome** *adj.*

down(e) *adv.* down I.85, 280sd etc.; I.406sd (**doun** *adv.*)

dowte *n.* valour, prowess II.1267 (**dought** *adj. & n.*)

dowt(e) *see also* **doute**

dowteles *adv.* without doubt I.167 (**douteles** *adv.*)

dowtere *n.* daughter I.101; *n.pl.* **dowterys** II.707, 1698 (**doughter** *n.*)

dowth *see* **doute**
dowty *adj.* valiant, strong II.488 (**doughti** *adj. & n.*)
dragonys *n.pl.* dragons II.35, 492 (**dragoun** *n.*)
drawe, drawyn *v.* pull, draw, attract, approach, turn, bring II.32, 764; II.698sd; *1sg.pr.* **drawe** I.989; *3sg.pr.* **drawyth** I.326, 397 etc.; *3?pl.pr.* **drawe** II.610; *imp.sg.* **drawe** II.772; *pr.p.* **drawyng** I.1032sd; *1sg.pa.* **drowe** I.17; *p.p.* **drawe** I.319, 553, 606, **drawyn** II.543sd (**drauen** *v.*)
dred *ppl.adj.* frightening, terrible II.488 (**dreden** *v.*)
dred(e), dreed *n.* fear, terror, danger II.1279, 1357, 2A118; I.145, 148 etc.; II.1745; **withoutyn drede** assuredly II.809 (**dred(e** *n.*)
drede *v.* fear I.939 (**dreden** *v.*)
dredfull, -fful *adj.* awesome, terrible 2A81; 2A82 (**dredeful** *adj.*)
dresse *v.* prepare, go II.1917; *imp.pl.* **dresse** I.381; *p.p.* **to deth is dressyd** is put to death II.925 (**dressen** *v.*)
dreve, drevyn *see* **dryve**
drynes *n.* dryness II.896 (**drienes(se** *n.*)
drynk(e) *n.* drink II.900, 903; II.901 (**drink(e** *n.*)
drynke *v.* *3sg.pr.subj.* drink I.821; *3sg.pr.* **drynkyth** I.817 (**drinken** *v.*)
dryve, dryvyn *v.* drive, throw, strike II.774; II.35; *imp.sg.* **dryve** II.767; *3sg.pa.* **droff** II.1684; *p.p.* **dreve** II.770, **drevyn** II.1389 (**driven** *v.*)
droff *see* **dryve**
drowe *see* **drawe**
duke *n.* ruler, lord I.2 (**duk** *n.*)
dullyth *v.* *3sg.pr.* becomes dazed/sleepy II.1344 (**dullen** *v.*)
dur, durst *see* **dare**
dwelle, dwellyn *v.* live, dwell I.6, II.947 etc.; I.120, II.1378; *1pl.pr.* **dwell** II.1669; *3pl.pr.* **dwelle** II.1015; *pr.p.* **dwellynge** II.1495 (**dwellen** *v.*)
dwellyng *vbl.n.* habitation, dwelling-place II.714 (**dwellinge** *ger.*)
dwere *n.* doubt II.1610 (**dwere** *n.*)

ease *see* **ese**
ech(e) *pron.* each I.282, 662sd; I.164sd, 662sd etc. (**ech** *pron.*)
ech(e) *adj.* each, every I.110; I.34, 66 etc. (**ech** *pron.*)
echon *pron.* each one I.726, 885, 979, II.597 (**ech on** *pron.phrase*)
edyfy *v.* establish (itself), be exalted I.417, 1A3 (**edifien** *v.*)
eer *see* **er(e)** *conj.*
eerly *see* **erthely**
efne *see* **hevyn**
egal *adv.* equally I.847 (**egal** *adj.*)
ey *n.* eye I.356, 501; *n.pl.* **eyn(e)** I.85 (alternative wording), 438, 438sd, II.1142sd; I.958; **haue eyn** set eyes II.1702 (**eie** *n.1.*)
eyd *n.* heed II.911 (**hed** *n.2.*)
eyn(e) *see* **ey**
eyr *n.* air II.1052 (**air** *n.1.*)
eyre *n.* heir I.156 (**heir** *n.*)

eyther *adj.* either, each II.692 (**either** *pron.*)

eyzil *n.* vinegar II.898 (**aisel** *n.*)

eke *conj.* also 3A14 (**ek** *adv.* and *conj.*)

eld *adj.* old I.708 (**old(e** *adj.*)

elde *n.* old people II.407 (**elde** *n.*)

eleccyon *n.* election 3A34 (**eleccioun** *n.*)

ellys *adj.* **not ellys but** nothing other than I.736, 740 (**elles** *adj.*)

ellys *adv.* else, otherwise I.1070, II.717, 1203, 1832 (**elles** *adv.*)

empere *n.* rule, dominion II.1055 (**empire** *n.*)

emperour *n.* emperor II.275, 312 etc.; *n.poss.* **emperorys** II.280, **emperourys** II.277 (**emperour** *n.*)

encheson, incheson *n.* pretext, reason, cause I.585; II.305 (**enchesoun** *n.*)

enclosyd *p.p.* joined I.70 (see note to I.70–2) (**enclosen** *v.*)

ende, hende *n.* end I.702, 778 etc.; I.502 (**ende** *n.*)

endles, endeles, hendles *adj.* endless II.1418, 1494, 1922, 2A84; II.1379, 1422, 1890; II.1426 (**endeles** *adj.*)

endlesly *adv.* for ever, eternally II.301 (**endelesli** *adv.*)

eneryth, inheryte *v.* inherit I.118; I.370 (**enheriten** *v.*)

engynes *n.pl.* contrivances, designs I.50 (**engin** *n.*)

enherytawns, inerytawns *n.* inheritance I.157; I.100 (**enheritaunce** *n.*)

enmye *n.* enemy I.701; *n.pl.* **enmyes** II.1397 (**enemi** *n.*)

ensure *v.* *1sg.pr.* assure, pledge I.370; *p.p.* **ensuryd** I.40 (**ensuren** *v.*)

entent, intent *n.* purpose, wish, desire I.92, 290 etc.; II.24, 294 etc. (**entente** *n.*)

enteryth *v.* *3sg.pr.* enters I.342sd, 518sd, II.249sd, 486sd; *p.p.* **enteryd** II.1sd, 81 (**entren** *v.*)

enterly *adv.* sincerely, wholeheartedly I.680 (**enterli** *adv.*)

envye *n.* envy I.113, 712 (**envie** *n.*)

envyous *adj.* malicious II.1421 (**envious** *adj.*)

eqwall *adj.* equal I.689 (**equal** *adj.*)

er *conj.* or II.1203 (**er** *conj.2.*)

er(e) *adv.* before II.198; II.101 (**er** *adv.*)

er(e), eer, or *conj.* before I.681 (**er þan**), II.1220 (**er þat**); II.1935; II.1167; I.204, 276 etc. (**er** *conj.1.*)

erand, herand, erdon *n.* message, errand, business II.374; II.730; I.930; *n.pl.* **errandys** II.728 (**erend(e** *n.*)

erde *n. see* **erth(e)**

erde *see also* **here** *v.*

erdon *see* **erand**

ere, here *n.* ear II.99, 101; I.990sd; *n.pl.* **erys** II.1510, 1625, 1627, **herys** I.85 (alternative wording) (**ere** *n.1.*)

ere *see also* **here** *pl.pron.poss.*

eresye *n.* heresy I.998 (**heresie** *n.*)

eretyk *n.* heretic, one in opposition to the current faith I.170, 309 (**heretik(e** *n.*)

ermyn *n.* ermine (fur) I.105 (**ermin** *n.*)

erre *v.* sin, go astray II.30; *3pl.pr.* **erre** II.55 (**erren** *v.1.*)

errour *n.* heresy, sin, false belief II.60, 307; *n.pl.* **errouris** I.212 (**errour** *n.*)

erth(e), **erde**, **herd** *n.* earth, ground II.292, 1049; II.216; I.976sd; I.943 (**erthe** *n.1.*)

erthely, **eerly** *adj.* earthly II.1051; I.401 (**ertheli** *adj.*)

erthequake *n.* earthquake II.1581 (**erthe** *n.1.*)

erthqwave *n.* earthquake II.1053 (**erthe** *n.1.*)

ese, **ease** *n.* benefit, comfort II.396, 743; **in ease** at peace II.1938 (**ese** *n.*)

est *n.* east II.1629 (**est** *n.*)

ete *v.* eat I.700, 707 etc.; *3sg.pr.* **etyth** I.817, 2A64sd, **etyht** 2A117, **ete** I.518sd, 821; *1pl.pa.* **ete** I.674; *p.p.* **ete** I.667, 711, 772, **etyn** I.664, 683, 715, 783 (**eten** *v.*)

eternal(l) *adj.* everlasting I.118; I.687 (**eternal** *adj.*)

eternalyté *n.* **by eternalyté** ?everlastingly 3A5 (see note) (**eternalite** *n.*)

evangelyst *n.* evangelist (Matthew) 3A25 (**evangelist** *n.*)

ever *see* **evyr**

every, **euery**, **heuery** *adj.* every I.305, 306 etc.; II.1779; I.361 (**everi** *pron.*)

everychon(e), **euerychon** *pron.* everyone I.809, II.39 etc.; I.964; I.21 (**everich-on** *pron.*)

everydel *adv.* entirely, totally I.784, II.159 (**everi-del** *n. & adj.*)

evyl *adj.* wicked, difficult, awkward II.317, 1615 (**evil** *adj.*)

evyl *adv.* badly, unluckily II.454, 459, 751 (**evil(e** *adv.*)

evyldoere *n.* evildoer, criminal II.318 (**evil-doere** *n.*)

evyn *n.* evening; **both(e) evyn and morn/morwyn** always, at all times, continually I.450, II.910, 1473 (**eve(n** *n.*)

evyn, **euyn**, **hevyn** *adv.* even, just, indeed II.1302, 1522 etc.; II.1658; II.1811 (**even** *adv.*)

evyr, **ever** *adv.* ever, always I.780, 800 etc.; I.8, II.1932 (**ever** *adv.*)

evyrlastynge *adj.* eternal I.120 (**ever-lasting** *ppl.*)

evyrmor(e), **heuermore** *adv.* eternally, forever II.955; II.225, 1375 etc.; II.1414; **for evyrmore** I.782 (**ever-mo(r** *adv.*)

examyne *v.* examine, question II.603 (**examinen** *v.*)

exawmpyl, **exawmple**, **exawnpyl** *n.* example, token, instance I.825; I.385; I.736; *n.pl.* **exawmplys** I.740 (**exaumple** *n.*)

excede *v.* exceed, transcend I.60, 178; *3sg.pr.* **excedyth** I.756; *3pl.pr.* **excede** I.169, II.60 (**exceden** *v.*)

excellent, **excyllent** *adj.* illustrious II.406; II.27, 378 (**excellent** *adj.*)

except *prep.*, *conj.* except I.762sd, II.377sd (**except** *ppl.*)

excyllence, **excillens** *n.* greatness, dignity, superiority 3A2; II.50 (**excellence** *n.*)

excyllent *see* **excellent**

excuse *n.* defence, justification I.999 (**excuse** *n.*)

excuse *v.* defend, clear, excuse II.441, 453, 729 (**excusen** *v.*)

exys *n.pl.* axes I.658 (**ax(e** *n.*)

exorte *v.* encourage, urge, cry out I.116; *1pl.pr.* **exorte** I.413 (**exhorten** *v.*)

expedyent *adj.* advisable, expedient I.532 (**expedient** *adj.*)

expelle *v.* drive away II.1899 (**expellen** *v.*)

experyence *n.* proof; **shewyd experyence** demonstrated I.420 (**experience** *n.*)

exposytour *n.* expositor, one who explains or comments II.1sd (**expositour** *n.*)

expres *v.* declare, tell II.1915; *imp.sg.* **expresse** 2A76 (**expressen** *v.*)

expres *adj.* open, clear II.1789 (**expres** *adj.*)

faccyon *n.* fashion I.80 (**facioun** *n.*)

face *n.* face, presence I.925, 1064 etc.; **make good face** put on a friendly appearance I.648 (**face** *n.*)

fade *v.* grow pale I.1064 (**faden** *v.*)

fadyr *n.* father I.665, 686sd etc.; *n. poss.* **faderys** II.289, 294 etc.; *n.pl.* **faderys** II.713 (**fader** *n.*)

faye, feye *n.* faith, belief II.1077; II.817 (**feith** *n.*)

fayl *n.* **withowtyn fayl** without doubt, certainly I.843 (**faile** *n.*)

fayl(e) *v.* fail, be unsuccessful, run out I.249,-638; I.46, 190, 453 (**failen** *v.*)

fayn, fawe *adj.* glad II.999, 1767; II.93 (**fain** *adj.*)

fayn *adv.* willingly, gladly, eagerly I.990, 1041 etc. (**fain** *adv.*)

fayr *adv.* **fayr and wel** wholly, fully I.991 (**fair(e** *adv.*)

fayr(e) *adj.* fine, beautiful, dear, pure II.1040, 1743, 2A58; II.425, 1408 (**fair** *adj.*)

fayrest *adj.* most beautiful I.16 (**fair** *adj.*)

falle *v.* fall, go down, (+ **on**) attack, (+ **fro**) abandon, (+ **to**) join I.297, 406sd etc.; *1sg.pr.* **falle** II.1352; *3sg.pr.* **fallyth** I.824sd, II.1150sd; *3pl.pr.* **falle** I.976sd; *p.p.* **falle** II.405; (see note to II.1657–9 for II.1659) (**fallen** *v.*)

fals(e) *adj.* deceitful, faithless, treacherous, wicked I.228, 229 etc.; II.442 (**fals** *adj.*)

false *v.* pervert, misrepresent I.52 (**falsen** *v.*)

falsnesse *n.* deceitfulness, imposture II.399 (**falsnesse** *n.*)

fare *v.* go, act, behave; **weyl/evyl mot(e) þu fare** good/bad luck go with you II.248, 454; *pl.pr.* **fare** II.739, 1407 (**faren** *v.*)

farewel *interj.* goodbye I.255, 645 etc. (**faren** *v.*)

fast *v.* *3sg.pa.* **fasted** I.28 (**fasten** *v.2.*)

fast *adv.* firmly, soundly, quickly, greatly I.268, 297 etc. (**fast(e** *adv.*)

favorabyl *adj.* partial, unfairly well-disposed II.624 (**favourable** *adj.*)

favour *n.* goodwill, leniency II.431 (**favour** *n.*)

fawe *see* **fayn** *adj.*

fawth *n.* lack, deficiency I.811 (**faute** *n.*)

fech(e) *v.* fetch, carry off II.1233; II.1014; *3pl.pr.* **fecch** 1A17sd; *p.p.* **fett** II.1644 (**fecchen** *v.*)

fede *v.* feed I.753, 759 etc.; *imp.pl.* **fede** I.810; *p.p.* **fed** I.806 (**feden** *v.*)

feet *see* **foot**

feye *see* **faye**

feyn *v.* hesitate I.175 (**feinen** *v.*)

feyn, fyne *adj.* fine, excellent, sheer I.72, 73; I.69 (**fin** *adj.*)

feyn (see note to II.1700)

feyr *see* **fyre**

feyt *see* **foot**

feyth *n.* faith, trust, belief I.730, II.29 etc.; **in feyth** truly II.1254 (**feith** *n.*)

fekyll *adj.* treacherous II.1714 (**fikel** *adj.*)

fela *n.* man, lad, companion, fellow (used contemptuously) II.138, 204, 775; *n.pl.* **felawys** I.883, 901 etc., **felawus** I.97 (**felau(e** *n.*)

felachep *n.* company, gang I.92 (**felauship(e** *n.*)

felde *n.* country II.1570 (**feld** *n.*)

fele *adv.* **to fele** too much I.137, 146 (**fele** *adv.*)

felle *n.* skin; **flesch and felle** the whole body II.1434, 1898 (**fel** *n.1.*)

felle *v.* destroy, overthrow I.224, 584, 603; *3sg.pr.* **fellyth** II.65 (**fellen** *v.*)

felle *adj.* cruel, fierce, dangerous I.8, II.1014, 1613 (**fel** *adj.*)

fend(e), fynd *n.* devil, fiend II.548; I.802, II.917, 1372; I.426; *n.poss.* **fendes** II.1684, **fendys** I.890, 2A44; *n.pl.* **fendys** II.947, 1014 etc., **fyndys** II.1682, 2A104 (**fend** *n.*)

fende *v.* save 2A34 (**fenden** *v.*)

fenne *n.* **be fryth and fenne** (lit. 'by wood and marsh') everywhere 2A18 (**fen** *n.*)

fer *adj.* far 2A103 (**fer** *adj.*)

fer(e) *n.* fear I.862, II.355, 1562; I.884, 904, II.1234 (**fer** *n.1.*)

ferdere, ferther(e), fordere *adv.* further I.183; II.1639; **ferthere þan** beyond what I.873; I.43 (**ferther** *adv.*)

fere *n.* companion, equal I.1020 (**fere** *n.1.*)

fere *n.* **in fere** in company, together I.632, II.1554, 3A15 (**fere** *n.2.*)

fere *v.* *1sg.pr.* am afraid I.785 (**feren** *v.1.*)

fere *adj.* bold, proud II.794 (**fer** *adj.2.*)

ferful *adj.* frightened I.927 (**ferful** *adj.*)

ferre *adv.* far II.528 (**fer** *adv.*)

fers *adj.* pressing, important II.1613 (**fers** *adj.*)

ferther(e) *see* **ferdere**

fervent *adj.* ardent, keen I.679 (**fervent** *adj.*)

fesyk *n.* medical science II.89 (**phisik(e** *n.*)

fest *v. imp.sg.* fasten, set, fix II.763, 771; *p.p.* **fest** II.685, 3A27 (or 'firmly'; cf. **fast** *adv.*) (**fasten** *v.1.*)

fest(e) *n.* feast, festival II.916 (or 'fast'; see note); II.1634 (**feste** *n.*)

fete *see* **foot**

fett *see* **fech(e)**

fewe *adj.* **at wordys fewe** without more ado I.827 (cf. **feue** *indef. pron.*)

fewté *n.* fealty, loyalty II.1723 (**feuté** *n.*)

fy *interj.* fie! (expressing contempt, ridicule, etc.) II.1244, 1538, 1568 (**fi** *int.*)

fyght, fyth, fytyn *v.* fight II.1554; I.91, 654; II.790sd (**fighten** *v.*)

fygure *n.* symbol, figure I.675 (**figure** *n.*)

fylth *n.* corruption, wickedness II.1407 (**filth** *n.*)

fynd(e), fyndyn *v.* find, discover I.582, 1051, II.1206; II.117, 337 etc.; II.1398, *1A7*; *1sg.pr.* **fynd** I.987, **fynde** II.306, 575 etc., *2sg.pr.* **fyndyst** II.1454; *3sg.pr.* **fyndyth** I.916sd, 928sd, 952sd; *1pl.pr.* **fynde** I.226, II.1803; *p.p.* **founde** II.288, **fownd(e)** II.701; I.998, II.1714, 1802, 1822 (**finden** *v.*)

fynd(ys) *see* **fend(e)**

fyne *see* **feyn** *adj.*

fyre, feyr *n.* fire I.6, 320 etc.; I.964sd (**fir** *n.*)

fyrst *adv.* first, at first I.319, 363 etc. (**first** *adv.*)

fyrst, fryst *ord.num.* first (as *adj.*) I.24, II.698, *3A24*, (as *n.*) I.398sd, 406sd, II.181sd; I.438sd (**first** *ord.num.*)

fyth, fytyn *see* **fyght**

five *num.* five (occurs only as roman numeral, II.786sd)

flamys *n.pl.* flames II.490 (**flaume** *n.*)

fle *v.* escape, flee I.323, 734 etc.; *imp.pl.* **fleth** *2A35*, 37; *p.p.* **fled** *3A28* (**flen** *v.1.*)

fled *see* **fle**

flem *v.* banish, put to flight I.890 (**flemen** *v.1.*)

flesch(e) *n.* flesh (see also **felle**) I.678, 763 etc.; I.697, 927, II.36, 784 (**flesh** *n.*)

fleschly *adj.* **fleschly lorde** physical presence of (their) lord II.1738 (**fles-li(ch** *adj.*)

fleth *see* **fle**

flynt *n.* flint II.490 (**flint** *n.*)

flytt *v.* escape, move away, depart II.1286; *2pl.pr.?subj.* **flytt** II.1639; *p.p.* **flytt** *2A41* (**flitten** *v.*)

flok *n.* company *3A26* (**flok** *n.1.*)

flokkys *n.pl.* tufts of wool (for stuffing) I.77 (**flok** *n.2.*)

flom *n.* river II.1394 (**flum** *n.*)

floure *n.* flower, child *2A15*; *n.pl.* **flowrys** I.405, 410sd (**flour** *n.*)

flowe *n.* flood II.1401 (**flou** *n.*)

flowre *v.* flourish *2A38* (**flouren** *v.*)

flowrys *see* **floure**

fo(o) *n.* enemy II.942, 1230; II.1372, 1432; *n.pl.* **fon(e)** II.4; II.1430 (**fo** *n.*)

fode *v.* feed, nourish II.987 (**foden** *v.1.*)

fol *see* **ful** *adv.*

folde *n.* **in many folde** much, far I.127 (**folde** *n.2.*)

fole *n.* foal *1A8*, 17sd (**fole** *n.*)

fole, fool *n.* fool II.156; II.819 (**fol** *n.*)

folé *n.* falsehood, harm II.386 (**folie** *n.*)

fole *see also* **ful** *adj.*

folwe, folwyn *v.* follow I.11, 601, 675; I.604, II.1453; *3pl.pr.* **folwyn**

II.130; *pr.p.* **folwyng** I.778sd, 884sd; *imp.sg.* **folwe** I.1009; *imp.pl.* **folwyth** I.279; *3pl.pa.* **folwyd** *3A*16 **(folwen** *v.***)**

folwerys *n.pl.* followers, disciples I.545, 578 **(folwer** *n.***)**

fon(e) *see* **fo(o)**

fonge *v.* *2pl.pr.subj.* undertake, begin I.131 **(fongen** *v.***)**

fonnyng *vbl.n.* error II.410 **(fonning** *ger.***)**

foo *see* **fo(o)**

food *n.* food II.1634 **(fode** *n.1.***)**

fool *see* **fole, fool** *n.*

foot, fote *n.* foot (including 12-inch measure) I.68, II.1362 (see note); I.442sd, II.109, 762, *2A*24; *n.pl.* **feet** I.719, 721 etc., **feyt** II.963, **fete** I.361, 669 etc. **(fot** *n.***)**

fop *n.* fool II.164 **(fop(pe** *n.***)**

for *conj.* because, for, since I.13, 60 etc. **(for** *conj.***)**

for(e) *prep.* for, on account of, despite, as, to I.35, 42 etc.; I.948, II.119; **for me** as far as I am concerned I.537, II.606 etc.; **for to** (introducing a simple infinitive = 'to') I.13, 131 etc. **(for** *prep.***)**

fordere *see* **ferdere**

forfare *v.* be lost, be damned *2A*5 **(forfaren** *v.1.***)**

forfett *v.* sin *2A*42 **(forfeten** *v.***)**

forgete *v.* *imp.sg.* forget II.825 **(foryeten** *v.***)**

forgeve, forgyf(f) *v.* *imp.sg.* forgive II.801; II.1080, 1151; II.800; *1sg.pr.* **forgyf** II.392; *p.p.* **forgove** II.836, **forȝovyn** II.1377, 1388 **(foryeven** *v.***)**

forgo *v.* give up, lose I.837 **(forgon** *v.***)**

forkys *n.pl.* forked sticks II.698sd **(forke** *n.***)**

forlorn *p.p.* lost, damned II.297, 1380, 1472 **(forlesen** *v.***)**

forme *n.* shape, likeness, (outward) form, manner I.678, 708, 756 **(forme** *n.***)**

formest *adv.* in front, first I.964sd **(formest** *adv.***)**

form-faderys *n.pl.* ancestors, forefathers I.737 **(form(e-fader** *n.***)**

fors *n.* strength, force; **with fyne fors** with sheer strength II.1327 **(force** *n.***)**

forsake *v.* give up, deny, reject, decline, abandon I.53, 239 etc.; *1sg.pr.* **forsake** I.441; *2sg.pr.subj.* **forsake** I.833; *1sg.pa.* **forsoke** II.224; *3pl.pa.* **forsoke** II.207; *p.p.* **forsake** I.961, II.215, 218 **(forsaken** *v.***)**

forseyd *adj.* just spoken I.375 (cf. **for(e-said** *ppl.***)**

forsothe *adv.* truly, indeed I.233, 975, 1042, II.1931 **(forsoth** *adv.***)**

fortefye, fortyfye *v.* confirm, strengthen, make more certain, maintain, I.58, 166 etc.; I.55; *3sg.pr.* **fortyfyet** I.714; **Aȝens ... to fortefye** to resist/go against II.632 **(fortifien** *v.***)**

forth(e) *adv.* forward, out, onward, forth, afterwards I.187, 208sd etc.; II.969, 1368, 1370; **ryth forth** straight on I.136; **forth teche** make known II.133 **(forth** *adv.***)**

forthryght *adv.* at once, fully II.1596, 1658, *1A*41 **(forth-right** *adv.***)**

forthwith *adv.* straightaway, immediately I.990sd, II.89sd (**forth-with**
   adv.)
forward *adv.* forwards I.1032sd (**for(e-ward** *adv.*)
fote *see* **foot**
foulyng *n.* vile thing/person II.454 (**fouling** *ger.1.*)
founde *see* **fynd(e)**
foure *num.* four I.38 (as roman numeral I.398sd, 406sd, II.786sd) (**four**
   num.)
fourty *num.* forty I.28 (**fourti** *num.*)
fowle *adj.* vile, evil, ugly 2A104 (**foul** *adj.*)
fowlyd *p.p.* polluted, defiled 2A18 (**foulen** *v.1.*)
fownd(e) *see* **fynd(e)**
frayd *p.p.* frightened, terrified II.1578 (**fraien** *v.1.*)
fre *adj.* noble, free, clean II.275, 584 etc. (**fre** *adj.*)
freke *n.* creature II.917 (**freke** *n.*)
frelté *n.* frailty, weakness II.885 (**freleté** *n.*)
frenchep *n.* friendship II.480 (**frendship(e** *n.*)
frend(e) *n.* friend I.645, 777 etc.; I.256, 607 etc.; *n.pl.* **frendys** I.415, 498
   etc., **fryndys** II.1369 (**frend** *n.*)
fryst *see* **fyrst** *ord. num.*
fryth *n.* forest, wood; **be fryth and fenne** everywhere (see **fenne**) 2A18
   (**frith** *n.2.*)
fro(m) *prep.* from I.44, 64 etc.; I.235, 819 etc.; as regards I.358 (**from** *prep.*)
ful, fole *adj.* full I.1073, 2A17; II.702 (**ful** *adj.*)
ful, fol, wul *adv.* very, fully, most I.15, 36 etc.; II.1157; II.1760 (**ful** *adv.*)
fulffille, fulfylle, fullfylle *v.* perform, carry out, fulfil 2A95; I.270, 383
   etc.; II.619; *2pl.pr.* **fulfylle** II.1107; *p.p.* **fulfyllyd** I.949 (**ful-fillen** *v.*)
fulleche *adv.* fully I.930 (**fulli** *adv.*)
fullyth *v. 3sg.pr.* becomes full II.1345 (**fullen** *v.1.*)
furryd *p.p.* furred, edged/lined with fur I.105, 164sd etc. (**furren** *v.*)

gadere *v. imp.sg.* gather I.92 (**gaderen** *v.*)
gaf, ȝaff *see* **gef**
galle *n.* gall (a bitter drink) II.898 (**galle** *n.1.*)
game *n.* pastime, fun, happiness, entertainment, scheme, situation II.189,
   471 etc. (**game** *n.*)
gan *see* **gynnyth**
gardener *n.* gardener II.1870 (**gardiner** *n.*)
garmentys *n.pl.* clothes I.964sd (**garnement** *n.*)
gast *see* **gef**
gate *n.* gate I.398 (see textual note); *n.pl.* **gatys** II.534, 1016sd etc., **ȝatys**
   II.1019 (**gate** *n.1.*)
gatt *n.* way; **gon oure gatt** leave, depart II.1649 (**gate** *n.2.*)
gebettys *see* **jebet**
gef, geve, ȝeve, ȝevyn, gyf *v.* give I.176; I.609; I.376, 541 etc.; II.712;

Glossary

283

I.232, 292 etc.; *1sg.pr.* **ʒeve** I.770, II.664, **gyf** II.33, 481, 1180, 1212; *2sg.pr.* **gevyst** II.424; *3sg.pr.* **ʒyvyth** I.762sd, ?**gyf** I.56; *imp.sg.* **gef** II.755, **geve** I.964, **gyf** I.89, II.752; *imp.pl.* **ʒevyth** I.813, **gevyth** II.21, **gyf(f)** II.346, 1213; I.61; *pr.p.* **ʒevyng** II.11; *2sg.pa.* **gast** II.1535; *3sg.pa.* **gaf** II.507, **ʒaff** II.185, 1395, *1A*18

gentyl *see* **jentyl**

gest *n.* visitor, guest II.519 (**gest** *n.*)

gete, gett, ?**ʒet** *v.* obtain, get I.23; I.104; ?**ʒet** get *or* yet ('in addition') II.141 (**geten** *v.*)

gett *n.* fashion II.907 (**get** *n.1.*)

gevyst, gevyth *see* **gef**

gyde *n.* guide I.389 (**gide** *n.*)

gyde *v.* lead II.971 (**giden** *v.*)

gyf *see* **gef**

gylt *n.* misdeed, guilt II.307 (**gilt** *n.1.*)

gylty *adj.* guilty II.668 (**gilti** *adj.*)

gyltles *adj.* guiltless, blameless II.644 (**giltles** *adj., adv., n.*)

gynnyth *v. 3sg.pr.* begin (or as *aux.*) II.886; *pr.pl.* **gyn(ne)** II.895, 1505; I.1027; *1sg.pa.* **gan** I.22 (see note); *2sg.pa.* **gunne** II.1412; *3sg.pa.* **gan** II.506, 1402 etc.; *3pl.pa.* **gun** II.1700; *p.p.* **gunne** II.1410 (**ginnen** *v.*)

gyrdyl *n.* girdle, belt I.731, 732 (**girdel** *n.*)

gyrdyn *v. 3pl.pa.* girded I.672; *p.p.* **gyrt** tied I.824sd (**girden** *v.*)

gyse *n.* fashion, manner (of behaving), state of affairs I.208sd, II.113 (**gise** *n.*)

glad *adj.* joyful, happy, glad II.265, 343, *1A*44 (**glad** *adj.*)

gladly *adv.* **doth gladly** be merry II.697 (**gladli** *adv.*)

glas *n.* glass II.1689 (**glas** *n.*)

gle *n.* happiness; **beth glad with gle** rejoice II.1492 (**gle** *n.*)

gleyvis, gleyvys *n.pl.* weapons of the halberd or lance type I.658; I.964sd, II.15 (**glaive** *n.*)

glyde *v.* move, pass II.1326 (**gliden** *v.*)

glorye *n.* **kynge of glorye** king of heaven II.1021, 1038 (**glorie** *n.*)

gloryous *adj.* magnificent, illustrious II.58, *3A*13 (**glorious** *adj.*)

glotenye *n.* gluttony II.504 (**gloteni(e** *n.*)

glove *n.* glove I.620 (**glove** *n.*)

go(n), gone, goo(n) *v.* walk, move, travel, depart, come, behave I.183, 359 etc.; I.205, 887 etc.; I.366, II.1452; I.351; II.1083; *1sg.pr.* **go** II.1687, *2A*4; *2sg.pr.* **gost** I.1000; *3sg.pr.* **goth** I.208sd, 280sd etc.; *pl.pr.* **go** I.637, 811 etc., **gon** I.478sd, 494sd etc.; *sg./pl.subj.* **go** I.187, 580 etc.; *imp.sg.* **go** I.201, II.232, 240; *imp.pl.* **go** II.864, *1A*5, 6, **goth** I.467, II.1742, **goht** II.1305; *pr.p.* **goyng** I.406sd, II.1112; *3sg.pa.* **went** II.99; *p.p.* **go** II.40, 528, **gon(e)** I.977, II.1229 etc.; II.1429 (**gon** *v.*)

God, god *n.* Christian and heathen god I.95, 149 etc.; II.45, 390; *n.poss.* **Goddys** I.41, 294 etc. (**God, god** *n.1.*)

gode, good *n.* good, (worldly) possessions II.1 (see note); I.823, *2A*91; *n.pl.* **godys** II.1236; **a word of good** a friendly word II.719 (**god** *n.2.*)

gode, good(e) *adj.* good II.564, 1882; I.18, 221 etc.; II.1480 (**god** *adj.*)

godhed(e) *n.* divine nature, divinity I.689, 720, 724; II.1693 (**godhede** *n.*)

goht, goyng *see* **go(n)**

gold(e) *n.* gold (coins/money) I.1012, II.1310, 2A90, 91; II.1623, 1634 etc. (**gold** *n.*)

gonge *n.* (cess) pit II.1425 (**gang, gong** *n.*)

good(e) *see* **gode, good** *n.* and **gode, good(e)** *adj.*

goodly *adj.* splendid, excellent I.69 (**godli** *adj.*)

goodly *adv.* splendidly II.1546 (or *adj.*) (**godli** *adv. 2.*)

goodman *n.* master, sir (as form of address) II.196 (**godman, god-man** *phr. & n.*)

goodnesse *n.* goodness I.429 (**godnes(se** *n.2.*)

goon *see* **go(n)**

goostly *see* **gostly**

gospel *n.* gospel 3A35 (**gospel** *n.*)

gost *n.* spirit, spiritual being (devil) II.1410, 1577 (**gost** *n.*)

gost *see also* **go(n)**

gostly, goostly *adj.* spiritual, of the spirit I.356, 358 etc.; I.495 (**gostli** *adj.*)

goth *see* **go(n)**

governawns *n.* rule, authority I.215; **in governawns** under (my) control II.43 (**governaunce** *n.*)

gowne *n.* coat (outer garment) I.81 (see note), 164sd; *n.pl.* **gownys** I.406sd (**goune** *n.*)

grace, gras *n.* mercy, forgiveness, (heavenly) grace I.439, 922 etc.; II.1842 (**grace** *n.*)

gracyous *adj.* merciful I.511, 1069, II.1895, 1936 (**gracious** *adj.*)

graffe *see* **grave**

gramercy, gromercy *interj.* many thanks, thank you II.560, 1115; I.439 (**gramerci** *n. & int.*)

gras *see* **grace**

grave, graue, graffe *n.* grave, tomb, sepulchre II.1086, 1121 etc.; II.1209, 1478 etc.; II.1273 (**grave** *n.1.*)

gravyd *p.p.* buried II.1692 (**graven** *v.1.*)

graunt(e) *see* **grawnt**

grawnt *v.* give, allow, permit, agree, consent, grant I.518; *1sg.pr.* **graunt** II.769, 1099, **grawnt** II.828, 1122, 1596; *1pl.pr.* **graunte** II.1276; *3sg.pr.subj.* **graunt** II.1703; *imp.sg.* **graunt** II.1877; *imp.pl.* **grawnt** I.61; *p.p.* **grawntyd** I.893, II.618, 1116 (**graunten** *v.*)

grede *v.* lament, mourn II.1868 (**greden** *v.*)

greet *see* **gret(e)**

greff *n.* distress II.1540; **take this at no greff** do not be displeased at this, do not take this amiss 1A22 (**gref** *n.*)

gres *n.* ground (lit. 'grass') II.1692 (**gras** *n.*)

gret(e), grett, greet *adj.* great, large, important I.2, 79 etc.; I.89, II.1693, 2A6, 3A2; I.45, II.893 etc.; II.773 (**gret** *adj. & adv. & n.*)

grete *v.* greet II.1089; *1pl.pr.* **grete** II.907, 909; *imp.sg.* **gret** I.256; *imp.pl.*
   grete II.479; *p.p.* **gret with gode** ?welcomed, ?honoured II.1 (see note)
   (**greten** *v.2.*)

gretyng *vbl.n.* greeting II.380 (**greting(e** *ger.*)

gretlye, **grettly** *adv.* greatly, very much I.714; I.36 (**gretli** *adv.*)

grett *see* **gret(e)**

gretter(e), **grettyr** *adj.* greater II.1911; II.1498, 1907; II.1862 (**gret** *adj.* &
   adv. & *n.*)

grettest *adj.* greatest I.388 (**gret** *adj.* & *adv.* & *n.*)

grettly *see* **gretlye**

grevaunce, **grevans**, **grevauns** *n.* harm, hardship, offence, annoyance,
   pain II.1410; I.445; I.54, 59, 456, II.41 (**grevaunce** *n.*)

grevyth *v.* *3sg.pr.* annoys, oppresses, saddens II.499, 2A67 (**greven** *v.*)

gromercy *see* **gramercy**

ground(e), **grownd(e)**, **growunde** *n.* ground, earth, place II.1546;
   II.1425, 1564; II.1348; II.1716, 1801, 1824; II.1312 (**ground** *n.*)

gun(ne *see* **gynnyth**

ȝa *adv.* yes (and as an exclamation) I.483, 631 etc.

ȝaff *see* **gef**

ȝatys *see* **gate**

ȝe *pl.pron.subj.* you

ȝef *see* **if(f)**

ȝeld *v.* *1sg.pr.* give, offer I.688

ȝerd *n.* garden (of Gethsemane) II.206 (*OED* **Yard** *sb¹*)

ȝerdys *n.pl.* yards (a measure of three feet) I.81 (*OED* **Yard** *sb²*)

ȝere *n.* year II.6, 9; *n.pl.* **ȝere** II.1443, **ȝerys** II.341

yet *conj.* yet, even so I.107

ȝet(t), **ȝit(t)** *adv.* yet, still, nevertheless, in addition I.17, 80 etc.; II.1879;
   II.962, 1057 etc.; II.931, 955 etc.

ȝet *see also* **gete**

ȝeve, **ȝevyn**, **ȝevyng**, **ȝevyth**, **ȝyvyth** *see* **gef**, **geve** *etc.*

ȝyf *see* **if(f)**

ȝyng *n.* the young II.407

ȝys *adv.* yes II.178

ȝit(t) *see* **ȝet(t)**

ȝon *adj.* yonder 1A5

ȝondyr *adv.* over there, yonder II.1129

ȝou, **ȝow** *pl.pron.obj.* you, yourselves II.235, 246 etc.; I.4, 63 etc. (all
   examples of **ȝou** are expansions of abbreviations)

ȝour(e), **ȝowre** *pl.pron.poss.* your I.1, 21 etc.; I.63, 196 etc.; I.374, 435,
   II.1884 (all examples of **ȝour** are expansions of abbreviations)

ȝourself *pron.* yourself II.708 (**ȝour-** abbreviated)

ha *see* **a**

habyl *adj.* able I.366 (**able** *adj.*)
habytacyon *n.* dwelling-place I.366, **han habytacyon** live, dwell I.447 (**habitacioun** *n.*)
habundawns *see* **abundauns**
had(de), haddyst *see* **haue**
hald *see* **holde** *v.*
half *adj.* half II.278 (**half** *adj.*)
half-brother *n.* spiritual brother 3A15 (see note to 3A14–16) (**half-brother** *n.*)
hall *see* **al** *adj.*
halle *n.* house, dwelling-place, hall I.480, II.192 etc. (**hal(le** *n.*)
halpe *see* **help(e)** *v.*
hals *n.* neck II.1319 (**hals** *n.*)
halse *v.* embrace, cling to II.854sd (**halsen** *v.2.*)
halt *see* **holde** *v.*
han *see* **haue** *and* **a(n)**
hand(e), hond(e) *n.* hand, side, control I.686sd, 1013 etc.; I.137; I.839, II.657, 658sd; I.608, II.1032, 1247, 1331; *n.pl.* **handys** I.739, 741 etc., **hond(e)** I.673; II.466, **hondys** I.544, II.666 (**hond(e** *n.*)
handmay *n.* handmaiden, servant II.991 (cf. **hond(e** *n.*)
hange, hangyn, honge *v.* hang (on the cross) II.691, 786sd, 1095; II.31, 790, 790sd; II.923; *2sg.pr.* **hangyst** II.784, 792; *3sg.pr.* **hangyth** II.257sd, 868, 1004, 1147; *imp.pl.* **hang(e)** II.860; II.788; *pr.p.* **hangyng** I.85; *3sg.pa.* **hynge** II.1436; *p.p.* **hangyd** II.695, 722, **hangyn** I.319, 606, 1011, II.34, **hongyn** I.571 (**hongen** *v.*)
happend *v.* *3sg.pa.subj.* happened II.1218 (**happenen** *v.*)
hard(e) *adj.* unfeeling, onerous, harsh, grievous I.1046, II.1501; II.1440 (**hard** *adj.*)
harde *adv.* tightly, firmly II.1411 (**harde** *adv.*)
hardely *adv.* certainly II.1255 (**hardili** *adv.*)
hardy *adj.* bold, resolute II.23, 29 (**hardi** *adj.*)
harlat, harlot *n.* scoundrel II.1538; II.446, 731 (**harlot** *n.*)
harry *see* **arryn**
harrow, herrow *interj.* harrow (a cry of distress) II.1027; II.1424 (**harou** *interj. & n.*)
hasayd *see* **asay**
haske, haskyd, haskyng *see* **aske**
hast *see* **haue**
hast(e) *n.* **haue/had gret hast** are/were in a great hurry I.965, II.901; **in hast(e)** quickly, hurriedly, presently I.199, 202 etc.; I.266; **in (h)al(l) þe hast þat** as quickly as I.206, 477, II.370, 375 (**hast(e** *n.*)
hasty *adj.* speedy, sudden I.335 (**hasti(e** *adj.*)
hastyly *adv.* quickly, without delay I.674, 743, 749 (**hastili(e** *adv.*)
hate *n.* hatred I.712 (**hate** *n.*)
hath *see* **haue**

haue, have, han, a, an *v.* have I.273, 361 etc.; I.406sd, 579, 621; I.100, 107 etc.; I.29, 252 etc.; I.80; *1sg.pr.* **haue** I.109, 163 etc., **have** I.140, 680 etc.; *2sg.pr.* **hast** I.778, 783 etc., **ast** I.777; *3sg.pr.* **hath** I.33, 40 etc.; *1pl.pr.* **haue** I.507, 651 etc., **have** I.391, II.326, **han** I.98, II.123 etc.; *2pl.pr.* **haue** I.344, 965 etc., **have** I.1022, **han** I.447, II.176 etc., **an** II.302; *3pl.pr.* **haue** I.1043, 1044 etc., **han** I.451, II.709 etc., **hath** II.1393; *imp.sg.* **haue** I.427, II.887, 1080, **have** I.1075; *imp.pl.* **haue** I.88, 639 etc., **have** I.1031, II.1234; *1sg.pa.* **had** I.29, 32 etc.; *2sg.pa.(subj.)* **haddyst** I.995, II.473, 733, 1548; *3sg.pa.(subj.)* **had** I.252, II.40 etc., **hadde** I.773; *pl.pa.(subj.)* **had** II.901, 1030, 1074, 1565; *p.p.* **had** II.994, 1163sd taken, 1549, 1768 (**haven** *v.*)

hawe *n.* haw; **gyf not an hawe** care nothing for II.33 (**haue** *n.2.*)
he *pron.* he (**he** *pron.1.*)
hed, heed *n.* head I.164sd, 669 etc.; II.1344, 1588; *n.pl.* **hedys** I.164sd, 208sd (**hed** *n.1.*)
hed(e) *n.* heed; **take/takyth hed(e)** consider, pay attention, take care, look after I.18, 21, etc.; I.181, 329 etc. (**hed** *n.2.*)
hede *v.* heed, be careful about II.1621 (**heden** *v.2.*)
hedyr *adv.* hither, here I.384, 978 etc. (**hider** *adv.*)
heed *see* **hed**
hefly *see* **hevynly**
hef(f)ne *see* **hevyn**
hey(e), hy, hy3(e) *adj.* high, important, lofty, tall I.87, 253 etc.; I.1013; II.883; II.1576; II.1056; (as *n.*) **in heye** quickly I.1013, **on hey** clearly II.440, **on hy** above II.883 (**heigh** *adj.*)
heye *adv.* on high, high up II.31 (**heighe** *adv.*)
heyest, hyest *adj.* sovereign, greatest, topmost II.50; I.68 (as *n.*) *3A*39 (**heigh** *adj.*)
heyl(e) *interj.* hail (a salutation originally wishing good health) I.257, 599 etc.; II.90 (**heil** *interj.*)
heylyng *pr.p.* greeting, saluting II.89sd (**heilen** *v.*)
heldyn *v.* *3pl.pr.* look II.1122sd (**holden** *v.2.*)
hele *v.* *imp.sg.* heal, cleanse *3A*6 (**helen** *v.*)
helle *n.* hell I.1, 2 etc. (**helle** *n.*)
helme *n.* helmet II.1311 (**helm** *n.*)
help(e) *v.* help II.1155sd, 1158, 1161, 1455; II.1599, *1A*41; *3sg.pr.* **helpyth** I.1016, II.777; *3sg.pr.subj.* **help(e)** II.529; ?I.539, ?II.870; *imp.sg.* **help(e)** II.808; II.816; *imp.pl.* **help** I.990sd; *3sg.pa.* **halpe** II.868 (**helpen** *v.*)
helpe *n.* succour, assistance II.1007, 1354 (**help** *n.*)
helthe *n.* (spiritual) health, welfare I.348, *1A*49; **with helthe ... grete** wish prosperity to II.1089 (**helth(e** *n.*)
hem *pl.pron.obj.* them, themselves (**hem** *pron.pl.*) (*see also* **them, þem**)
hem *see also* **hym**
hende *see* **ende**
hendyth *v.* *3sg.pr.* ends II.916 (**enden** *v.*)

hendles *see* **endles**

hens *adv.* hence II.225, 345, 1664 (**hennes** *adv.*)

her(e), hire *pron.obj.obl./poss.* her II.844; I.104, 105 etc.; 2A37 (**hir(e** *pron.1.* and *pron.2.*)

her(e) *adv.* here II.854sd; I.164sd, 170 etc. (**her** *adv.*)

herand *see* **erand**

herborwe *v.* lodge, shelter, harbour I.86 (**herberwen** *v.*)

herd *see* **erth(e)**

herd(e) *see* **here** *v.*

here *v.* hear I.140, 321 etc.; *2sg.pr.* **heryst** II.163, 166; *2pl.pr.* **heryth** II.174; *3pl.pr.* **here** I.976sd, **heryn** II.298; *2pl.pr.subj.* **heryn** I.1036; *imp.sg.* **here** II.564; *imp.pl.* **here** II.1227, **heryth** I.177, **heryght** II.1673; *1sg.pa.* **herd** I.555, II.150 etc.; *3sg.pa.* **herd** I.509; *2pl.pa.* **herd** I.1026; *p.p.* **herd** I.617, II.176, **erde** II.302 (**heren** *v.*)

here, ere *pl.pron.poss.* their I.53, 164sd etc.; I.662sd (**her(e** *pron.poss.pl.*)

here *see also* **ere** *n.*

hereafter *adv.* hereafter, in the future II.1203 (**her-after** *adv.*)

hereby *adv.* nearby II.1329 (**her-bi** *adv.*)

herein(ne) *adv.* in this (matter), here within II.556, 1369; II.190, 1841 (**her-in(ne** *adv.*)

hereto *adv.* to this II.616 (**her-to** *adv.*)

heryght *see* **here** *v.*

heryng *vbl.n.* hearing I.358 (**hering(e** *ger.*)

herk(e) *v. imp.sg./pl.* listen, take heed (and as an exclamation to attract attention) II.1200, 1627; II.1584, 1618, 1A18 (**herken** *v.*)

herrow *see* **harrow**

hert(e) *n.* heart I.718, 847 etc.; I.197, 399 (perhaps *pl.*) etc.; *n.poss.* **hertys** I.679; *n.pl.* **hertys** I.374, 1051, II.1938 (**herte** *n.*)

herty *adj.* **with herty wylle** readily, willingly II.978 (**herti** *adj.*)

hertyly *adj.* heartfelt, deep II.986, 1838 (**hert(e)li(e** *adj.*)

hertyly *adv.* friendlily, cordially II.1132 (**hert(e)li(e** *adv.*)

hes(e) *see* **his**

heuery *see* **every**

heve *v. imp.pl.* heave, raise II.1141 (**heven** *v.*)

heuermore *see* **evyrmor(e)**

hevy *adj.* heavy, sad, grief-stricken I.1076, II.1356, 1828, 1859 (**hevi** *adj.*)

hevy *adv.* **beryth hevy of** is heavily burdened with II.721 (**hevi** *adv.*)

hevyn, hef(f)ne, efne *n.* heaven I.132, 156 etc.; I.13, 22 etc.; I.947; I.852 (**heven** *n.*)

hevyn *see also* **evyn** *adj.*

hevynes *n.* sadness, gloom II.1899 (**hevines(se** *n.*)

hevynly, hefly *adj.* heavenly, divine I.372, 403; I.400 (**hevenli** *adj.*)

hy, hy3(e) *see* **hey(e)** *adj.*

hy(e) *v.* hurry, hasten I.206; I.268, 476; *imp.sg.* **hy3** II.1881; **al þe hast þat I kan hy** all the speed that I can muster I.206 (**hien** *v.*)

hyde *n.* skin II.944 (**hide** *n.1.*)

hyde *v.* hide I.339; *imp.pl.* **hyde** II.716; *p.p.* **hyd** II.718 (**hiden** *v.*)

hyest *see* **heyest**

hyght *p.p.* promised II.1657 (**hoten** *v.1.*)

hylle *v.* cover *1A*34 (**hilen** *v.*)

hylle *see* **ill**

hyllys, hillis *n.pl.* hills II.715; II.1505 (**hil(le** *n.*)

hym, hem *pron.obj.* him, himself I.6, 7 etc.; ?I.230, 240, ?II.1237; (as *subject*) *2A*79 (**him** *pron.*)

himself, hymself *pron.* himself I.208sd; I.164sd, 757 etc. (**him-self** *pron.*)

hynge *see* **hange**

hire *see* **her(e), hire**

his, hes(e) *pron.poss.* his, its I.31, 33 etc.; I.455; I.36, 46 etc. (**his** *pron.1.*)

ho(o) *pron.interr. and rel.* who I.541, II.185 etc.; they who I.169

hoberd *n.* knave, rascal II.897, 905 (**hoberd** *n.*)

hod *n.* hood II.157; *n.pl.* **hodys** I.164sd, 244sd (**hod** *n.*)

hol, hool *adj.* complete, cured, undivided, healthy, unharmed I.818, 990sd; I.1003, II.101, 153, 425 (**hol(e** *adj.2.*)

holde *n.* captivity, prison I.1044, II.660 (**hold** *n.2.*)

holde, holdyn, hald *v.*consider, hold (out), keep faith, stand firm I.138, 149, 739, II.1309; II.1036; II.666; *1sg.pr.* **hold(e)** II.1630; II.1331, 1528, *2A*102; *3sg.pr.* **halt** II.685sd; *imp.sg./pl.* **hold** I.741, II.657 (**holden** *v.1.*)

holde *see also* **old(e)**

holy *adj.* holy, divine, blessed I.1034, II.502 etc. (**holi** *adj.2.*)

holyday *n.* festival day, holy day II.1093 (**hali-dai** *n. & phr.*)

holond *n.* linen cloth from Holland I.73 (**Holand** *n.*)

hom *adv.* home, back II.478, 1190 (**hom** *adv.*)

homage *n.* allegiance II.1723 (**homage** *n.*)

homward *adv.* homeward, back home II.1303 (**homward** *adv.*)

hond(e), hondys *see* **hand**

honderyd, hunderyd *num.* hundred II.1244; II.1242, 1246 (as roman numeral II.1244 (second and third instances), *2A*58) (**hundred** *card.num.*)

honge, hongyn *see* **hange** *v.*

honor, honour *n.* reverence, worship I.688; I.402 (**honour** *n.*)

honowre *v.* honour, worship I.382; *p.p.* **onowryd** II.1932 (**honouren** *v.*)

hoo *see* **ho(o)**

hool *see* **hol**

hoold *see* **old(e)**

hoot *adj.* hot *2A*112 (**hot** *adj.*)

hope *n.* hope I.145, 148 etc. (**hope** *n.1.*)

hope *v.* *1sg.pr.* hope, trust I.504 (**hopen** *v.1.*)

hors *n.* horse II.125, 256; *n.pl.* **hors** I.553, II.32 (**hors** *n.*)

hosyn *n.pl.* hose I.70 (see note to I.70–2) (**hose** *n.*)

hoso *pron.* whosoever I.389, 817 etc.

hosoevyr *pron.* whosoever I.7

host *n.* Eucharistic wafer, host I.936sd (**host(e** *n.4.*)
houre, oure *n.* hour I.23; I.745, 749, II.242, 521 (**houre** *n.*)
houre *see* **our(e)**
hous *n.* house I.472, 510sd, 513, 518sd; **cownsel/cowncel(l) hous** meeting house, place of assembly I.288sd, 518sd, II.603sd, 656sd (**hous** *n.*)
how *interr. and conj.adv.* how I.163, 581 etc. (**hou** *interrog. & conj.adv.*)
howe *see* **owe**
howth *see* **aught**
humanyté *n.* human nature, manhood I.721 (**humanité** *n.*)
humylyté *n.* humility I.385 (**humilité** *n.*)
hunderyd *see* **honderyd**
hurt *v. 3pl.pr.subj.* injure II.287 (**hurten** *v.*)

I *pron.* I (**ich** *pron.*)
i-ches *v. 3sg.pa.* chose (see note) II.1685 (?**ichesen** *v.*)
if(f), yf, ʒef, ʒyf *conj.* if II.293, 347 etc. II.1548, *1A*10, 40, *2A*87; I.91, 103 etc.; I.173, II.29; I.299, 601 etc. (**if** *conj.*)
ignorans *n.* **of myn ignorans** in my ignorance (of what I was doing) II.1154 (**ignoraunce** *n.*)
ill, hylle *adj.* wicked I.218; *2A*33 (**il(le** *adj.*)
ylle *adv.* **ful ylle** with great displeasure II.1097, **ryght ylle** most wrongly *2A*53 (**il(le** *adv.*)
immaculat, inmaculate *adj.* spotless, pure I.723; I.1033 (**immaculat(e** *adj.*)
in *adv.* in I.145, 491 etc. (see note to I.873–4) (**in** *adv.*)
in *prep.* in, on I.6, 8 etc. (**in** *prep.*)
incheson *see* **encheson**
incomperhensibele *adj.* (as *n.*) boundless, infinite being *3A*2 (**incomprehensible** *adj.*)
incressyd *p.p.* increased II.926 (**encresen** *v.*)
indede *adv.* truly, indeed, assuredly I.722, 937, II.88, 1160 (**dede** *n.*)
inerytawns *see* **enherytawns**
inf(f)ormacyon *n.* instruction, direction, information *3A*10; I.707 (**informacioun** *n.*)
inheryte *see* **eneryth**
inke *n.* ink II.874sd (**inke** *n.*)
inmaculate *see* **immaculat**
innovmerabyl *adj.* innumerable, without number I.54 (**innombrable** *adj.*)
inow *see* **anow** *n.* and *adv.*
inportable *adj.* unbearable II.53 (**importable** *adj.*)
inqwere *v. 3sg.pr.subj.* make inquiry, investigate I.336 (**enqueren** *v.*)
instawnce, instawns *n.* persuasion, urging, request I.27; I.272, 505, **at his instawns** at his command 578 (**instaunce** *n.*)
intellygens *n.* news, information, comprehension I.273, 391, 756 (**intelligence** *n.*)

intencyon *n.* purpose, inclination I.31, 47, 63, 237 (**entencioun** *n.*)
intende *v. 1sg.pr.* intend II.1883; *3pl.pr.* **intendyn** II.6 (**entenden** *v.*)
intent *see* **entent**
interpretacyon *n.* explanation I.709 (**interpretacioun** *n.*)
into *prep.* into, to (**in-to** *prep.*)
yron *n.* iron (fetters) I.547 (**iren** *n.*)
is *see* **be(n)**
i-schrewe *v. imp.sg.* ?deform I.85 (see note to I.85–6) (cf. *OED* **Shrew** *v.*)
it, yt *pron.* it I.23, 77 etc.; I.728, 769, II.734, 886, 2A55; (+ 'is') **tys** it is
    I.990sd (**hit** *pron.*)
iwys *adv.* certainly, indeed I.727, 1067 etc. (**iwis** *adv.*)

japyn *v. 3pl.pr.* **japyn with** stupidly follow, fool with II.496 (**japen** *v.*)
jebet *n.* gallows I.571; *n.pl.* **gebettys** II.31 (**gibet(e** *n.*)
jentyl, gentyl *adj.* gracious, kind, noble (and as a common form of polite
    address) I.1067, II.863 etc.; II.1131 (**gentil** *adj.*)
jentylman *n.* man of noble or gentle birth I.71, II.678 (**gentil-man** *n.*)
jentylnesse *n.* graciousness, generosity II.1115 (**gentilnes(se** *n.*)
jentylwoman *n.* woman of noble or gentle birth I.102 (**gentil-woman** *n.*)
jewge *n.* judge, man of law I.166, 175, 211, 1006; *n.pl.* **jewgys** I.195, 223
    etc. (**juge** *n.*)
jewge *v.* administer, rule, sentence I.550, II.367; *2sg.pr.subj.* **jewge** II.546
    (**jugen** *v.*)
jewgement, jugement, jwgement *n.* trial, judging, sentence, verdict,
    opinion I.292, 330 etc.; I.176, 232 etc.; II.571 (**jugement** *n.*)
joy(e) *n.* happiness, joy, rejoicing II.1171, 1500, 1900, 1910; I.399, 494 etc.;
    n.pl. **joyis** I.515 (**joi(e** *n.*)
joye *v.* rejoice in II.1471 (**joien** *v.*)
joyful *adj.* happy, glad II.1767, 1924, 1927 (**joiful** *adj.*)
jorné, jurney *n.* journey, day's work/combat I.401, 894, II.74; 1A43 (**jour-
    nei** *n.*)
jugement *see* **jewgement**
jurediccyon, jurysdyccyon, jurresdyccyon *n.* authority, control, power
    of judgment, area of authority II.348; II.368; II.71 (**jurisdiccioun** *n.*)
jurney *see* **jorné**
justyce, justyse *n.* judge II.1088; II.1616 (**justice** *n.*)
jwgement *see* **jewgement**

kachyd *p.p.* **kachyd a clowte** given a blow (see note) II.97, **cawth** taken
    II.1642 (**cacchen** *v.*)
kalle, kallyst *see* **calle**
kam *see* **com(e)**
kan *n.* jar, pot I.478sd (**canne** *n.*)
kan, kannat, kannot, kanst *see* **can**
kast *see* **cast**

ken, kynne *n.* kindred, fellow humans, race *2A*60; II.1025, *2A*16 (**kin** *n.*)
ken *v.* know II.201 (**kennen** *v.*)
kend(e), kynde *n.* nature, race, natural order, behaviour, way I.10, 111;
   I.229, 1070; II.1416 (**kinde** *n.*)
kend(e) *adj.* gracious, loving II.781; II.391, 835, 1196 (**kind(e** *adj.*)
kendnessys *n.pl.* acts of love/generosity I.1068 (**kindenes(se** *n.*)
kep *n.* care; **to hem takyth good kep** take good care of them I.812 (**kep** *n.*)
kepe, kepyn *v.* guard, keep, celebrate, retain, protect, look after I.190, 459
   etc.; II.1269; *3pl.pr.* **kepyn** II.299; *imp.sg.* **kepe** II.1361, **kepp** II.1349;
   imp.pl. **kepe** I.823, **kepyth** I.800, II.1307; *pr.p.* **kepyng** I.136; *p.p.*
   kept(e) II.660; I.365, 701, II.1277 (**kepen** *v.*)
kepere *n.* guardian, protector II.237 (**keper(e** *n.*)
kepyng *vbl.n.* custody I.1043 (**keping(e** *ger.*)
kerchy *n.* handkerchief, cloth II.742sd, 746 (**kerché** *n.*)
kest *see* **cast**
kylle *v.* kill II.33, 39 etc. (**killen** *v.*)
kynde *see* **kend(e)** *n.*
kyng(e) *n.* king I.306, 308 etc.; II. 1002, 1021 etc. (**king** *n.*)
kyngdham, kyngham *n.* kingdom, realm, rule I.132; II.331, 332, 334, 826
   (**kingdom** *n.*)
kynne *see* **ken**
kyrtyl *n.* dress, gown (see note) II.543sd (**kirtel** *n.*)
kys(se) *n.* kiss II.1878; I.642, II.962, 1169; *3sg.pr.* **kyssyth** I.840sd, 988sd
   (**kissen** *v.*)
knave *n.* commoner (or term of familiar address) II.1579; *n.pl.* **knavys**
   II.787 (**knave** *n.*)
knawe *v.* gnaw II.35 (**gnauen** *v.*)
knawe *see also* **knowe**
kne *n.* knee I.824sd; *n.pl.* **knes** I.406sd, 908sd, II.1150sd. *2A*48 (**kne** *n.*)
knelyn *v.* kneel II.781; *3sg.pr.* **knelyth** II.235sd; *pr.p.* **knelyng** I.920sd,
   II.377sd, 698sd (**knelen** *v.*)
knett, knyt(h) *p.p.* joined, united, secured, knotted II.1646; I.162, *3A*19;
   I.620 (**knitten** *v.*)
knew *see* **knowe**
knyght, knyth *n.* knight, soldier II.678, 1579; II.59, 789 etc.; *n.pl.* **knyghtys** II.1305, 1311sd, **knyhtys** II.1633, 1637, 1640, **knygtys** II.1122sd,
   knytys II.1103, 1110sd etc. (**knight** *n.*)
knyhtys *see* **knyght**
knyt(h) *see* **knett**
knyth, knytys *see* **knyght**
knok *n.* blow II.141 (**knok(ke** *n.*)
knop *n.* ornamental top-knot I.164sd (see note) (**knop(pe** *n.*)
knove *see* **knowe**
knowe *v.* know, understand, find out, recognise I.237, 282 etc.; *1sg.pr.*
   know I.559, II.356, **knowe** I.497, 516 etc.; *2sg.pr.* **knowyst** II.326, 436

etc.; *3sg.pr.* **knowyth** II.453; *1pl.pr.* **know(e)** I.433, II.1029; I.971, II.311, 386; *2pl.pr.* **knowe** II.360, 579, 581, **knove** I.1028; *3pl.pr.* **knowyth** I.195; *imp.sg.* **knowe** I.186; *pr.p.* **knowyng** II.339; *1sg.pa.* **knew** I.31, 648; *2pl.pa.subj.* **knew** I.1039; *p.p.* **knowe** I.204, **knowyn** II.294, **knawe** II.399 (**knouen** *v.*)

knowyng *vbl.n.* knowledge, experience, understanding, I.460, II.421 (**knouing(e** *ger.*)

kone *see* **can**

kow *n.* cow II.256 (**cou** *n.*)

kowdyst *see* **can**

kroune *see* **crowne** *n.*

labour *n.* activity, trouble I.646 (**labour** *n.*)

lady *n.* lady (as a form of address) I.1035, 1041 etc. (**ladi(e** *n.*) (*For* **Oure Lady** *see* List of proper names *etc.*)

lay *see* **ly(ne)**

layde *see* **ley(n)**

lake *n.* pit, grave II.518, 1580, 1845, 1857 (**lak(e** *n.*)

lakke *v. 3sg.pr.subj.* is lacking I.103 (**lakken** *v.*)

lambe *see* **lom**

lame *adj.* **betyn lame** beaten till you're crippled II.473 (**lame** *adj.*)

langorys, langoris, langowrys *n.pl.* sorrows, miseries, afflictions I.347; *1A*48; I.1057 (**langour** *n.*)

lanterne *n.* lantern II.98; *n.pl.* **lanternys** I.656, 964sd (**lantern(e** *n.*)

lappe *n.* lap II.1163sd (**lap(pe** *n.*)

large *adj.* **be a large fote** fully a foot II.762 (**large** *adj.*)

lasse *adj.* less II.984, **nevyr þe lasse** in no way reduced II.1693 (**les(se** *adj.comp.*)

last *adj.* last, final I.412, II.6, 9; **at þe last** finally I.32, *1A*43sd (**last(e** *adj.sup.*)

last *adv.* last, after the others I.764sd (**last(e** *adv.sup.*)

last(e) *v.* last, hold out, endure, continue I.547, II.768 (or *3pl.pr.subj.*), 1037; *2A*98; *3pl.pr.* **last** II.467 (**lasten** *v.*)

late *adj.* late I.396 (**lat(e** *adj.*)

late *see also* **lete** *v.*

latyng *vbl.n.* **withowte latyng** without delay, without interruption I.462 (**letting(e** *ger.*)

latyng *see also* **lete** *v.*

latt *adv.* shortly before, just now II.1534 (**lat(e** *adv.*)

lawe *n.* law (frequently the Mosaic law, the old law) I.91, 164sd etc.; *n.pl.* **lawys** I.168, 172 (**laue** *n.*)

lawful *adj.* legal, acceptable to the law II.634 (**laueful** *adj.*)

leccherous *adj.* lecherous, lascivious I.734 (**lecherous** *adj.*)

leche *n.* doctor, physician I.353, 372, II.1678 (**leche** *n.3.*)

leche *v.* anoint II.1674 (**lechen** *v.*)

lechory, lycherye *n.* lechery, fornication I.106, 111; I.89 (**lecheri(e** *n.*)

leddere, led(d)yr *n.* ladder II.874sd; II.1163sd; II.1163sd *n.pl.* **lederys** II.1155sd (**ladder(e** *n.*)

lede, ledyn *v.* lead, suffer, take, guide, control I.850, 1006 etc.; II.486sd; *1sg.pr.* **lede** I.935, II.985; *3sg.pr.* **ledyth** II.603sd; *3pl.pr.* **lede** I.1032sd, II.377sd, **ledyn** II.265sd; *2pl.pr.subj.* **lede** I.1030; *imp.pl.* **lede** II.369, 371, 478, 1138; *pr.p.* **ledyng** I.1032sd; *1sg.pa.* **leed** II.1468; *3pl.pa.* **leed** II.1589; *p.p.* **led** I.717, 861 (**leden** *v.*)

leed *n.* lead II.1356 (**led** *n.*)

leed *v. see* **lede**

lees *n.pl.* lies II.1684 (**li(e** *n.1.*)

leff *adv.* much, eagerly 2A121 (**lef** *adj. & adv.*)

lefful *adj.* lawful, permissible II.322 (**lefful** *adj.*)

left(e), lyfte, lefft *adj.* left II.695; I.137, 143, II.1264; II.688; II.1316 (**lift** *adj.*)

lefte *see* **leve** *v.*

ley(n) *v.* lay, place, wager, put (aside), give up II.1286, 1588; I.1013, II.157 etc.; *3sg.pr.* **leyth** II.1163sd; *3pl.pr.* **ley** I.988sd; *imp.pl.* **ley** I.547; *1pl.pa* **leyd** II.112, 1562; *p.p.* **leyd(e)** I.189, II.1469, 1564, 1706; I.614, **layde** I.615, II.416 (**leien** *v.*)

leysere *adv.* ?slowly, ?at length II.790sd (see note) (cf. **leiser** *n.*)

leke, lych(e) *adj.* like II.543sd; I.288sd, 518sd, 900sd; I.636, II.111 (**lik** *adj.*)

lemys *n.pl.* limbs II.1700 (**lim** *n.1.*)

lende *v.* give I.609 (**lenen** *v.3.*)

lenger(e) *adj.* longer II.247; II.1193 (**lenger(e** *adj.*comp.)

lenth *n.* length; **in lenth and in brede** overall II.367 (**length(e** *n.*)

lepers *n.pl.* lepers II.425 (**lepre** *n.2.*)

lere *v.* teach, give (counsel), expound I.1023, II.461, 1609 (**leren** *v.*)

lernyd *p.p.* taught I.751; (as *adj.*) **lernyd** educated, scholarly, 3A9, 11 (**lernen** *v.*)

les *n.* lie II.1787 (**les(e** *n.*)

lese *v.* *2pl.pr.* lose, waste, ruin II.1239; *p.p.* **lore** taken away II.1852, **lorn(e)** II.1572, 2A102, 115; II.531 (**lesen** *v.4.*)

lesse *adj.* less, lower I.690 (**les(se** *adj.*comp.)

lesser *adj.* less; **Jamys þe Lesser** (St) James the Less 3A23 (**lesser(e** *adj.*)

lesse than *conj.* unless 2A7 (**les(se** *conj.*)

lesson *n.* lesson II.461 (**lessoun** *n.*)

lest, lyst *n.* desire II.1119; II.1116 (**list** *n.2.*)

lest *v.* last, endure, remain I.1046; *3sg.pr.* **lestyth** II.1016 (**lasten** *v.1.*)

lest *adj.* least, smallest I.434 (**lest(e** *adj.1.*)

lete *v.* allow, let, leave I.227, II.587, 615, 2A54; *3sg.pr.* **letyth** II.626sd; *2sg.pr.subj.* **lete** II.313, 635, 1452; *1pl.pr.?subj.* **let(e)** I.183; II.1095; *2pl.pr.?subj.* **let(e)** I.235; II.629, 1237; *imp.sg./pl.* **let(e)** I.115, 237 etc.; I.75, 90 etc., **lett(e)** II.1594; I.95, II.1760, **late** I.405, 535 etc.; *pr.p.* **latyng** I.928sd (**leten** *v.*)

lete, lett *v.* hinder, prevent, delay, linger II.1336; II.906, *1A*12; *imp.sg.* **lett** *1A*25 (**letten** *v.*)

leue, leve *n.* leave, permission II.5; I.662sd, II.1484, *1A*18 (**leve** *n.2.*)

leve *v.* leave, cease I.524, II.774sd, 1199sd; (*inf.* + it) **levynt** omit/pass over it I.778sd; *imp.pl.* **leve** II.863; *1sg.pa.* **lefte** I.19; *1pl.pa.* **lefte** stopped at II.6; *p.p.* **levyl** I.727; **leve of** stop II.774sd (**leven** *v.1.*)

leve, levyn *v.* live, dwell, remain I.748, 826; II.1390; *1sg.pr.* **leve** II.921; *3sg.pr.* **levyth** II.1749, 1752, **lyvyth** II.1812; *3pl.pr.* **levyn** I.851; *2pl.pr.subj.* **leve** I.747 (**liven** *v.1.*)

leve *v.* believe I.230 (**leven** *v.4.*)

levyng *vbl.n.* life, living, way of life I.734, 736, II.424 (**living(e** *ger.*)

levynge *adj.* living II.1547, 1773, 1897, 1926 (**living(e** *ppl.adj.*)

levyr *adv.* rather I.537, II.473 (**lef** *adj. & adv.*)

ly(ne) *v.* lie, remain, rest II.1425; I.928sd; *1sg.pr.* **ly3** II.1428; *3sg.pr.* **lyth** I.157, 171 etc.; *pr.p.* **lyeng** II.108; *3sg.pa.* **lay** I.38; *1pl.pa.* **loyn** II.111 (**lien** *v.1.*)

lycens, lysens *n.* permission II.664; II.1163 (**licence** *n.*)

lych(e) *adv.* similarly, alike I.208sd; I.637 (**like** *adv.*)

lych(e) *see also* **leke**

lycherye *see* **lechory**

lyest *v.* *2sg.pr.* **lyest upon** tell lies about II.1541 (**lien** *v.2.*)

lyf(f), lyve *n.* life I.822, 850 etc.; I.38, 717 etc.; II.997, 1012 etc.; **on lyve** alive II.1546, 1916; *n.pl.* **lyvys** II.1236 (**lif** *n.*)

lyfte *see* **left(e)**

ly3 *see* **ly(ne)**

lyght, lyth *adj.* light, nimble II.960; II.1665 (**light** *adj.2.*)

lyght *see also* **lyth** *v.*

lyghtnes *n.* brilliance *3A*3 (**lightnes(se** *n.1.*)

ly3 *see* **ly(ne)**

lykkenyd *p.p.* comparable to I.143 (**liknen** *v.2.*)

lyne *see* **ly(ne)**

lyppys *n.pl.* lips II.24, 895 (**lip(pe** *n.1.*)

lysens *see* **lycens**

lyst *v.* *3sg.pr.subj.* wants to II.443 (**listen** *v.1.*)

lyst *conj.* lest I.293 (**lest(e** *conj.*)

lyst *see also* **lest** *n.*

lyst(e) *v.* *imp.pl.* listen II.1200; II.1295 (**listen** *v.2.*)

lyth *n.* light I.16, 19; *n.pl.* **lytys** I.1032sd (**light** *n.*)

lyth *v.* alight, descend I.406sd; *1sg.pa.* **lyght** II.1444; *3sg.pa.* **lyth** II.1689 (**lighten** *v.2.*)

lyth *p.p.* lighted, lit I.656, 964sd (**lighten** *v.1.*)

lyth *see also* **lyght** *adj.*; **ly(ne)** *v.*

lytyl *n.* **a lytyl** a small amount, for a short time *2A*64sd; **a lytyl þerbesyde** near, nearby I.900sd (**litel** *n.*)

lytyl, lytil *adj.* little, small, short I.360, II.1601 etc.; I.288sd (**litel** *adj.*)

lytys *see* **lyth** *n.*

lyve, lyvys *see* **lyf(f)**

lyvyth *see* **leve, levyn**

lo(o) *interj.* lo, look! I.9, 96 etc.; II.442, 1280, 1288 (**lo** *interj.*)

lofte *n.* **on lofte** up high II.905 (**loft** *n.*)

logge *n.* dwelling, prison II.996, 1037, 1406 (see note), 1428 (**logg(e** *n.2.*)

loyn *see* **ly(ne)**

loke *n.* look II.222 (**lok** *n.4.*)

loke, lokyn *v.* look, see (to it), ensure I.774sd, II.780, 786sd, 1793; II.213sd, 866sd; *3pl.pr.* **lokyn** II.746; *imp.sg./pl.* **loke** I.80, 81 etc.; *pr.p.* **lokyng** I.686sd; *p.p.* **lokyd** considered I.361; **loke abowte** take heed, keep watch II.517 (**loken** *v.2.*)

loke *v. imp.pl.* lock, secure II.1290 (**loken** *v.1.*)

lokke *n.* lock II.1290 (**lok** *n.2.*)

lokkys *n.pl.* hair I.85 (**lok** *n.1.*)

lom, lomb(e), lambe *n.* lamb II.110; I.485, 518sd etc.; I.702, 703 etc.; I.663 (**lomb** *n.*)

lond(e) *n.* (dry) land, region, country I.868, II.270 etc.; II.581, 607, 1033 (**lond** *n.*)

long(e) *adj.* long I.69, 953; II.160 (**long** *adj.1.*)

long(e) *adv.* (for) long, for a long time II.750, 763, 772; I.126, II.420 etc.; **pulle/drawe hym long** pull him out to his full extent II.763, 772 (**longe** *adv.*)

longyth *v. 3sg.pr.* belongs to, is necessary for I.508 (**longen** *v.3.*)

lord(e) *n.* lord (often as a form of address) I.1, 9 etc.; II.1054, 1056, 2A40; *n.poss.* **lordys** I.407, 490, 1032sd; *n.pl.* **lordys** II.46, 90 etc. (**lord** *n.*) (*For* **Oure Lord** *see* List of proper names *etc.*)

lordly *adj.* appropriate to a lord II.21 (**lordli** *adj.*)

lore *n.* teaching, instruction I.11 (**lor(e** *n.2.*)

lore, lorn(e) *v. p.p. see* **lese**

lose *v.* loose, untie I.128 (**losen** *v.3.*)

lost *p.p.* lost, forfeited, ruined I.793, II.464 etc. (**losen** *v.2.*)

loth *n.* fault II.1730 (**loth** *n.*)

loth *adj.* dissatisfied, displeased II.1545 (**loth** *adj.*)

loue, love *n.* love I.422, 713 etc.; I.61, 108 etc.; *n.poss.* **lovys** I.62 (**love** *n.1.*)

love *v.* love I.363, 364; *3pl.pr.* **love** II.609, **lovyn** I.498; *2pl.pr.subj.* **loue** I.810; *3pl.pa.* **lovyd** 3A30; *p.p.* **louyd** II.1901 (**loven** *v.1.*)

lowd *adv.* ?publicly I.1026, **lowd and lowe** ?to all, ?at all times I.1026 (**loude** *adv.*)

lowe *adv.* ?privately I.1026 (see also **lowd**); (or *adj.*) deep I.15 (**loue** *adv.*)

lowlyté *n.* submission, humility II.1722 (**loulité** *n.*)

lowte, lowth *v.* bow, owe allegiance II.1034; II.489 (**louten** *v.1.*)

luminarye *n.* bright light, shining example 3A3; *n.pl.* **luminaryes** 3A17 (**luminari(e** *n.*)

mad *adj.* mad II.543sd, 1906 (**mad** *adj.*)

mad(e) *see* **mak(e)**

magesté *n.* magnificence, sovereignty II.171, 1935 (**magesté** *n.*)

may *v. 1/3sg.pr.* may I.20, 60 etc.; *2sg.pr.* **may** I.759, **mayst** I.156, 997 etc.; *pl.pr.* **may** I.135, 303 etc.; might *sg.pa.* **myth** I.560, II.606 etc., **myght** II.1498, 1905, 1911, 2A59; *pl.pa.* **myth** I.638, II.625, 1203, **myght** II.1497; *pa.subj.* **myth** I.982, 1041, II.533, **myght** II.1720 (**mouen** *v.3.*)

mayd(e) *n.* maiden, virgin II.969, 1382; I.41 (**maid(e** *n. & adj.*)

maydyn *n.* virgin (especially the Virgin Mary) II.796; *n.poss.* **maydenys** II.3, 1404, 2A15, **maydonys** II.1148 (**maiden** *n.*)

maynteyn *v.* preserve, support I.90 (**mainteinen** *v.*)

mayster, maystyr *n.* master, leader (and as a form of address) I.53, 602 etc.; I.598, 606 etc.; *n.poss.* **maysterys** I.584; *n.pl.* **maysterys** II.623 (**maister** *n.*)

maystryes *n.pl.* deceits, accomplishments, great deeds I.22, II.1332 (**maistri(e** *n.*)

mak(e), maken, makyn *v.* make, create, force, put on, pretend, celebrate I.788; I.35, 44 etc.; II.680; II.543sd, 874sd; *1sg.pr.* **make** I.258, II.59 etc.; *2sg.pr.* **makyst** II.425, 1849; *3sg.pr.* **makyth** I.230, 618; *1/2pl.pr.* **make** II.899, 908 etc.; *3pl.pr.* **make** I.212, II.518, **makyn** I.406sd, 988sd; *2/3sg.pr.subj.* **make** I.81, 84, 874, II.115; *imp.sg./pl.* **make** I.135, 883, II.519, 1485; *2sg.pa.* **made** I.1062; *3sg.pa.* **mad(e)** I.345, II.1914; II.11, 210, 1583; *p.p.* **mad(e)** I.29, 435 etc.; I.163, II.511 (**maken** *v.1.*)

makere *n.* creator I.356, 382, II.799 (**maker(e** *n.*)

maladyes *n.pl.* diseases I.371 (**maladi(e** *n.*)

malycyous *adj.* malicious, hostile I.50, 59 (**malicious** *adj.*)

man *n.* man, mankind I.5, 104 etc.; *n.poss.* **mannys** I.42, 110 etc.; *n.pl.* **men** I.740, II.111 etc.; *n.pl.poss.* **mennys** II.1092 (**man** *n.*)

manace, manas *n.* threat 2A101; 2A68 (**manace** *n.*)

maner *n.* kind (of), sort (of) I.146, 160 etc. (**maner(e** *n.*)

manhod *n.* manliness, human nature I.113, 690, II.848 (**manhed(e** *n.*)

many *adj.* many I.119, 127 etc.; (as *n.*) I.367, 631 (**mani** *adj. & n.*)

mankend(e), mankynd(e) *n.* mankind, human nature I.1075; II.885, 993, 1483; II.620; II.1492 (**man-kind(e** *n.*)

manly *adv.* like a man, valiantly II.109 (**manli** *adv.*)

mansclawth *n.* murder II.593 (**man-slaught** *n.*)

marchawnt *n.* merchant, dealer 2A105 (**marchaunt** *n.*)

masager, masanger(e), massanger(e) *n.* messenger I.255sd; II.240; I.164sd, 208sd etc.; II.89sd, 228, 235sd, 243sd; II.226 (**messager** *n.*)

massage *n.* message, errand I.258, 481; *n.pl.* **massagys** I.254 (**message** *n.1.*)

mater(e) *n.* case, business, (subject) matter II.312, 1221; I.4, 117 etc.; *n.pl.* **materys** I.119, 122 etc. (**mater(e** *n.*)

mawndé, maundé *n.* Paschal meal (Last Supper) I.508, 680, II.11, 13; I.459, 484 (**maundé** *n.2.*)

me *pron.obj.* me, myself (**me** *pron.2.*)

mech(e) *adj.* much, many II.823; I.569, 758, II.158, 1171 (**much(e** *adj.*)

mech(e) *adv.* much II.221; I.149, 403, II.415 (**much(e** *adv.*)

mede *n.* gift, bribery, reward, benefit I.852, II.20 etc.; **reward here mede** give them their just deserts I.852 (**mede** *n.*)

medytacyon *n.* meditation, prayer I.1034 (**meditacioun** *n.*)

meef *v. 3sg.pr.subj.* stirs up I.119; *p.p.* **mevyd** put forward II.674 (**meven** *v.*)

meen *see* **mene** *v.*

meende *see* **me(e)nde**

meet *see* **mete** *adj.*

meke *adj.* gentle, mild, humble I.983, 1033, II.110, *1A*38 (**mek** *adj.*)

mekel, mekyl *adj.* great II.1468; I.312, II.269 (**muchel** *adj.*)

mekely *adv.* humbly, patiently, politely I.471, 840sd, II.10, 19 (**mekli** *adv.*)

melyon *num.* million I.1012 (**milioun** *num.*)

melle *v.* meddle II.1614; **with myrþe to melle** to live in bliss, to experience happiness (lit. 'to be united with happiness') II.1375 (**medlen** *v.*)

membre *n.* limb, part of the body I.95; *n.pl.* **membrys** II.495 (**membre** *n.*)

memory, memorie *n.* remembrance, memorial I.795, 845; **haue memorie (on)** remember II.1020 (**memori(e** *n.*)

men *pron.* people I.86, 778sd etc. (**men** *pron.indef.*)

men *see also* **man**

me(e)nde *n.* mind, memory I.283, 800 etc.; I.1058; **haue/hast in mende** remember, bear in mind I.283, II.837, 887; *n.pl.* **mendys** thoughts I.25 (**mind(e** *n.*)

mene *n.* method, way I.219; *n.pl.* **menys** I.298, 577, 588, 630 (**mene** *n.3.*)

mené, meny *n.* body of retainers or followers II.866sd; I.653, 662sd (**meiné** *n.*)

mene, meen *v.* say, intend, mean I.716, 729; I.452; *p.p.* **ment** I.941 (**menen** *v.1.*)

mene *adj.* **in þe mene tyme** meanwhile, at the same time I.208sd, 244sd etc. (**mene** *adj.2.*)

meny *see* **mené**

ment *see* **mene** *v.*

meracle *n.* miracle, marvel II.429; *n.pl.* **meracles, -clis, -clys** II.421; I.229, II.502; I.295, II.409 (**miracle** *n.*)

mercy(e) *n.* mercy I.142, 149 etc.; I.414, 427 (**merci** *n.*)

mercyful *adj.* merciful I.152 (**merciful** *adj.*)

mere *n.* boundary (mark), ?place (see note) II.1712 (**mere** *n.3.*)

mery *adj.* happy, joyful I.594, II.952, 1818 (**miri(e** *adj.*)

merke *v. 1sg.pr.* afflict II.495 (**marken** *v.1.*)

merth(e) *see* **myrth(e)**

merveylis, mervaylys *n.pl.* wonders, marvels II.1051; I.522 (**merveille** *n.*)

merveylyth, merveyllys *v.pl.pr.* wonder, are surprised, are filled with awe II.875; I.36 (**merveillen** *v.*)

mervelous *adj.* strange, extraordinary I.25, 31 (**merveillous** *adj.*)

mesemyth *v.impers. 3sg.pr.* it seems to me I.398, 552, 572, II.196

mete *n.* food I.453, 753 etc. (**mete** *n.1.*)

mete *v.* meet I.280sd, 395 etc.; *3sg.pr.* **metyth** I.256sd, 410sd; *3pl.pr.* **metyn** II.718sd, **mett** I.288sd, **mete** *1A*43sd; *pr.p.* **metyng** I.478sd; *p.p.* **met** II.204 (**meten** *v.4.*)

mete, meet *adj.* fit, adequate, right II.690, 748, 759, 793 (**mete** *adj.*)

methynkyth *v.impers. 3sg.pr.* it seems to me I.23, II.586 etc.; *3sg.pa.* **methought** II.113 **methowut** II.102

mevyd *see* **meef**

my(n) *pron.poss.* my I.3, 6 etc.; I.25, 32 etc. (**min** *pron.*)

myd *adj.* **þe myd place** the middle (?of the 'place'; see note) I.288sd (**mid** *adj. & pref.*)

myddys *n.* middle (way) I.138 (**middes** *n.*)

mydnyth *n.* midnight II.16 (**mid-night** *n.*)

myght, myth *n.* strength, power II.1359, 1467 etc.; I.28, 434, 693, II.1656 (**might** *n.*)

myght *see also* **may**

myghtfful *adj.* powerful, mighty II.1726 (**mightful** *adj.*)

mylde *adj.* gentle, merciful II.1388, 1489 (**milde** *adj.*)

mylk *n.* milk II.1404 (**milk** *n.*)

myn *see* **my(n)**

myrth(e), merth(e) *n.* joy, happiness, bliss, rejoicing II.955, 1485 etc.; II.1375, 1379, 1750; II.1889; II.1000; *n.pl.* **myrthis** II.1398, **merthis** II.936, 994; **merthis þat ȝe make** be cheerful II.936 (**mirth(e** *n.*)

mys *n.* sin II.1080 (**mis** *n.*)

mys(se) *v.* lack, be lacking, fail I.12; I.640, II.1171; *1sg.pr.* **mys** II.955 (**missen** *v.1.*)

myschef(f), myscheve *n.* misfortune, suffering, harm II.339, 495, 570; *2A*84; I.569 (**mischef** *n.*)

myscheve *v.* ruin, harm I.526 (**mischeven** *v.*)

mysdede *n.* sin, wickedness II.836 (**misdede** *n.*)

myself, -sylf *pron.* myself I.124, 555 etc.; *2A*4 (**mi-self** *pron.*)

mysese *n.* suffering, trouble, hardship II.745 (**misese** *n.*)

myslevyng *vbl.n.* sin; **with myslevyng** sinfully, wickedly I.717 (**mis-living(e** *ger.*)

myst *n.* mist II.1050 (**mist** *n.1.*)

mystery *n.* sacrament, mystical truth I.677, 692 (**misteri(e** *n.*)

mytere *n.* mitre I.164sd (see note) (**mitre** *n.*)

myth *n. see* **myght**

myth *v. see* **may**

mythty *adj.* mighty II.810 (**mighti** *adj.*)

mythtyly *adv.* with great power/strength I.561 (**mightili** *adv.*)

mo *n.* more I.807, II.287, 1246; **non mo** any others II.287 (**mo** *n.*)

mo *adj.* more II.538, 588 etc. (**mo** *adj.*)

modyr *n.* mother I.1033, 1062 etc.; *n.pl.* **moderys** II.714 (**moder** *n.*)

mo(o)lde *n.* earth II.1778; II.495 (**mold(e** *n.1.*)

mon *v. pl.pr.* may II.190, 681 (**monen** *v.2.*)

monay, moné, mony(e) *n.* money 2A99; 2A57; I.83, 103 etc.; 2A106 (**monei(e** *n.*)

mone *n.* moon II.167 (**mon(e** *n.1.*)

mone *n.* sorrow, lamentation, mourning, weeping II.718, 1445, 1848 (**mon** *n.1.*)

moné, mony(e) *see* **monay**

monthis *n.pl.* months II.408 (**month** *n.*)

mood(e) *n.* attitude, mind, feelings, mood II.981, 1633; II.1481 (**mod** *n.*)

moolde *see* **mo(o)lde**

moost *see* **mo(o)st**

moralysacyon *n.* explanation, exposition I.141 (**moralizacion** *n.*)

more *n.* more, others II.128, 415, 508, 762 (**mor(e** *n.*)

more *adj.* more, greater, further, better I.122, 254 etc. (**mor(e** *adj.*)

more *adv.* more, longer, greatly I.127, 151 etc. (**mor(e** *adv.*)

morn *n.* morning; **bothe evyn and morn** always, at all times II.910, 1473 (**morn** *n.*)

morne *v.* mourn, grieve II.1847; *pr.p.* **mornyng** II.790sd (**mornen** *v.*)

mornyng(e) *vbl.n.* weeping, sorrow, lamentation II.863, 2A106; II.976, 1858, 1906; (as *adj.*) **mornyng** II.1481, 2A64 (**morning(e** *ger.*)

mortal(l) *adj.* deadly, subject to death I.368, 436 (see note); I.121 (see note), 130; **dedys mortal, mortall dedys** deadly sins I.368; I.130 (**mortal** *adj.*)

morwe *n.* morning II.1501 (**morwe** *n.*)

morwyn *n.* morning; **both evyn and morwyn** continually I.450 (see also **morn** and **evyn**) (**morn** *n.*)

most *adj.* most, greatest I.362, 451 etc. (**most** *adj.sup. & n.*)

mo(o)st, ?must *adv.* most I.70, 139 etc.; II.27; ?I.428 (see note) (**most** *adv.sup.*)

mot(e) *v. sg.pr.subj.* may II.454, 459, 1178; II.203, 248 etc.; *2pl.pr.subj.* **mote** II.1197, 1A30; must *1sg.pa.* **must(e)** I.122, 172 etc.; II.1868, **mut** II.644; *2sg.pa.* **must** I.629, II.257; *3sg.pa.* **must** I.204, 502 etc., **mut** II.645; *2pl.pa.* **must** I.318, 575 etc., **mut** II.1; *1/3pl.pa.* **must** I.162, 181 etc.; (with *pron.* 'I') **moty** may I II.102 (**moten** *v.2.*)

mothalle *n.* meeting–house, counsel hall II.230, 239, 246, 260 (**mot–halle** *n.*)

moty *see* **mot(e)**

mount, mownth *n.* hill I.900sd; II.696 (**mount** *n.1.*)

mowe *n.* grimace, face II.899, 908 (**moue** *n.2.*)

mownteynes *n.pl.* mountains II.715 (**mountain(e** *n.*)

mowth(e) *n.* mouth II.150, **mowth to mowth** face to face II.1929; **be mowthe** by confession II.368 (**mouth** *n.*)

multyplye *v.* multiply, increase II.28 (**multiplien** *v.*)
must(e) *see* **mot(e)**
must *see also* **mo(o)st**
mut *see* **mot(e)**

nay *n.* **is no nay** cannot be denied II.1512, 1786 (**nai** *n.*)
nay *interj.* no I.20, 473 etc.; **sey nay** deny, refuse I.20, 473, II.169, 200 (**nai** *interj.*)
nayl *n.* nail II.690, 767, 770, 773; *n.pl.* **nayles** II.512, **naylys** II.686, **naylis** II.1700 (**nail** *n.*)
naylyn *v.* nail II.746sd; *p.p.* **naylid** II.964, 1044, 1062 , **naylyd** II.1496, 1762 (**nailen** *v.*)
nakyd *adj.* naked II.680 (**naked** *adj.*)
name *n.* name, authority, behalf I.3, 407 etc.; *n.pl.* **namys** I.109 (**name** *n.*)
namyd *v.* *3sg.pa.* called, named II.878 (**namen** *v.1.*)
naterall, **naturall** *adj.* natural, according to man's nature I.66, 111; *3A38* (**natural** *adj.*)
ne *adv.* not II.1274 (**ne** *adv.*)
ne *conj.* nor II.243, 287, *2A43* (**ne** *conj.*)
necglygens *n.* negligence I.357 (**necligence** *n.*)
necke *n.* neck, shoulder II.698sd; *n.pl.* **neckys** I.244sd (**nekke** *n.*)
ned(e) *n.* necessity, need, distress, reason II.1124; I.146, 539 etc. (**ned(e** *n.*)
nedful *adj.* necessary II.129 (**ned(e)ful** *adj.*)
nedys *adv.* of necessity I.536, II.231 etc. (**nedes** *adv.*)
nedyth *impers.v.* *3sg.pr.* **what nedyth us** what necessity is there for us II.175 (**neden** *v.2.*)
neybore *n.* neighbour, fellow-man I.364; *n.pl.* **neyborys** I.399 (**neighebor** *n.*)
neyr *see* **ner(e)** *adv.*
neyth *v.* draw near I.49 (cf. **neighen** *v.1.*)
neyther *conj.* neither I.137 (**neither** *conj.*)
ner(e), **neyr** *adv.* near, nearly, almost II.569, 1225; I.315, 881 etc.; II.271 (**ner** *adv.2.*)
nere *conj.* nor I.114 (**ner** *conj.*)
nerhonde *adj.* near II.582 (**ner-honde** *adj.*)
ner-to *adv.* nearly II.97 (see note) (cf. **ner** *adv.2.*)
nevyr *adv.* never I.12, 32 etc. (**never** *adv.*)
new(e) *adj.* new I.50, 600 etc.; I.80, 103 etc. (**neue** *adj.*)
newly *adv.* once more II.1470 (**neuli** *adv.*)
ny, **ny3** *adv.* near, nearly, almost I.387, 392, 878; II.1443 (**neigh** *adv.*)
ny(e) *adj.* near I.398; I.429 (**neigh** *adj.*)
nyght *see* **nyth**
nygramancye, **nygramansye** *n.* sorcery, witchcraft II.272, 404; I.1015 (**nigromaunci(e** *n.*)
nyth, **nyght** *n.* night I.86, 480 etc.; II.1585, 1598, 1643, 1833 (**night** *n.*)

no *adj.* no I.64, 95 etc. (**no** *adj.*)
no *adv.* not, not at all I.43, 243 etc. (**no** *adv.*)
noȝt *see* **nowth** *adv.*
noyse *n.* noise I.1032sd, II.543sd (**noise** *n.*)
noyther *adj.* neither I.628 (**nouther** *pron.*)
non *adj.* no I.1032, 1070 etc. (**non** *adj.*)
non *adv.* not (at all) I.595, 626 (**non** *adv.*)
non(e), noon *pron.* none, no–one I.308, 353 etc.; II.1454; II.23 (**non** *pron.*)
nor *conj.* nor I.93, 137 etc. (**nor** *conj.*)
norsshere *n.* nourisher, encourager, nurse I.5 (**norisher(e** *n.*)
not *adv.* not I.20, 31 etc.; **not ellys but** nothing other than I.736, 740; ?not at
    all I.93 (**not** *adv.*)
nother *conj.* neither II.576, 1098, 1230 (**nouther** *conj.*)
nothyng(e), noþing *pron.* nothing I.60, 396, 849; II.1031; II.54 (**no–thing**
    pron.)
notwithstandyng *conj.* although I.16 (**not-with-stonding(e** *conj.*)
notwth *see* **nowth** *adv.*
nought *see* **nowth** *adv.* and *n.*
novmbyr *n.* **novmbyr of** many I.856 (**nombre** *n.*)
now *adv.* now I.9, 25 etc. (**nou** *adv.*)
nowth, nought *n. and pron.* nothing I.76, 94 etc.; *1A*46 (**nought** *n. and*
    pron.)
nowth, nought, notwth, noȝt *adv.* not, not at all I.79, 520 etc.; II.959;
    I.252, 1028; II.983 (emend.) (**nought** *adv.*)

o *num.* one, a I.533, 555 etc. (**o** *num.*)
o *prep.* (reduced form of various prepositions in unstressed position; see also
    a *prep.*) at, of (a) I.86, out of, from II.38 (**o** *prep. 1 and 2*)
o *interj.* oh! O (in invocation) I.343, 443 etc. (**o** *interj.*)
obecyon *n.* difficulty, obstacle, problem II.306 (**obecion** *n.*)
obedyens *n.* obedience I.464, II.381 (**obedience** *n.*)
obedyent *adj.* obedient I.1066 (**obedient** *adj.*)
obeyth *see* **abey**
oblé *n.* sacramental wafer I.686sd (**oblé** *n.*)
odyr *see* **other(e)** *adj.*
of *adv.* off II.99, 205, 679 (**of** *adv.*)
of(f) *prep.* of, about, from, by, through I.1, 2 etc.; I.69 *2A*64; **browt of**
    dawe II.149 (see **a** *prep.*); **of þis** from this time I.682 (**of** *prep.*)
of-corde *see* **acorde**
offens *n.* wrong, crime II.648 (**offens(e** *n.*)
offere *v.* offer (the eucharist at the mass), dedicate I.948; *p.p.* **offeryd** I.946,
    *3A*20 (**offren** *v.*)
offyce *n.* duty (of an official position) II.654 (**office** *n.*)
ofte *adv.* often, frequently I.153, II.128 (**oft(e** *adv.*)
oftyn *adv.* often, many times I.801 (**often** *adv.*)

oftyn-times *adv.* often, many times II.123 (**often-times** *adv.*)

oyle *n.* **oyle of mercy** salvation I.893 (see note) (**oil(e** *n.*)

oynement, onyment *n.* ointment II.1727, 2A23, 50, 54; II.1182 (**oine-ment** *n.*)

old(e), holde, hoold *adj.* old, ancient I.208sd, 617, 684; I.699; (as *n.*) I.47; I.164sd; **old(e)/hoold lawe** law of Moses, Old Testament I.684; I.699; I.164sd; **aftyr þe old gyse** according to the old law (or 'old-fashioned'?) I.208sd (see note) (**old(e** *adj.*)

omnypotent *adj.* all-powerful II.1726 (**omnipotent(e** *adj.*)

on *pron.* one, someone I.26, 178 etc.; **many on** many, many a one II.37, 1398, 1441 (**on** *pron.* and **mani on** *phr.*)

on *num.* one I.162, II.1594, 3A16; **in on** together, in unity 3A19 (**on** *num.* and **in-on** *adv. & adj.*)

on *adv.* on I.1009, II.194 etc. (**on** *adv.1.*)

on, vn *prep.* on, in, against I.24, 88 etc.; I.866 (**on** *prep.*)

onclose *see* **vnclose**

ondothe *v. imp.pl.* undo, open II.1019

onesté *n.* good name/reputation, honourable position I.111 (**honesté** *n.*)

onhangyd *adj.* unhanged II.446

ony *see* **any**

onyment *see* **oynement**

onys *adv.* once I.473, 863 etc.; (as *n.*) (**all(e)**) **at onys** (all) together, at the same time I.406sd, 413 etc. (**ones** *adv.* and **at ones** *phr.*)

onythynge *see* **anythyng**

only *adv.* only, solely I.724, II.340, 1A20 (**onli** *adv.*)

onlose *v.* **onlose hese lyppys** open his mouth, start talking II.24 (*OED* **Unloose** *v.*)

onowryd *see* **honowre** *v.*

ontyl(le) *prep.* to 3A4; II.452 (*OED* **Until** *prep.* and *conj.*)

onto(o), vnto *prep.* to I.89, 207 etc.; II.1521; I.82, 592 (*OED* **Unto** *prep.* and *conj.*)

opyn *adj.* **with opyn syght** clearly II.1043, 1902, 1912; **with opyn voys/speche** openly II.1789, 1919 (**open** *adj.*)

opyn *adv.* openly, publicly II.134 (**open** *adv.*)

opynly *adv.* generally, publicly, openly II.399, 403, 2A78 (**openli** *adv.*)

oppyn *v. imp.pl.* open II.716 (**openen** *v.*)

oppynyon *n.* belief; **fals oppynyon** heresy I.239 (**opinioun** *n.*)

oppressyon *n.* harm, injury I.234 (**oppressioun** *n.*)

or *conj.* or I.28, 77 etc. (**or** *conj.*)

or *see also* **er(e)** *conj.*

oratory *n.* oratory, ?chapel I.288sd (see note) (**oratori(e** *n.*)

ordeyn *v.* prepare, make ready, arrange, appoint, ordain I.482, 489 etc.; *imp.sg.* **ordeyn** I.484, 655, 661; *1sg.pa.* **ordeyn** II.1185; *p.p.* **ordayned** 1A21, **ordeyned** I.911 (**ordeinen** *v.*)

ordenawnce, ordenawns, ordenauns *n.* plan, decree, preparation, fate I.443; I.57, 458 etc.; *3A*24 (**ordinaunce** *n.*)

orryble *adj.* fearful, foul II.486sd, *2A*101 (**horrible** *adj.*)

ost *n.* host, army II.1578 (**host(e** *n.*)

oth *n.* oath II.211; *n.pl.* **othys** I.89, 95 (**oth** *n.*)

other, othyr, tother *pron.* (the) other I.774sd, II.782sd; I.846; II.1163sd; *poss.* **otherys** I.282, 848 (**other** *pron.*)

other(e), othyr, odyr, tother *adj.* other I.363, 740 etc.; I.285, II.133; I.523; I.964sd; II.195sd (**other** *adj.*)

ouer, ouyr *prep.* over I.85 (alternative wording), 164sd; II.181sd (**over** *prep.*)

ouerest *adv.* on top, uppermost II.486sd (**overest** *adv.*)

ouyrlede *v.* overpower, master I.538 (**overleden** *v.*)

ovyrthrow *v.* throw down, fall down, overturn I.561; *imp.pl.* **ovyr- throwyth** II.717; *1pl.pa.* **ovyrthrewyn** II.107 (**overthrouen** *v.*)

our(e), houre *pron.poss.* our I.234, II.40, 654, 1219; I.121, 133 etc.; I.98, 520 **oure** ours II.126 (**our(e** *pron.*)

oure *see also* **houre** *n.*

out *interj.* alas, shame II.173, 1027; **out on/upon** shame on, a curse on II.524, 795, 1537 (**out(e** *interj.*)

out(e), owth, owt(e) *adv.* out I.15, 786 etc.; *3A*4; I.418, II.1065, *1A*4; **all owt** openly, fully *2A*94; **owte** departed, gone II.1733 (**out(e** *adv.*)

out/outh/owth/owt(e) of *prep.* out of I.1, 244 etc.; I.804, 1032sd; I.925, II.1857; I.510sd, II.1057 etc.; II.1599 (**out(e of** *prep.*)

outborn *p.p.* born II.347 (see note)

owe, howe *v.* *1sg.pr.* owe, ought II.1722; I.358 (**ouen** *v.*)

owyn *adj.* own I.364, 528 etc. (**ouen** *adj.*)

owt(e), owth *see* **out . . . of** *prep.* and **out(e)** *adv.*

owth *pron.* anything I.727 (**ought** *pron.*)

owth *see also* **aught**

ox(e) *n.* ox II.125; II.1690 (**oxe** *n.*)

pace, pas(se) *v.* go, pass, escape, surpass I.235, II.557, 635; I.244, II.313; I.327, *2A*97; *1sg.pr.* **passe** *2A*63; *3sg.pr.* **passeth** II.1074, **passyth** I.410sd, II.1191, 1500, 1830; *3pl.pr.* **passe** I.82; *p.p.* **passyd** II.258, **past** I.204, 276, II.754 (**passen** *v.*)

page *n.* servant II.248 (**page** *n.1.*)

pay *v.* pay I.611, II.848; *1pl.pa.* **payd** II.124 (**paien** *v.*)

payment *n.* payment, fee, paying I.73, 373, 613 (**paiement** *n.*)

payn *see* **peyn(e)**

pale *adj.* pale II.1170, 1551 (**pal(e** *adj.*)

palpable *adj.* clear, evident I.214 (**palpable** *adj.*)

paradys(e) *n.* heaven II.1370; II.829, 998, 1399 (**paradis(e** *n.*)

parayl *n.* way, means, apparel, physical appearance I.195, 636 (**ap(p)areil** *n.*)

pardon *v.* forgive; **pardon me for to say** excuse me for saying I.225 (**pardounen** *v.*)

park *n.* park, enclosed area I.900sd (see note) (**park** *n.*)

parlement *n.* assembly, council I.941 (**parlement(e** *n.*)

part(e) *n.* part, portion, task, side, share I.20, 231 etc.; I.67 (**part** *n.*)

partabyl *adj.* **to ben partabyl** to be able to share I.796 (**partable** *adj.*)

parte *v.* part II.961; *3pl.pr.* **partyn** I.662sd (**parten** *v.*)

partenere *n.* sharer, partaker II.1159 (**partener(e** *n.*)

party *n.* **on his party** for his part I.539, 655 (**parti(e** *n.*)

pas *n.* pace, way II.265, 1694 (**pas(e** *n.1.*)

pas(e) *see also* **pace**

Pasch(e) *n.* Passover (feast) I.486; **Pasche day** II.582, 661 (**pask(e** *n.*)

Paschal(l) *adj.* **Paschal(l) lomb(e)** lamb eaten at the Passover I.518sd, 683, 702, 752; I.485, 743 (**pascal(e** *adj.*)

passe, passeth *etc. see* **pace**

passyon *n.* suffering, passion (of Christ) I.681, 795 etc. (**passioun** *n.*)

path(e), patthe *n.* path, way I.495; I.157; I.144, 148; *n.pl.* **pathys** I.135, **patthis** I.164 (**path** *n.*)

patryarke *n.* bishop *3A24* (**patriark(e** *n.*)

pees *n.* peace I.499 (**pes** *n.*)

peyn *v.* torture, torment, afflict, trouble II.1701; *1sg.pr.* **peyn** I.920; *3sg.pr.* **peyneth** II.858, **peynyth** II.42, 501 (**peinen** *v.*)

peyn(e), payn *n.* punishment, pain, suffering, penalty I.312, 436 etc.; I.12, 120, II.857; **in payn** under penalty of forfeiting II.1236; *n.pl.* **peynes** I.8, 922 etc., **peynys** I.899 (**pein(e** *n.*)

peynde *v.* suffer, languish II.886 (see note) (?**peinen** *v.*; ?**pinen** *v.*; cf. **pinden** *v.*)

peyre *n.* pair I.69 (**paire** *n.1.*)

pekyd *adj.* pointed-toed I.69 (see note) (**piked** *adj.*)

pelere *n.* pillar II.681, 696sd (**piler(e** *n.*)

pellys *n.pl.* robes, cloaks I.208sd (**pal** *n.*)

penawns *n.* penance I.131, 155 (**penaunce** *n.*)

penne *n.* pen II.874sd (**penne** *n.*)

pens *n.pl.* pennies (small silver coins) II.124, *2A58* (**peni** *n.*)

pepyl(l) *n.* or *n.pl.* people I.21, 36 etc.; I.88, II.344, 403 (**peple** *n.*)

peraventure *adv.* perhaps, maybe II.431 (**paraventur(e** *adv.*)

perdure *v.* continue I.368 (**perduren** *v.*)

pere *n.* equal II.44, 1054 (**per** *n.*)

pereles *adj.* peerless, without equal II.1055 (**perles** *adj.*)

perfectly *adv.* perfectly, righteously I.145 (**parfitli** *adv.*)

perfyth *adj.* perfect, full I.424 (**parfit** *adj.*)

peryl *n.* danger, peril II.1217; *n.pl.* **perellys** I.870 (**peril** *n.*)

periory *n.* false swearing, perjury I.114 (**parjuri(e** *n.*)

perysch *v.* die I.534 (**perishen** *v.*)

persecucyon *n.* torment, suffering, tribulation I.49, 444 (**persecucioun** *n.*)

perseverawns *n*. **in perseverawns** continually, with constancy I.365 (**perseveraunce** *n*.)

person(e) *n*. person, self I.1035, 2A124; I.364, 404; *n.pl*. **personys** people, persons I.559, 964sd, II.4 (**persoun(e** *n*.)

perverte *v*. *3sg.pr*. leads astray, misguides I.218 (**perverten** *v*.)

pes *n*. peace I.165, II.1686; **in pes** unmolested, safe II.606, 611 (**pes** *n*.)

pety *n*. pity I.1075 (**pité** *n*.)

petyful *adj*. merciful, compassionate I.1067 (**pitéful** *adj*.)

peusawns *n*. crowds, numbers I.521 (**puissance** *n*.)

pyght(e) *p.p*. set, fixed, appointed, placed II.1680, 2A72; II.967 (**picchen** *v*.)

pylle *v. imp.?pl*. pluck II.191 (see note to II.189–93) (**pilen** *v*.)

pynne *v*. shut, imprison 2A116 (**pinnen** *v*.)

pynnacle *n*. pinnacle (of the temple) I.30 (**pinacle** *n*.)

pyt(t), **pitt** *n*. pit, grave II.1121; II.1285; II.1832; **helle pytt** the depths of hell 2A47, 103, 110 (**pit** *n*.)

place, **plas(e)** *n*. house, place, acting-area ('platea') I.35, 244sd etc.; 2A71; I.487; *n.pl*. **placys** I.419 etc. (**place** *n*.)

play *see* **pley** *v*.

playn *adj*. full I.40 (**plein(e** *adj*.)

playn *see* **pleyn** *adv*.

plas(e) *see* **place**

platys *n.pl*. coins I.619, II.14 (**plat(e** *n*.)

pley *n*. pleasure, joy II.1399; *n.pl*. **pleys** II.998 (**plei(e** *n*.)

pley, **play** *v*. perform, play, act II.190; I.22; *3sg.pr*. **pleyth** II.486sd; *p.p*. **pleyd** II.486sd (**pleien** *v*.)

pleyn *adj*. plain, clear II.1205, 1920 (**plain(e** *adj*.)

pleyn, **playn** *adv*. openly, clearly, directly II.612, 998 etc.; I.867, 893 (**plain(e** *adv*).

plenté *n*. abundance I.51; **mete plenté** a large quantity of food 2A59 (**plenté** *n*.)

plentévous *adj*. plentiful, copious I.64 (**plentévous** *adj*.)

plesande *see* **plese**

plesauns, **plesawns** *n*. will, desire, pleasure II.34; I.98, 104, 270, 363; **take þat to plesawns** take pleasure in that I.406 (**plesaunce** *n.1*.)

plesaunt *adj*. pleasant, enjoyable I.110 (**plesaunt(e** *adj*.)

plese *v*. plese I.245; *3sg.pr*. **plesyth** I.849, II.972; *3sg.pr.subj*. **plese** I.273, (with *pron*.) **plesyt** may it please I.225; *2pl.pr.subj*. **plese** II.1936; *pr.p*. **plesyng(e)** I.504; *1A40*, **plesande** I.139; *p.p*. **plesyd** II.113 (**plesen** *v*.)

plesyng *vbl.n*. satisfaction, liking I.507, 596 (**plesing(e** *ger*.)

ply *v*. follow, agree to I.208 (**plien** *v.1*.)

plyght *n*. way, manner II.1836 (**plight** *n*.)

plyght, **plyth** *v*. *1sg.pr*. promise, assure II.1282; II.1094 (**plighten** *v*.)

poer *see* **pore** *adj*.; **power(e)** *n*.

poynt *n.* part I.434; *n.pl.* **poyntys** laces I.72, elements, arguments II.404 (**pointe** *n.1.*)

pore, poer, power *adj.* poor I.88, 468, *1A*20, *2A*61; I.513, II.786sd, *2A*56; *2A*60 (**povre** *adj.*)

possyble *adj.* capable, possible I.211, 214 (see notes) (**possible** *adj.*)

poverté *n.* poverty I.64, 75 (**poverté** *n.*)

pounde *n.pl.* pounds II.1566 (**pound(e** *n.1.*)

power *adj. see* **pore**

power(e), poer *n.* might, power, capacity I.340, 584 etc.; I.167, 171 etc.; II.348, 568, 617; *n.pl.* **powerys** resources, powers I.211 (**pouer(e** *n.*)

pray *n.* power, captivity II.850 (**prei(e** *n.2.*)

pray, prey(n) *v.* pray, request, beg II.1091, 1621; II.975; II.782; *1sg.pr.* **pray** I.460, 530 etc., **prey** II.735, 1132, 1158; *3sg.pr.* **prayth** I.908sd, **prayt** I.247, *1pl.pr.* **pray** I.839, II.864, 910, 1933, **prey(e)** II.230, 723, *3A*7; II.732; *2sg.pr.subj.* **pray** I.200; *imp.sg.* **pray** I.202, ?II.1633; *3sg.pa.* **prayd** II.239 (**preien** *v.*)

prayere, prayour *n.* prayer, request I.903, II.981; II.1604, *2A*31 (**preier(e** *n.*)

prate *v.* talk uselessly, blab II.1650 (**praten** *v.*)

praty *adj.* worthy II.240 (**prati(e** *adj.*)

precept *n.* instruction, law, commandment I.93, 1066; *n.pl.* **preceptys** I.750, **precepptys** I.742 (**precept(e** *n.*)

precepte *p.p.* ordained I.699 (**precepten** *v.*)

preche *v.* preach I.742, 1026 etc.; *p.p.* **prechyd** I.419, II.134 (**prechen** *v.*)

precher *n.* teacher, expositor *3A*11 (**prechour** *n.*)

prechyng *vbl.n.* preaching, teaching I.218, II.133 etc. (**preching(e** *ger.*)

precyous *adj.* sacred, precious, of great worth I.393, 752, 760, II.1482 (**precious(e** *adj.*)

pref *v.* make a trial of, prove, demonstrate, show II.543; *3pl.pr.* **preue** II.1054; *p.p.* **prevyd** I.191 (**preven** *v.*)

prey(n) *see* **pray** *v.*

prelat *n.* ecclesiastical dignitary, bishop I.165 (**prelat(e** *n.*)

pres *n.* **put . . . in pres** thrust (oneself) forward (into a fight, a mob, etc.) II.98, 1242 (**presse** *n.*)

presence, presens *n.* presence I.265, II.23, 1934; I.260, 268 etc.; **se þi/his/ 3our presence/presens** come before you/him, see you/him face to face I.260, 265 etc. (**presence** *n.*)

present *v.* represent, deliver up, present I.284; *1sg.pr.* **present** I.209; ?*3sg.pr.* **present** claims I.295 (see note); *imp.pl.* **present** II.371 (**presenten** *v.*)

present *adj.* present I.75, 90 etc. (**present(e** *adj.*)

present *adv.* now, here I.174, 188 etc.; ?I.938 (see note); **present beforn** in the presence of I.287 (**present(e** *adv.*)

preserve *v.* *3sg.pr.subj.* protect, save II.3 (**preserven** *v.*)

presydent *n.* leader, ruler *3A*14 (**president** *n.*)

preson *n.* prison I.240, 546, *2A*112 (**prisoun** *n.*)

presonde *p.p.* imprisoned II.593 (**prisounen** *v.*)

pressyd *p.p.* assailed, oppressed II.927 (**pressen** *v.*)

prest *adj.* manifest, unremitting II.976 (**prest** *adj.*)

prest *adv.* at once II.1530 (**prest** *adv.*)

presthood *n.* clergy, priests I.948 (**presthed(e** *n.*)

prestys *n.pl.* priests I.238, 518sd etc. (**prest** *n.3.*)

presume *v.* presume, assume a right, act presumptuously I.768, II.23 (**presumen** *v.*)

presumpcyon *n.* over-confidence (in God's mercy) I.160 (**presumpcioun** *n.*)

pretendyth *v. 3sg.pr.* claims (to be) I.41 (**pretenden** *v.*)

prevayll *see* **provayl(e)**

preudent *see* **prudent**

preue *see* **pref**

preuély, preuyly, prevély, prevyly *adv.* secretly, privately I.661, II.891; II.1293; II.1833, 2A128sd; II.1625 (**privéli(e** *adv.*)

prevy *adj.* secret, confidential I.104, 298 etc. (**privé** *adj.1.*)

prevyd *see* **pref**

price *n.* penalty, payment II.585; **most of price** of greatest worth I.686 (**pris** *n.1.*)

pride, pryde *n.* pride I.75, 76, 111; I.386 (**prid(e** *n.2.*)

primat *n.* chief priest I.209 (**primat(e** *n.1.*)

prime *n.* prime (a time between 6a.m. and 9a.m., or at 6a.m. or 9a.m.) II.242, 247 (**prim(e** *n.*)

prynce, prince *n.* prince, chief ruler I.296, 418 etc.; I.2, 21; *n.pl.* **princys** I.591, II.90 etc., **pryncys** I.296, II.623; **prynces** II.89sd, **prynsesse** I.599 (**prince** *n.*)

pryncipal *adj.* most important I.203 (**principal** *adj.*)

pryncypaly *adv.* chiefly I.172 (**principalli(e** *adv.*)

procede, prosede *v.* continue, go on, proceed with I.853, II.6, 17; I.183; *3sg.pr.* **procedyth** I.442sd; *pl.pr.* **procede** I.499, II.1251; *3sg.pr.subj.* **procede** I.179, 187 etc. (**proceden** *v.*)

processyon *n.* procession II.1sd, 3A10 (**processioun** *n.*)

proferre *v.* advance, promote II.57 (cf. **preferren** *v.*)

profyr *v. 3sg.pr.subj.* offer I.596 (**profren** *v.*)

profytable *adj.* beneficial, profitable II.56 (**profitable** *adj.*)

promese *n.* assertion, promise I.874; *n.pl.* **promessys** II.59 (**promis(se** *n.*)

promysyst *v. 2sg.pa.* promised I.1062 (**promisen** *v.*)

prongys *n.pl.* agonies I.1060 (see note) (**pronge** *n.*)

properyd *p.p.* appointed (specifically) I.165 (**propren** *v.*)

prophecy, prophesé, prophesey, prophesye *n.* prophecy I.854, II.777; I.383; I.888; I.705 (**propheci(e** *n.*)

prophecy(e), prophesy *v.* prophesy II.187; II.183; I.704; *1sg.pr.* **prophesye** I.125; *1sg.pa.* **prophecyed** I.352 (**prophecien** *v.*)

prophete *n.* prophet I.479, II.500 etc.; *n.poss.* **prophetys** I.383; *n.pl.* **prophetys** I.857, *3A*39 (**prophet(e** *n.*)

prophete *v. 1pl.pr.* profit, prosper I.520 (**profiten** *v.*)

proporcyon *n.* due form; **of proporcyon** in proportion I.78 (**proporcioun** *n.*)

prose *n.* **for a prose** as a plain statement I.177 (**prose** *n.*)

prosede *see* **procede**

prossesse *n.* **procede be prossesse** continue in the same way I.224 (**proces** *n.*)

provayl(e), prevayll *v.* be superior/efficacious I.193; I.251; I.841; *3pl.pr.* **provaylys** I.37 (**prevailen** *v.*)

provyde, provide *v.* make provision, provide, arrange, ordain I.122, 165 II.; I.51 (**providen** *v.*)

provynce, province *n.* territory, district, province II.76; II.1117 (**province** *n.*)

prow *n.* benefit, advantage, honour II.1098, 1134 (**prou** *n.*)

prudens *n.* wisdom, shrewdness I.60 (**prudence** *n.*)

prudent, preudent *adj.* wise I.257, II.45; I.209 (**prudent** *adj.*)

pulle, pullyn *v.* pull, tear at, drag II.746sd; II.181sd, 696sd, 698sd, 746sd; *3pl.pr.* **pulle** II.461sd, **pullyn** I.988sd; *imp.sg./pl.* **pul(le)** II.751; II.760, 763 (**pullen** *v.*)

punche *v.* pierce II.1701 (**pouncen** *v.*)

purcatorye *n.* purgatory II.1042 (**purgatori(e** *n.*)

pure *adj.* pure, perfect *3A*3 (**pur(e** *adj.*)

purpyl *adj.* crimson, purple II.698sd (**purpel** *n.*)

purpos(e) *n.* purpose, intention *1A*36; I.46, 250 etc. (**purpos** *n.*)

purpose *v. 1sg.pr.* intend, be determined I.39; *imp.pl.* **purpose** I.138 (**purposen** *v.*)

purs(e) *n.* purse, money bag II.1646; I.83 (**purs(e** *n.*)

pursewe *v.* hunt down, persecute I.1051 (**pursuen** *v.*)

puruyauns, purvyaunce, purvyauns *n.* preparation, provision I.35; I.497; I.101 (**purveiaunce** *n.*)

put, puttyn *v.* put, place I.527, 536 etc.; II.601; *2pl.pr.* **put** II.53; *3pl.pr.* **put** II.698sd, **puttyn** II.698sd; *3pl.pr.subj.* **put** II.1242; *imp.sg./pl.* **put** I.116, 323, 730, 991; *3sg.pa.* **put** II.98; *p.p.* **put** I.286, II.670 etc.; **put on** impute to I.536, II.559; **put up** sheathe II.100 (**putten** *v.*)

quake *see* **qwake**

quyk, qwycke, qweke *adj.* living, live II.1898, 1926; II.1547; I.86, (as *n.*) II.172 (**quik** *adj.*)

qwake, quake *v.* shake, tremble II.1860; II.1505; *3sg.pr.* **qwakyth** I.904, 927, II.1049; *pr.p.* **qwakyng** I.884 (**quaken** *v.*)

qwan *see* **whan** *conj.*

qwarel *n.* quarrel, dispute I.610 (**querele** *n.*)

qwat *see* **what** *pron.*

qweche *see* **wech(e)** *pron.*
qweke *see* **quyk**
qwelle *v.* kill II.1433 (**quellen** *v.*)
qwene *n.* queen 3A22 (**quen(e** *n.2.*)
qwere *n.* choir, company 3A13 (**quer** *n.*)
qwere *see* **wher(e)** *adv.* and *conj.*
qwest *n.* judicial meeting, trial, assise II.1628 (**quest(e** *n.*)
qwethynge *adj.* speaking II.1898 (**quethen** *v.*)
qwhat *see* **what** *pron.*
qwher *see* **wher(e)** *adv.* and *conj.*
qwych *see* **wech(e)** *pron.*
qwycke *see* **quyk**
qwyght *p.p.* *see* **qwyte**
qwyl *see* **whyl(l)**
qwyppys *see* **whippe**
qwyte, qwyght *adj.* free II.587; II.1914 (**quite** *adj.*)
qwytte *v.* acquit, excuse II.1518 (**quiten** *v.*)

ray *adj.* made of a kind of striped cloth I.244sd (see note) (**rai(e** *adj.*)
rather *adv.* sooner I.871 (**rather(e** *adv.comp.*)
rave *v.* act madly/foolishly, become distraught I.1027, II.1154, 1583 (**raven** *v.1.*)
ravyn *n.* crow II.1575 (**raven** *n.*)
rawnsom *n.* ransom II.848 (**raunsoun** *n.*)
rebuke *n.* shame, reproach II.507; *n.pl.* **rebukys** I.56 (**rebuke** *n.*)
receyve, reseyve *v.* receive (the sacrament), take I.722, 726, 755, 758; I.754; *imp.pl.* **reseyve** II.92; *3sg.pr.subj.* **receyve** 2A8; *p.p.* **reseyvyd** I.770sd (**receiven** *v.*)
recomende *v.* *1sg.pr.* commend I.253 (**recommenden** *v.*)
record(e) *n.* witness, testimony, record II.212, 338; II.1776 (**record(e** *n.*)
record(e) *v.* testify, remember II.344; I.338 (**recorden** *v.*)
recure, recuryn *v.* obtain, cure, regain I.433, 517; II.300; *3sg.pa.* **recuryd** I.38 (**recuren** *v.*)
red, reed *adj.* red I.208sd, II.1005; II.1749 (**red** *adj.*)
rede, reed *n.* advice, counsel I.541; II.1620 (**red** *n.1.*)
rede *adv.* quickly, readily II.1449 (see note) (**rad(e** *adv.*)
rede *see also* **redyn**
redem *v.* redeem, save I.892; *p.p.* **redemyd** I.942 (**redemen** *v.*)
redy *adj.* ready, prepared I.261, 406sd etc. (**redi** *adj.3.*)
redy *adv.* conveniently II.1280 (**redi** *adv.*)
redyn *v.* advise, read II.874sd; *1sg.pr.* **rede** I.194, II.1077 (**reden** *v.1.*)
redolens *n.* fragrance I.406 (**redolence** *n.*)
redresse *v.* set right, amend I.367 (**redressen** *v.*)
redrure *n.* harshness, rigour I.373 (**reddour** *n.*)
reducyd *p.p.* brought back, recalled I.932 (**reducen** *v.*)

reed *see* **red** *adj.*; **rede** *n.*

refeccyon *n.* sustenance, nourishment 3A36 (**refeccioun** *n.*)

reforme *v.* 2pl.pr. put right, amend I.129 (**reformen** *v.*)

refuse *v.* reject, deny I.997; 3sg.pa. **refusyd** II.506 (**refusen** *v.*)

regyon *n.* district, territory II.367 (**regioun(e** *n.*)

rehers *v.* repeat, enumerate, speak I.117, 288; *p.p.* **rehercyd** I.695 (**rehersen** *v.*)

rehersall, rehersayl *n.* speech, words I.375, 3A12 (**rehersail(le** *n.*)

reyn *n.* kingdom, rule I.565, 796 (**regne** *n.1.*)

reyn *n.* reign, exist, live I.173; *1sg.pr.* **reyne** II.487; *3sg.pr.subj.* **reyn** I.170; *3sg.pa.* **reyned** II.1401 (**regnen** *v.*)

reynes *n.* fine linen cloth (from Rennes) I.74 (**rainees** *n.*)

reynes *n.pl.* loins I.672, 731 (**reine** *n.2.*)

reyse *v.* raise II.1011, (*inf.* + 'it') **reysynt** I.562, II.806; *p.p.* **reysed** II.1494 (**reisen** *v.1.*)

rekenyng *vbl.n.* **to make rekenyng** to give an account II.160 (**rekening(e** *ger.*)

reknyd *p.p.* named, counted up; **reknyd be rowe** individually one after another II.1041 (**rekenen** *v.*)

relacyon *n.* **make/gyf** (. . .) **relacyon** give an account I.258, II.346 (**relacioun** *n.*)

releve *v.* relieve, aid 1A20 (**releven** *v.*)

remeffe, remeve *v.* remove, depart, move off I.122; I.907; *imp.sg.* **remeve** I.922; *p.p.* **remevyd** II.1823 (**remeven** *v.*)

rememberawns *n.* memory I.25 (**remembrawns** *n.*)

remembyr *v.* 3pl.pr. remember, recall, reflect on, consider II.746; *imp.sg.* **remembyr** 2A127; *imp.pl.* **remembre** I.121, 189, 285, **remembyr** I.886; *p.p.* **remembryd** I.47 (**remembren** *v.*)

remeve, remevyd *see* **remeffe**

remyssyon *n.* forgiveness, pardon I.40 (**remissioun** *n.*)

rend(e) *v.* tear (apart), wound II.36; I.1060; *p.p.* **rent** I.95, II.940 etc. (**renden** *v.*)

renne, rennyn *v.* run, hasten, come, flow I.804, II.854sd, 1792; I.1032sd; *1sg.pr.* **renne** II.1794; *1pl.pr.* **renne** II.1797; *3pl.pr.* **rennyn** I.25; *pr.p.* **rennyng** II.89sd, 543sd, 1142sd (**rennen** *v.1.*)

renown *n.* distinction, reputation II.814 (**renoun** *n.*)

repent *v.* feel regret, be sorry, repent I.179, 328, 994; *1pl.pr.subj.* **repent** I.293, 535 (**repenten** *v.*)

replye *v.* 2pl.pr.subj. respond I.710 (see note) (**replien** *v.1.*)

repref(f), repreve *n.* reproof, censure, rebuke, scorn, disgrace I.84; I.116; I.527; *n.pl.* **reprevys** I.51; **withowt repreff** without dispute 1A24 (**repreve** *n.*)

repreff *v.* 3pl.pr. reprove, rebuke, censure I.76; *3sg.pr.subj.* **repreve** I.91 (**repreven** *v.*)

reprevable *adj.* blameworthy I.219 (**reprevable** *adj.*)

repreve *see* **repref(f)** *n.*; **repreff** *v.*

request *n.* desire, wish II.483, 1118 (**request(e** *n.*)

requyryth *v. 3sg.pr.* requires, demands II.88 (**requeren** *v.*)

reseyve, reseyvyd *see* **receyve**

resemblauns *n.* appropriateness, likeness I.67 (see note to I.66–7) (**resemb-launce** *n.*)

resyn *see* **ryse**

resystens *n.* opposition I.379, II.384 (**resistence** *n.*)

reson *n.* good sense, understanding, rational thought I.28, 213 etc.; **is reson** is reasonable/appropriate I.572, 2A128; (**resoun** *n.2.*)

reson *see also* **ryse**

resonable *adj.* reasonable, moderate I.623 (**resonable** *adj.2.*)

resorte *v.* come, return I.408; *pr.p.* **resortyng** I.662sd (**resorten** *v.*)

rest, resste *n.* rest, repose I.920, 953, II.523; 2A111 (**rest(e** *n.1.*)

rest *v.* rest, sleep, be at ease, delay, stay, dwell, pause I.480, II.87 etc. *3sg.pr.* **restyth** II.310 is vested, 2A64sd (**resten** *v.1.*)

restore *v.* restore, give back II.854; *imp.sg.* **restore** I.432 (**restoren** *v.*)

returne *v.* return, go back 2A46 (**returnen** *v.*)

reve *v.* steal, snatch (away) II.892; *p.p.* **revid** II.1509 (**reven** *v.*)

reverens, reuerens *n.* honour, veneration I.512, 758, II.27; I.404, II.1199sd **do reuerens** bow (**reverence** *n.*)

reverent *adj.* honoured I.245, 1037, II.25 (**reverent(e** *adj.*)

revyfe *v.* revive, give life again to I.422; *3sg.pr.* **revyfe** I.197 (**reviven** *v.*)

rew(e) *v.* regret, mourn, grieve, feel compassion I.650; II.1166, 1203, 1497 (**reuen** *v.1.*)

reward *v.* reward I.7, 10, 852 (**rewarden** *v.*)

reward(e) *n.* reward II.121; I.518 (**reward** *n.*)

rewelerys *n.pl.* leaders, authorities I.317 (**reuler(e** *n.*)

rewful *adj.* pitiful II.703 (**reuful** *adj.*)

rewly *adj.* woful II.543sd (**reuli** *adj.1.*)

rewthe *n.* shame, pity II.630 (**reuth(e** *n.*)

ryalté *n.* magnificence, sovereign dignity/state I.446 (**roialté** *n.*)

ryches *n.* wealth 2A119, 3A1 (**riches(se** *n..*)

ryde *v.* ride I.384, II.1606, 1A35; *3sg.pr.* **rydyth** 1A43sd; *3sg.pr.subj.* **ryde** II.1322; *imp.pl.* **rydyth** II.1647 (**riden** *v.*)

ryght *see* **ryth** *adj.* and *adv.*

ryme *v. 3sg.pr.subj.* agree, match, be in proportion (see note to I.77–8) I.79 (**rimen** *v.1.*)

rynggyng *adj.* noisy II.487 (**ringen** *v.2.*)

ryse, rysyn *v.* rise, get up I.865, II.111 etc.; I.976sd, II.696sd etc.; *3sg.pr.* **ryseth** II.990, **rysyth** 2A128sd; *3pl.pr.* **rysyn** I.976sd; *3sg.pr.subj.* **ryse** II.1274; *imp.pl.* **ryse** I.957; *p.p.* **resyn** II.1478, 1487 etc., **reson** II.1211, **rysyn** II.1449, 1809 (**risen** *v.*)

ryth *n.* right I.216, 548, II.704 (**right** *n.*)

ryth, ryght *adj.* right, straight, true, proper I.135, 137 etc.; II.1677 (**right** *adj.*)

ryth, ryght *adv.* truly, just, very, at all, directly II.27, 136 etc.; II.1045, 1952 etc. (**right(e** *adv.*)

rythful *adj.* righteous II.251 (**rightful** *adj.*)

rythwysnesse *n.* justice, right II.57 (**right-wisnes(se** *n.*)

ro *n.* roe-deer II.1665 (**ro** *n.1.*)

roberych *n.* rubric, stage-direction I.828sd (**rubrich(e** *n.*)

rochand *n.* ?regent, ruler II.487 (see note) (cf. **rochand** *n.*)

rode, rood *n.* cross I.764, II.3 etc.; II.1821 (**rode** *n.5.*)

root *n.* **on root** upright, firm II.1363 (see note to II.1362–7) (**rote** *n.4.*)

rop *n.* rope II.763, 771; *n.pl.* **ropys** II.698sd, 765 (**rop** *n.2.*)

rowe *n.* row, order; **reknyd be rowe** individually one after another II.1041 (**reue** *n.2.*)

rownd *adv.* round; **vnclose rownd abowtyn** be opened up (by drawing back curtains around the sides) I.662sd; **rownd abowth** around II.89sd (**round(e** *adv.*)

rownde *adj.* round I.1001 (**round(e** *adj.*)

rowth *n.* gang, company II.95, 487 (**rout(e** *n.1.*)

rowth *v.impers. 3sg.pa.* (with present meaning) **Of here acusyng me rowth nowth** Their accusing is of no concern to me II.286 (see note) (**recchen** *v.2.*)

sabath *n.* the Jewish sabbath II.1138 (see note) (cf. **Sabat** *n.*)

sacryd *p.p.* consecrated I.685, 814 (**sacren** *v.*)

sacryfyce *n.* sacrifice, offering I.684, 686 (**sacrifice** *n.*)

sad *adj.* sorrowful I.884sd, II.1904 (**sad** *adj.*)

sadde *adv.* sorrowfully II.1861 (**sad** *adv.*)

sadelys *n.pl.* saddles II.1645 (**sadel** *n.*)

sadly *adv.* carefully, seriously II.1618 (**sadli** *adv.*)

saff *adj.* safe II.265 (**sauf** *adj.*)

say(e), sayd, sayn, sayng *see* **sey(e)**

sayn *see also* **se(n)**

sake *n.* **for . . . sake** out of consideration for I.909, 958 etc. (**sake** *n.*)

saluacyon *n.* salvation, deliverance I.42 (**savacioun** *n.*)

salve *n.* healing ointment II.1719, 3A6; *n.pl.* **salvys** II.1674 (**salve** *n.1.*)

salvyn *v.* heal I.347, 1A48; *imp.sg.* **salve** amend 2A14 (**salven** *v.*)

same *pron.* same I.342, 409, II.219, 1350 (**sam(e** *pron.*)

same *adj.* same I.662, 708 etc. (**sam(e** *adj.*)

Sarazyn *n.* Saracen, Arab I.164sd (see note) (**Sarasin(e** *n.*)

satan *n.* satin I.105 (**satin** *n.*)

saue, save, sawe *v.* save, rescue, protect, redeem, retrieve II.1221, 1381 etc.; I.570, 824 etc.; I.1024; *3sg.pr.subj.* **save** II.1138; *imp.sg.* **saue** I.1003; *p.p.* **savyd** I.698, 912 etc. (**saven** *v.*)

savyng *conj.* except that I.208sd, 406sd (**saving** *prep.*)

savyour *n.* saviour II.58, 1736 (**saveour** *n.*)
saw *see* **se(n)**
sawe *n.* word, remark, saying, decree II.320, 1641 (**sau(e** *n.2.*)
sawe *see also* **saue**
scafald, schaffald(e), shaffald, skaffald, skafhald *n.* stage, scaffold II.377sd; II.543sd, 696sd; II.1sd; II.866sd; II.235sd, 880sd; I.208sd; *n.pl.* **schaffaldys** II.1sd, **skaffaldys** II.1311sd (**scaffold** *n.*)
schafftys *n.pl.* spears II.1334 (**shaft** *n.2.*)
schake *see* **shake**
schal *see* **xal(l)**
schame *see* **shame**
schapyn *v.* (?*inf.*) devise, cause II.1335 (see note to II.1332–5) (**shapen** *v.*)
schapman *n.* merchant, dealer I.618; *n.pl.* **chapmen** I.623 (**chap-man** *n.*)
sche *see* **she**
schent *see* **shende**
schep *n.pl.* sheep I.810
schewyn(g) *see* **shew(e)**
schon *see* **shon**
schonde *n.* ruin, destruction II.1335 (**Shond** *sb¹.*)
schrewde *see* **shrewde**
schuld *see* **xal(l)**
sclayn *see* **sle(n)**
sclep *see* **slepp**
sclepe, sclepyng *see* **slepe**
scorgys *n.pl.* whips, scourges II.456 (**scourge** *n.*)
scorn, skorn(e) *n.* taunt, indication of contempt II.909; a contemptible thing I.23; **hast þu scorn/skorne** do you disdain II.165; II.447, 731 (**scorn** *n.*)
scorn *v.* deride, jeer at II.1573; *pr.p.* **skornyng** II.698sd (**scornen** *v.*)
scrypture *n.* the Bible *3A*39 (**scriptur(e** *n.*)
se *n.* seat II.914 (**se** *n.2.*)
se(n) *v.* see, understand, behold, discover, ensure I.109, 198 etc.; I.299, 605 etc.; *1sg.pr.* **se** I.501, II.956 etc.; *2sg.pr.* **seyst** I.961, II.796; *3sg.pr.* **seyth** I.22, II.858; *1pl.pr.* **se** I.188; *2pl.pr.* **se** II.195, 970; *3pl.pr.* **se** I.438, **seen** I.406sd; *imp.sg.* **se** II.556; *imp.pl.* **se** I.492, II.623, 867, 1107; *1sg.pa.* **saw** II.1925 **sey** II.198, 938; *3sg.pa.* **sey** II.1172; *1pl.pa.* **saw** II.1823, 1834, **sowe** I.631; *p.p.* **sen** I.1022, **sene** I.153, **seen** I.454, **seyn** II.1916, **sayn** II.1523 (**sen** *v.1.*)
seal(e), sele *n.* seal II.1284; II.1296; II.1281 (**sel(e** *n.3.*)
seche *see* **such(e)**
second, secunde *ord.num.* second I.920sd; I.364 (**second** *num.*)
seel *see* **sel**
seen *see* **se(n)**
sees *see* **ses(e)**
sefne *see* **sevyn**

sey(e), seyn, say(e), sayn *v.* say, tell, explain, speak I.473, 555 etc.; I.531, II.815; I.452, 775sd etc.; I.225, 314 etc.; II.1075; I.733; *1sg.pr.* **say** I.18, II.172 etc., **saye** II.1741, **sey** I.537, II.169, 213, 1350; *2sg.pr.* **seyst** I.776, II.162 etc.; *3sg.pr.* **seyth** I.42, 305 etc., **seyt** 2A128sd; *1pl.pr.* **say** II.670, 1524, **sey** II.599, **seye** II.178, **seyn** II.652, 668; *2pl.pr.* **say** I.269, II.590 etc., **sey** II.659, 669, **seyn** II.322, 481; *2pl.pr.subj.* **say** I.471; *imp.sg.* **sey** II.127, 229, 1883, **say** I.91, 530; *imp.pl.* **sey** II.372, 1642, 1644, 1782, *1A11*; *pr.p.* **seyng** I.164sd, 208sd etc., **sayng** I.256sd, 442sd; *1sg.pa.* **seyd** II.223; *3sg.pa.* **seyd** I.559, II.106 etc., **sayd** II.1755; *1pl.pa.* **seyd** II.105; *3pl.pa.* **seyd** II.1822, **seydyn** I.858; *p.p.* **seyd** I.20, 191 etc., **seyde** I.617, **sayd** II.414, 711 (**seien** *v.1.*)
sey, seyst, seyth *see also* **se(n)**
seyl *see* **sel**
seyn *n.* sign I.106
seyn *see also* **se(n)**; **sey(e)**
seynt, sen *n.* saint, holy one II.1347; II.790sd (**seint(e** *n.*)
seyse *n.* assise I.114
seke *v.* seek, search, look for, afflict, find, come I.219, 476 etc.; *1sg.pr.* **seke** I.1035; *1pl.pr.* **seke** I.969, 981; *2pl.pr.* **seke** I.968, 977; *imp.sg.* **seke** II.1741; *1sg.pa.* **sowght** II.1903, **sowth** 2A49; *1pl.pa.* **sowth** II.104; *p.p.* **sowth** I.77, 97 etc., **sought** II.930, **sowght** 2A19 (**sechen** *v.*)
sekyr *adj.* sure, certain I.782, II.1278, 1282 (**Sicker** *a.* and *adv.*)
sekyr *adv.* truly II.1632 (**Sicker** *a.* and *adv.*)
sekyrly *adv.* surely, certainly II.1266
sel, seyl, seel *n.* time I.786, 989, II.181; II.116; II.161 (**sel(e** *n.1.*)
seldyst *see* **selle**
sele *v.* seal II.1273; *1sg.pr.* **sele** II.1285; *imp.pl.* **sele** II.1289; *p.p.* **selyd** II.1277 (**selen** *v.*)
sele *see also* **seal(e)**
selle *v.* sell I.106, 586 etc.; *3sg.pr.* **sellyth** 2A100; *2sg.pa.* **seldyst** II.256; *3sg.pa.* **solde** II.13, 496, 1775; *1sg.pa.subj.* **solde** 2A87; *p.p.* **solde** I.649, 777, 783, 1042 (**sellen** *v.*)
semyth *v.impers.* *3sg.pr.* seems II.902, 1048; **as semyth me** as it seems to me I.394 (*see also* **mesemyth**) (**semen** *v.2.*)
semly *adj.* splendid, fine II.236 (**semeli** *adj.*)
sen *n.* *see* **seynt**
sen(e) *see* **se(n)**
send(e) *v.* send I.466; I.632, II.394, 2A28; *3sg.pr.* **sendyth** I.34, II.380, 566; *3sg.pr.subj.* **send** II.539, **sende** II.988; *2pl.pr.subj.* **sende** I.194; *imp.pl.* **send** I.186, 337; *sg./pl./pa.* **sent** II.119, 388, 576, 1A23; *p.p.* **sent** I.246, 252 etc. (**senden** *v.2.*)
sensyble *adj.* apparent to the senses I.209 (see note to I.209–10) (**sensible** *adj.*)
sensual *adj.* physical I.28 (**sensual** *adj.*)
sensualyté *n.* sensuality, physical indulgence I.153 (**sensualité** *n.*)

sentens *n.* words, meaning, opinion, statement I.378, 744, II.427 (**sentence** *n.*)

senues *n.pl.* sinews II.768

separacyon *n.* **make separacyon** separate itself I.44 (**separacioun** *n.*)

septer *n.* sceptre II.698 sd (**ceptre** *n.*)

sepulcre *n.* sepulchre, tomb II.1199sd, 1732 (**sepulcre** *n.*)

ser(e), syr *n.* sir I.274, 289 etc.; I.3, 185 etc.; II.1268, 1300 etc.; *n.pl.* **serys** I.177, 241 etc.

serge *n.* search II.80 (**serch(e** *n.*)

seryattly *adv.* in succession, one after another I.754 (**seriatli** *adv.*)

sertayn, serteyn *adj. see* **certayn** *adj.*

sertayn, serteayn, serteyn *adv. see* **certeyn** *adv.*

serteynly *adv.* truly II.1626 (**certainli** *adv.*)

sertys *adv.* certainly, indeed II.1610 (**certes** *adv.*)

servaunt *n.* servant I.514, II.934; *n.pl.* **seruauntys** I.121, **servauntys** I.117 (**servaunt** *n.*)

serve *v.* obey, serve, give allegiance to I.11, 462; *1sg.pr.* **serue** II.986; *3sg.pr.subj.* **serve** I.7, II.491; *p.p.* **servid** treated II.1511 (**serven** *v.1.*)

servyce *n.* attention, service I.830, 833 (**servis(e** *n.*)

ses(e), sesse, ces *v.* cease, stop, end II.1240, 1585, 1590; I.247; I.675; II.100; *imp.pl.* **sees** II.21, 470 (**cesen** *v.*)

sessyon *n.* legal assembly, session (of a court) I.114 (**sessioun** *n.*)

set(t), settyn *v.* set, place, put, fix, arrange, value, sit II.1155sd; I.804sd, II.1938; II.181sd, 790sd, 874sd, (*inf.* + 'it') **settynt** II.152; *3sg.pr.* **settyth** I.840sd, 908sd; *3pl.pr.* **settyn** II.698sd; *2sg.pr.subj.* **sett** I.93; imp.sg. **sett** I.94, **sette** I.76; imp.pl. **set** II.779, 787, **sett** II.1281; *pr.p.* **settyng** II.790sd; *3sg.pa.* **sett** II.101; *p.p.* **set** I.663, II.782sd, **sett** I.66, II.905, 1296, 1645; **sette hem at nowth** pay no heed to them I.76, **sett not be** have no regard for I.93 (**setten** *v.*)

sete *n.* seat II.1087 (**sete** *n.2.*)

sethyn *see* **sythyn** *conj.*

seuere *v.* separate, distinguish I.216 (see note) (**severen** *v.*)

sevyle *adj.* civil (law) I.94 (see note) (**civil(e** *adj.*)

sevyn, sefne *num.* seven I.130; II.1914; (as roman numeral II.1680, 1843, 2A34, 41) (**seven** *num.*)

sew(e) *v.* seek, follow, go 2A12; I.148, II.562; *pr.p.* **sewyng** I.738 (**seuen** *v.1.*)

sewre *see* **sure**

shaffald *see* **scafald**

shake, schake *v.* shake, tremble II.1582; I.899, 928; *p.p.* **shake** II.1506 (**shaken** *v.*)

shal *see* **xal(l)**

shame, schame *n.* shame, disgrace 2A13, 80; I.286, 322; **haue grett shame** be greatly ashamed 2A13 (**shame** *n.*)

shameful *adv.* ignominiously, shamefully I.1068

shamfast *adj.* shy, bashful I.99 (**shamefast(e** *adj.*)
shamful, shameful *adj.* ignominious, shaming II.794, 1235; I.568 (**shameful(le** *adj.*)
shamfully *adv.* ignominiously, shamefully II.966; 2A72 (**shamefulli** *adv.*)
shape *v.* go, escape II.1237 (**shapen** *v.*)
sharp(e) *adj.* sharp II.1140; II.514 (**sharp** *adj.*)
she, sche *pron.* she I.102, 108, II.543sd, 2A38; II.537, 539, 543sd, 742sd (**she** *pron.*)
shede *n.* sheath I.991
shende *v.* ruin, destroy, damn, disgrace 2A88; *p.p.* **shent** I.315, 534, 730, 996, **schent** I.1068, II.569
shert *n.* shirt I.73 (see note), II.543sd; *n.pl.* **shertys** II.656sd, **shyrtys** I.406sd
shete *n.* (winding-)sheet, shroud II.1798, 1802, 1806
shete *v. imp.sg.* shoot 3A4
shew(e), shove, shewyn *v.* show, make known, display, present, reveal I.692, II.431; I.373, 825, 898, II.20sd, 1051; I.147; I.164sd; *1sg.pr.* **shewe** I.709; *3sg.pr.* **shewyth** I.208sd, 295, 696; *3pl.pr.* **schewyn** I.244sd; *imp.sg.* **shewe** I.1015; *pr.p.* **shewyng** I.385, 662sd, II.377sd, **schewyng** I.518sd; *1pl.pa.* **shewyd** II.9; *p.p.* **shewyd** I.420, 677, II.8, 387 **shewyth** II.273 (see note)
shyneth *v. 3sg.pr.* shines II.1409
shyrtys *see* **shert**
shytt *p.p.* shut, confined, secured 2A45, 112
shon, schon *n.pl.* shoes I.128; I.69, 673, 735, 738
short *adj.* brief, short I.124, 241 etc.
shortly *adv.* for a short time, briefly II.774sd
shove *see* **shew(e)**
show *v. imp.sg.* shove, thrust II.1142; *3sg.pr.* **showyth** II.1142sd
shrewde, shrewyd, schrewde *adj.* bad, difficult, injurious, dangerous II.529; II.523; I.525
shrylle *adj.* loud, clear II.1760
shryve *v.* confess II.1919
syde *n.* side, part I.142, 143 etc.; *n.pl.* **sydys** II.1729
syde *adj.* long I.85 (see note) (**Side** *a.*)
syght, syth(te) *n.* sight, spectacle II.956, 959 etc.; I.432, II.102 etc.; II.64
sylk *n.* silk II.698sd
sylver, syluer, sylvyr *n.* silver I.612, 619, II.1623, 2A97; I.72; 2A90
sympyl *adj.* poor, common, ordinary I.468, II.790sd
symulacyon *n.* deceit, pretence II.273
syn *conj.* since, seeing (that) I.1073, II.199 etc.
syn(ne) *n.* sin I.232; I.5, 13 etc.; *n.pl...* **synnys** 2A6
synagog *n.* synagogue II.135
syndony *n.* fine linen cloth, shroud II.1180 (see note)
synful *adj.* sinful, wicked I.716, II.221 etc.

syng *v.* sing, cry I.8; *3pl.pr.* **synggyn** I.410sd
synke *v.* sink, fall *2A*83
synners *n.pl.* sinners I.10
synnyst *v. 2sg.pr.* sin I.154; *3sg.pa.* **synnyd** II.1061; *p.p.* **synnyd** II.250
syr *see* **ser(e)**
systeryn, systerys *n.pl.* sisters II.1672, 1782; II.1697; *n.poss.* **systerys**
    II.1688
syt(t), syttyn *v.* sit, be placed, be fitting/appropriate, remain I.770sd,
    II.654; I.790, II.1284; II.1574; *3sg.pr.* **syttyth** I.394, II.235sd, 656sd, 1087;
    imp.pl. **syt** I.827; *pr.p.* **syttyng(e)** I.518sd, 662sd, II.716; *2A*69
syth(e) *adv.* afterwards II.18; I.295
syth(e) *conj.* since, seeing that I.24, 391; II.961
syth(te) *n. see* **syght**
sythe *v.* sigh II.1860
sythyn *adv.* then, afterwards I.549, 766sd, 840sd, II.515
sythyn, sethyn *conj.* since, seeing that I.768; II.550, *1A*27
skaffald(ys), skafhald *see* **scafald**
skarlet *adj.* scarlet, bright red I.164sd (see note)
skylle *n.* capability, (good) sense *2A*29, 55
skyp(pe) *v.* jump, skip, escape II.509; II.463
skorgyn *v.* scourge, beat II.696sd; *imp.pl.* **skorge** II.682; *p.p.* **skorgyd**
    II.698sd
skorn(e) *see* **scorn** *n.*
skornfully *adv.* scornfully, contemptuously II.866sd
skornyng *see* **scorn** *v.*
slake *v.* bring to an end, diminish, abate II.888, 897, *3A*8
slawe *adj.* slow, sluggish I.330
sle(n) *v.* kill, slay II.917, 1761; II.323; *3pl.pr.* **slew** II.1003; *p.p.* **slayn**
    II.1527, 1772, 1812, **sclayn** II.1009
slepe *v. 1sg.pr.* sleep II.1358; *2sg.pr.* **slepyst** I.917; *imp.sg.* **sclepe** I.918; *pr.p.*
    slepyng II.549, **sclepyng** I.916sd, 952sd
slepp, sclep *n.* sleep II.1346; I.954
smal(e) *adj.* small, narrow I.87; I.79
smert *adj.* keen, severe II.948
smet *see* **smyte**
smyte *v.* strike, hit I.990, II.141sd; *3sg.pr.* **smytyth** I.990sd, **smyth** I.992;
    imp.pl. **smyth** I.625 (see note); *2sg.pa.* **smet** II.205; *p.p.* **smet(e)** II.514,
    689; I.992
so(o) *adv., conj.* so, thus, such, as I.7, 10 etc.; II.1511
soch *see* **such(e)**
socowre *n.* help, aid *2A*28 (**Succour** *sb.*)
sodeynly *adv.* all of a sudden, straightaway I.453, 518sd etc.
soevyr *see* **what(t)**
sofer(e), sofre, suffer, suffyr, suffre *v.* suffer, allow, accept, undergo
    I.1054; I.1050; I.474, 952, 1065; I.970; II.472, 1499; II.853; *1sg.pr.* **suffre**

I.681; *3sg.pr.* **soferyth** II.1058, **sufferyth** II.949; *3pl.pr.* **sufferyn** II.963; *imp.pl.* **sofre** I.828; *1sg.pa.* **sufferyd** II.1891; *3sg.pa.* **suffryd** II.1501; *p.p.* **soferyd** II.1386, **sofryd** II.1441

soferauns *n.* permission, grace II.5

sofreynes *see* **sovereyn** *n.*

softyd *p.p.* soothed, alleviated II.1725, 1728

sokelyng *n.*?honeysuckle, ?clover I.668, 715 (see note to I.667–70)

sokyn *p.p.* sucked II.1404

sokyng *vbl.n.* **ȝevyn sokyng** provide milk II.712

solace, solas *n.* comfort, delight II.1465, 1889; I.1038

solde *see* **selle**

solemnyté *n.* **for þe solemnyté** because of the religious importance II.661

som(e), sum *pron.* some I.294, 355, II.252; I.57, 359 etc.; *1A6;* **all and som** every bit II.252

som(e), sum *adj.* some I.536, 582 etc.; I.523, 585; I.104, 542 etc.

somdel, sumdel *adv.* somewhat, a bit II.180; *2A7*

somewhath, somwhat *n.* a certain amount, something II.132; II.508

somtyme *adv.* at a certain time II.1185

son(e) *n.* son I.41, II.66, 1165, 1168; I.26, 294 etc.; *n.poss.* **sonys** II.973

son(e), soon *adv.* at once, soon I.299; I.29, II.49 etc.; II.1085

sonest *adv.* soonest I.451

songe *n.* song *2A64*

sonn-bem *n.* sunbeam *3A18*

sonne *see* **sunne**

sool *n.* sole I.68

soon *see* **son(e)** *adv.*

sopere *n.* supper I.482

sore *adj.* grievous, severe, great II.62, 852 etc.

sore *adv.* intensely, much, greatly, grievously, earnestly, hard I.650, 904 etc.

sory *adj.* distressed, sad, sorry, grievous I.793, II.1402 etc.

sorwatorie *n.* ?sorrowing, ?suffering II.1019 (see note)

sorwe *n.* distress, grief, suffering, lamentation I.12, 785 etc.

sorwef(f)ul *adj.* sad, grieving, doleful I.1047, II.718; *2A30*

sorwyn *v.* grieve, mourn II.1865

soserye *n.* sorcery, witchcraft II.402

sote *see* **swete** *adj.*

sotely, sotylly *adv.* craftily, inconspicuously I.647; I.650sd

soth *n.* truth II.1746

soth *adj.* true II.213

sothfast *adj.* true II.1409

sotyl(le) *adj.* cunning, crafty, cleverly contrived I.576, 653, II.404; I.27 (**Subtle** *a.*)

sotylté *n.* cleverness, cunning, ingenuity, trick, scheme I.59, 119, 523, II.422; *n.pl.* **sotyltés** I.540

souereyn, sovereyn *n.* lord I.205, 245; II.78; *n.pl.* **sofreynes** (a term of polite address to the audience) II.1

sovereyn *adj.* sovereign, supreme, excellent II.50, 58 etc.

sought *see* **seke**

soule, soulys *see* **sowle**

sowe *v.* sow, spread, beget I.13, II.1402

sowe *see also* **se(n)**

sowght *see* **seke**

sowle, soule *n.* soul I.417, 892 etc.; I.44, 714; *n.pl.* **sowlys** I.23, 121, 1024, **soulys** II.20, 287

sowle-drynk *n.* spiritual drink, refreshment for the soul II.1008

sownde *adj.* unharmed I.1003

sowth *see* **seke**

space, spas *n.* time, while I.264, 489; II.263

spak *see* **speke**

spare *v.* spare, hold back, deal gently with I.1074; *3sg.pr.subj.* **spare** 2A7; *imp.sg./pl.* **spare** I.1005, II.440 etc.

spas *see* **space**

spech(e) *n.* speech, speaking, words I.778sd; II.1673, 1789, 1919

specyal *adj.* particular II.1673 (but see note)

specyfye *v.* set out, lay down precisely I.708

spede *v.* further, prosper, hasten, fulfil I.930, II.231, 370, 1A30; *3sg.pr.subj.* **sped** II.761; *imp.sg.* **sped** I.787; *p.p.* **sped** II.374

speke, spekyn *v.* speak I.200, 350 etc.; I.694sd, II.523sd; *2sg.pr.* **spekyst** II.138, 434 etc.; *3pl.pr.* **spekyth** I.398sd; *3pl.pr.subj.* **speke** I.202; *imp.sg.* **spek** II.164, 438, 454; *1sg.pa.* **spak** II.1930; *3pl.pa.* **spoke** I.857; *p.p.* **spoke** II.833

spelle *n.* words, talk 2A125

spelle *v.* relate, declare I.4

sperd *p.p.* fastened, bolted II.534 (**Spar** *v¹.*)

spere *n.* spear II.514, 1139, 1142sd, 1701

spetously *adv.* shamefully, cruelly I.1044 (**Spitously** *adv.*)

spyes *n.pl.* spies, informers I.337

spyl, spyll(e) *v.* destroy, spoil, kill, perish, spill II.475; I.220; I.914, II.567 etc.; *p.p.* **spylt** II.309

spyryte *n.* spirit, soul II.915; *n.pl.* **spyritys** 2A36

spyteful *adj.* shameful II.1892

spyttyn *v.* spit II.181sd

splayed *p.p.* opened out, displayed I.105 (**Splay** *v¹.*)

spoke *see* **speke**

spot *n.* spot, blemish I.703

spovse *n.* spouse, bride I.892

sprede *v.* lay out, cover I.406sd, 731

spryng *v.* arise I.410

staf(f) *n.* staff, rod I.739; I.164sd; *n.pl.* **stauys** I.741, **stavys** I.673

stage *n.* scaffold, platform, stage I.164sd
stake *n.* stick, post II.1330, 1442; **stele stake** sword II.1330
stalke *v.* creep, walk stealthily II.1340
stall *n.* stall, shed II.1691
stand, standyn, stond(e), stondyn *v.* stand II.786sd; II.750; I.671, II.658; I.174, 610 etc.; II.377sd, 1036; *1sg.pr.* **stonde** *3A9*; *2sg.pr.* **standyst** II.126, **stondyst** II.435, 1846; *3sg.pr.* **standyth** *1A5*, **stant** II.361, **stondyth** *2A96*; *1pl.pr.* **stounde** II.1611; *2pl.pr.* **stondys** II.665; *3pl.pr.* **stande** II.1122sd; *pr.p.* **standyng** II.109, 656sd, **stondyng** I.164sd; *3sg.pa.* **stod** II.110; *1pl.pa.* **stodyn** I.671
stauys, stavys *see* **staf(f)**
stedfast *adv.* unshakenly, steadfastly I.428
stedfastly *adv.* unshakenly, firmly I.442, II.299
stey *v.* ascend II.1884
stele *n.* steel II.1311
stele *v.* steal II.1294, 1298, 1323; *3pl.pr.subj.* **stele** II.1209; *p.p.* **stolyn** II.1832, 1845, 1852
stele *adj.* steel II.1330
steppys *n.pl.* footsteps I.738
stylle *adj.* unmoving, quiet II.111, 435 etc.
stylle *adv.* yet, still, always I.906, 952sd etc.
stynk *n.* stench I.790
styrte *v.* go, escape II.512; *2sg.pr.subj.* **styrte** I.199
stod, stodyn *see* **stand**
stody *v. imp.sg.* think carefully, consider I.999
stol *n.* stool, seat II.181sd, 698sd; *n.pl.* **stolys** I.288sd
stolyn *see* **stele** *v.*
stomachere *n.* stomacher I.74 (see note)
stomblyd *p.p.* stumbled II.1442
ston *n.* stone I.1046, II.1188 etc.; *n.pl.* **stonys** I.29, II.1508
stond(e), stondys, stondyng, stondyst, stondyth, stounde *see* **stand**
stowte *adj.* strong, valiant II.515
strawnge, straunge *adj.* odd. unusual II.102, 117; I.964sd
streyth *adv.* directly, straight II.1013
strengere *adj.* stronger I.127
strete *n.* street I.469, II.1735
stryff *n.* violence, dispute II.1386, 1739, *3A32*
stryvyn *v.* quarrel, struggle II.790sd
strok, strook *n.* blow, beating II.1386; II.1739
strong *adv.* firmly, boldly II.1241
strong(e) *adj.* strong, resolute, severe, grievous I.955, II.472, 633, 765; II.79, 842, 886, 922
stuffe *v.* stuff I.78
submyt *v. imp.pl.* **submyt egal** yield equally (to each other) I.847

substawns *n.* reality, importance, essential quality I.362, 757 (see notes to I.362 and 755–8)

subuertyd *p.p.* undermined, overthrown II.127

such(e), seche, soch, swech(e), swych *adj.* such II.1454, 1848, 1849, 2A81; II.1581, 1858; I.563; II.1051; I.401, II.807; I.353; 2A119

sudary *n.* head-cloth II.1803, 1806

suerly *see* **surely**

suete *see* **swete** *adj.*

suffer, suffyr, suffre, sufferyd, sufferyn, sufferyth, suffryd *see* **sofer(e)**

sum *see* **som(e)** *adj.*, **som(e)** *pron.*

sumdel *see* **somdel**

sunne, sonne *n.* sun II.1409, 1689; II.167

suppe *v.* sup, eat I.682

suppoce *see* **suppose**

supporte *n.* assistance, aid I.411

suppose, suppoce *v. 1sg.pr.* believe, understand II.1047; I.1055

sure, sewre *adj.* sure, certain, safe, secure I.644, 747, II.1127, 1254; II.1123

surely, suerly *adv.* truly, certainly I.197; II.1106 definitely

susteyn *v.* uphold, bear, endure I.172, 1057

sustenauns, sustenawns *n.* food, nourishment II.36; I.755

swech(e) *see* **such(e)**

swerd *n.* sword I.989, 991 etc.; *n.pl.* **swerdys** I.658, 964sd, II.15

swere, sweryn *v.* swear II.1553; II.116; *p.p.* **sworn** II.354, 733, 1074

swet *n.* sweat II.740

swete *v. 1sg.pr.* sweat I.936

swete, suete, sote *adj.* sweet, pleasant I.667, 1037 etc.; I.713; 2A23

swych *see* **such(e)**

swonge *v.* swoon, faint II.798sd; *pr.p.* **swuonyng** II.790sd

sworn *see* **swere**

tabbard *n.* tabard, a loose over-garment usually without sleeves and open down the sides I.164sd, 208sd (see notes and Introduction); *n.pl.* **tabardys** I.244sd

tabyl, table *n.* tablet, wooden board, table II.874sd; I.662sd

tayle *n.* retinue, band of followers I.17 (see note)

take *v.* take, receive, capture, arrest, accept, take away, offer I.181, 221 etc.; *1sg.pr.* **take** I.500, 592 etc.; *3sg.pr.* **takyth** I.824sd, 828sd etc.; *1/2pl.pr.* **take** I.669, 920 etc.; *3pl.pr.* **take** II.377sd, **takyn** ?I.662sd, II.1163sd; *2sg./pl.pr.subj.* **take** II.544, 724, 1105, 1249; *imp.sg.* **take** I.910, 933 etc., **takyht** II.266; *imp.pl.* **take** I.322, 608 etc., **takyth** I.18, 21 etc.; *pr.p.* **takyng** II.698sd; *1sg.pa.* **took** II.1416; *3sg.pa.* **toke** II.19, 1577; *1/3pl.pa.* **toke** II.16, 206; *2sg.pa.subj.* **took** II.1871; *p.p.* **take** II.89sd, 93 etc., **takyn** I.544, ?II.1sd

takyng *vbl.n.* capture I.1032sd

takke *v.* fasten II.512; *p.p.* **takkyd** II.775 (see note)

Glossary

tale *n.* story, news, tale II.1621, 1931; *n.pl.* **talys** II.1653, 1670
talk *v.* talk, speak, say I.280; *3pl.pr.* **talkyn** II.84
tame *adj.* tame *1A*38
tary *v.* delay, remain I.126, II.376; *1sg.pr.* **tery** II.243; *2sg.pr.subj.* **tery** II.233; *imp.pl.* **tary** II.1606, **taryeth** II.979
taske *?v.*, *?n.* ?engage in/try out; ?job of work II.1366 (see note to II.1362–7)
tast *n.* taste, flavour II.903
teche *v.* teach I.740, 1023, etc.
techer *n.* teacher, expositor *3A*9
techyng *vbl.n.* instruction, teaching I.811
tekele *v.* *3pl.pr.* tickle I.86
tell(e), tellyn *v.* tell, reckon up, report, speak, work out II.1670; I.222, 269 etc.; I.593; *1sg.pr.* **telle** I.969, 975 etc.; *3sg.pr.* **tellyth** II.89; *1/2pl.pr.* **telle** II.316, 415, 1816; *3pl.pr.* **tellyth** II.63; *2sg.pr.subj.* **telle** II.168; *imp.sg.* **tel(l)** II.330; *2A*94, **telle** I.249, 266 etc.; *imp.pl.* **telle** I.470, 968 etc.; *1sg.pa.* **told(e)** I.983; II.1460; *3sg.pa.* **tolde** II.219, 1777, 1788; *p.p.* **told(e)** I.1047, II.312, 422; I.140, II.1653; obtain, receive (money) I.587, 605
temperal *adj.* temporal, secular I.195
temperawnce *n.* moderation, sobriety I.213
tempyl, temple *n.* temple, the temple in Jerusalem I.561, II.804; I.1022, II.135 etc.; *n.pl.* **templys** I.457
tempt *v.* tempt I.39; *3sg.pa.* **tempte** I.27
temptacyon *n.* temptation II.503, *3A*28
ten *num.* ten II.408, 734 (as roman numeral I.964sd)
tendyth *v.* *3sg.pr.* goes to, intends *2A*95 (see note) (**Tend** *v¹.* or *v².*)
tery *see* **tary**
teryeng *vbl.n.* delay I.659, II.458, 1193
terys *n.pl.* tears II.1839
term *n.* proverb, saying I.58; *n.pl.* **termys** I.617
termynable, termynabyle *adj.* conclusive, final, finally concluded I.216; II.51 (see notes) (**Terminable** *a.*)
testament *n.* covenant, agreement (between God and man) I.799
testefy *v.* assert as true I.52
testymonyall *n.* witness, corroboration I.377
testymonye *n.* evidence, proof II.634
testymonye *v.* bear witness I.338
tetys *n.pl.* breasts II.712
than, þan *conj.* than II.1499, 1864 etc.; I.127, 348 etc.
than(ne), þan(ne) *adv.* then I.324, 525 etc.; II.86, 991; I.9, 21 etc.; I.320
thank(e) *n.* thanks, gratitude I.277, II.419, 726; II.120; **kan/cone ... thank(e)** give thanks to I.277, II.419; II.120
thanke *v.* *1sg.pr.* thank II.1376, *2A*40; *pr.p.* **thankyng** I.692
thankyng *v.* *pr.p.* thanks, gratitude I.688
þar *v.* *2pl.pr.* need I.750 (**Tharf, thar** *v.*)

324 Glossary

that, þat *pron.* that II.1151; I.139, 406 etc.
that, þat *rel.pron.* that, which, who 2A99, 3A16, 23, 26, 38; I.1, 14 etc.; he who, that which, what 2A99; I.404, II.213 etc.
that, þat *adj.* that 2A101; I.470, 476 etc.
that, þat *conj.* that II.412, 1044 etc.; I.8, 80 etc.
the, þe *pron.* thee I.486, 944 etc.; I.78, 91 etc.
the, þe *def.art.* the I.36, 297 etc.; I.5, 14 etc.
the, þe *v. see* **then**
thedyrward *adv.* towards that place I.494sd
thef(f), þeff *n.* thief (and as a term of abuse) II.659, 837; II.923, 1541; II.583, 592; *n.poss.* **thevys** I.1020; *n.pl.* **thevys** II.667, 788 etc.; **þevys** II.786sd, **þewys** II.656sd
they, thei, þei *pron.* they I.195, 410sd etc.; I.1051, II.802; I.107, 120 etc.
them, þem *pl. pron.obj.* them I.406sd, II.656sd etc.; I.804sd, II.92 etc. (*see also* **hem**)
then, the, þe *v.* prosper, thrive II.1265; (in asseveration) **so mote I/moty the** II.102, 203, 769, 1258; (in imprecation) **evyl mot(e) he/þu the/þe** II.751; II.459 (**Thee** *v¹.*)
þer(e) *pron.poss.* their I.406sd, II.1311sd etc.; I.84
ther(e), þer(e) *adv.* there, where II.665; I.112, 178 etc.; I.6, 22 etc.; I.14, 19 etc.
þeratte *adv.* of it II.20
þerbesyde *adv.* a lytyl **þerbesyde** nearby, near to it I.900sd
þerby *adv.* from it I.675, by it, nearby II.1292
theref(f)ore, therfore, þerfor(e) *adv.* therefore I.181; 3A31; II.114, 350 etc.; I.633, 749; I.15, 154 etc.
þerin *adv.* there, in that, in it I.134, 267 etc.
þerof *adv.* of/from/about that I.579, 782 etc.
þeron *adv.* on/about that, on it II.157, 417, 746sd
þerto *adv.* for/to/about that, that, in addition I.582, II.141 etc.
þerupon *adv.* upon/about that I.406sd, 768
þerwhylys *adv.* during that time II.790sd
þerwith *adv.* with it II.1614
thes *see* **this** *pron.*
these, þese *adj.* these I.162, 280 etc.; I.159, 365 etc.
þese *pron.* these I.118, II.1790
þese *see also* **this** *adj.*
thevys, þevys, þewys *see* **thef(f)**
thi, thy(n), þi(n), þine *pron.poss.* thy, thine II.1935; 1A37, 2A87; II.433, 437 etc.; I.78, 85 etc.; I.82, 85 etc.; (used absolutely) II.622
thyng(e), þing(e) *n.* thing, matter (often collective = 'things') I.66, 285 etc.; II.1032, 1034, 1A46; I.345, II.158 etc.; II.28; *n.pl.* **thyngys** I.213, II.166
thynke, thynkyn *v.* think, consider, believe, be of the opinion, intend 2A81; II.225; *1sg.pr.* **thynke** 2A12; *2sg.pr.* **thynkyst** II.471; *2pl.pr.*

Glossary

thynk(e) II.177, 302, 904; II.303; *imp.sg.* **thynk** I.1076; *2pl.pa.* **thowth** I.1053

thynkyth, þinkyth *impers.v. 3sg.pr.* **how thynkyth/þynkyth ȝow** how does it seem to you? II.1252; II.1125

thyrknes *n.* (spiritual) darkness *3A*27

thyrlyd *p.p.* pierced I.1058

this, thes, þis *pron.* this I.233, 763 etc.; I.188; I.20, 103 etc.

this, þese, þis *adj.* this I.341, 723 etc.; I.799; I.2, 47 etc.

þiself(f) *pron.* thyself I.1003, 1074 etc.; *2A*125

þo(o) *pron.* those I.76, 172 etc.; II.60

tho, þo *adj.* those II.42, 712; I.17, II.32 etc.

tholyd *v. 1/3sg.pa.* suffered, endured II.1314, 1448, 1675

thondyr-blast *n.* clap/crash of thunder II.552

thonge *n.* thong, lace I.128

þornys *n.pl.* thorns II.698sd

thorwe, þour, thurwe, þurwe *prep.* through II.687, 688 etc.; II.689; II.80; I.693

thou, thow *see* **thu**

þough *see* **thow**

thought, thowth, þowth *n.* thought, intention, anxiety I.733, 761 etc.; II.253; II.797

þour *see* **thorwe**

thow, þough, þow *conj.* though I.1020, II.937, 1692; II.1764; I.75, 79 etc.

thowsand *num.* thousand I.23, II.33 etc.; *n.pl.* **thowsandys** II.405

thowth, þowth *n. see* **thought**

thowth *v. see* **thynke**

thrall *n.* while, space of time II.1601

thrawe *see* **throwe**

thre *num.* three I.81, II.4 etc. (as roman numeral: II.790sd, *2A*58)

thred *see* **thryd(de)**

thretty *num.* thirty I.619, II.124 etc. (as roman numeral: II.14)

thryd(de), thred *ord.num.* third II.1207, 1211 etc.; I.562, 866 etc.; II.689

thryes *adv.* three times I.27, 876

thryfte *n.* prosperity, fortune (in mild oath **be my thryfte**) II.116

throwe *v. 1sg.pr.* throw II.1039; *p.p.* **thrawe** I.240

thrust *n.* thirst II.893, 895, 897

thu, þu, thou, thow *pron.* thou II.1935; I.84, 484, 511, 873, 954, II.811; *3A*1; I.411, 783 (abbreviated forms I.76, 80 etc.)

thurwe, þurwe *see* **thorwe**

thus, þus *adv.* thus, so, in this way I.179, II.487, 1928, *1A*19; I.9, 52 etc.

tydandys *n.pl.* tidings II.564, 1545, 1768 (**Tiding** *sb.*)

tyde *n.* time, while II.1260, 1605, *2A*63

tydyng *n.* news, information I.493, 1036; *n.pl.* **tydyngys** I.600, 1047 etc.

tyed *p.p.* tied, tethered *1A*8

tyl(l) *conj.* until I.248, 775sd etc.; II.988

tyl(le) *prep.* to II.822; I.472, II.1637
tyme *n.* time I.49, 96 etc.; *n.pl.* **tymes** I.123, II.134, 219, **tyme** II. 734
tys *see* **it**
tyxt *n.* text, saying I.47
to *num. see* **two**
to(o) *adv.* too, as well I.117, 137 etc.; II.1290
to(o) *prep.* to I.4, 5 etc.; I.353, II.1591, 2A66; **to plesawns** as a pleasure I.406 (*see* **plesauns**), **lyth not to me** is not my responsibility II.365
togedyr *adv.* together I.682, 722 etc.
toke *see* **take**
told(e) *see* **tell(e)**
tombe *n.* tomb, sepulchre II.1189
tomorwe *adv.* tomorrow I.748, II.74
tomorwyn *n.* tomorrow II.1093
tonge, tounge *n.* tongue, voice II.464; II.1915
tonyght *adv.* tonight II.1360
too *n.* toe II.943
too *see also* **to(o)** *prep.* and *adv.*
took *see* **take**
top *n.* top II.943
torchis, torchys *n.pl.* torches I.964sd; I.656
to-rent *p.p.* sorely wounded, lacerated II.943
torn *p.p.* lacerated II.1005, 1381, 2A104
torne *n.* change of fortune II.529
to-shake *v. 1sg.pr.* smash to pieces, shatter II.1334
tother *see* **other** *pron.*; **other(e)** *adj.*
to-torn *p.p.* sorely rent, lacerated II.938
tounge *see* **tonge**
towaly *n.* towel I.824sd, 828sd
toward *prep.* toward I.900sd
towch(e) *v.* touch II.677, 1708; II.1231; *imp.sg.* **towche** II.1879
towche *n.* touch, glancing blow II.99
town *n.* town, village, inhabited place I.34, II.1570
towre *n.* tower, high place II.1886; *n.pl.* **towrys** I.457
trace *n.* way, manner of life 2A46
tray *v.* betray II.1413
trayn *n.* deceit, falsehood II.1556
traytour, traytorys *see* **tretore**
tras *v.* devise, plot out 2A69
tre *n.* tree, the cross I.405, 1011 etc.; *n.pl.* **tres** II.1506
treson, tresson *n.* treachery, treason, betrayal I.58, 558 etc.; 2A81
tresorere *n.* treasurer 3A22
tresour, tresoour, tresure *n.* treasure, money, wealth I.62; 2A97; I.112
tres(s)pace, trespas *n.* sin, crime, offence I.176, 184 etc.; I.1055; II.311, 400 etc.

trespacyd *v. 3sg.pa.* sinned, transgressed I.1052; *p.p.* **trespacyd** I.551, 761

tretore, tretour(e), tretowre, traytour *n.* traitor, betrayer, deceiver II.583; I.309, 970 etc.; I.1005, II.468; I.55; II.1414, 2A75 etc.; *n.pl.* **tretorys** II.48, **tretowrys** II.42, **traytorys** II.32, 55

trew(e), trowe *adj.* true, real, genuine, faithful I.446, II.427, 1206; I.516, 801 etc.; II.1400

trewly, truly *adv.* truly, indeed, rightfully II.95, 125 etc.; II.1786

trewth(e), trowth *n.* truth I.43, 192 etc.; I.222, 328, 423; II.293; *n.pl.* **trewthis** I.171, 423; **of/in trewth** truly I.233, II.1043; **with trewth** justly I.192

try(e) *v.* find out, ascertain, prove, test I.303; I.171, II.73; *p.p.* **tryed(e)** I.43; I.423

trybulacyon *n.* distress, affliction, suffering I.388, 449, 1050

tryst *see* **trost(e)**

trobelyd *p.p.* annoyed, vexed II.127

trobyl *n.* affliction, distress I.456

trone *n.* throne II.716, 1444

trost *n.* trust, belief I.58, 152

trost(e) *v.* trust, believe, be sure I.156; II.1783; *1sg.pr.* **trost** II.1137; *imp.pl.* **trost** II.1928, **tryst** II.445, **trostyth** II.1786

trow(e) *v. 1sg.pr.* believe, think, am sure I.594; I.650, II.290 etc.

trowe *see also* **trew(e)**

trowth *see* **trewth(e)**

truly *see* **trewly**

turne *v.* turn, change I.56, 794, II.710; *3sg.pr.* **turnyth** II.706sd, 718sd; *2pl.pr.subj.* **turne** II.1077; *pr.p.* **turnyng** II.1163sd; *p.p.* **turnyd** converted, seduced II.343

tweyn *num.* two I.19, 159 etc.

twelve *num.* twelve (occurs only as roman numeral, I.33)

twyes *adv.* twice I.875

twynne *v.* part asunder, break II.928

two, to *num.* two I.72, 79; II.340, 788, 1A6; **atoo** in two II.1507 (as roman numeral: I.164sd, 208sd etc.)

vayn *adj.* worthless, empty II.1557

varyable *adj.* inconstant, unreliable, untrustworthy I.217 (see note)

varyauns, varyawns *n.* diversity, variety, discord, conflict I.65; I.212 (see notes to ll. 65–87 and 211–12)

vath *interj.* (exclamation of contempt) yah! II.803 (**Vah** *int.*)

veyn *n.* vein II.766

veynglory(e) *n.* pride, self-glorification I.32; II.504

velany *n.* wickedness, disgrace II.1150

venge *v.* avenge I.59

vengeance *n.* vengeance I.454

veray, very *adj.* true, real, thorough, unqualified I.376, 422; I.697, 703 etc.

veryly(e) *adv.* truly, indeed I.409, 501 etc.; I.769
vertu *n.* goodness, virtue, power I.116, 695, II.1002, *2A*11
vertuis *adj.* virtuous, good I.736
vesyte, vicyte, vycyte *v.* visit I.487; I.372; I.400
vessel *n.* container, receptacle (fig. 'a person') *3A*34
vetaylys *n.pl.* food, provisions I.492
vicyte, vycyte *see* **vesyte**
vyl *see* **wyl(l)**
vmbyl *adj.* humble I.847
vn *see* **on** *prep.*
vnbegete *adj.* not conceived, unbegotten I.774
vnborn *adj.* not born I.774, 995, *2A*120
vnbownde *p.p.* released II.1679
vnclose, onclose *v.* reveal, open, draw back I.62, 662sd, II.377sd; I.518sd; *imp.pl.* onclose I.958 (**Unclose** *v.*)
vndyr, vndre *prep.* under II.83, 1299 etc.; I.45
vndyrstand, vndyrstonde *v.* understand, attend to I.720; I.142; *1sg.pr.* **vndyrstand** II.364; *2sg.pr.subj.* **vndyrstande** I.729; *imp.sg.* **vndyr-stonde** II.605; *imp.pl.* **vndyrstande** II.580
vndyrtake *v.* *1sg.pr.* vow, venture to assert II.209
vndre *see* **vndyr**
vnete *adj.* un-eaten I.727
vnkende *adj.* wicked I.700
vnkendely *adv.* cruelly, wrongly I.1018
vnkendenesse *n.* harshness, ill-will I.898
vnlokyn *adj.* open, unlocked II.1406
vnlosne *v.* *imp.pl.* set free, untie *1A*9
vnpynne *v.* unbolt, unfasten II.1024
vnqwyt *adj.* unrequited II.507
vnrecurabyl *adj.* unrecoverable, irremediable II.626
vnryth *adv.* or *n.* wrongfully; wrong I.1017
vnto *see* **onto(o)**
voys *n.* voice II.696sd, 1760, 1789, (emendation) *3A*40
vowchsaffe *v.* agree, permit, bestow II.1272; *1sg.pr.* **vowche ... save** II.1186; *2sg.pr.subj.* vowchesave II.1877
up, vp *prep.* up I.625, 787 etc.; II.1534, 1691; **smyth up** (see note to I.625); **sped up** hasten I.787; **put up** sheathe II.100
upholden *v.* maintain II.636
upon, vpon *prep.* on, upon, about I.30, 393 etc.; I.384, 571 etc.
upryth *adv.* full length, prostrate II.108
vpward *adv.* up, upwards I.686sd
us, vs *pron.obj.* us I.179, 268 etc.; I.282, 405 etc.
vse *v.* *imp.pl.* use, practise I.389; *p.p.* **vsyd** II.285
vttyrly *adv.* totally, absolutely II.506

wace *see* **be(n)**

way(e) *see* **wey(e)**

wayle *v.* cry out, lament I.451

wayten *v.* keep watch II.1271

wake, wakyn *v.* arouse, awake, keep watch, watch over I.597, II.1329, 1486, 2A111; II.1270

walk(e) *v.* walk I.134, 145, 278; I.880, 959 etc.; *pr.p.* **walkyng(e)** I.867; II.1737; *imp.pl.* **walkyth** I.491

walterid *p.p.* covered, soaked II.1339 (**Walter** *v.*¹)

wan *see* **wyn(ne)**

ware, whare *adj.* watchful, cautious, prepared, careful I.574, 635 etc.; I.327

ware *see also* **be(n)**

wark *see* **werk(e)**

warly *adv.* cautiously II.1142sd

warnyn *v.* warn II.517

warnyng *vbl.n.* warning I.770

was(e) *see* **be(n)**

wassche *v.* wash, wet I.831; *1sg.pr.* **wasch(e)** II.1839; II.643; *3sg.pr.* **wasshyth** I.840sd; *imp.sg.* **wasch(e)** 2A15; I.839; *p.p.* **wasschyd** I.844

wasshyng *vbl.n.* washing, cleansing I.841

wast *adj.* useless, needless, in vain II.902, 1035

watyr *n.* water I.469, 478sd etc.

watt *n.* creature II.117

wax *n.* wax II.1280, 1285, 1288

waxe *v.* grow, become II.960; *3pl.pr.* **waxe** II.1053

we, whe *pron.* we I.98, 179 etc.; I.288

wech(e), whech(e), which(e), wich(e), wyche, qweche, qwych *(rel.)* *pron.* which, who I.496, 775sd, 911; I.514, 632 etc.; I.4, 387, 430, II.1812; I.798, II.160, 268, 1185; I.190, II.44, 1002, 1772; II.1804, 1913, 1A2, 2A74, 123; I.164sd, 175 etc.; I.26; I.362; I.814; II.1775

wech(e), whech, wich *adj.* which, what sort of I.521; I.744, 891; I.859; I.425

weche *v.* keep watch over, stay awake I.902, II.1214

wechecrafte *see* **wichcraft**

wede *n.* clothing, costume II.1sd

wedyr *n.* bad weather II.1050

weel *see* **wel** *adv.*

weelaway *see* **wellaway**

wey *adv.* (shortened form of 'away') **do wey** cease, stop II.819

wey(e), way(e) *n.* means, way, path I.141, 163 etc.; II.639, 734, 2A35; I.470, 592 etc.; II.1737; *n.pl.* **weys** I.133, II.505, 1A12; **to go his way** to die II.866

weyl *see* **wel** *adj.* and *adv.*

wel, weyl *adj.* well I.255, 991; II.563

Glossary

wel, weel, weyl, well(e), wele *adv.* well, well! I.241, 256 etc.; II.953; I.964sd, II.114 etc.; II.1307; 2A127; I.849, II.1048 etc.
welcom(e) *interj., adj.* welcome!, welcome II.1464, 1467; I.289, 511 etc.
welcome *v.* welcome, greet I.405, 510sd
welcomyng *vbl.n.* welcoming, reception I.490
wele *n.* well-being, happiness II.1297 (**Weal** *sb¹.*)
wele *see also* **wyl** *v.*; **wel** *adv.*
welyn *see* **wyl**
well *see* **wyl** *v.*; **wel** *adv.*
wellaway, weelaway *interj.* (exclamation of distress) alas! I.8; II.214
welle *see* **wel** *adv.*
welthe *n.* happiness, well-being II.1297
wend *see* **wenyth**
wend(e) *v.* go II.1133; I.254, 281, II.1135; *1pl.pr.* **wende** II.958; *imp.sg.* **wende** II.1740; *imp.pl.* **wendyth** II.1734
wenyth *v.* *3sg.pr.* thinks II.156; *1sg.pa.* **wend** thought II.530
went *see* **go(n)**
wepe, wepyn *v.* weep, lament II.1847, 1850 etc.; II.213sd; *3sg.pr.* **wepyth** II.1837sd; *imp.pl.* **wepe** II.1463, **wepyth** II.707, 708; *pr.p.* **wepyng** I.442sd, II.698sd
wepyng(e) *vbl.n.* weeping, lamentation I.1041; II.975, 987
wepynge *adj.* lamenting, weeping II.1740, 1839, 2A27
wepon *n.* (as *n.pl.*) weapons I.964sd; *n.pl.* **weponys** I.1032sd
werd(e), werld(e), world(e) *n.* world I.2, 96 etc.; I.816; II.332; II.295, 1472; II.1056; II.1567, 1582; *n.poss.* **werdys** I.702
were *see* **be(n)**
weryd *v.* *3sg.pa.* drove II.1682 (**Were** *v.*)
weryn *see* **be(n)**
werk(e), wark *n.* work, deed, action II.931, 1048, 1071; I.311, 2A118; II.1070; *n.pl.* **werkys** I.36, 37 etc.
werk(e) *v.* work, carry out, perform I.535, 2A82; II.494, 2A68, 76; *1sg.pr.* **werke** II.978; *3sg.pr.* **werke** I.322, 325, **werkyth** I.229; *imp.pl.* **werkyth** 1A28; *1pl.pa.* **wrought** II.1387; *p.p.* **wrought** II.931, 977 etc., **wrougth** II.426, 429, **wrouth** I.548, **wrowth** I.522, II.269 etc.
werkyng *vbl.n.* actions, conduct, behaviour I.360, 1016
werld(e) *see* **werd(e)**
werme *n.* serpent II.1412
wers *adj.* worse II.530
werst *adj.* (as *n.*) worst II.274
west *adv.* west II.1629
wete, wetyn *v.* know I.348, 990 etc.; I.1036, II.187; *3pl.pr.* **wete** II.802; *1sg.pa.* **wyst** I.988, 1056 (*?subj.*), II.1153 (**Wit** *v¹.*)
wete *adj.* wet II.1338
whan *adj.* sickly II.1551, dark II.1053
whan *adv.* when II.342

whan, qwan *conj.* when I.44, 49 etc.; I.406sd, 976sd etc. (all **qw-** forms are expansions of abbreviations except I.406sd)

whar *v. imp.pl.* watch, look II.186 (**Ware** *v¹.*)

what, qwat, qwhat *pron. interr.* and *rel.* what I.18, 150 etc.; I.828; II.659 (the **qw-** form in I.828 is an expansion of an abbreviation)

what(t), whath *adj.* what, whatsoever, what kind (of) I.22, 466 etc.; 2A75; I.193; **what tyme** when II.1sd; **what man soevyr** whoever, whichever man 2A93

what *interj.* (often *interr.*) what!, what? I.487, II.138 etc.

whath *see* **what(t)** *adj.*

whatso *pron.* whatever I.485, II.1090, 1321

whe *see* **we**

whech *see* **wech(e)** *adj.*

whech(e) *see* **wech(e)** *pron.*

whedyr *adv.* whither, where II.1856, 1A35

whedyr *see also* **whether**

wheyle *see* **whyle**

whele *v. imp.sg.* or *pl.* spin, turn, circle around II.191 (see note)

whelpe *n.* puppy, child II.1353 (see note)

wher(e), qwere, qwher *adv.* and *conj.* where I.496, 789 etc.; I.39, 77 etc. II.1872; II.216

wher-as, where-as *adv.* where, wherever I.650sd; II.41

where *see also* **be(n)**

whereon *rel.adv.* on which II.722

wheresoever, wheresoevyr *conj.* wherever II.1800; II.1669

wher(e)fore *adv. interr.* and *rel.* for which reason, therefore, why I.354, 395 etc.; I.3, 129 etc.

whether, whethyr, whedyr *pron.* and *conj.* whether, which of the two I.778sd, II.482; II.595, 1121; I.748

why *adv.* why I.109, 147 etc.

which(e) *see* **wech(e)** *pron.*

whyl(l), qwyl *conj.* while II.467, 1181; II.1602; II. 486sd

whylde *see* **wyld(e)**

whyle, wheyle, wyle *n.* while, time I.241, II.87, 542; I.173; II.602

whyle *see also* **wyle** *n.*

whylys *conj.* while I.1000

whylt *see* **wyl**

whipyng *vbl.n.* wiping II.743

whypyth *see* **wype**

whippe *n.* whip II.465; *n.pl.* **whyppys** II.461sd, 466, **qwyppys** II.682

whysshe *v.* wish 2A120

whit *see* **with**

whyt *see* **wight** *adj.*

whyte, white *n.* and *adj.* white I.164sd, II.486sd; I.208sd, 964sd

whith *n.* creature, person II.1907; *n.pl.* **whithtys** II.1654; **wytys** II.1064

who *interr.* and *rel.pron.* who, one who II.223, *1A*18, *2A*99, 113
whoys *see* **whose**
whom *pron.obj.*, *interr.* and *rel.* whom I.689, 968 etc.
whose, whoys *pron.poss.* whose I.128; I.121
whoso *pron.* whoever I.11
wich *see* **wech(e)** *adj.*
wich(e), wyche *see* **wech(e)** *pron.*
wichcraft, wychecrafte, wechecrafte *n.* witchcraft, magic I.228; I.1015; I.325
wyckyd, wykkyd *adj.* wicked, evil II.1064, 1412 etc.; II.705
wyde *adj.* wide I.387, II.940 etc.
wyde *adv.* wide I.337
wyf(f) *n.* woman, wife I.420, II.486sd, etc.; II.536, 1385, 1740; *n.pl.* **wyfys** II.1238
wight, whyt *adj.* fierce, violent, quick II.1682; II.235
wykkyd *see* **wyckyd**
wyl, wele, wole, wul *v. 1sg.pr.* will, wish I.62, 442 etc.; I.472, 602 etc.; I.278, 590 etc.; *2A*32; *2sg.pr.* **whylt** II.214, 460, **wylt** I.91, 466 etc., **wolt** I.1069, **wolte** I.459; *3sg.pr.* **wyl** I.220, 224 etc., **wyll** II.1340, *2A*99, **wele** I.473, ?654, ?824, **wol** I.547, II.407, **wole** I.11, 116 etc.; *pl.pr.* **wyl** I.106, 107 etc., **wole** I.367, 521 etc.; *1pl.pr.* **wyll** II.906, 1650, 1814, **welyn** II.636; *2pl.pr.* **wele** II.627, 1256, **wolyn** II.600, **wolne** II.639; *3pl.pr.* **wele** I.1024, **wul** II.1817; *3sg.pr.subj.* **wyl** *1A*43sd, **wylle** II. 192, **wol** II.540; *2pl.pr.subj.* **wole** II.211; *3pl.pr.subj.* **wyl** I.778sd, ?**well** II.768, **wolne** I.778sd; *1/3sg.pa.* **wold** I.396, 587 etc., **wolde** I.784, 990 etc.; *2sg.pa.* **woldyst** I.1065; *1/2pl.pa.* **wolde** II.105, 651; *1pl.pa.* **wold** II.17, 1702; *3sg.pa.subj.* **wold** I.1048 (for detailed discussion of forms see *OED* **Will** *v¹*.)
wyl(l), wylle, vyl *n.* will, desire, intention II.289, 477 etc.; II.978, 1705, *1A*28; I.474, 625 etc.; I.916; *n.pl.* **wyllys** II.7
wyld(e), whylde *adj.* wild, uncontrolled, distracted I.553; II.32, 552; II.1490
wyle, whyle *n.* trick, device II.450, 529; II.1130
wyle *see also* **whyle** *n.*
wyll *see* **wyl** *v.*; **wyl(l)** *n.*
wylle *adj.* wild, perplexed *2A*27
wylle *see also* **wyl** *v.*; **wyl(l)** *n.*
wylt *see* **wyl**
wyn(ne) *v.* gain, win over, overcome, regain, save *2A*25; *2A*119; *1sg.pa.* **wan** I.24; *p.p.* **wonnyn** II.1676, **wunne** II.1408
wynde *n.* wind II.1304
wynde *v.* wrap, enclose II.1181; *1sg.pr.* **wynde** II.1418; *p.p.* **wounde** II.1426, 1799, 1804, **woundyn** II.1373
wynke *n.* nap, short sleep II.1367 (see note to II.1362–7)
wynnynge *vbl.n.* money-making, gain *2A*108

wyntyr *n.pl.* years II.1145
wype *v.* wipe II.1142sd; *3sg.pr.* **whypyth** I.840sd, II.742sd
wysdam *n.* wisdom I.112
wyse *n.* way, manner I.139, 150 etc.
wyse *adj.* wise II.79, 827 etc.
wysest *adj.* wisest I.222
wysly, wysely *adv.* prudently II.1251; I.535
wyst *see* **wete** *v.*
wyth *adv.* quickly II.1133 (**Wight** *a.*)
with, whit *prep.* with I.18, 20 etc.; I.395; (as *adv.*) II.512, 518 (all examples
　except I.395 are expansions of abbreviation)
withal(l) *adv.* with I.78; II.1183
wythin, withinne *adv.* and *prep.* in, inside I.480; I.241, 264 etc.
without(h), withoutyn, withowt(e), withowth, withowtyn *prep.*
　without I.379, II.151 etc.; I.304, II.247; I.83, 160 etc.; II.1730, 1A2, 24;
　I.462, 703, II.309; I.260; I.416, 843 etc.
withstonde *v.* withstand II.1245
wytys *see* **whith**
wytness(e) *n.* evidence, witness II.175; II.143, 148
wytnessyth *v.* *3sg.pr.* bears witness 3A39
wytt, witt *n.* sense, mind, understanding II.1635, 2A43; II.1830; *n.pl.*
　wyttys I.710, II.1509, **wittys** II.1617
wo(o) *n.* misery, suffering I.649, 785 etc.; I.455, II.941 etc.
wode *see* **wood**
woful *adj.* miserable, sorrowful I.54, 443 etc.
wol(e) *see* **wyl**
wold(e), woldyst *see* **wyl**
wolde *n.* hill; **whithtys on wolde** men on earth II.1654
wolyn *see* **wyl**
wolle *n.* wool I.77
wolne, wolt(e) *see* **wyl**
woman *n.* woman I.1076, II.193sd etc.; *n.pl.* **women** I.1033, II.698sd etc.
wombys *n.pl.* wombs II.711
wondyr, woundyr *n.* marvel, surprise 2A65; II.1515, 1826; *n.pl.* **wondrys**
　II.65, **woundrys** II.68
wondyr *adj.* marvellous, wonderful I.291, II.422, 426
won(n)e, wonyn *v.* dwell, live II.522; I.789; II.941; *3pl.pr.* **wone**
　II.494
wonnyn *see* **wyn(ne)**
woo *see* **wo(o)**
wood, wode *adj.* mad, infuriated I.819, II.253 etc.; I.988sd
woodmen *n.pl.* madmen I.1027
woot *see* **wot(e)**
worchep(e), wurchep *n.* respect, honour, veneration I.570, II.584 etc.;
　I.402; II.1569, 1572

worchep(e), **wurchep(e)** *v.* worship, venerate II.1081; II.786; II.1466; II.1473; *1sg.pr.* **worchep** I.691, **wurchep** *2A*48

word(e), **wourd**, **wurd(e)** *n.* word, speech I.311, 733 etc.; I.614, 814, II.372; instructions *1A*15; *2A*43; II.1683, 1759; *n.pl.* **wordys** I.52, 695 etc. **wurdys** II.919, 1480; **at a worde** I.614, **at wordys fewe** I.827 without more ado; **a word of good** a friendly word II.719

wore, **worn** *see* **be(n)**

world(e) *see* **werd(e)**

worth *adj.* worth *2A*57

worthy *adj.* worthy, deserving I.128, 312 etc.

wot(e), **woot** *v.* *1sg.pr.* know I.494; II.1146; II.953, 1688; *2sg.pr.* **wotyst** I.934, II.1204, **wotysst** *2A*128

wounde *n.* wound II.1314, 1675, 1715, *3A*36; *n.pl.* **woundys** I.54, II.940 etc.

wounde, **woundyn** *see* **wynd** *v.*

woundyr *v.* *1sg.pr.* wonder *2A*113

woundyr *adv.* exceptionally, marvellously II.1050

woundyr *see also* **wondyr** *n.*

woundyrful *see* **wundyrful**

woundrys *see* **wondyr** *n.*

wourd *see* **word(e)**

wrake *n.* injury, harm II.516

wrappyd *p.p.* enveloped, sunk II.1373, *2A*2

wrecche *n.* wretched/miserable creature II.1856, *2A*2; *n.pl.* **wrecchis** II.1343

wreche *n.* misery, wretchedness II.1676

wreke *v.* deliver, rescue II.1026 (**Wreak** *v.*)

wreth *n.* wrath, anger I.113

wretyn *see* **wryte**

wry *v.* deviate, err I.144

wryngyn *pr.p.* wringing II.698sd

wryte *v.* write II.874sd, 877; *2pl.pr.* **wryte** state II.876; *p.p.* **wretyn** II.874sd, 879

wrong(e) *n.* wrong, evil, suffering I.216, II.631 etc.; I.129

wrong(e) *adv.* astray, wrong, unjustly I.811; II.82, 1078, *2A*62

wroth(e) *adj.* angry, sorrowful II.1544, 1731; II.1304

wrought, **wrougth**, **wrouth**, **wrowth** *see* **werk(e)** *v.*

wul *see* **ful** *adv.*; **wyl** *v.*

wundyrful, **woundyrful** *adj.* marvellous, amazing, II.1045, 1048, 1621; II.1931

wunne *see* **wyn(ne)**

wurchep *see* **worchep(e)** *n.* and *v.*

wurchepe *see* **worchep(e)** *v.*

wurd(e), **wurdys** *see* **word(e)**

xad *p.p.* shed I.798
xal(l), **schal** *v. 1sg. pr.* shall, will I.50, 51 etc.; II.1624, 1636; II.393; *2sg.pr.*
  xalt I.154, 445 etc., **xal(le)** I.831, 835, 876; I.482; *3sg.pr.* **xal** I.8, 12 etc.,
  schal I.145, 899, **shal** II.1473; *1pl.pr.* **xal** I.179, 266 etc., **xul** II.1269, 1270
  etc.; *2pl.pr.* **xal** I.111, 140 etc., **xall(e)** I.845; I.299, **xul** II.1310, 1374 etc.;
  3pl.pr. **xal** I.53, 54 etc., **xul(e)** I.775sd, 804sd etc.; II.774sd, **xuln**
  II.782sd; should, would *1/3sg.pa.* **xuld(e)** I.361, 401 etc.; II.277, 305 etc.,
  schuld I.715; *2sg.pa.* **xuldyst** I.939, II.389 etc.; *1pl.pa.* **xuld(e)** I.402, 567
  etc.; II.1771; *2/3pl.pa.* **xuld** I.362, 376 etc.; *2sg.pa.subj.* **xulde** II.197
xamefullest *adj.* most shameful/ignominious II.61
xul(e), **xuld(e)**, **xuldyst**, **xuln** *see* **xal(l)**

yet *see* **yet** *under* ȝ
yf *see* **if(f)**
ylle *see* **ylle** *under* i
yn *see* **in** *adv.*
yron *see* **yron** *under* i
ys *see* **be(n)**
yt *see* **it**

LIST OF PROPER NAMES AND
DRAMATIS PERSONAE

References are given here to proper names that appear in the text or stage directions (sd), and to speakers' names (sn). All line references are given for names occurring in the text and stage directions unless they are numerous, when a single reference followed by 'etc.' is given. One line reference only is normally given for speakers' names, followed by 'etc.' if the name occurs more than once.

Aaron I.665 the archetypal high priest, brother of Moses.
Abraham II.1367sd, 1400sn, 1400 the patriarch Abraham
Adam I.24, II.1367sd, 1368, 1376sn, 1402; *n.poss.* **Adamys** II.848, **Adamis** II.1385 Adam
Affraunt II.1226, **A. (quartus/4)** II.1264sn, 1312sn, **Quartus Miles** II.1246sn, 1362sn, 1528sn, 1584sn, 1648sn the fourth of Pilate's knights who watch the sepulchre
Alius miles 2 II.1047sn; **Alius m. 3** II.1051sn the two knights with the Centurion at the Crucifixion
Amaraunt II.1256, **Ameraunt** II.1258sn, **A. (primus)** II.1328sn, **Amorawnt** II.1224, **Primus Miles** II.1240sn, 1344sn, 1503sd, 1504sn, 1544sn, 1592sn, 1604sn, 1664sn the first of Pilate's knights who watch the sepulchre
Andreas 2A81sn, **Andrewe** 3A15 the apostle Andrew, brother of Peter
Angelus I.937sn, **an aungel** I.936sd; **Angelus** II.1734sn, **Aungelus** II.1846sn in *Passion* I the angel which comforts Christ in Gethsemane; in *Passion* II the angel at the sepulchre
Anima Cayn 5AAi the soul of Cain
Anima Christi II.993sn etc., 1367sd, 1439sd, **the sowle** II.1016sd the soul of Christ
Annas I.164sd etc., 165sn etc., 167 etc.; II.1sd etc., 18 etc., 120sn etc. the high priest Annas
Annys *n.poss.* II.1698 of Anne, mother of the Virgin Mary, Mary Salome and Mary Jacobi
Aramathy *see* **Joseph of Aramathia**
Arfexe I.199, 205sn the name given to the Saracen messenger in *Passion* I; *see also* **Massanger(e)**

Arphaxat II.1225, **Arfaxat (secundus)** II.1256sn, 1260sn, 1336sn, **Secundus Miles** II.1242sn, 1350sn, 1512sn, 1560sn, 1596sn the second of Pilate's knights who watch the sepulchre
Artyse II.641 the name given to Pilate's servant who brings him water to wash his hands

Baptyst *see* **John Baptyst**
Barabas II.592, 656sd, 657, 659, 663 the convicted murderer Barabbas
Baramathie *see* **Joseph of Aramathia**
Bartholomeus 2A93sn, **Bertylmew** 3A28 the apostle Bartholomew
Bedlem II.359, 1382 Bethlehem
Beliall II.1424sn, **Belyall** II.1027sn, 1592 the devil Belial
Betany I.880 Bethany (for **Betanyward** see Glossary)
Burgensis 1A18sn, 27sn, **þe burgeys** 1A17sd the citizen in charge of the ass and foal

Cayme 5AAiisd Cain
Cayphas I.186 etc., 208sd etc., 209sn etc., II.1sd etc., 18 etc., 130sn etc. the high priest Caiaphas
Calvary II.1805, **Caluerye** II.696, 1112, **Kalvarye** II.725 Calvary
Candas 3A22 queen Candace
Caryoth *see* **Judas (Caryoth)**
Centurio II.1043sn, 1055sn, **Senturyo** II.1067sn the centurion
Cephas 3A24 Peter (*see also* **Petrus**)
Contemplacio II.1sn the prologue, Contemplation, of *Passion* II
Cosdram II.1226, **C. (tertius)** II.1262sn, **Cosdran (3)** II.1320sn, **Tertius Miles** II.1244sn, 1356sn, 1520sn, 1576sn the third of Pilate's knights who watch the sepulchre
Cryst I.26, 119, 410sd etc., II.37 etc., 698sd etc., 3A16, 20, **Crist** 5AAiisd, **Cryst Jhesu(s)** II.1001, 2A10; II.741, 1930; *n.poss.* **Crystys** II.874sd, 1589, 1799, 1818, 3A36 Christ (*see also* **Fily altissimi, Jhesus, Oure Lord**)

Davyd I.411, 427 king David, one of the ancestors of Christ
Demon I.1sn, 779sn, **þe devyl** I.778sd, II.543sd Lucifer/Satan; **Demon** II.524sn, **a devyl** II.523sd a devil in hell (*see also* **Lucifer, Satan**)
Dysmas II.665, 693, 819sn Dismas, the saved thief

Egythp I.666 Egypt
Eua II.1367sd, 1384sn, **Eue** II.1368, 1385, **Eve** I.24 Eve
Euangelyst *see* **John þe Euangelyst**

Fily altissimi 3A5 the son of the highest, Christ (*see also* **Cryst, Jhesus, Oure Lord**)

Galylé I.868, II.80 etc., **Galelye** II.347, 356, 361 Galilee

Gamalyel I.543sn etc. one of the leaders of the opposition to Christ
Gylle II.1261 Jill

Hely II.889 the prophet Elias
Herowdys II.1sd, 21sn, 353, 377sd, 576, **Rex Herowdys** II.58sn, **Rex**
II.86sn, **Herowde Rex** II.390sn, **Rex Herowde** II.414sn, 446sn, 454sn,
Herowd(e) II.565; II.25, 366, 378, þe H. II.377sd, 433sd, þe **Herownd**
II.469sd, þe **Herowndys** II.20sd; *n.poss.* þe **Herowdys** II.377, 377sd the
tetrarch, Herod Antipas
Hierusalem *see* **Jherusalem**

Israel I.666, II.871 another name for the patriarch Jacob, hence the people of
the Jews, the land of Israel

Jacobi *see* **Maria Jacobi**
Jacobus maior *2A*85sn, **Jamys** *3A*17 the apostle James the Great, brother of
John the Evangelist, one of the sons of Zebedee, traditionally one of the
sons of Mary Salome
Jacobus minor *1A*31sn, *2A*101sn, **Jamys þe Lesser** *3A*23 the apostle James
the Less, traditionally the first bishop of Jerusalem and one of the sons of
Mary Jacobi, brother of Simon Zelotes and Jude
Jakke II.1261 Jack
Jesmas II.665, 695, **Jestes** II.815sn Gestas, the damned thief
Jestes *see* **Jesmas**
Jewys I.166 etc., 778sd etc.; II.14 etc., 193sd etc., **Jewus** II.878, **Juwys**
II.249sd the Jews (*see also* **Primus Judeus**, *etc.*)
Jewry I.257, **Juré** II.237, 328 the Jews, Judea
Jherusalem I.443, II.10, *3A*20, **Hierusalem** II.707, **Jherosolyman** *3A*23
Jerusalem
Jhesus I.178 etc., 495sn, 686sd etc., 825sn, 991sn, II.63 etc., 89sd etc., 134sn
etc., *1A*1sn, *2A*27sn etc., **Jhesu** I.187 etc., 415sn etc., 908sd, 964sd, II.15
etc., 265sd etc., *1A*43sd, *2A*10 Christ (*see also* **Cryst**, **Fily altissimi**,
Oure Lord)
John Baptyst I.125, 352; *3A*37, **John Baptist** II.1367sd, **John þe Baptyst**
I.704, II.37, **John** II.1392, **Johannes Baptista** I.125sn, II.1392sn the
prophet John the Baptist
John þe Euangelyst I.342sd, **John** I.478sd, II.973, 1795, **sen John** II.790sd,
Jhon *3A*17, **Jon** II.844, **Johannes** I.463sn etc., II.863sn etc., 968sd etc.,
*2A*77sn, **Johannes apostolus** I.375sn, **Johanne** II.984sd the apostle John
the Evangelist, brother of James the Great, one of the sons of Zebedee,
traditionally one of the sons of Mary Salome
Jordon II.1394 Jordan
Joseph I.26 Joseph, husband of the Virgin Mary
Joseph of Aramathia II.1079sn, **Joseph ab [Aramathia]** II.1115sn,
Joseph ab Aramathy II.1156, **Joseph of Baramathie** II.1099, 1104,

Joseph II.1109, 1112, 1122sd etc., 1160sn etc., 1178, 1192 Joseph of Arimathea

Judas (Caryoth) I.582sd etc., 582sn etc., 585 etc., II.13 etc., 249sd, 250, 2A53sn, 121sn, 128sd Judas Iscariot

Judas *see also* **Thadeus**

Judé II.359 the land of Judea

Judeorum *n.poss.* II.874sd of the Jews

Juré *see* **Jewry**

Kalvarye *see* **Calvary**

Lazare I.38 Lazarus, traditionally brother of Mary Magdalene and Martha

Leyon I.194, 265sn etc., **Leon** I.201, 313sn, **Lyon** I.207, 244sd, 275 one of the Pharisees or secular judges in opposition to Christ in *Passion* I (*see also* **Pharaseus**)

Leprows *see* **Symon (Leprows)**

Longeys II.1130sd, 1131, 1139, 1142sd, 1143sn, **Longeus** II.1135sn Longeus or Longinus who pierced Christ's side at the crucifixion

Lucifer I.1 Lucifer (*see also* **Demon**, **Satan**)

Mahound II.390, **Mahownd(e)** II.58, 1347, (?*n.poss.*) 1353, 1359; II.26, 43 Mahomet, seen as a heathen god or devil

Malchus I.990sd, **Malcus** II.98, (*n.poss.*) 101 servant of the high priest

Maria Jacobi II.1671sd, 1688sn, 1718sn, 1774sn, **Maria Jacoby** II.1754sn Mary Jacobi, sometimes called Mary Cleophas, traditionally daughter of Anne and Cleophas and therefore half-sister to the Virgin Mary; mother of Simon, Jude, James the Less and Joseph the Just

Maria Magdalene I.1033sn, 1041sn, II.855sn etc., 1671sd etc., 2A1sn, 40sn, **Maria Magdalyn** II.1895sn, **Maria** II.1874, **Marye Magdalene** I.1032sd, **Mary Mavdelyn** 2A9, **Mary Mawdelyn** 2A64sd, **Mary** II.1879, **Marie Magdalene** II.1939sd, **Magdalen** II.1672sn, **Mawdelyn** I.40, 1039 Mary Magdalene, traditionally sister of Martha and Lazarus

Maria Salome II.1671sd, 1696sn etc., **Mary Salomé** II.1696 Mary Salome, traditionally daughter of Anne and Salome and therefore half-sister to the Virgin Mary; mother of John the Evangelist and James the Great

Maria Uirgo I.1045sn, **Maria Virgo** II.859sn, 1168sn, **Marya** I.1039sn, **Maria** II.791sn etc., 984sd, **Mary** II.1164, 1176; *n. poss.* **Maryes** I.26 the Virgin Mary (*see also* **Oure Lady**)

Maryes *n.pl.* II.790sd, 1199sd Mary Magdalene, Mary Salome and Mary Jacobi, the latter reference probably also including the Virgin Mary

Massanger(e) II.90sn, 234sn, 244sn; II.227sn, **Masanger(e)** I.273sn; I.245sn, **Masager** I.253sn, 257sn, 269sn the messenger; in *Passion* I called **Arfexe** (*q.v.*) (NB Only speakers' name references are given here; for others see Glossary, *s.v.* **Masager**.)

Mathew 3A25, **Matheus** 2A89sn the apostle Matthew

Moyses I. 168, 215, 665 Moses

Nazarenus II.874sd the Nazarene
Nazareth I.178 etc., II.63 etc., 89sd Nazareth
Nychodemus II.1155sd, 1160, 1163sd, **Nichodemus** I.1059sn etc.,
Nicodemus II.1156sn Nichodemus, one of the secret followers of Christ
Noes *n.poss.* II.1401 of Noah

Olyvet (mount of) I.900sd, 908sd, 920sd the Mount of Olives
Omnes [I.342sn], II.178sn, 672sd all, the crowd (*see also* **Populus**)
Oure Lady I.1032sd, II.790sd etc.; **Oure Ladys** *n.poss.* II.1163sd (of) the
Virgin Mary (*see also* **Maria Uirgo**)
Oure Lord I.406sd etc., II.798sd, *3A*30; **Oure Lordys** *n.poss.* I.1032sd (of)
Christ (*see also* **Fily altissimi, Jhesus, Cryst**)

Petyr I.342sd etc., 809 etc., II.195sd, 213sd, 1744, 1771, *1A*43sd, *3A*14,
Petrus I.459sn etc., II.198sn etc., 1797sd, 1801sd, 1817sd, *2A*73sn; **Petro**
II.1765sd the apostle Peter
Pharao I.700 Pharaoh
Pharaseus *n.pl.* I.288sd; **Pharasy** I.233 the Pharisees (*see also* **Leyon,
Rewfyn**)
Phelypp *3A*21, **Philippus** *1A*22sn, 35sn, *2A*97sn the apostle Philip
Pilat(e) II.346sn etc., 1521; II.302sn, **Pylat(e)** II.1sd etc., 240sn etc., 278
etc.; II.18, **Pilatt** II.1532, **Pylatt** II.1636sn, 1648, **Pilatus** II.1279sd,
1284sn etc., 1627sd, **Pylatus** II.1272sn Pilate, the Roman governor of
Judea
Populus II.598sd the crowd, the people (*see also* **Omnes**)
Poul *3A*33 the apostle Paul
Prima ancilla II.194sn, 200sn, **þe woman** II.193sd; **Secunda ancilla**
II.196sn, **þe tother woman** II.195sd the two servant girls who accuse
Peter
Prima mulier II.699sn; **Secunda mulier** II.703sn; **to women** II.698sd
representatives of the women who mourn Christ's sufferings on the road
to Calvary
Primus apostolus *1A*14sn one of the apostles who fetch the ass, probably
Jacobus minor (*q.v.*)
Primus ciues (de Jherusalem) I.399sn, 407sn; **Secundus c.** I.401sn,
[411sn]; **Tertius c.** I.403sn; **Quartus c.** I.405sn representatives of the
inhabitants of Jerusalem who welcome Christ at his entry into the city
Primus doctor II.150sn etc.; **Secundus d.** II.154sn etc.; **Tertius d.**
II.158sn; **Primus doctor (Annas)** I.185sn, 317sn; **Secundus d. (A.)**
I.189sn, 321sn; **Primus doctor (C/Cayphas)** I.225sn, 285sn, 325sn;
Secundus d. (C/Cayphas) I.233sn, 287sn, 329sn the learned advisers of
Annas and Caiaphas; only latterly in *Passion* I are they attributed to each
high priest separately; **Primus (doctor)** *3A*1sn etc.; **Secundus (doctor)**
*3A*5sn etc. the presenters of the procession of apostles, etc.

Primus Judeus II.138sn etc.; **Secundus J.** II.184sn etc.; **Tertius J.** II.186sn etc.; **Quartus J.** II.189sn etc. the tormenters of Christ

Primus miles II.50sn, 74sn; **Secundus m.** II.54sn, 78sn Herod's knights; **Primus miles** II.1111sn, 1127sn, 1139sn, **þe knyth** II.1130sd; **Secundus m.** II.1123sn; **to knytys** II.1110sd, **two knygtys** II.1122sd Pilate's knights who go to the cross with Joseph of Arimathea; **Primus Miles, Secundus M., Tertius M., Quartus M.** *see also* **Ameraunt, Arphaxat, Cosdram, Affraunt**

Primus pauper homo I.427sn, 439sn; **Secundus p.h.** I.431sn, 441sn the blind men healed by Christ

Quartus . . . *see* **Primus . . .**

Rewfyn I.194, 201, 207, 244sd, 261sn etc., 275, **Rufyne** I.981sn, 1009sn one of the Pharisees or secular judges in opposition to Christ in *Passion* I (*see also* **Pharaseus**)

Romaynes *n.pl.* I.526 the Romans

Rome II.1647 Rome

Salome *see* **Maria Salome**

Samaryan *3A*21 Samaria

Satan I.3, II.486sd, **Sathan** I.97, 426, II.487sn, 491, 528sn Satan (*see also* **Demon, Lucifer**)

Secundus . . . *see* **Primus . . .**

Seymon *see* **Symon (Leprows)**

Senturyo *see* **Centurio**

Sesar(e) I.308; I.184, 310, II.275, **Sezar** I.558 Caesar

Symeon Zelotes *3A*29, **Symon** *2A*105sn the apostle Simon Zelotes, traditionally brother of Jude and James the Less, son of Mary Jacobi

Symon (Leprows) I.478sd, 487sn, 494sd, 510sd, 511sn, 516, **Seymon** I.505 Simon the Leper

Symon(e) II.727sn, 735sn, 738sd; II.718sd Simon of Cyrene

Syon I.467, [495] mount Sion (see note to I.495)

Spiritus Paraclyté *3A*7 the Holy Spirit, the Paraclete (see note)

Tertius . . . *see* **Primus . . .**

Thadeus *2A*113sn, **Judas** *3A*30 the apostle Jude, traditionally brother of Simon Zelotes and James the Less, son of Mary Jacobi

Thomas II.1826sn, *2A*109sn, *3A*35 the apostle Thomas

Veronica II.739sn, **Veronyca** II.743 Veronica

Vxor Pilaty II.544sn, **Pylatys wyf(f)** II.543sd; II.536 Pilate's wife

Zelotes *see* **Symeon Zelotes**

LIST OF LATIN WORDS, PHRASES, ETC.
IN TEXT AND STAGE DIRECTIONS

apud Jherosolyman 3A23

Attolite portas, principes, vestras et eleuamini / porte eternales, et introibit rex glorie II.1017–18

Crucifigatur II.597 and 599

Et cantabit gallus II.199sd and 212sd

Et clamabunt II.345sd and 646sd

Et clamabunt omnes II.177sd

Et clamabunt omnes, voce magna, dicentes: II.672sd

Et percuciet super caput II.185sd

Explicit apparicio Marie Magdalene II.1938sd

Fily altissimi 3A5

Gloria laus I.410sd

Heloy, heloy / Lamazabathany II.881–2

Hic currunt Johannes et Petrus simul ad sepulcrum, et Johannes prius venit ad monumentum sed non intrat. II.1797sd

Hic est Jhesus Nazarenus rex Judeorum II.874sd

Hic faciant Pilatus, Cayphas et Annas priuatim inter se consilium. Quo finito dicat II.1627sd

Hic intrat Johannes monumentum dicens: II.1805sd

Hic parum deambulet a sepulcro dicens: II.1853sd

Hic Petrus loquitur omnibus apostolis simul collectis. II.1817sd

Hic quasi semi-mortua cadat prona in terram; et dicit Johannes: II.968sd

Hic ueniont ad sepulcrum Maria Magdalene, Maria Jacobi et Maria Salome et dicit Maria Magdalene: II.1671sd

In manus tuas, domine II.913

Maria Magdalene dicit Petro et ceteris apostolis: II.1765sd

Nunc consummatum est II.920

Omnes congregati Thomas II.1826sn

Petrus intrat monumentum et dicit Petrus: II.1801sd

Populus clamabit II.598sd

Quia in inferno nulla est redempcio. I.48

Quod vere filius dei erat iste. II.1046

Salue sancta parens II.1456

spectans II.1873sd

Spiritus Paraclyté 3A7

Tunc dormyent milites et ueniet Anima Christi de inferno cum Adam et Eua, Abraham, John Baptist et alijs II.1367sd

Tunc evigilabunt milites sepulcri et dicit Primus Miles: II.1503sd

Tunc ibunt ad sepulcrum Pilatus, Cayphas, Annas et omnes milites, et dicit II.1279sd

Tunc respicit Maria Magdalene in sepulcro dicens: II.1709sd

Tunc transiet Anima Christi ad resuscitandum corpus; quo resuscitato, dicat Jhesus: II.1439sd

Tunc transiet Maria ad templum cum Johanne, et cetera. II.984sd